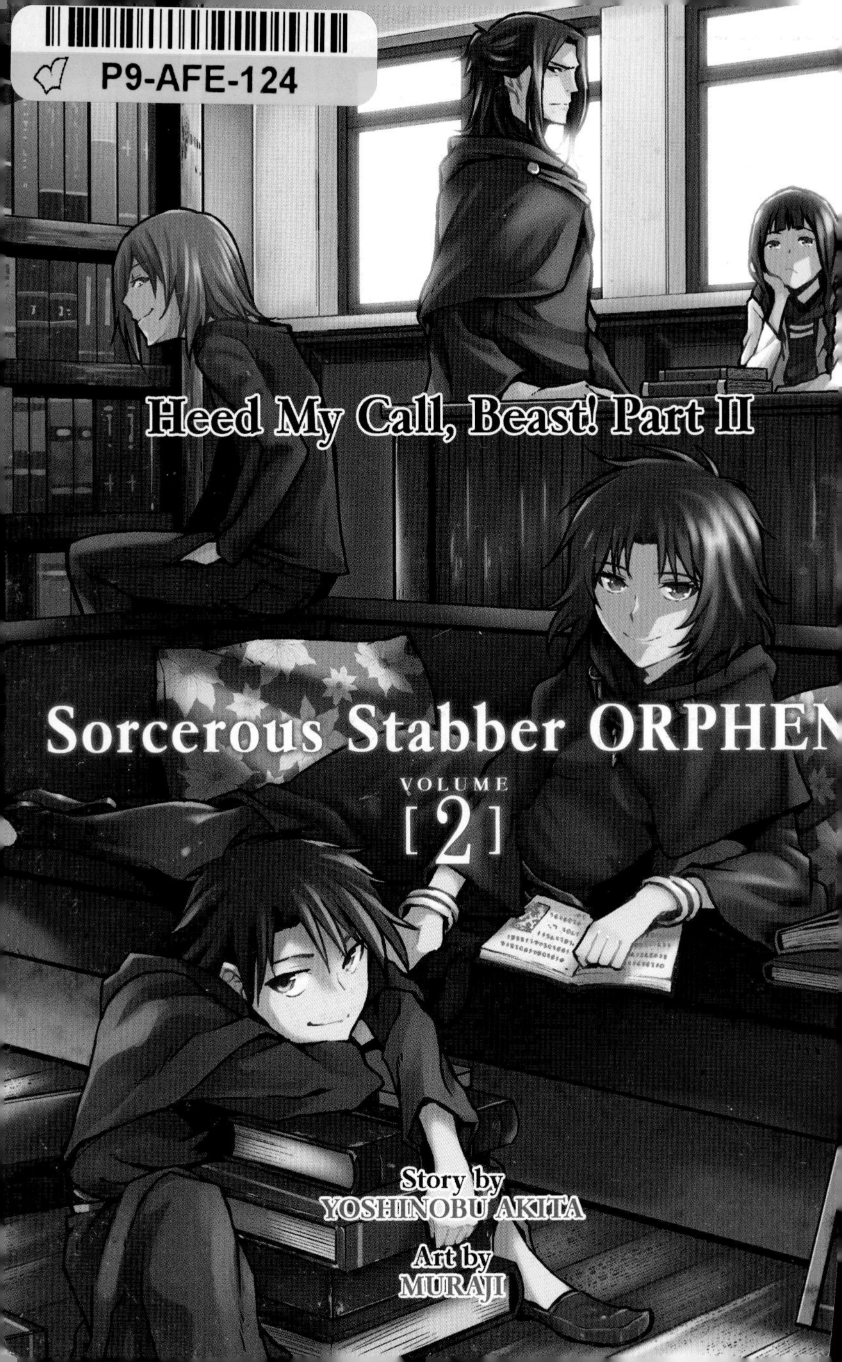
Heed My Call, Beast! Part II
Sorcerous Stabber ORPHEN
VOLUME
[2]
Story by
YOSHINOBU AKITA
Art by
MURAJI

Sorcerous Stabber ORPHEN
CONTENTS

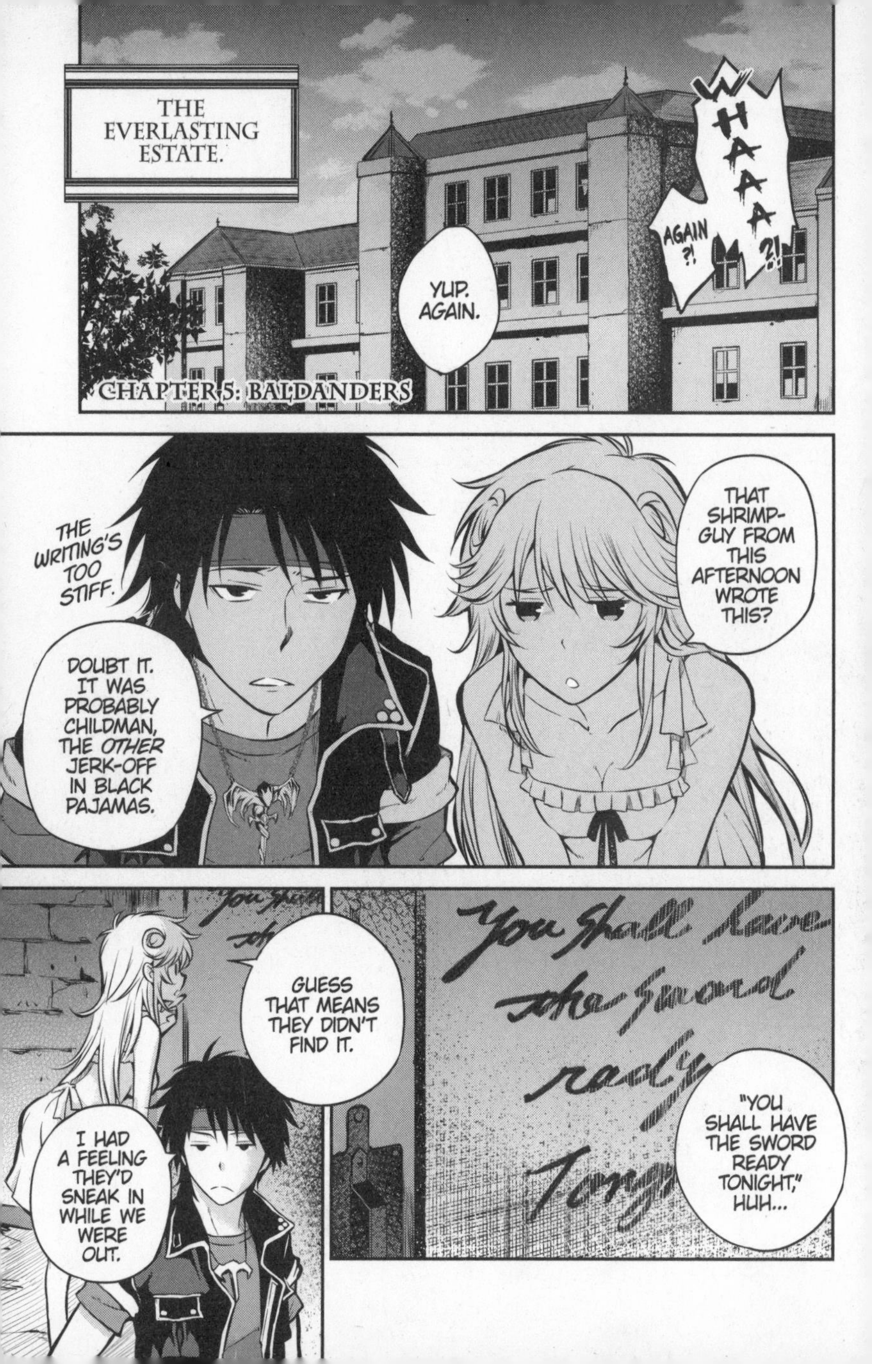
THE EVERLASTING ESTATE.
WHAAAA?!
AGAIN?!
YUP. AGAIN.
CHAPTER 5: BALDANDERS
THAT SHRIMP-GUY FROM THIS AFTERNOON WROTE THIS?
THE WRITING'S TOO STIFF.
DOUBT IT. IT WAS PROBABLY CHILDMAN, THE *OTHER* JERK-OFF IN BLACK PAJAMAS.
"YOU SHALL HAVE THE SWORD READY TONIGHT," HUH...
GUESS THAT MEANS THEY DIDN'T FIND IT.
I HAD A FEELING THEY'D SNEAK IN WHILE WE WERE OUT.

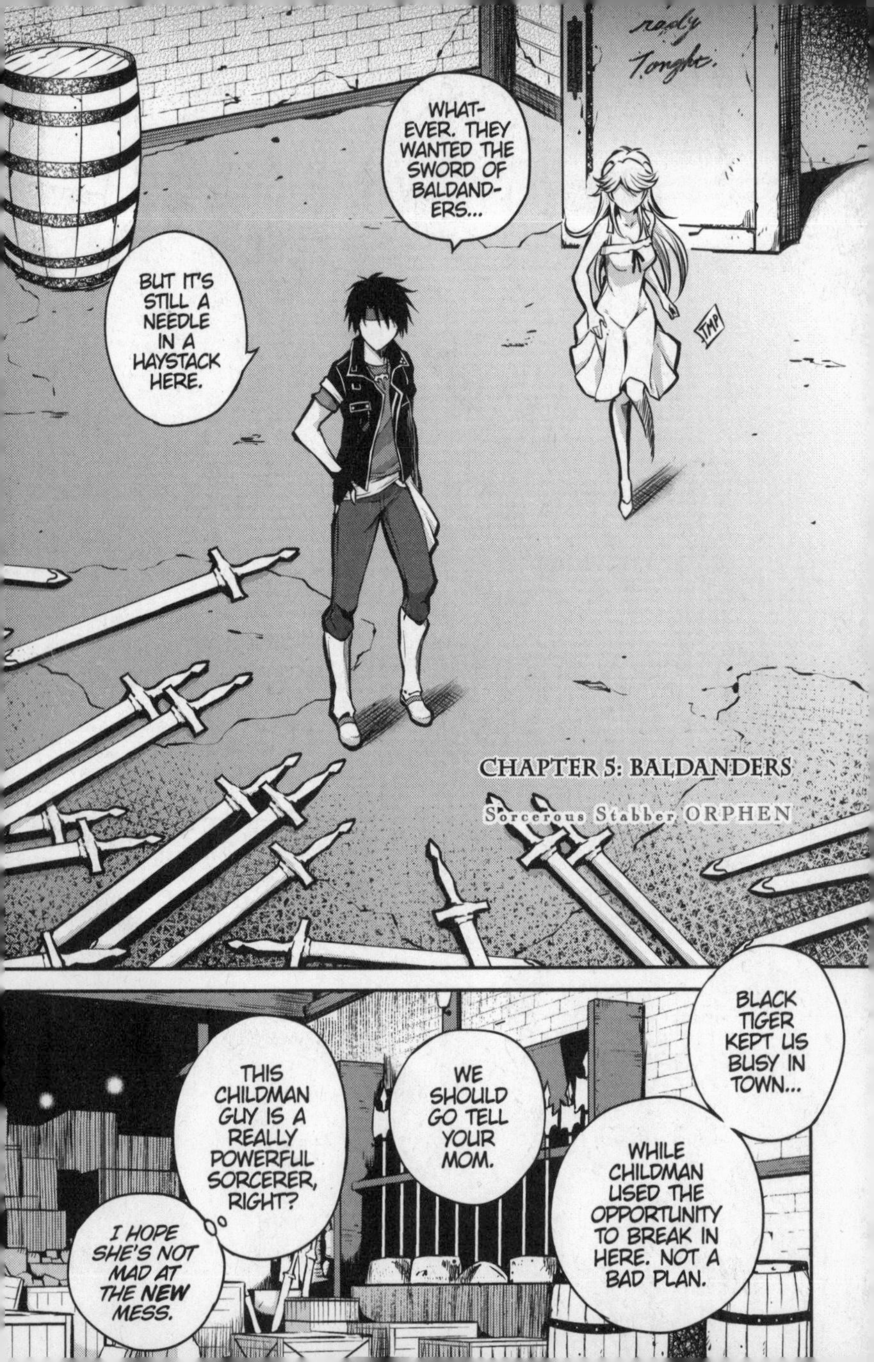
WHAT-EVER. THEY WANTED THE SWORD OF BALDAND-ERS...
BUT IT'S STILL A NEEDLE IN A HAYSTACK HERE.
TMP
CHAPTER 5: BALDANDERS
Sorcerous Stabber ORPHEN
BLACK TIGER KEPT US BUSY IN TOWN...
WHILE CHILDMAN USED THE OPPORTUNITY TO BREAK IN HERE. NOT A BAD PLAN.
WE SHOULD GO TELL YOUR MOM.
THIS CHILDMAN GUY IS A REALLY POWERFUL SORCERER, RIGHT?
I HOPE SHE'S NOT MAD AT THE NEW MESS.

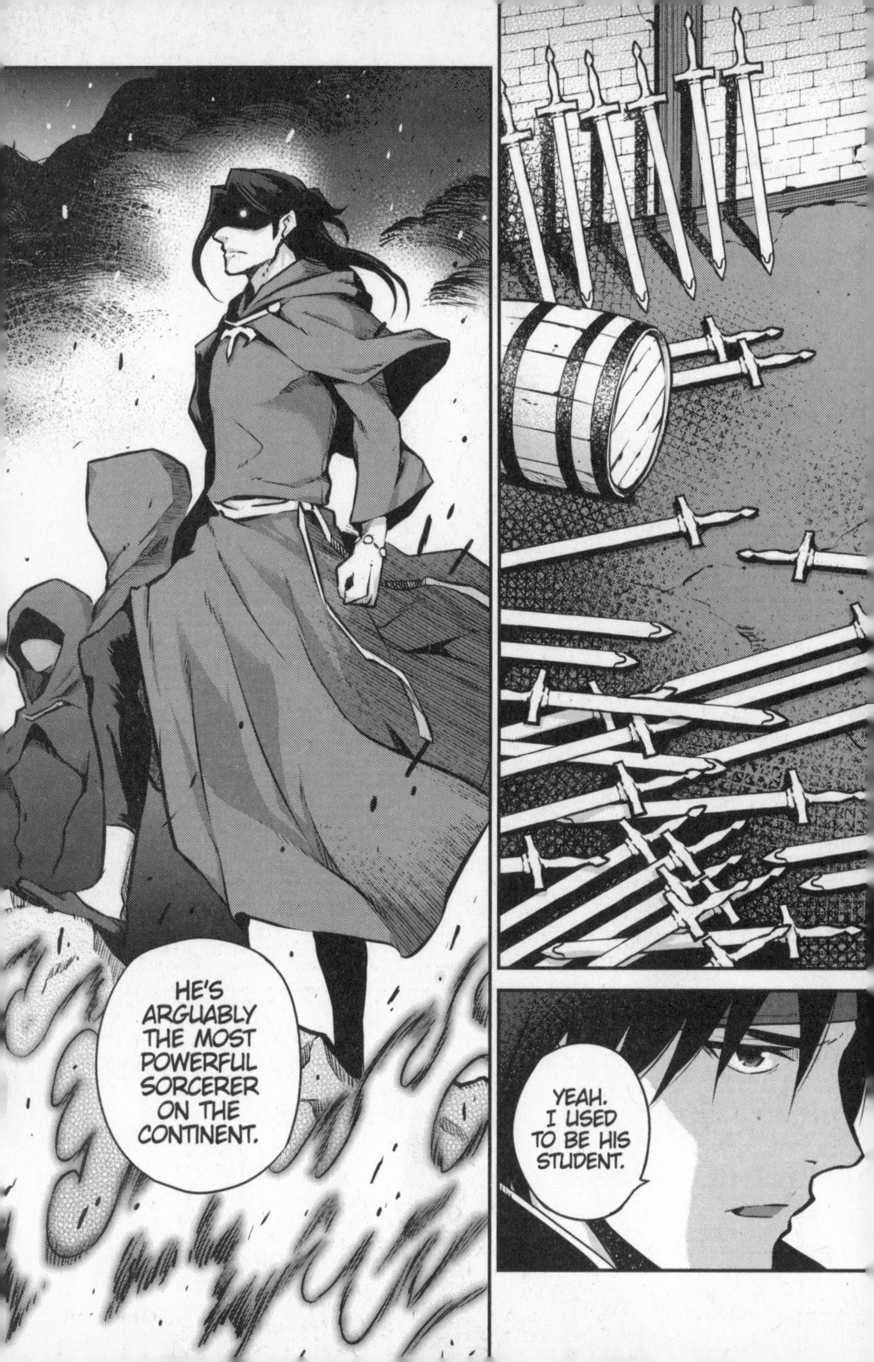
YEAH. I USED TO BE HIS STUDENT.
HE'S ARGUABLY THE MOST POWERFUL SORCERER ON THE CONTINENT.

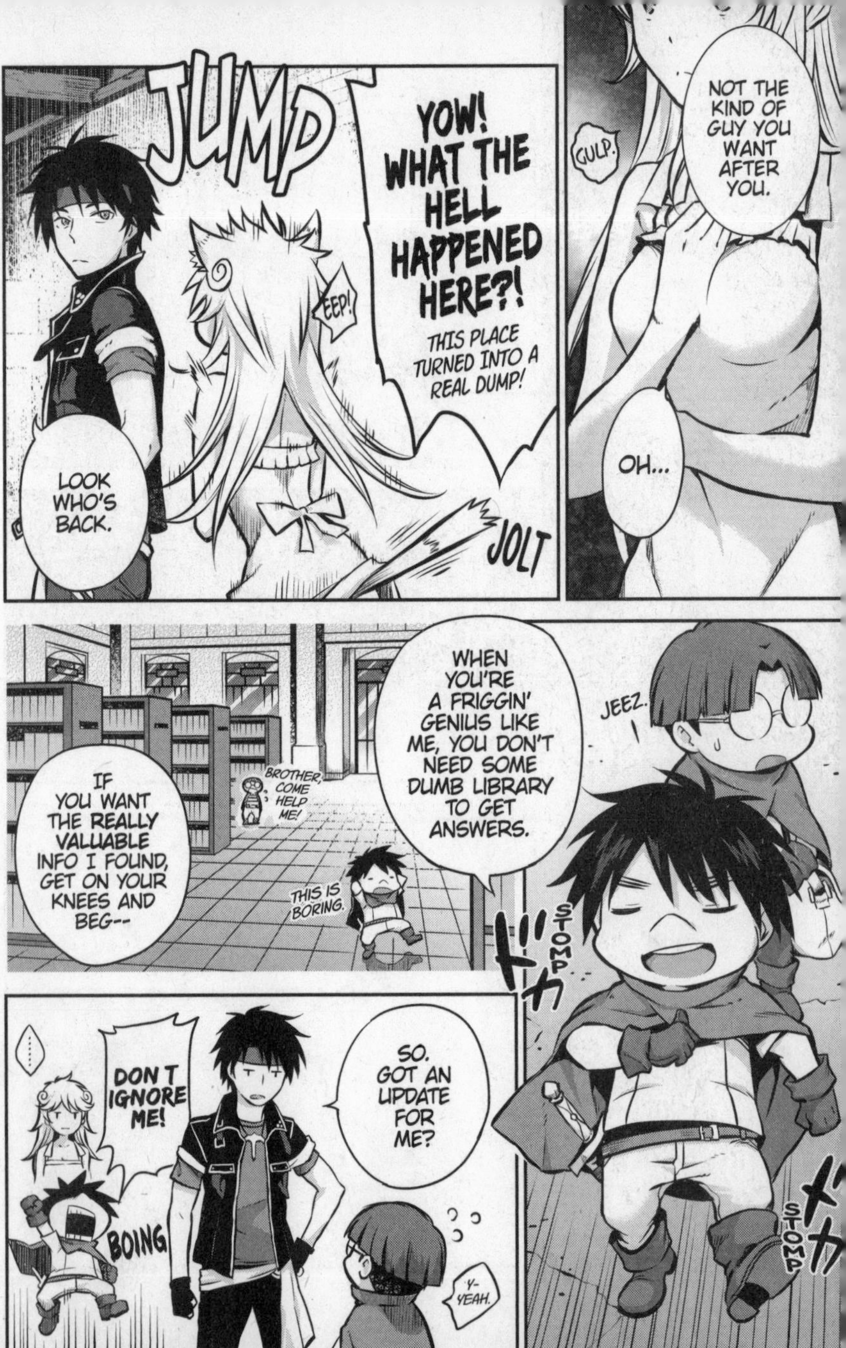
NOT THE KIND OF GUY YOU WANT AFTER YOU.
GULP.
OH...
YOW! WHAT THE HELL HAPPENED HERE?!
THIS PLACE TURNED INTO A REAL DUMP!
JUMP
EEP!
JOLT
LOOK WHO'S BACK.
JEEZ.
STOMP
STOMP
WHEN YOU'RE A FRIGGIN' GENIUS LIKE ME, YOU DON'T NEED SOME DUMB LIBRARY TO GET ANSWERS.
BROTHER, COME HELP ME!
IF YOU WANT THE REALLY VALUABLE INFO I FOUND, GET ON YOUR KNEES AND BEG--
THIS IS BORING.
SO. GOT AN UPDATE FOR ME?
Y-YEAH.
DON'T IGNORE ME!
...
BOING

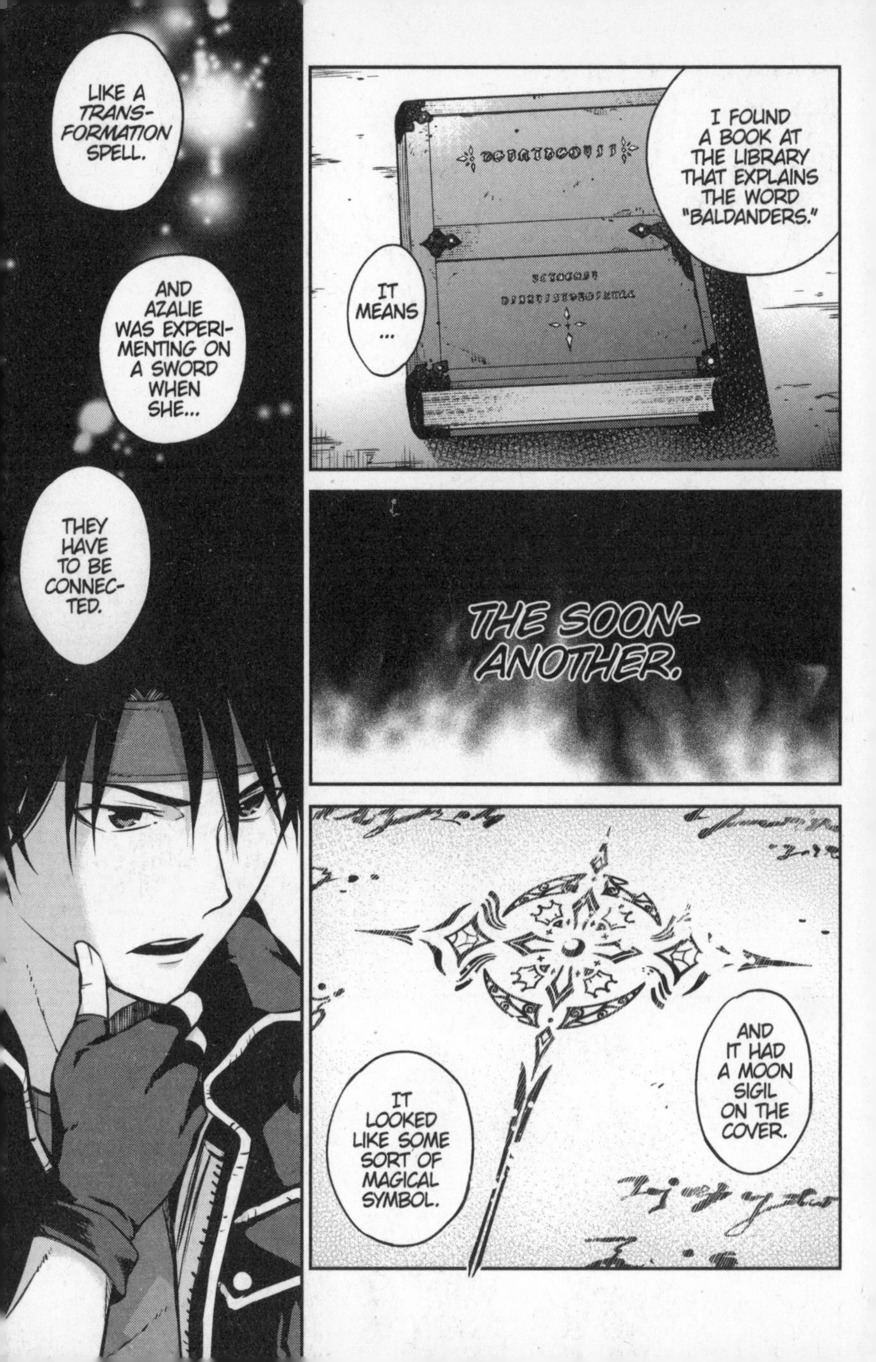
I FOUND A BOOK AT THE LIBRARY THAT EXPLAINS THE WORD "BALDANDERS."
IT MEANS ...
THE SOON-ANOTHER.
AND IT HAD A MOON SIGIL ON THE COVER.
IT LOOKED LIKE SOME SORT OF MAGICAL SYMBOL.
LIKE A *TRANS-FORMATION* SPELL.
AND AZALIE WAS EXPERI-MENTING ON A SWORD WHEN SHE...
THEY HAVE TO BE CONNEC-TED.

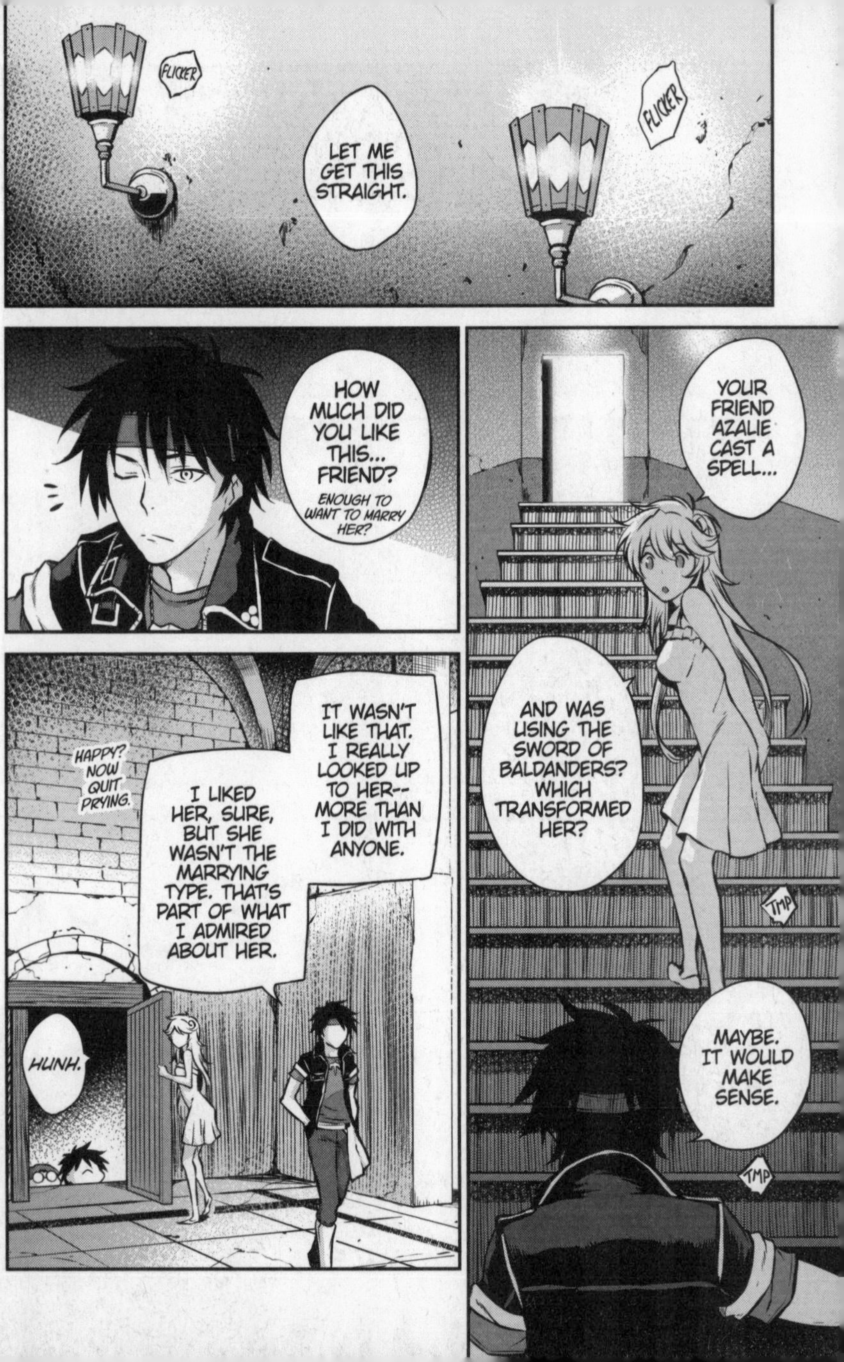
FLICKER
LET ME GET THIS STRAIGHT.
FLICKER
YOUR FRIEND AZALIE CAST A SPELL...
AND WAS USING THE SWORD OF BALDANDERS? WHICH TRANSFORMED HER?
TMP
MAYBE. IT WOULD MAKE SENSE.
TMP
HOW MUCH DID YOU LIKE THIS... FRIEND?
ENOUGH TO WANT TO MARRY HER?
IT WASN'T LIKE THAT. I REALLY LOOKED UP TO HER-- MORE THAN I DID WITH ANYONE.
I LIKED HER, SURE, BUT SHE WASN'T THE MARRYING TYPE. THAT'S PART OF WHAT I ADMIRED ABOUT HER.
HAPPY? NOW QUIT PRYING.
HUNH.

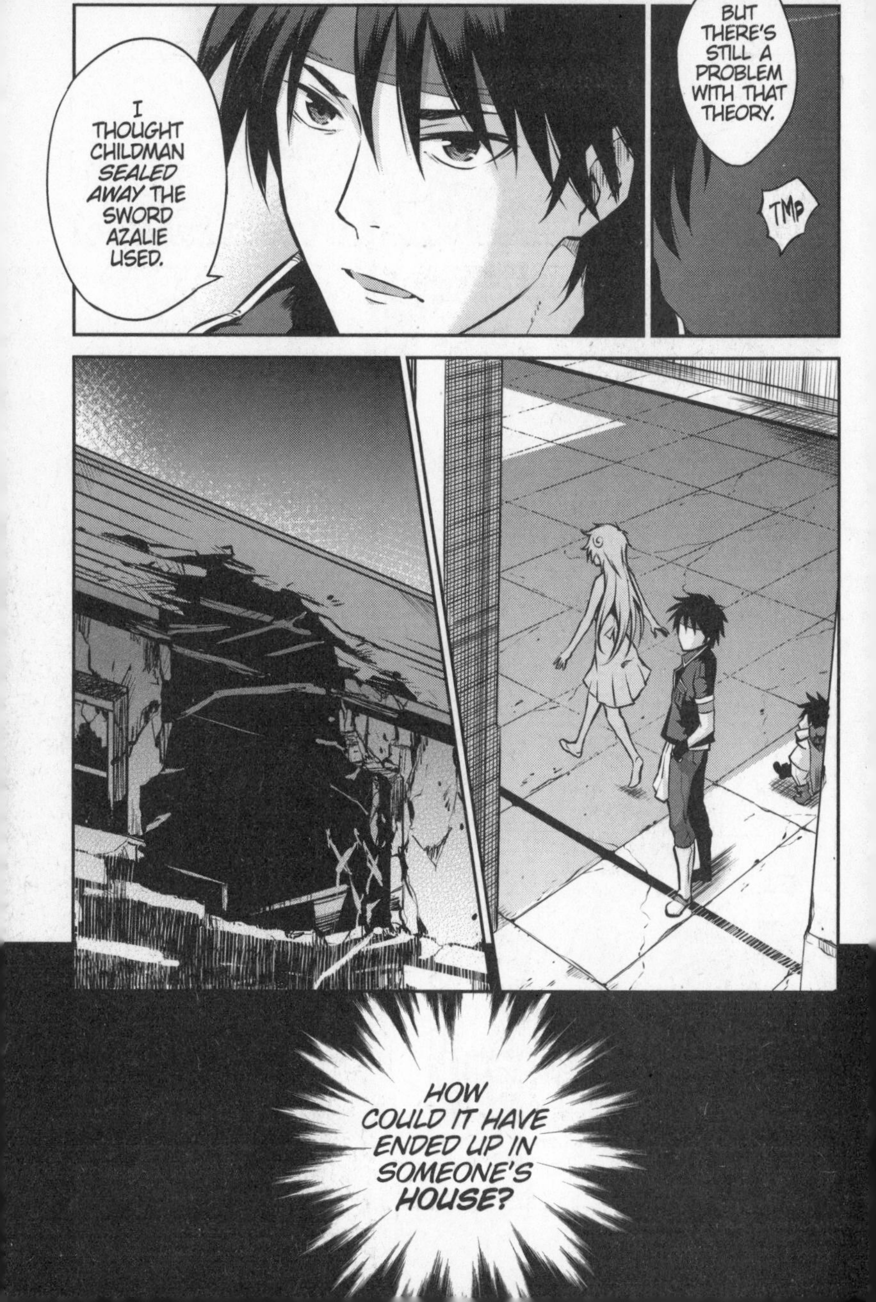
BUT THERE'S STILL A PROBLEM WITH THAT THEORY.
TMP
I THOUGHT CHILDMAN SEALED AWAY THE SWORD AZALIE USED.
HOW COULD IT HAVE ENDED UP IN SOMEONE'S HOUSE?

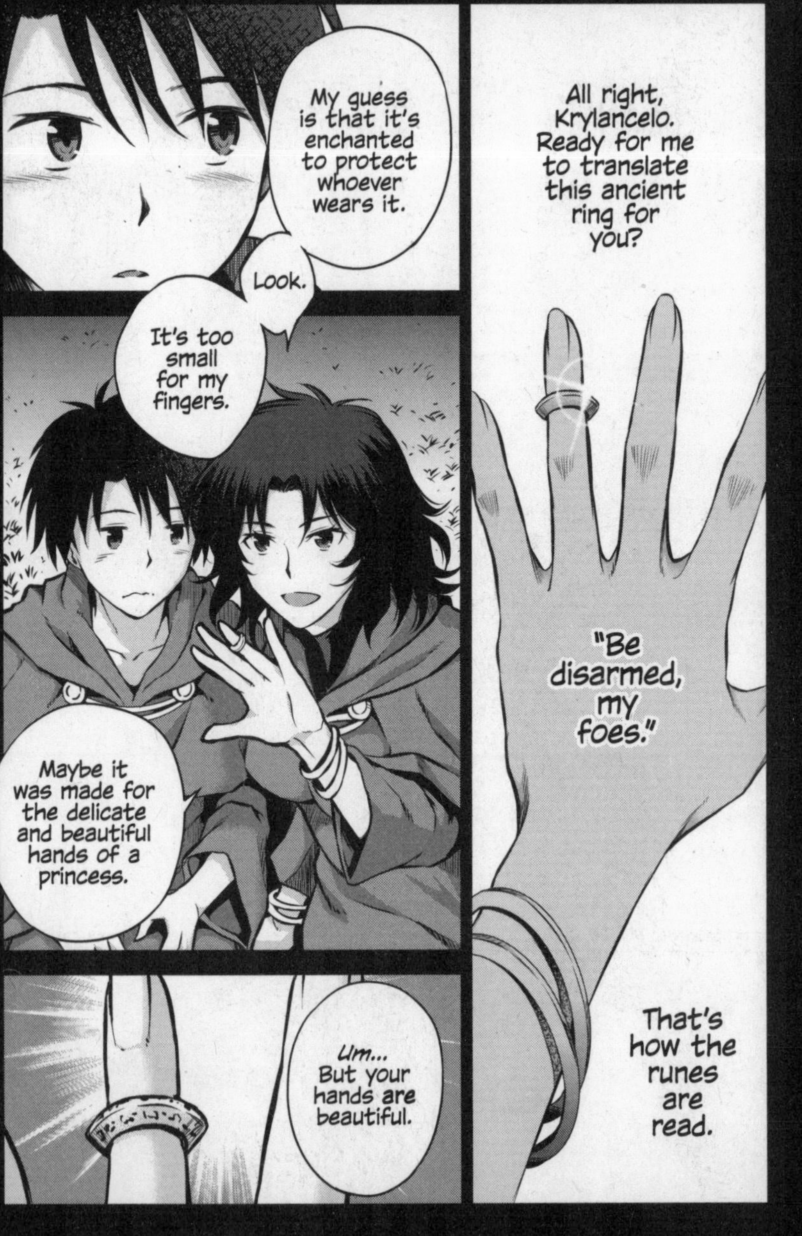
All right, Krylancelo. Ready for me to translate this ancient ring for you?
"Be disarmed, my foes."
That's how the runes are read.
My guess is that it's enchanted to protect whoever wears it.
Look.
It's too small for my fingers.
Maybe it was made for the delicate and beautiful hands of a princess.
Um... But your hands are beautiful.

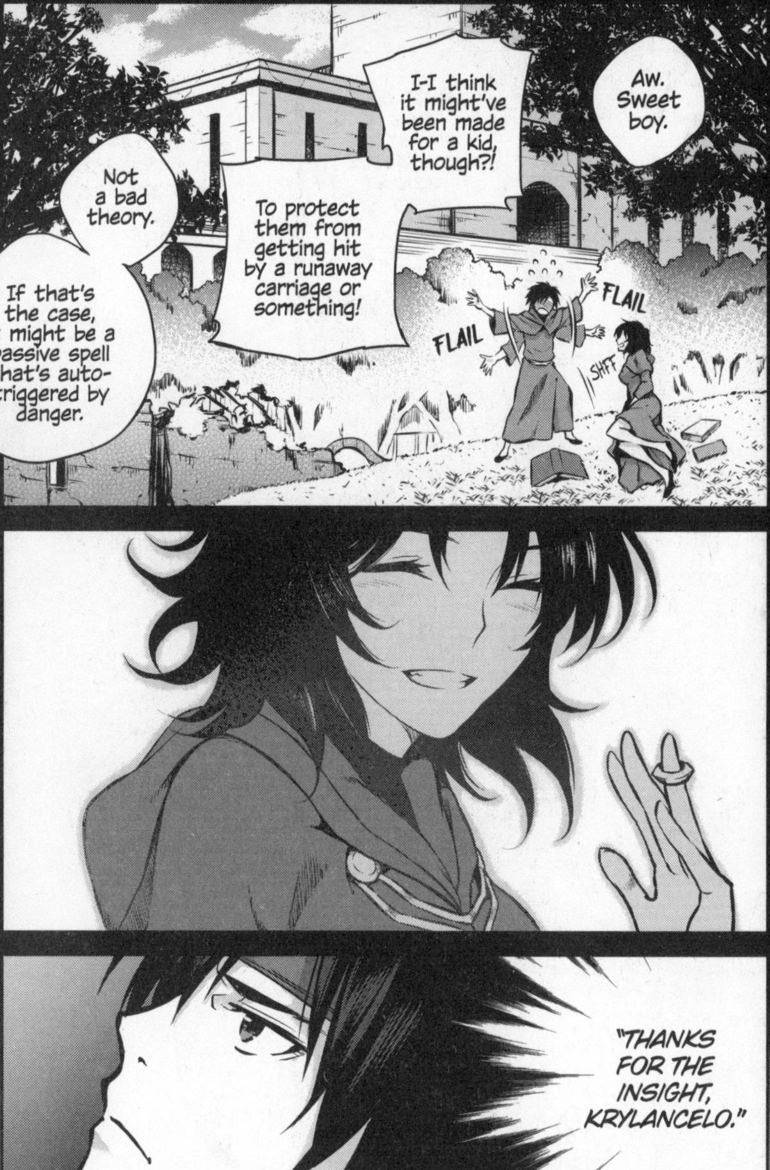
Aw. Sweet boy.
I-I think it might've been made for a kid, though?!
To protect them from getting hit by a runaway carriage or something!
FLAIL
FLAIL
SHFF
Not a bad theory.
If that's the case, it might be a passive spell that's auto-triggered by danger.
"THANKS FOR THE INSIGHT, KRYLANCELO."

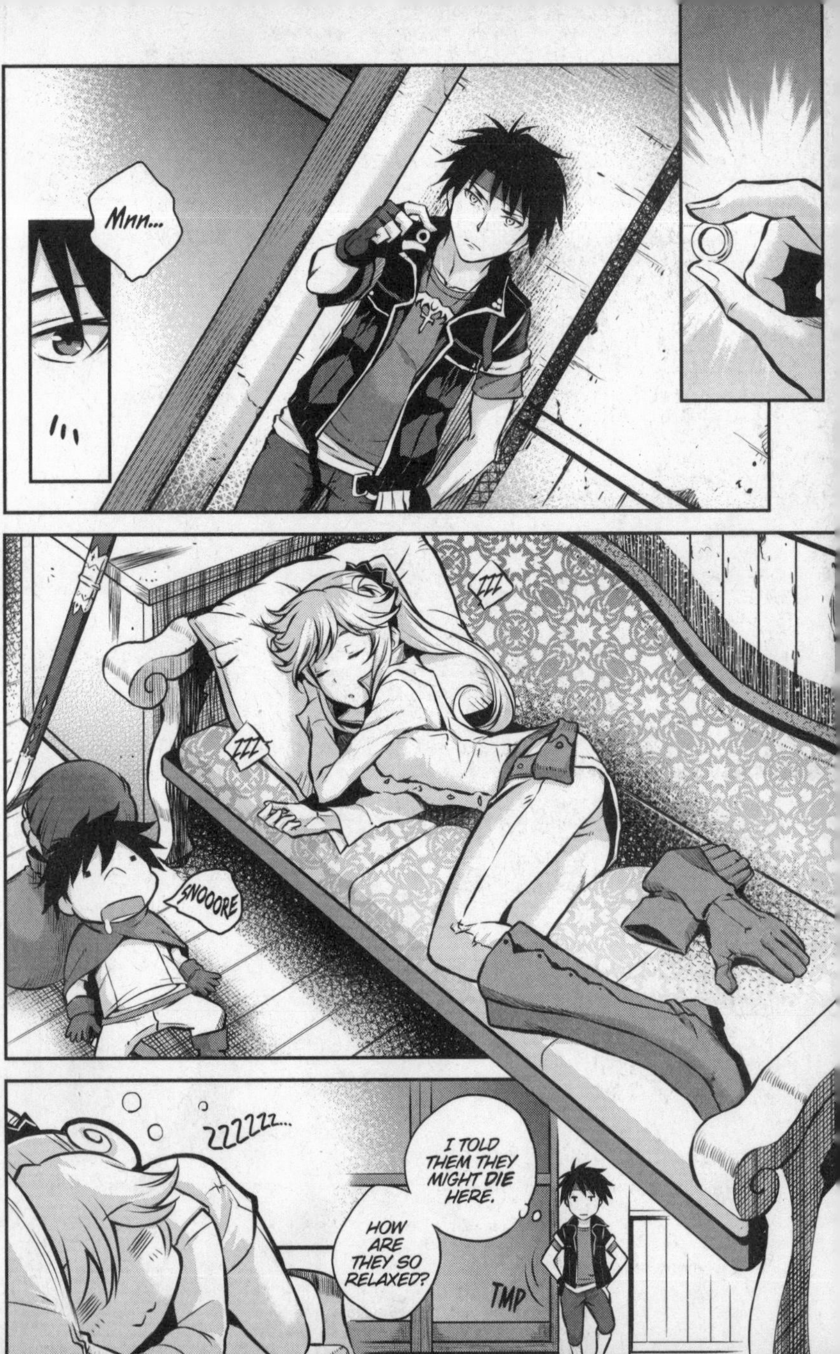

Mnn...
ZZZ
ZZZ
SNOOORE
I TOLD THEM THEY MIGHT DIE HERE.
HOW ARE THEY SO RELAXED?
TMP
ZZZZZZ...

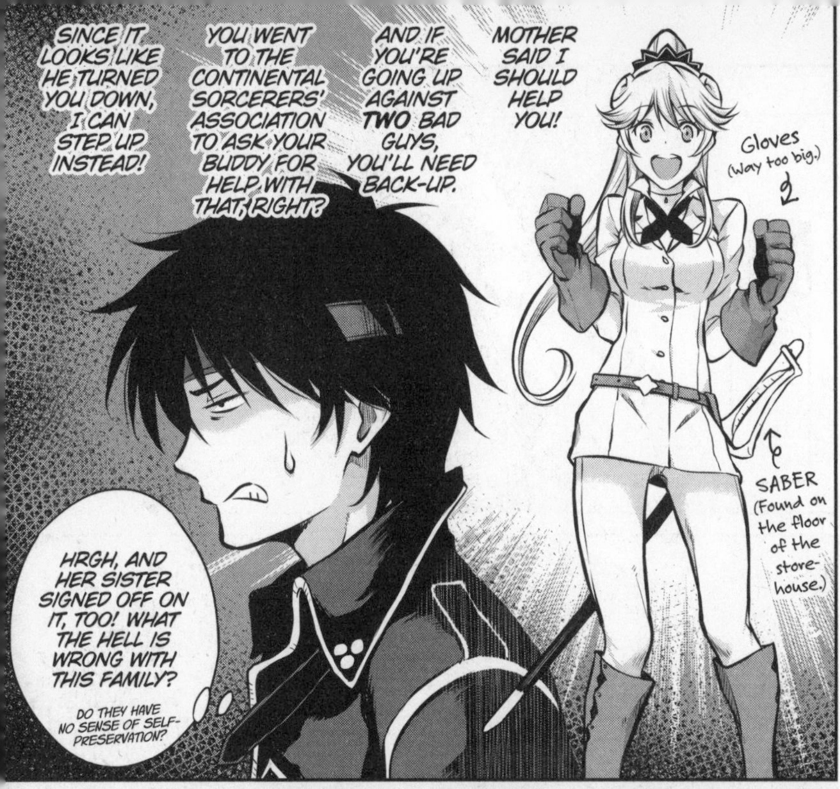
MOTHER SAID I SHOULD HELP YOU!
AND IF YOU'RE GOING UP AGAINST **TWO** BAD GUYS, YOU'LL NEED BACK-UP.
YOU WENT TO THE CONTINENTAL SORCERERS' ASSOCIATION TO ASK YOUR BUDDY FOR HELP WITH THAT, RIGHT?
SINCE IT LOOKS LIKE HE TURNED YOU DOWN, I CAN STEP UP INSTEAD!
Gloves (Way too big.)
SABER (Found on the floor of the storehouse.)
HRGH, AND HER SISTER SIGNED OFF ON IT, TOO! WHAT THE HELL IS WRONG WITH THIS FAMILY?
DO THEY HAVE NO SENSE OF SELF-PRESERVATION?

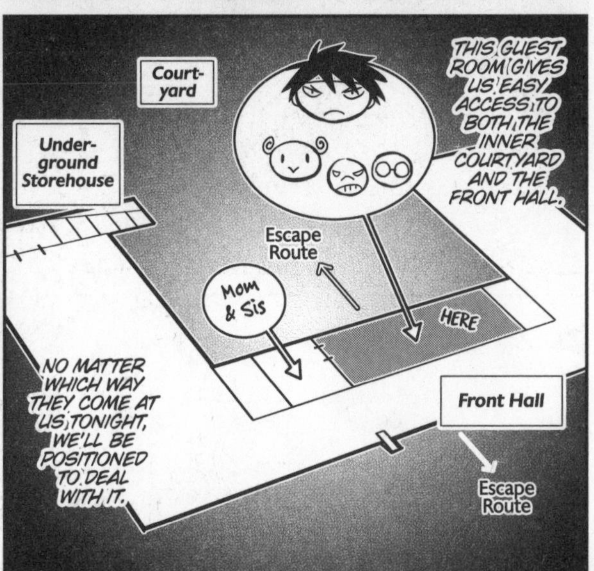
THIS GUEST ROOM GIVES US EASY ACCESS TO BOTH THE INNER COURTYARD AND THE FRONT HALL.
Court-yard
Under-ground Storehouse
Escape Route
Mom & Sis
HERE
Front Hall
Escape Route
NO MATTER WHICH WAY THEY COME AT US TONIGHT, WE'LL BE POSITIONED TO DEAL WITH IT.

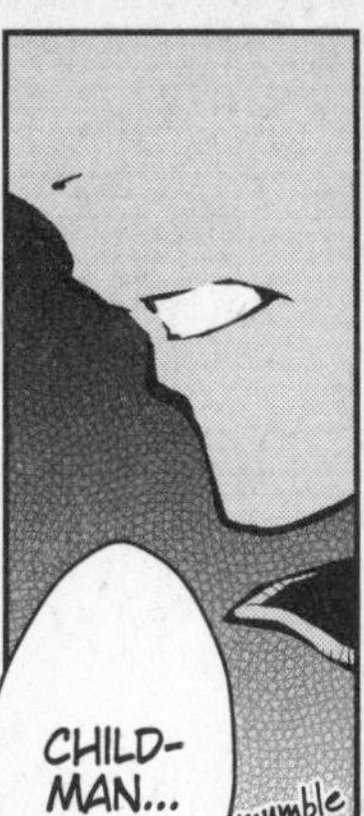
CHILD-MAN...
mumble

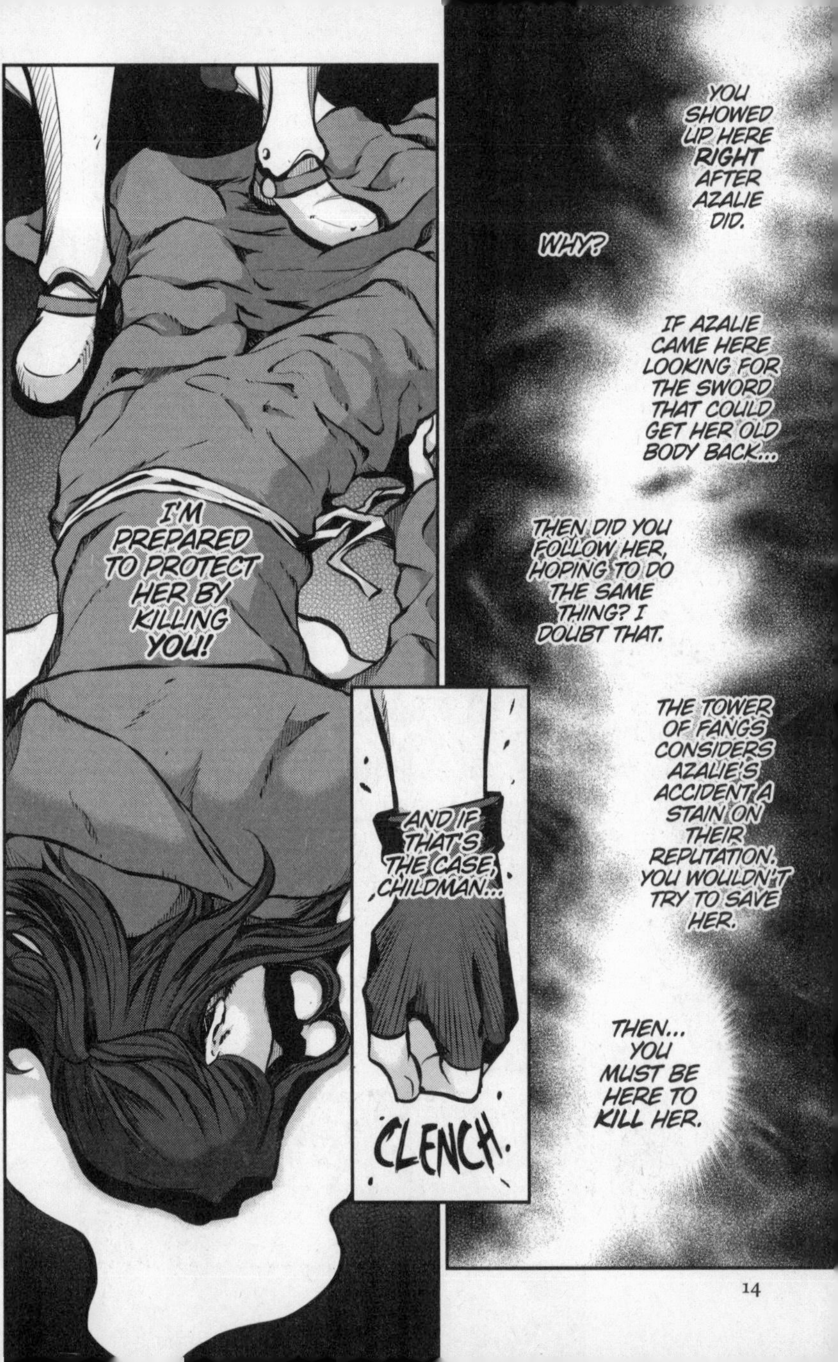
YOU SHOWED UP HERE RIGHT AFTER AZALIE DID.
WHY?
IF AZALIE CAME HERE LOOKING FOR THE SWORD THAT COULD GET HER OLD BODY BACK...
THEN DID YOU FOLLOW HER, HOPING TO DO THE SAME THING? I DOUBT THAT.
THE TOWER OF FANGS CONSIDERS AZALIE'S ACCIDENT A STAIN ON THEIR REPUTATION. YOU WOULDN'T TRY TO SAVE HER.
THEN... YOU MUST BE HERE TO KILL HER.
AND IF THAT'S THE CASE, CHILDMAN...
CLENCH.
I'M PREPARED TO PROTECT HER BY KILLING YOU!

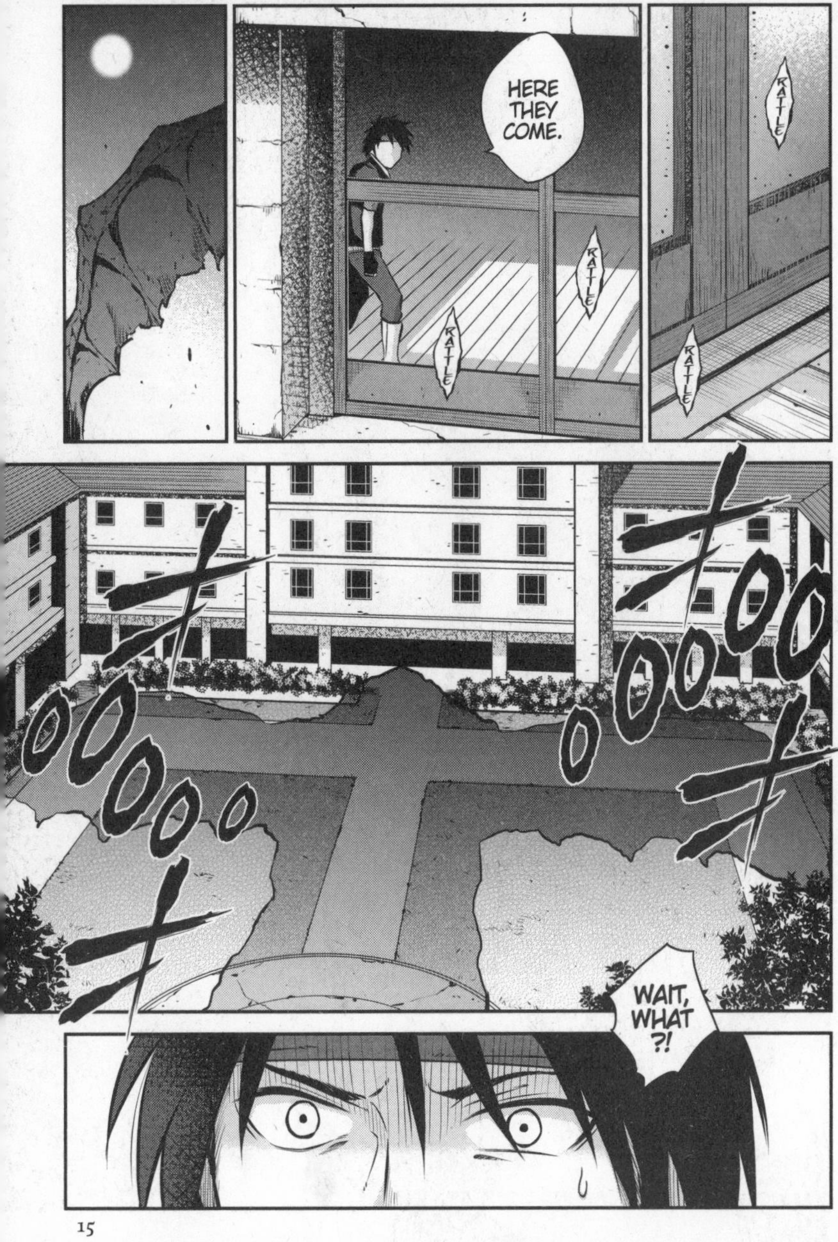
RATTLE
RATTLE
HERE THEY COME.
RATTLE
RATTLE
WAIT, WHAT?!

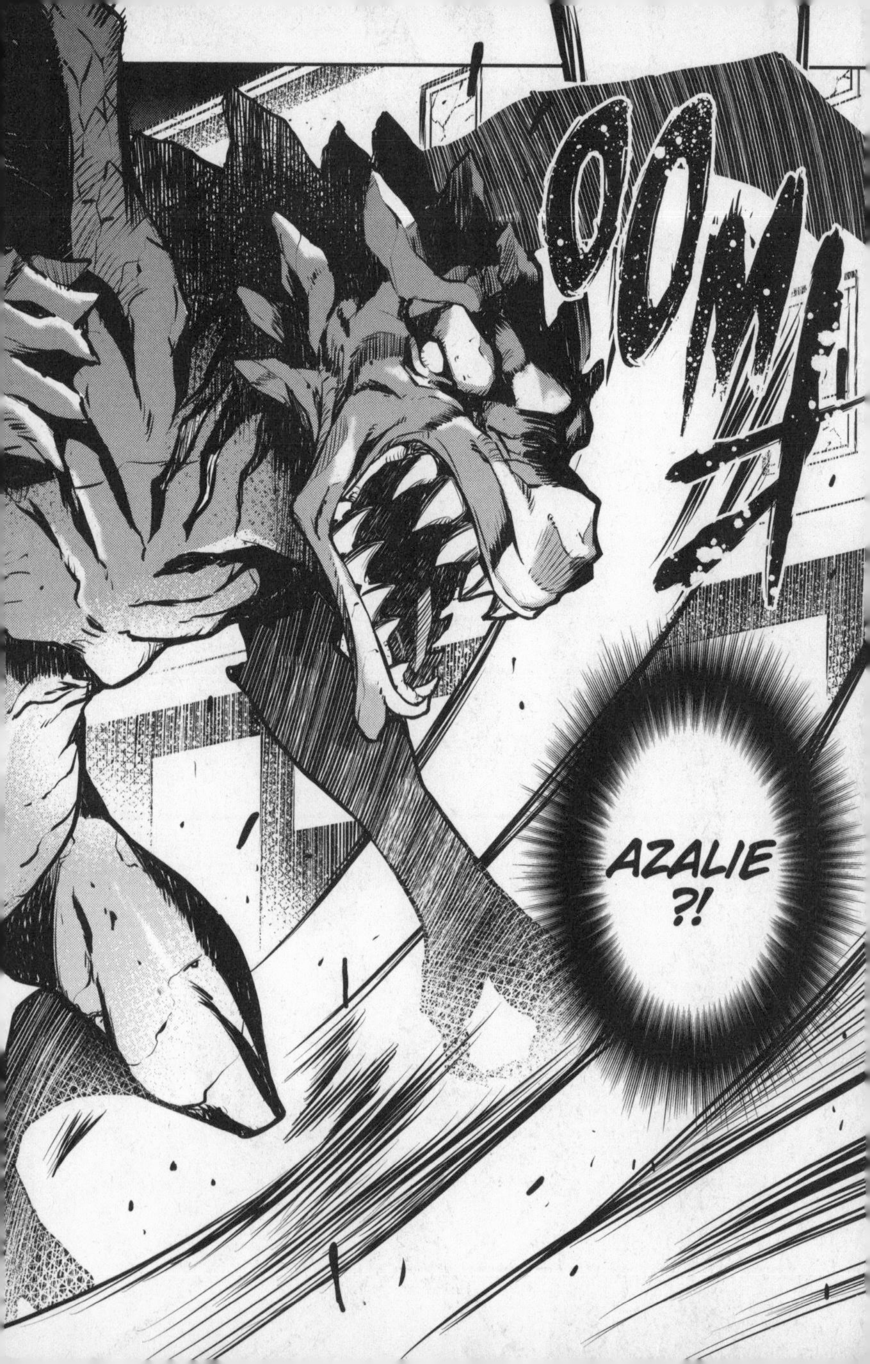
OOM!
AZALIE ?!

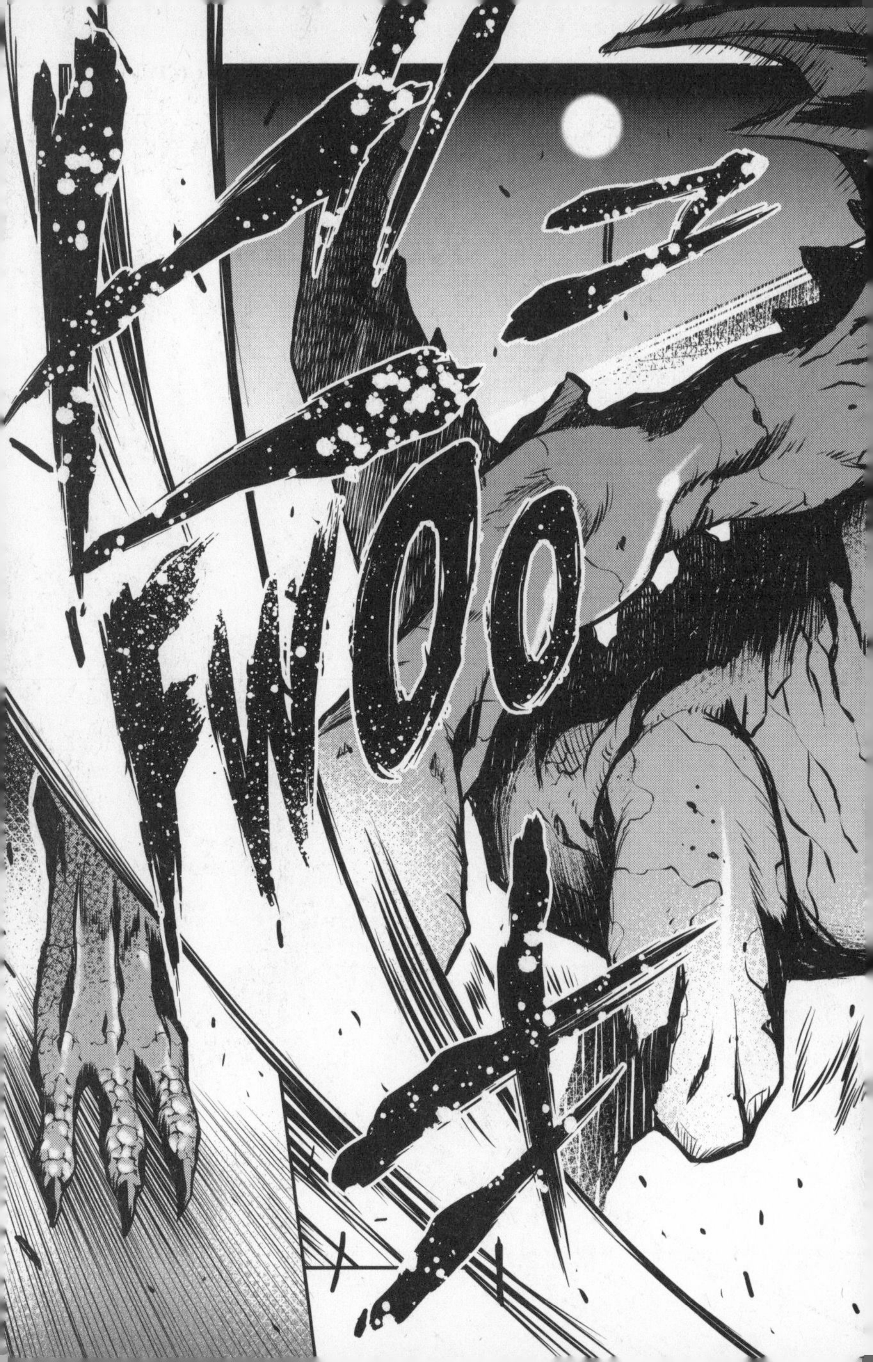
FWOO

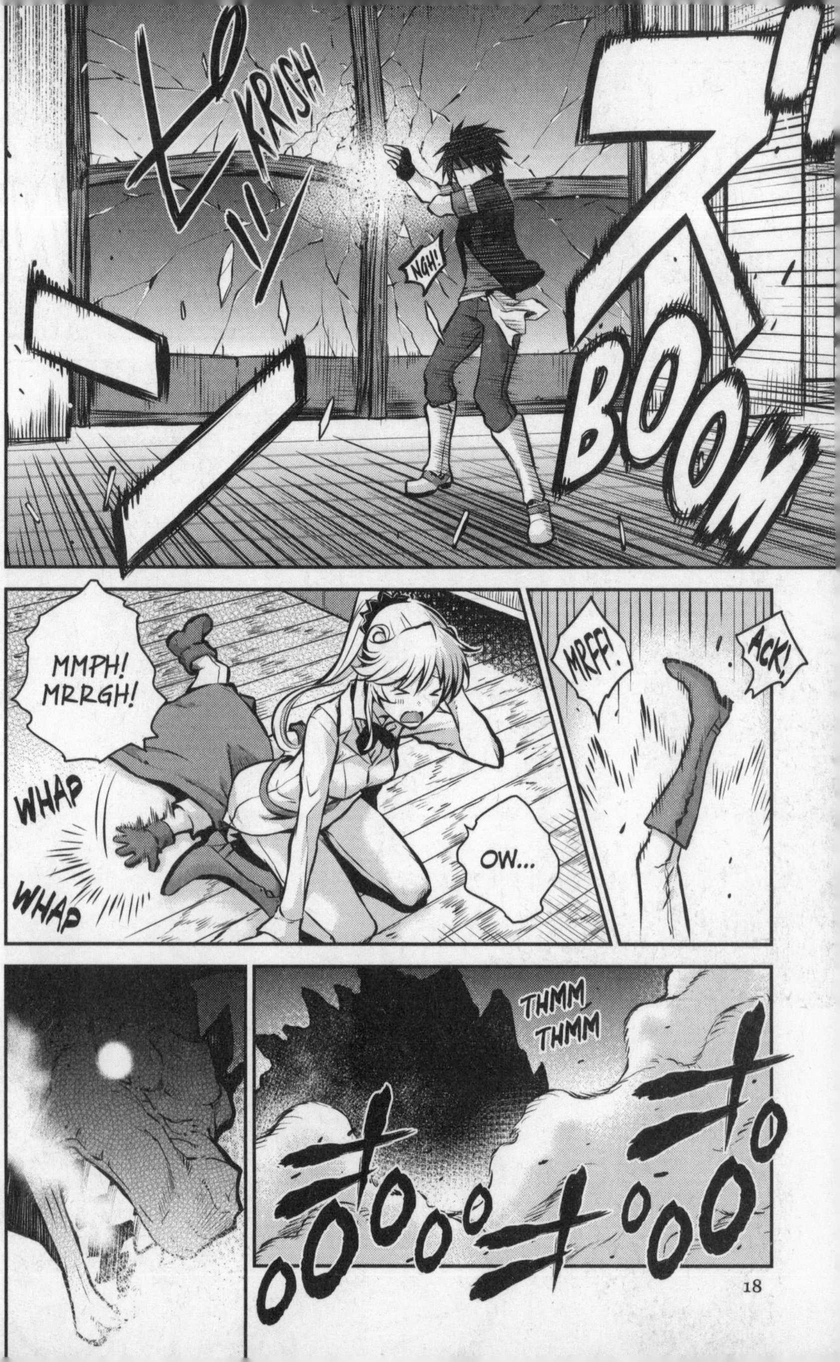
BOOM
NGH!
KRISH
ACK!
MRFF!
OW...
MMPH! MRRGH!
WHAP
WHAP
THMM
THMM

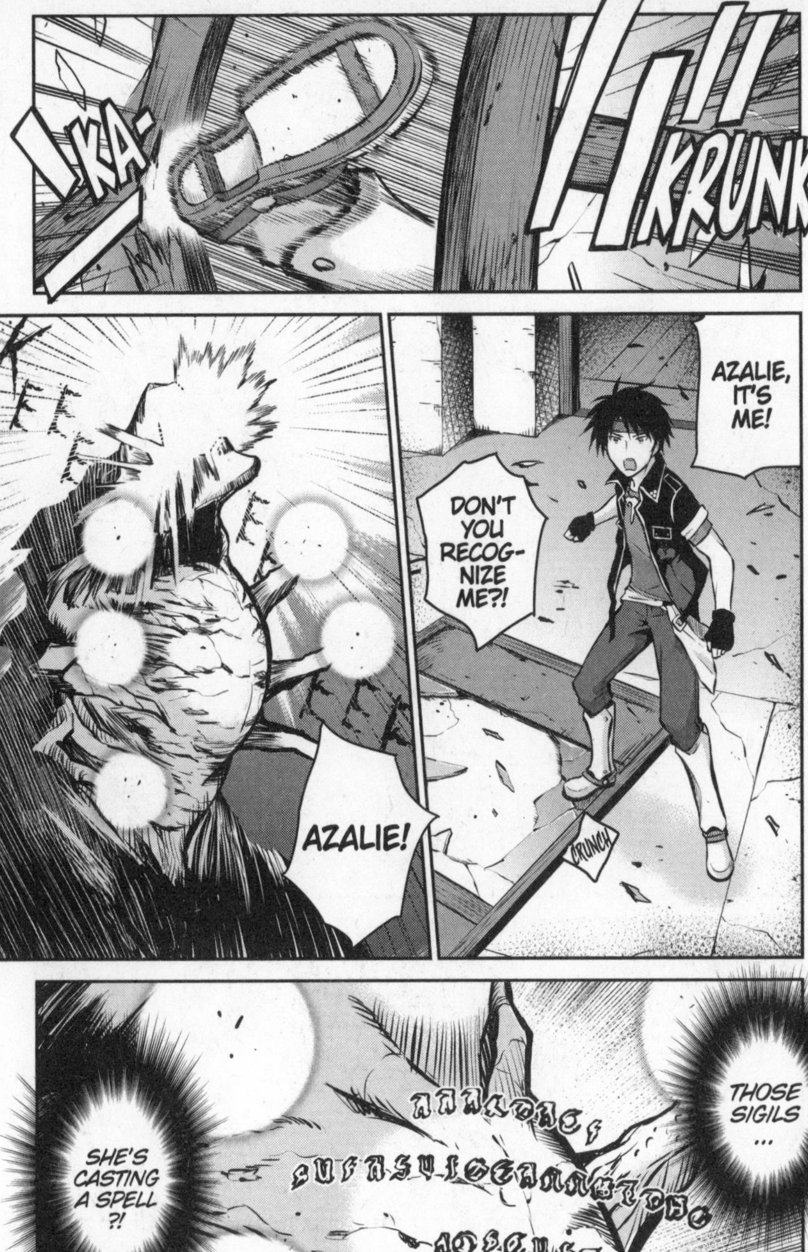
KA-
KRUNK
AZALIE, IT'S ME!
DON'T YOU RECOGNIZE ME?!
CRUNCH
AZALIE!
THOSE SIGILS...
SHE'S CASTING A SPELL?!

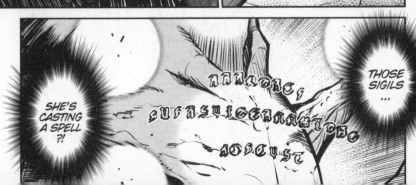

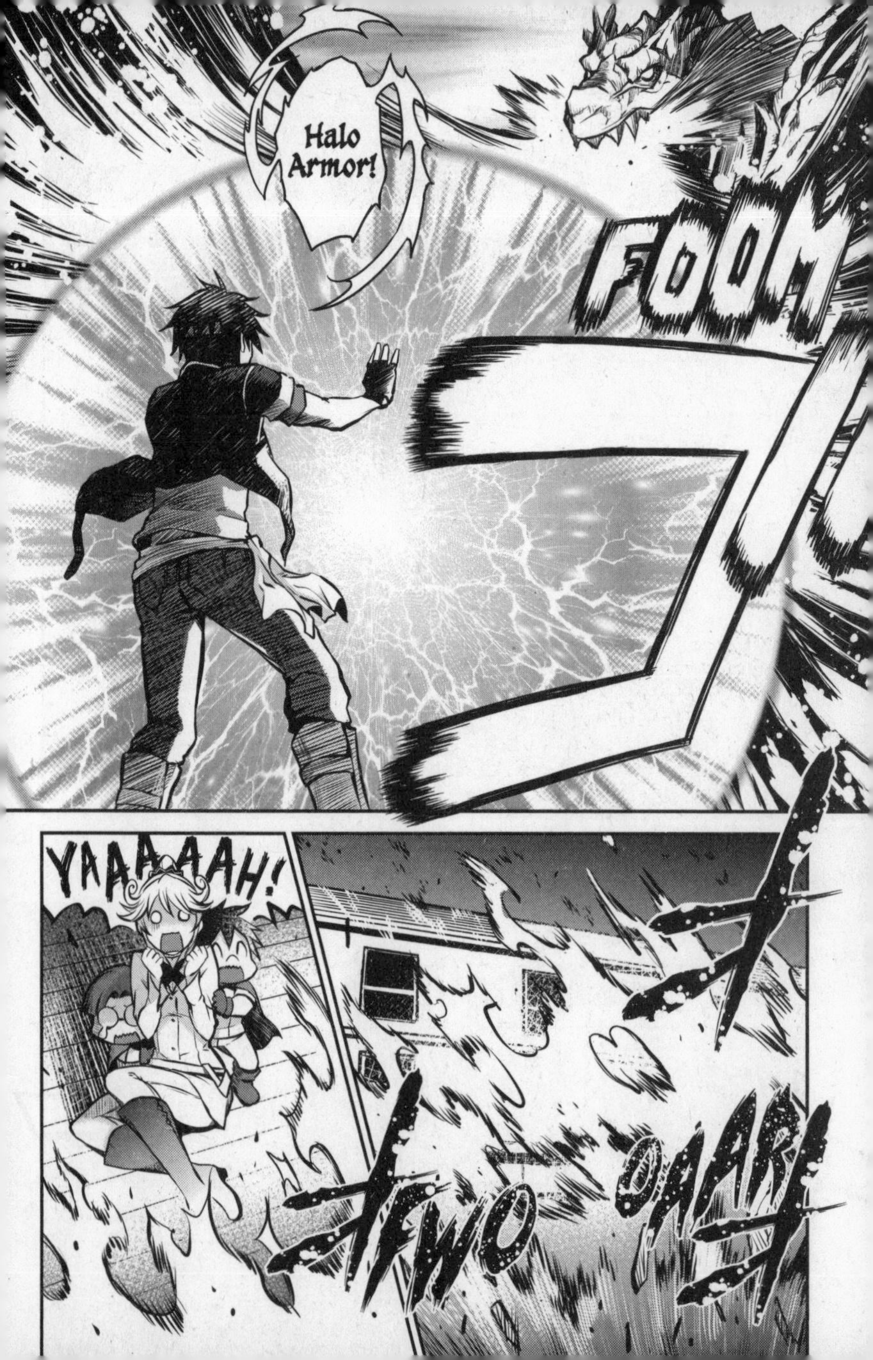
Halo Armor!
FOOM
FWOOAR!
YAAAAAH!

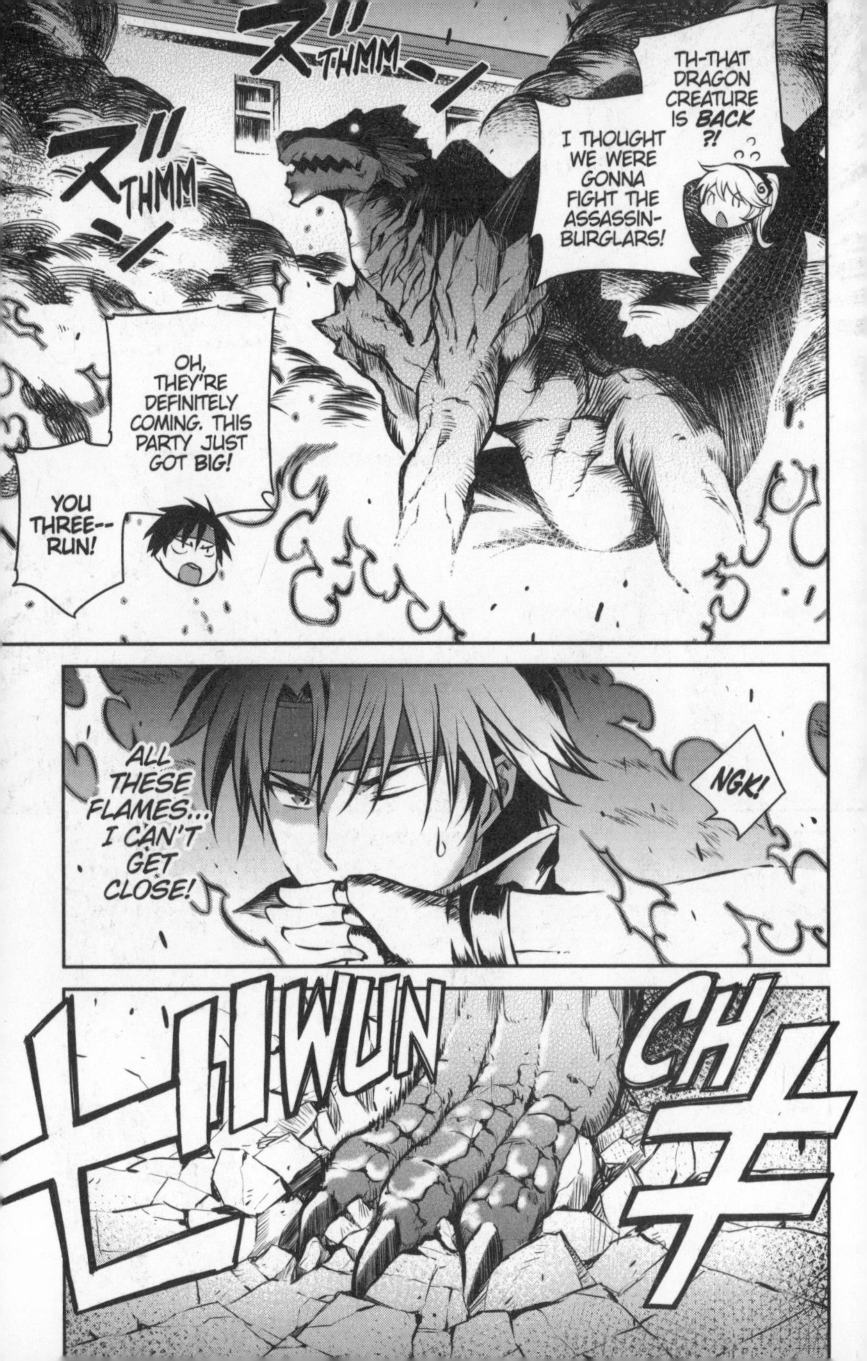
THMM
THMM
TH-THAT DRAGON CREATURE IS BACK?!
I THOUGHT WE WERE GONNA FIGHT THE ASSASSIN-BURGLARS!
OH, THEY'RE DEFINITELY COMING. THIS PARTY JUST GOT BIG!
YOU THREE--RUN!
NGK!
ALL THESE FLAMES... I CAN'T GET CLOSE!
CH
WUN

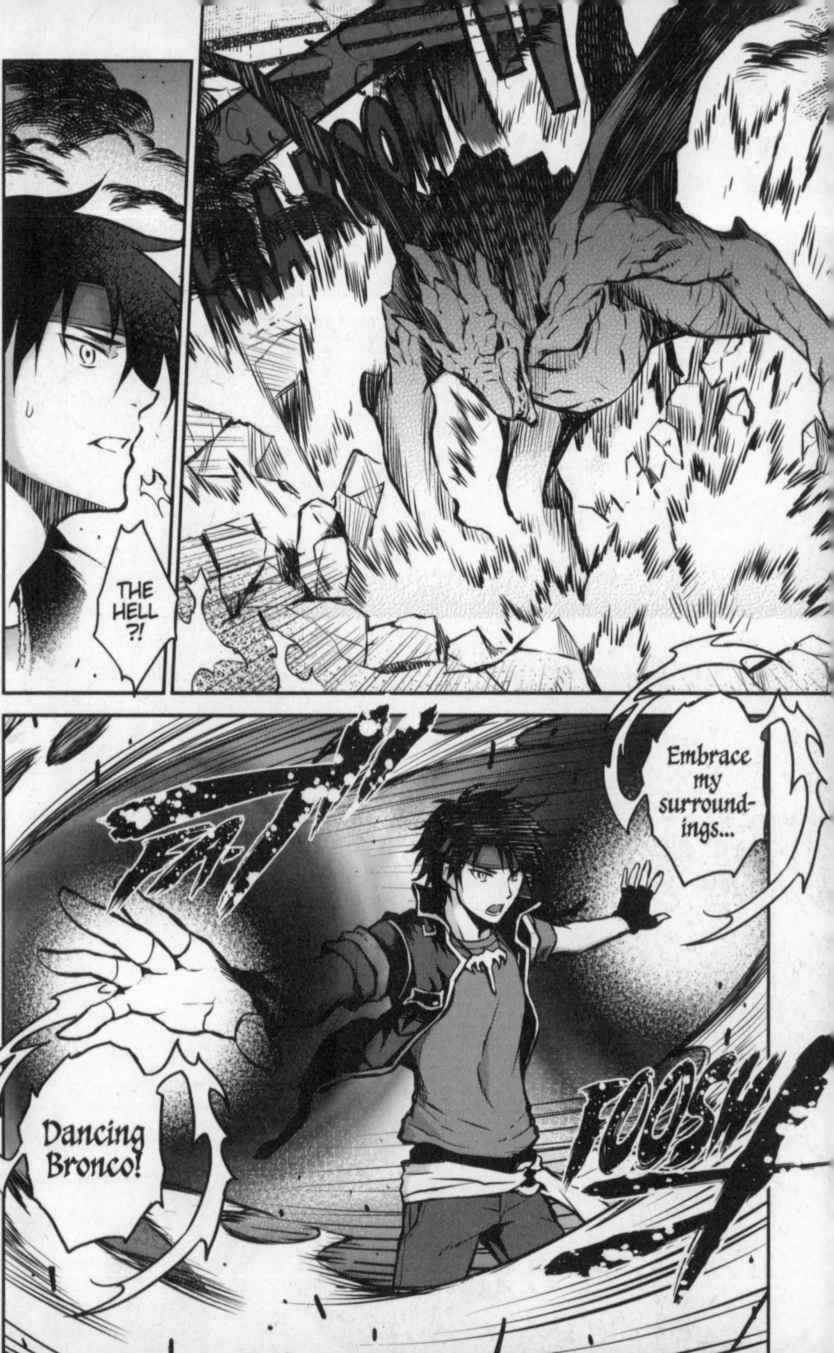
THE HELL ?!
Embrace my surroundings...
Dancing Bronco!
FOOSH

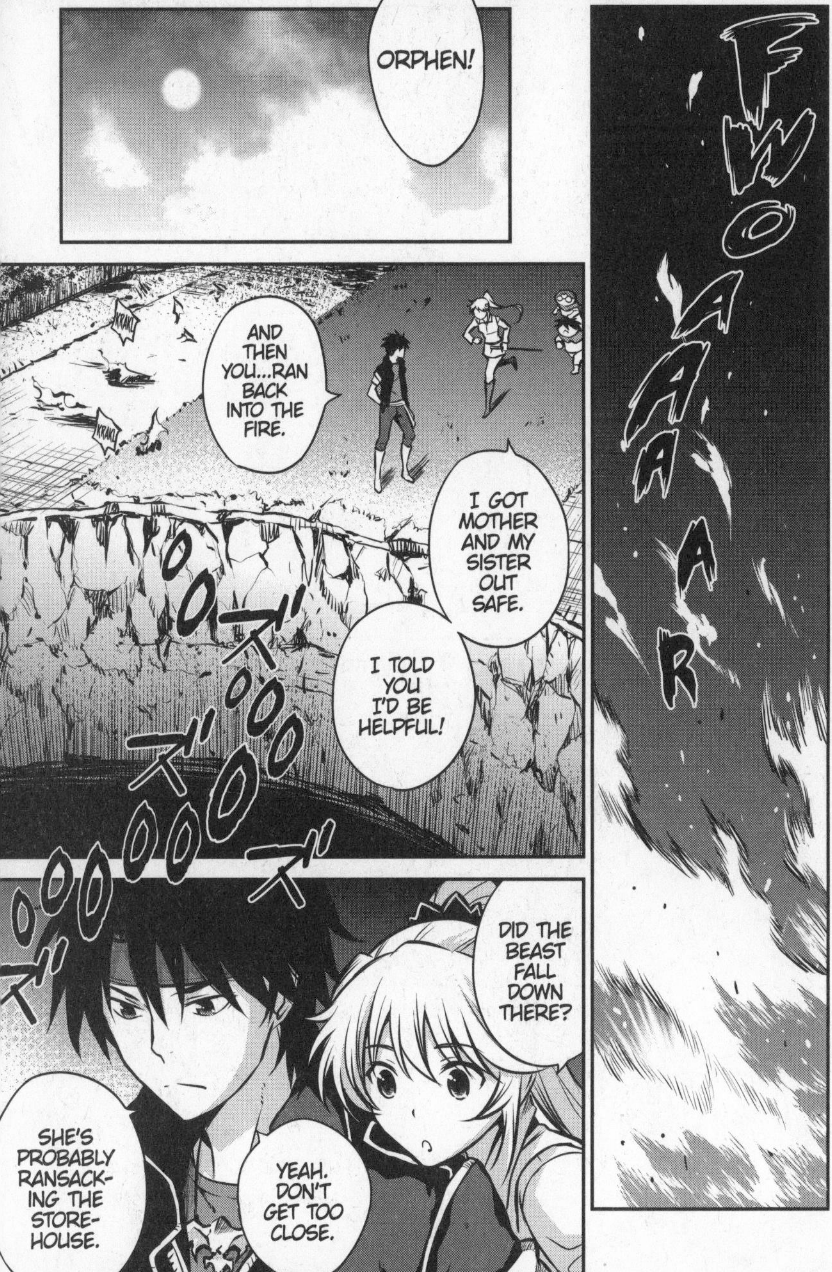
FWOAAAAR
ORPHEN!
KRAK!
KRAK!
AND THEN YOU...RAN BACK INTO THE FIRE.
I GOT MOTHER AND MY SISTER OUT SAFE.
I TOLD YOU I'D BE HELPFUL!
DID THE BEAST FALL DOWN THERE?
YEAH. DON'T GET TOO CLOSE.
SHE'S PROBABLY RANSACK-ING THE STORE-HOUSE.

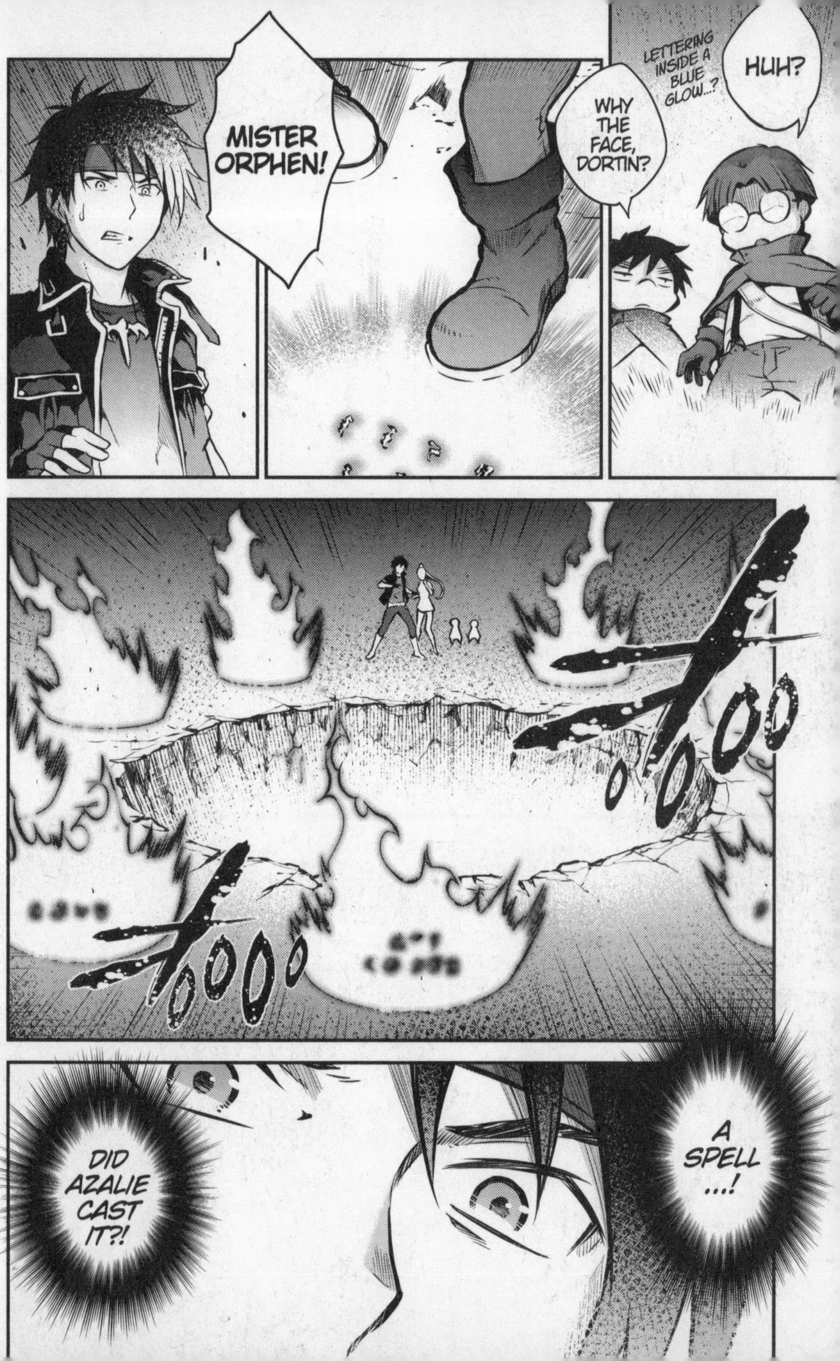
HUH?
LETTERING INSIDE A BLUE GLOW...?
WHY THE FACE, DORTIN?
MISTER ORPHEN!
A SPELL ...!
DID AZALIE CAST IT?!

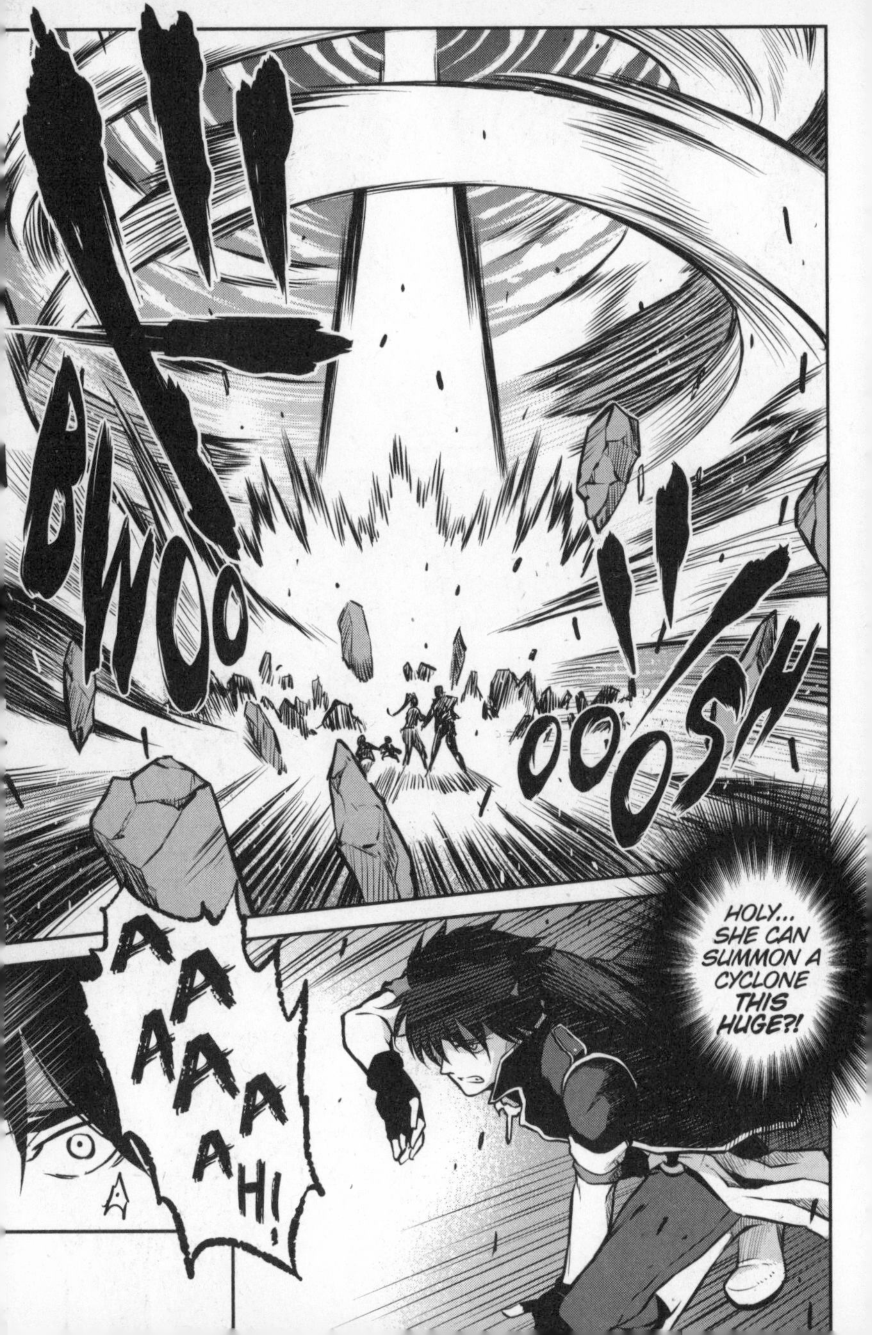
BWOOOOOSH!!!
HOLY... SHE CAN SUMMON A CYCLONE THIS HUGE?!
AAAAAAAH!

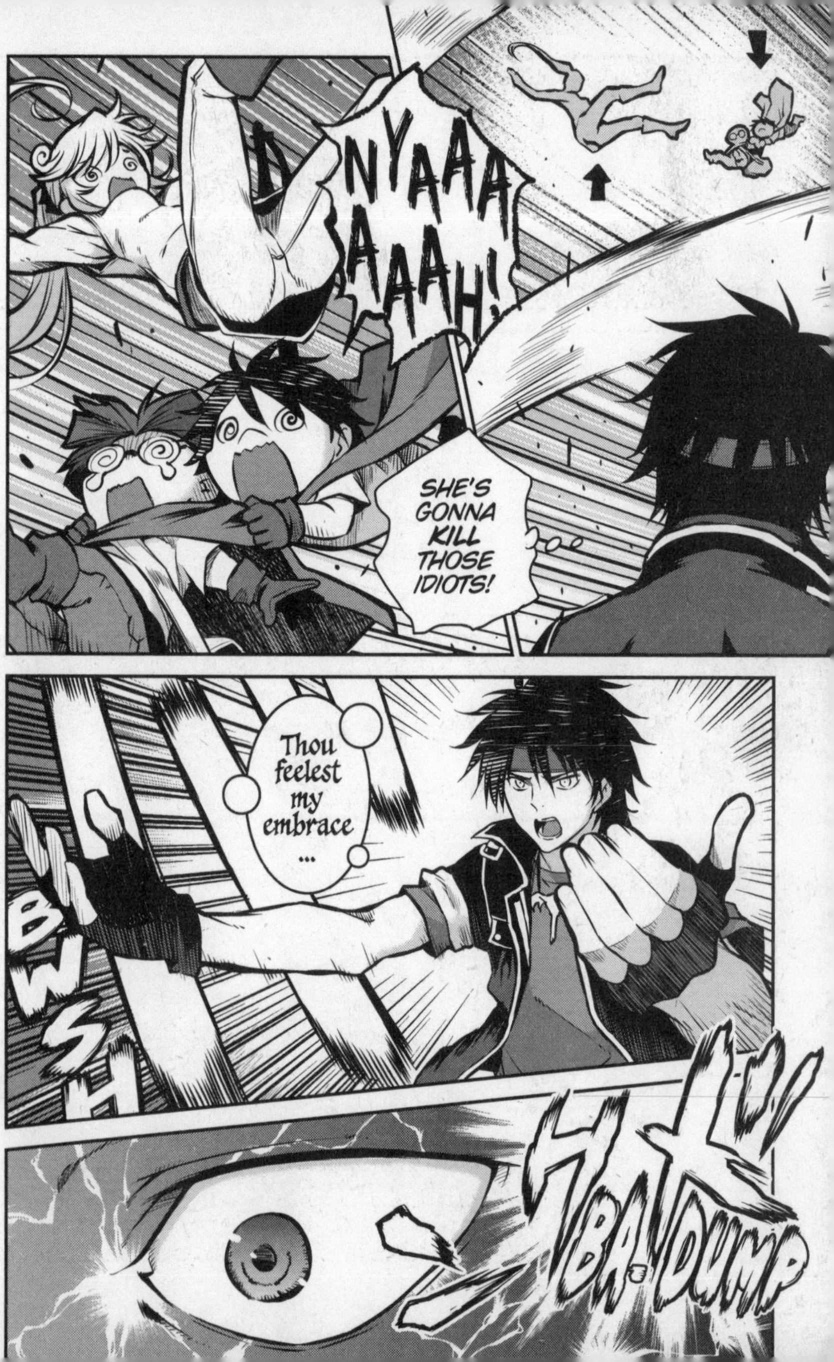
D
NYAAAAAAH!
SHE'S GONNA KILL THOSE IDIOTS!
Thou feelest my embrace ...
BWSH
BA-DUMP

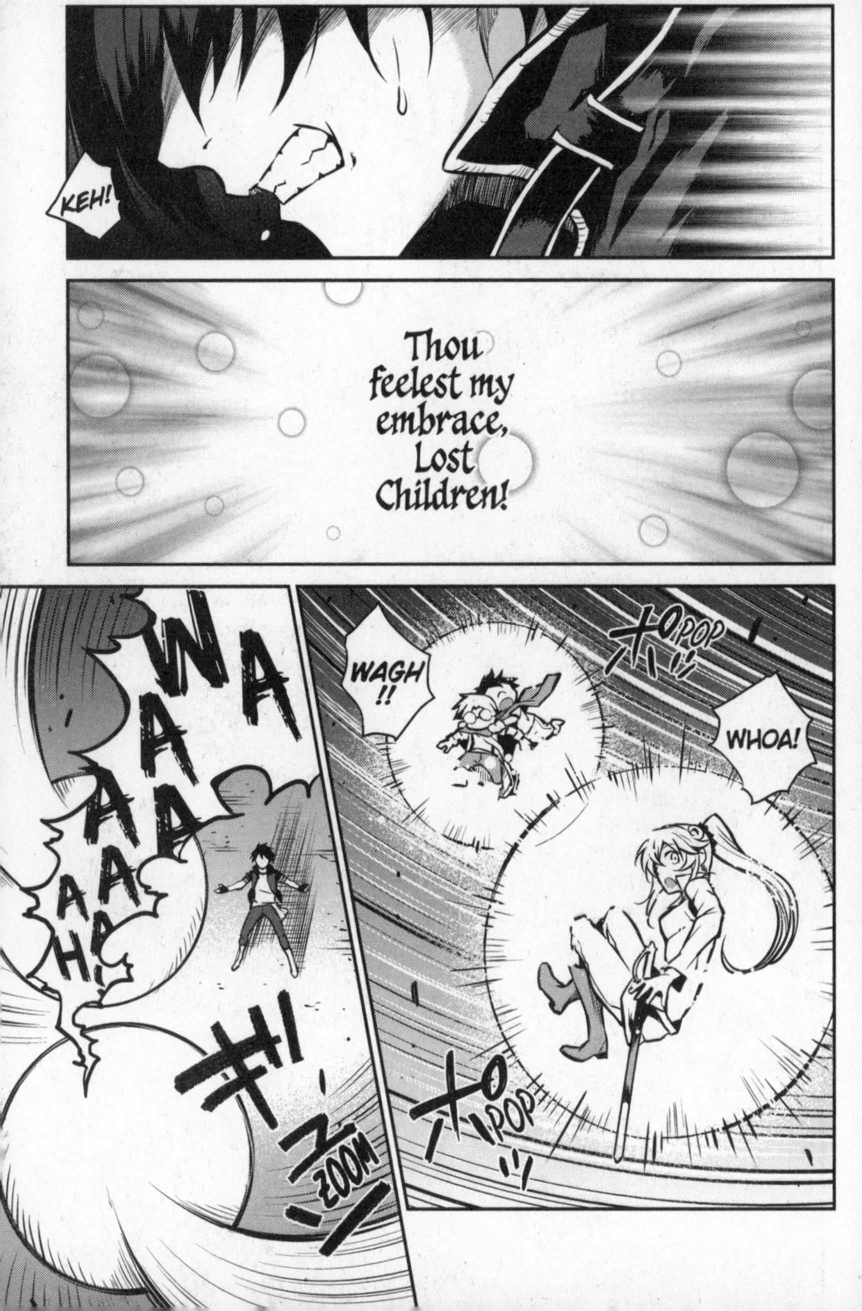
KEH!
Thou feelest my embrace, Lost Children!
POP
WAGH!!
WHOA!
POP
WAAAAAAAH!
ZOOM

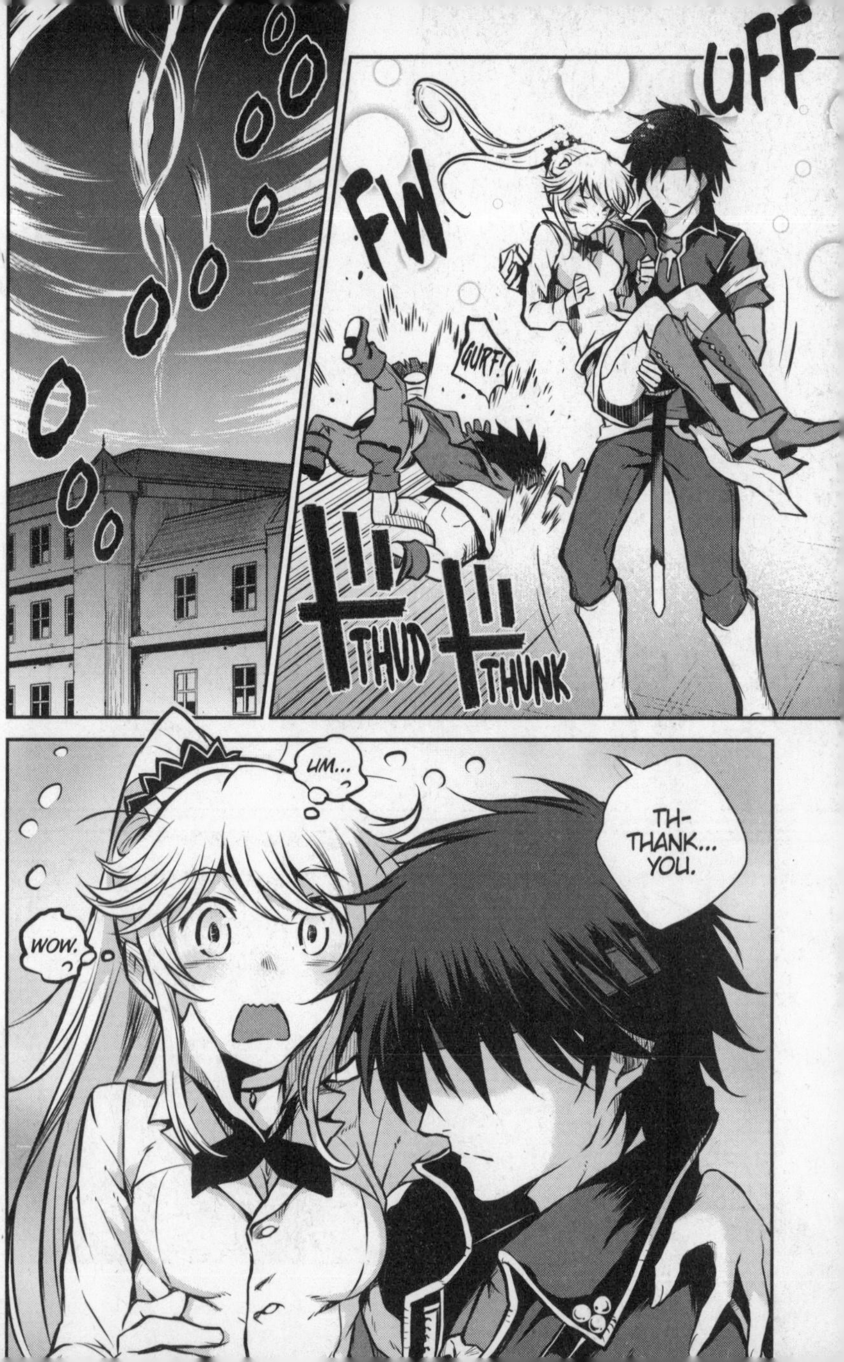
UFF
FW
GURF!
THUD
THUNK
UM...
TH-THANK... YOU.
WOW.

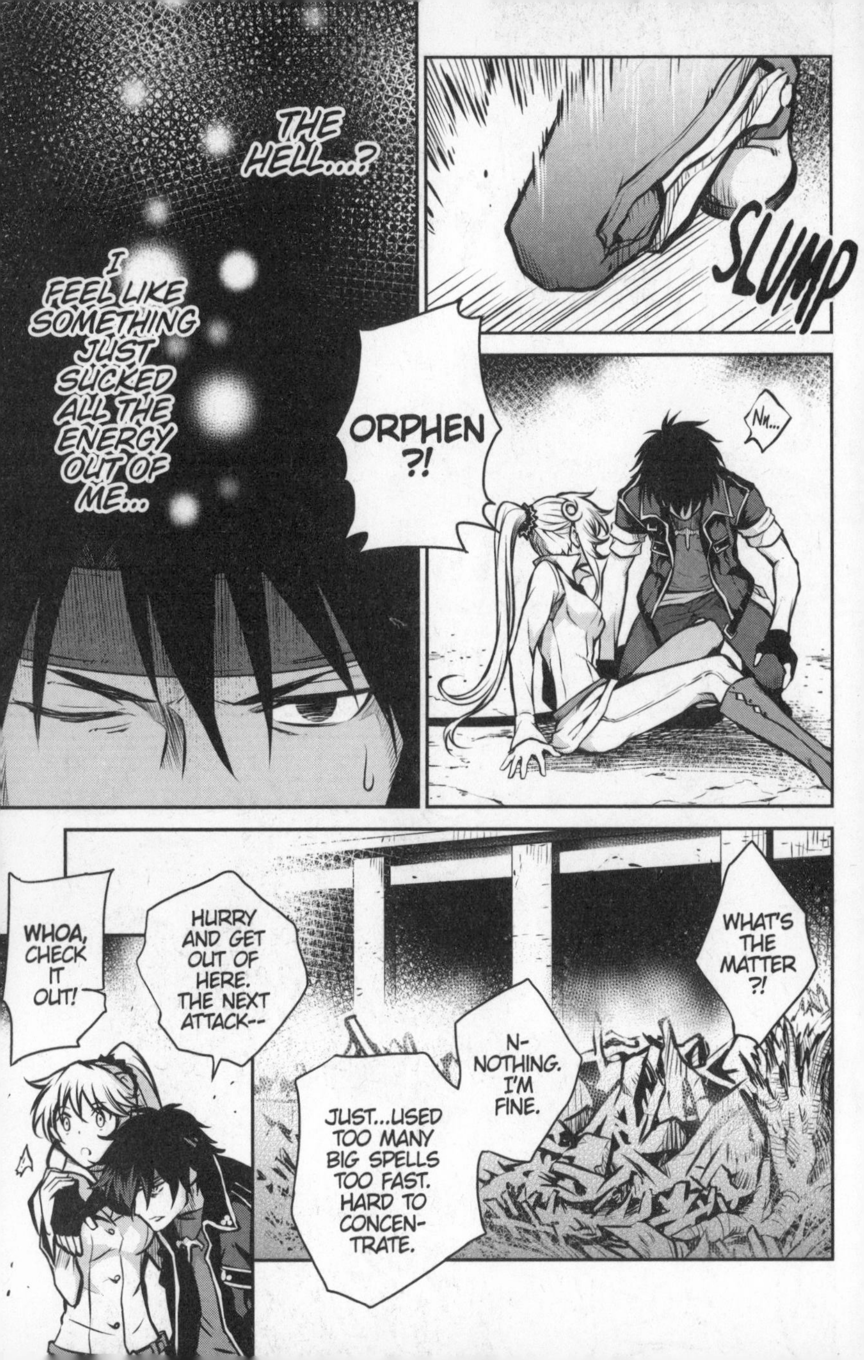
SLUMP
ORPHEN ?!
Nn...
THE HELL...?
I FEEL LIKE SOMETHING JUST SUCKED ALL THE ENERGY OUT OF ME...
WHAT'S THE MATTER ?!
N-NOTHING. I'M FINE.
JUST...USED TOO MANY BIG SPELLS TOO FAST. HARD TO CONCEN-TRATE.
HURRY AND GET OUT OF HERE. THE NEXT ATTACK--
WHOA, CHECK IT OUT!

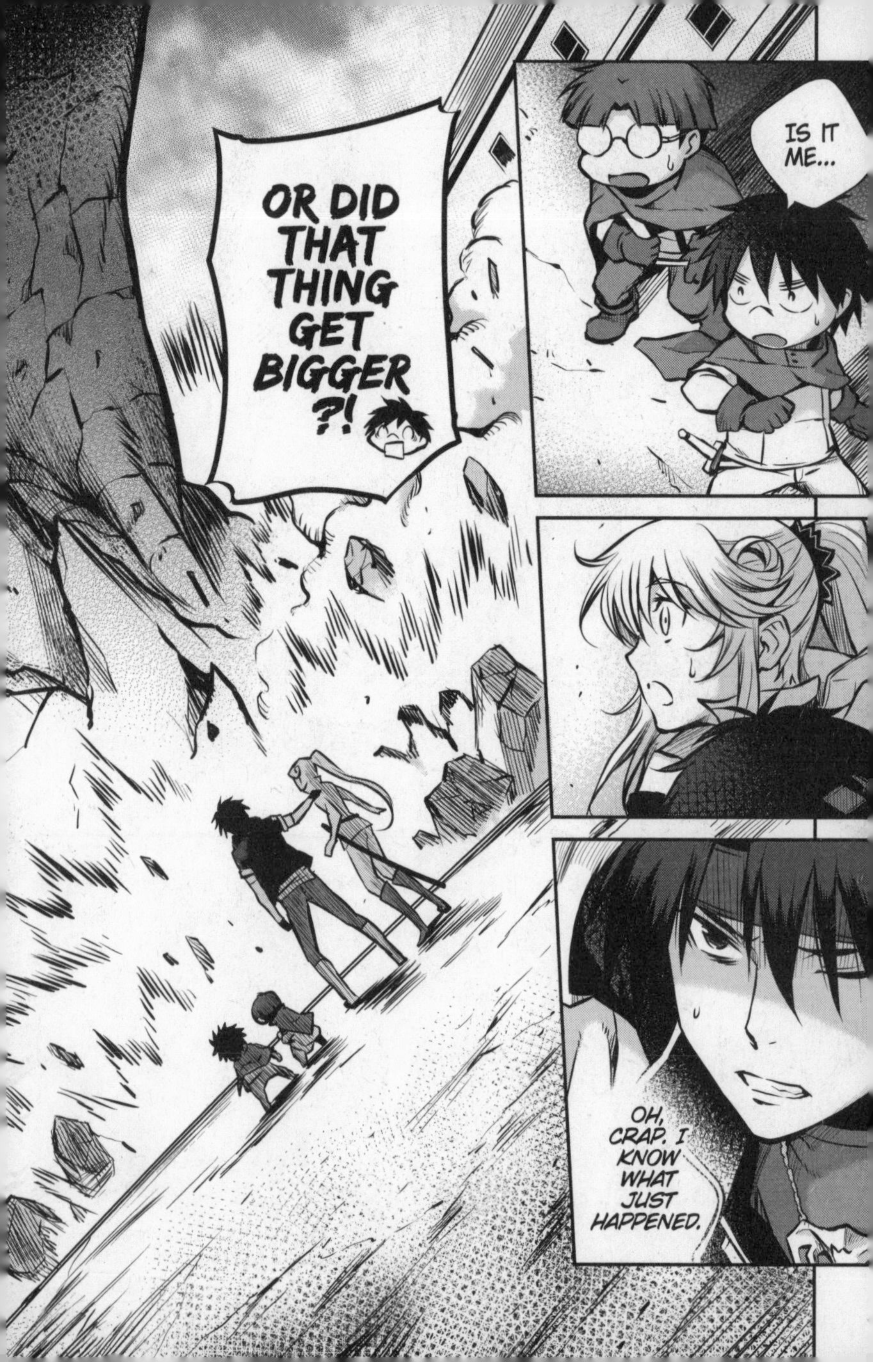
IS IT ME...
OH, CRAP. I KNOW WHAT JUST HAPPENED.
OR DID THAT THING GET BIGGER?!

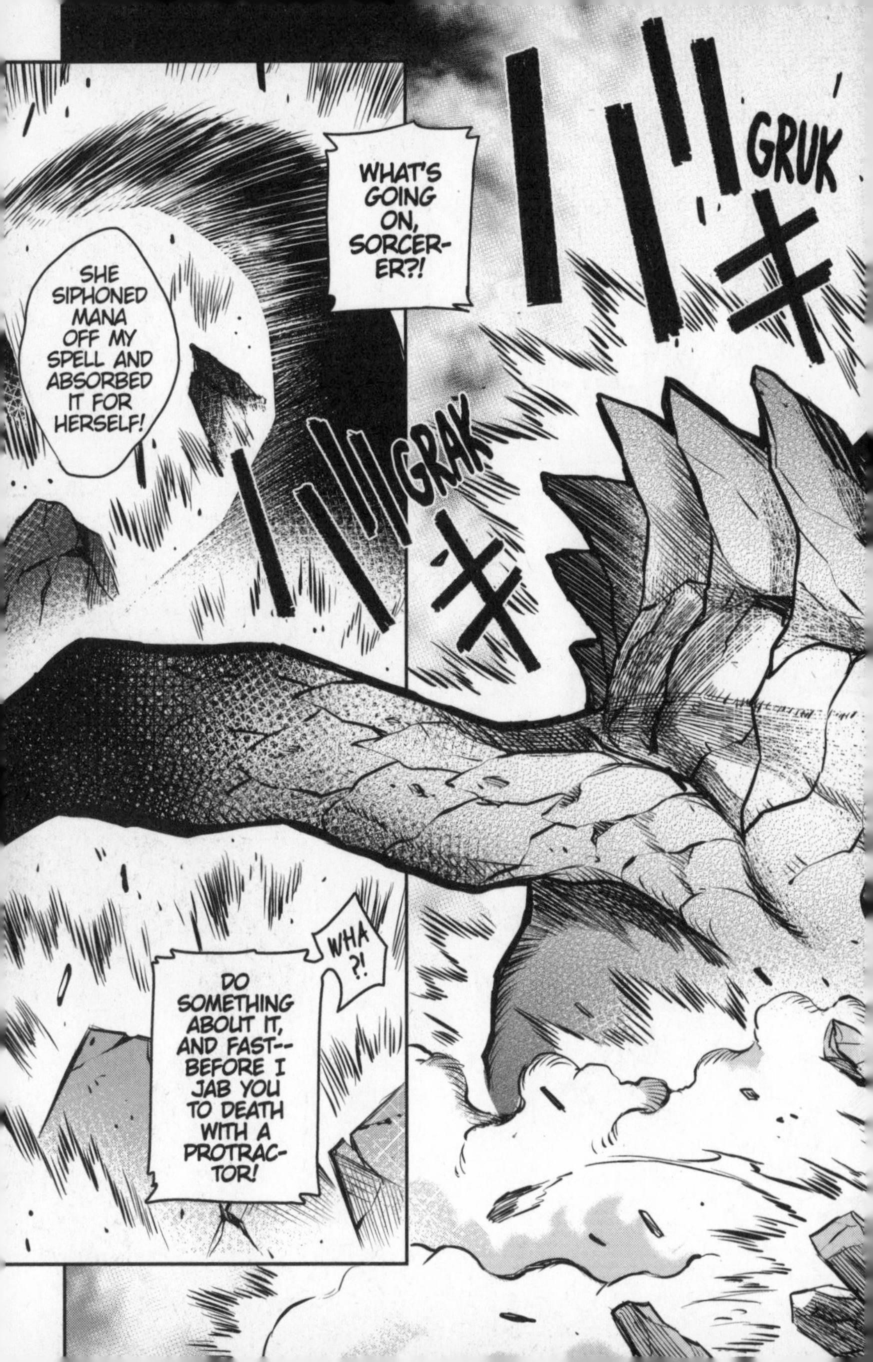
GRUK
GRAK
WHAT'S GOING ON, SORCERER?!
SHE SIPHONED MANA OFF MY SPELL AND ABSORBED IT FOR HERSELF!
WHA?!
DO SOMETHING ABOUT IT, AND FAST--BEFORE I JAB YOU TO DEATH WITH A PROTRACTOR!

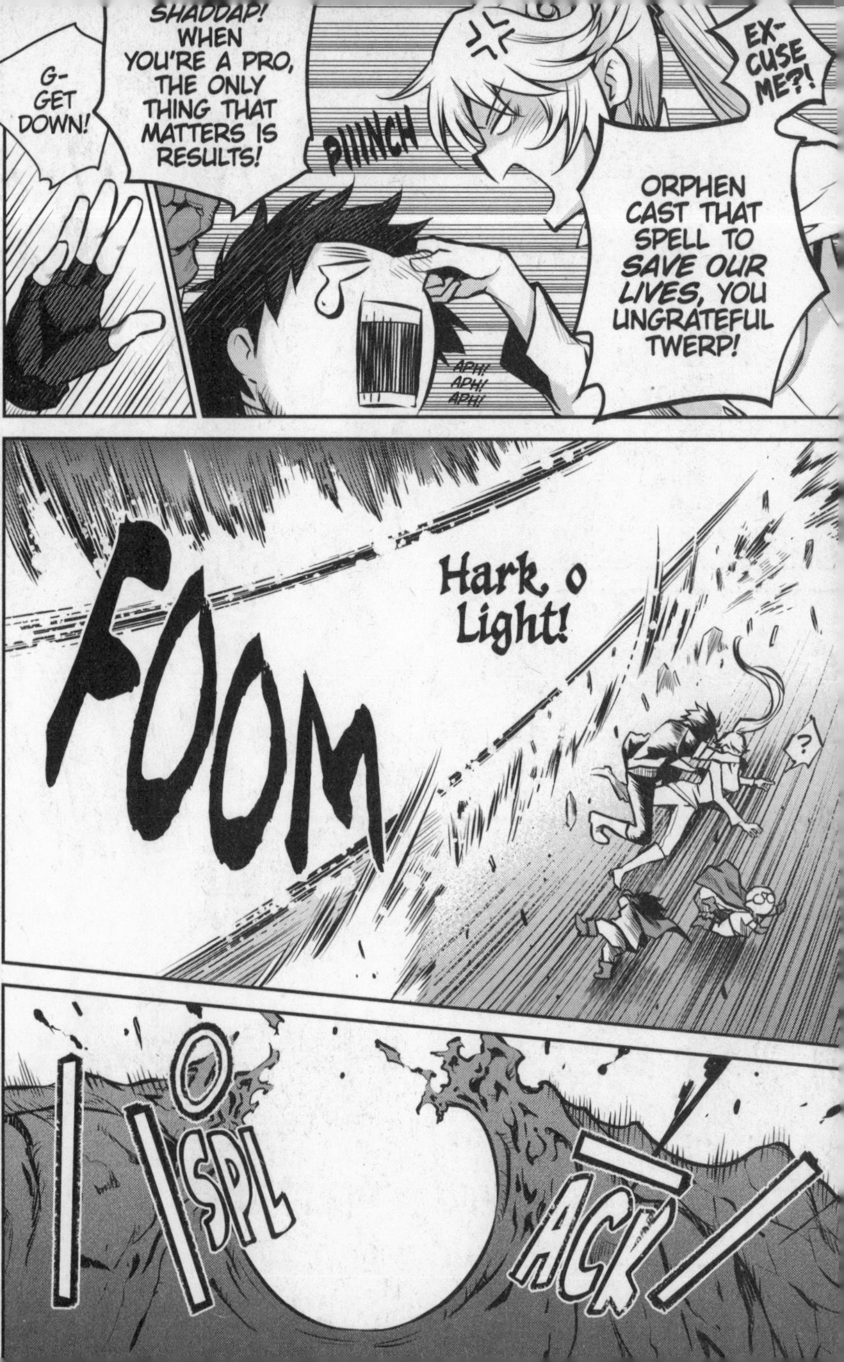
EX-CUSE ME?!
SHADDAP! WHEN YOU'RE A PRO, THE ONLY THING THAT MATTERS IS RESULTS!
PIIINCH
ORPHEN CAST THAT SPELL TO SAVE OUR LIVES, YOU UNGRATEFUL TWERP!
G-GET DOWN!
APH! APH! APH!
Hark, o Light!
FOOM
?
SPLACK

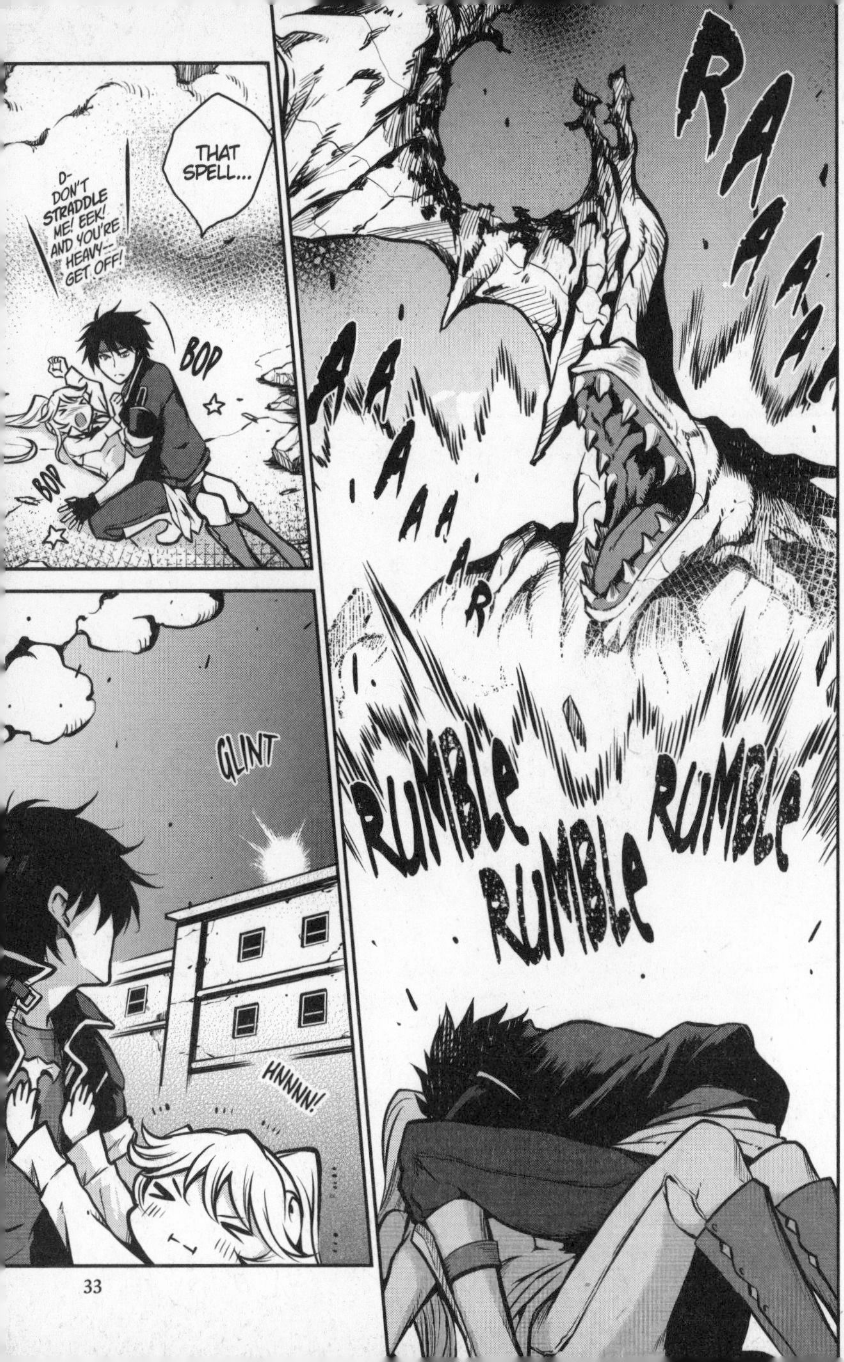
RAAAAAAA
AAAAAAR
RUMBLE RUMBLE
RUMBLE RUMBLE
THAT SPELL...
D-DON'T STRADDLE ME! EEK! AND YOU'RE HEAVY-- GET OFF!
BOP
BOP
GLINT
HNNNN!

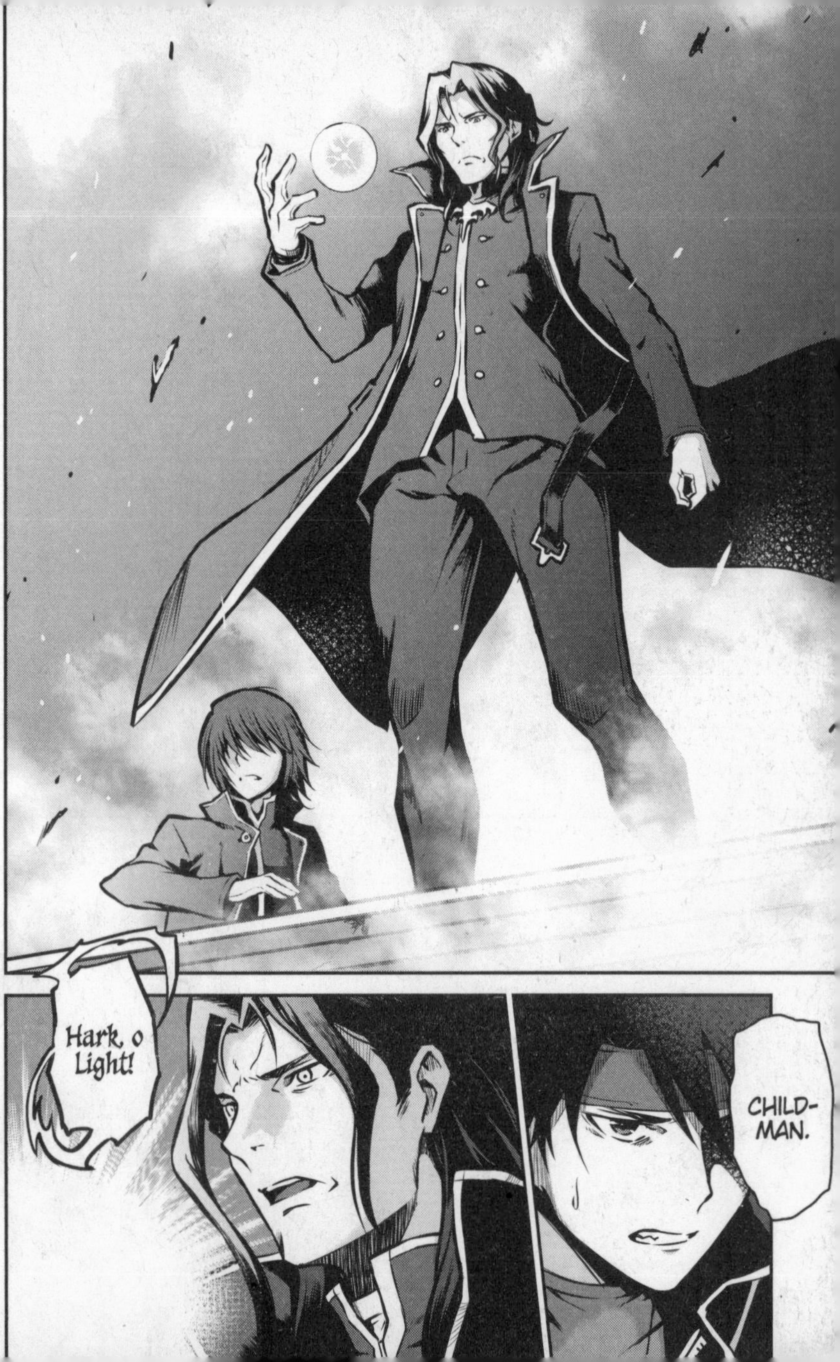
CHILD-
MAN.
Hark, o
Light!

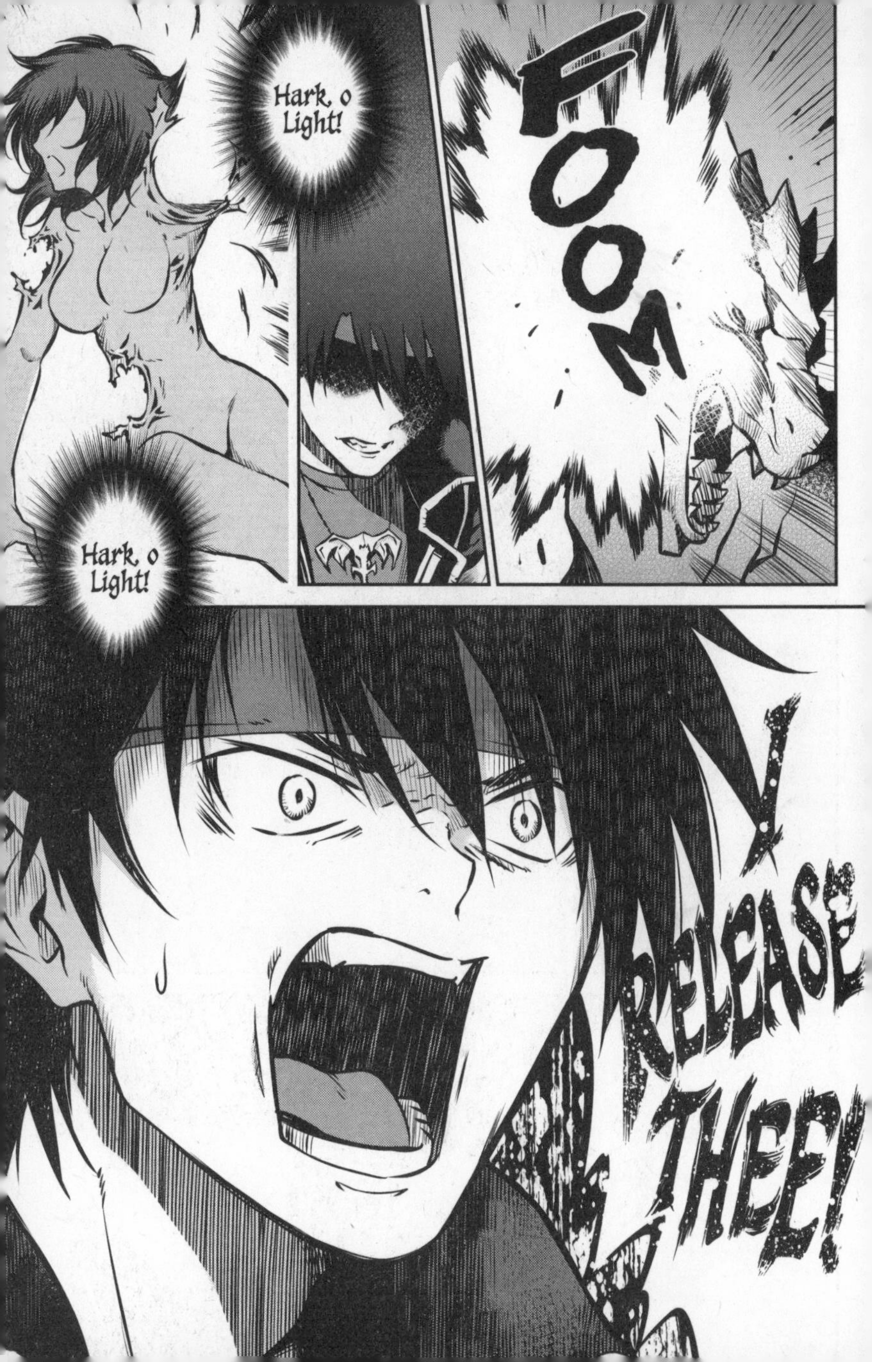
FOOM
Hark, o Light!
Hark, o Light!
RELEASE THEE!

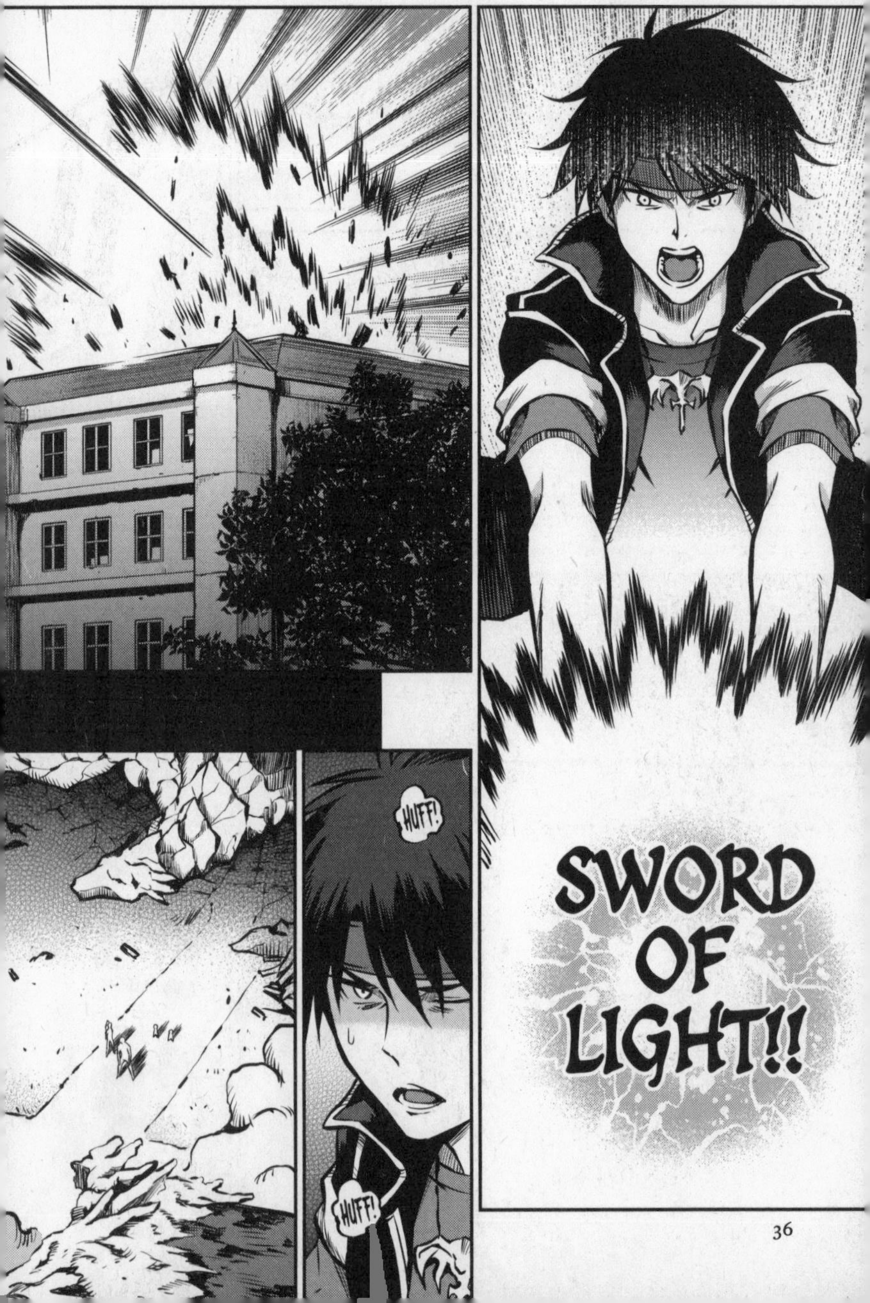
SWORD OF LIGHT!!
HUFF!
HUFF!

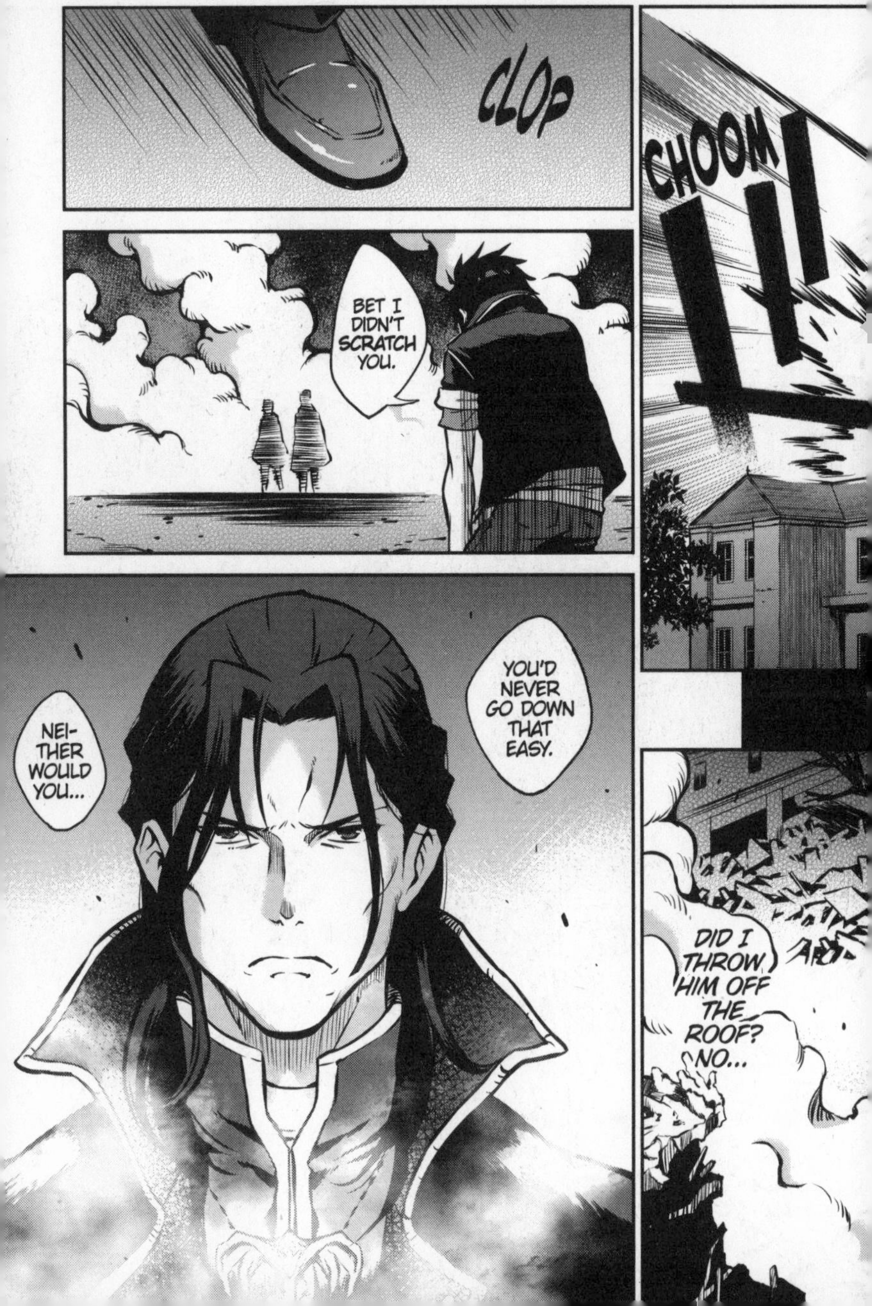
CHOOM!!
CLOP
BET I DIDN'T SCRATCH YOU.
DID I THROW HIM OFF THE ROOF? NO...
YOU'D NEVER GO DOWN THAT EASY.
NEI-THER WOULD YOU...

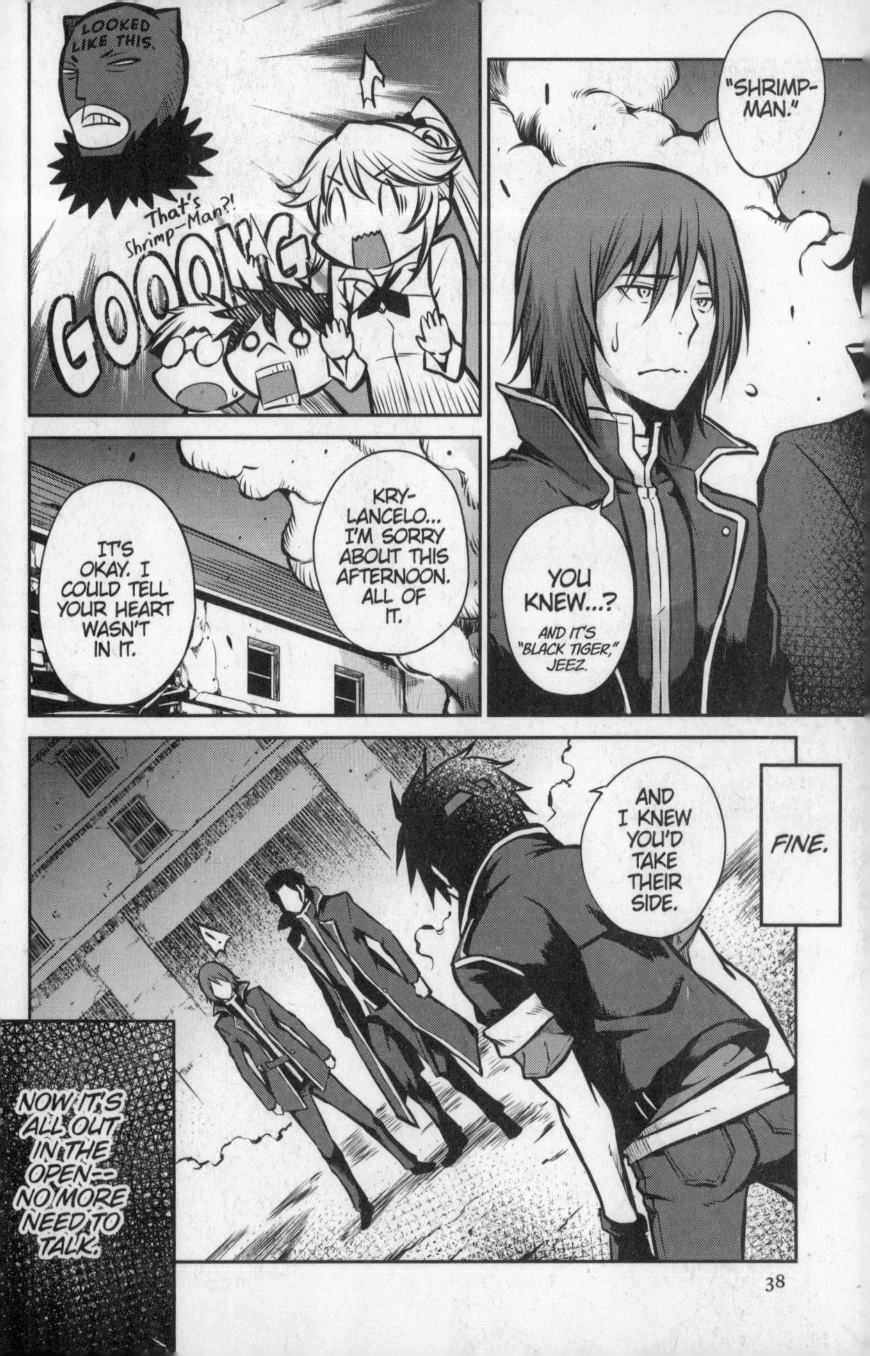
"SHRIMP-MAN."
YOU KNEW...?
AND IT'S "BLACK TIGER," JEEZ.
LOOKED LIKE THIS.
That's Shrimp-Man?!
GOOONG
KRY-LANCELO... I'M SORRY ABOUT THIS AFTERNOON. ALL OF IT.
IT'S OKAY. I COULD TELL YOUR HEART WASN'T IN IT.
FINE.
AND I KNEW YOU'D TAKE THEIR SIDE.
NOW IT'S ALL OUT IN THE OPEN— NO MORE NEED TO TALK.

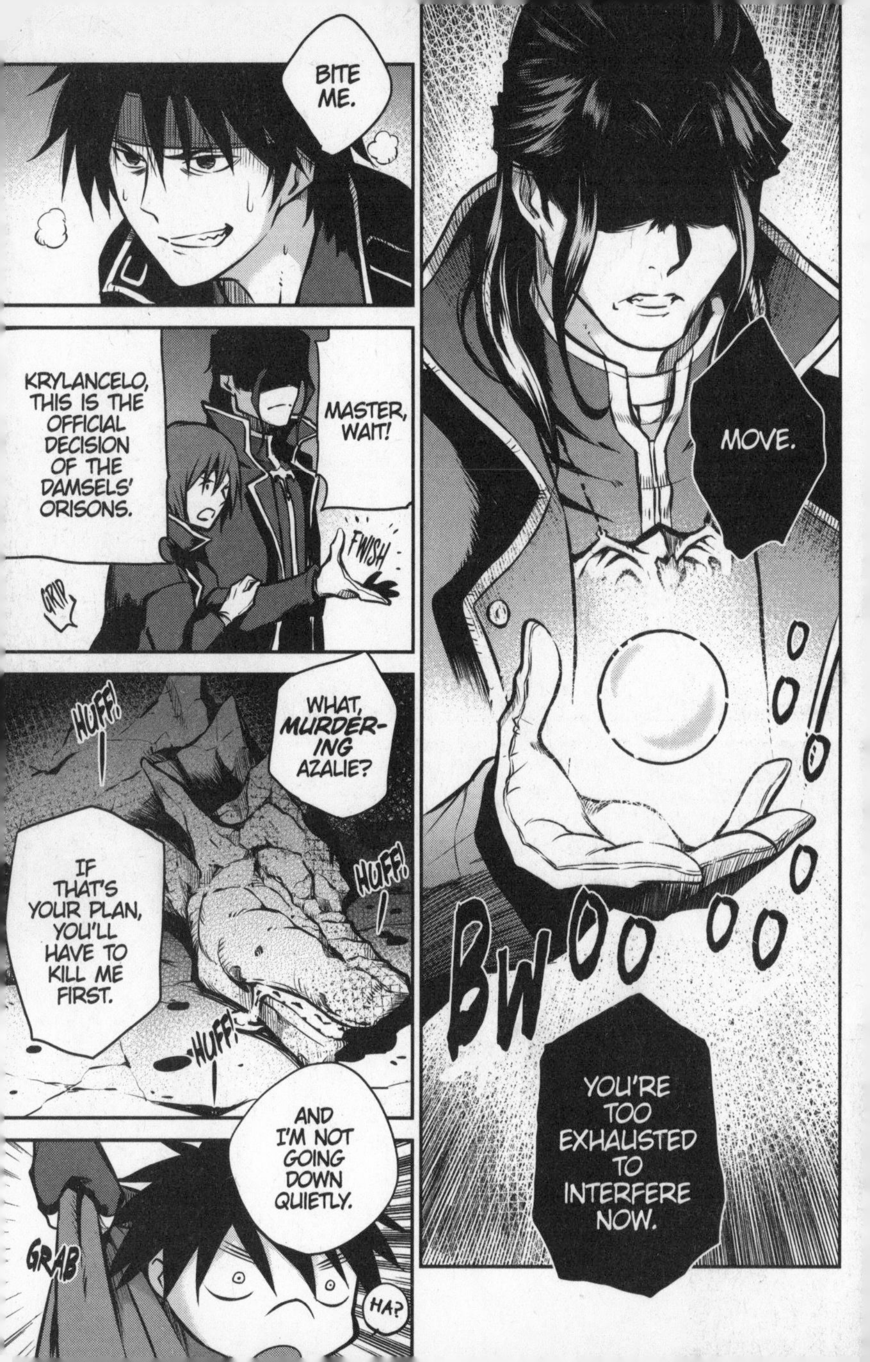
MOVE.
BWOOOOOOO
YOU'RE TOO EXHAUSTED TO INTERFERE NOW.
BITE ME.
MASTER, WAIT!
KRYLANCELO, THIS IS THE OFFICIAL DECISION OF THE DAMSELS' ORISONS.
FWISH
GRIP
WHAT, MURDERING AZALIE?
HUFF!
HUFF!
IF THAT'S YOUR PLAN, YOU'LL HAVE TO KILL ME FIRST.
HUFF!
AND I'M NOT GOING DOWN QUIETLY.
GRAB
HA?

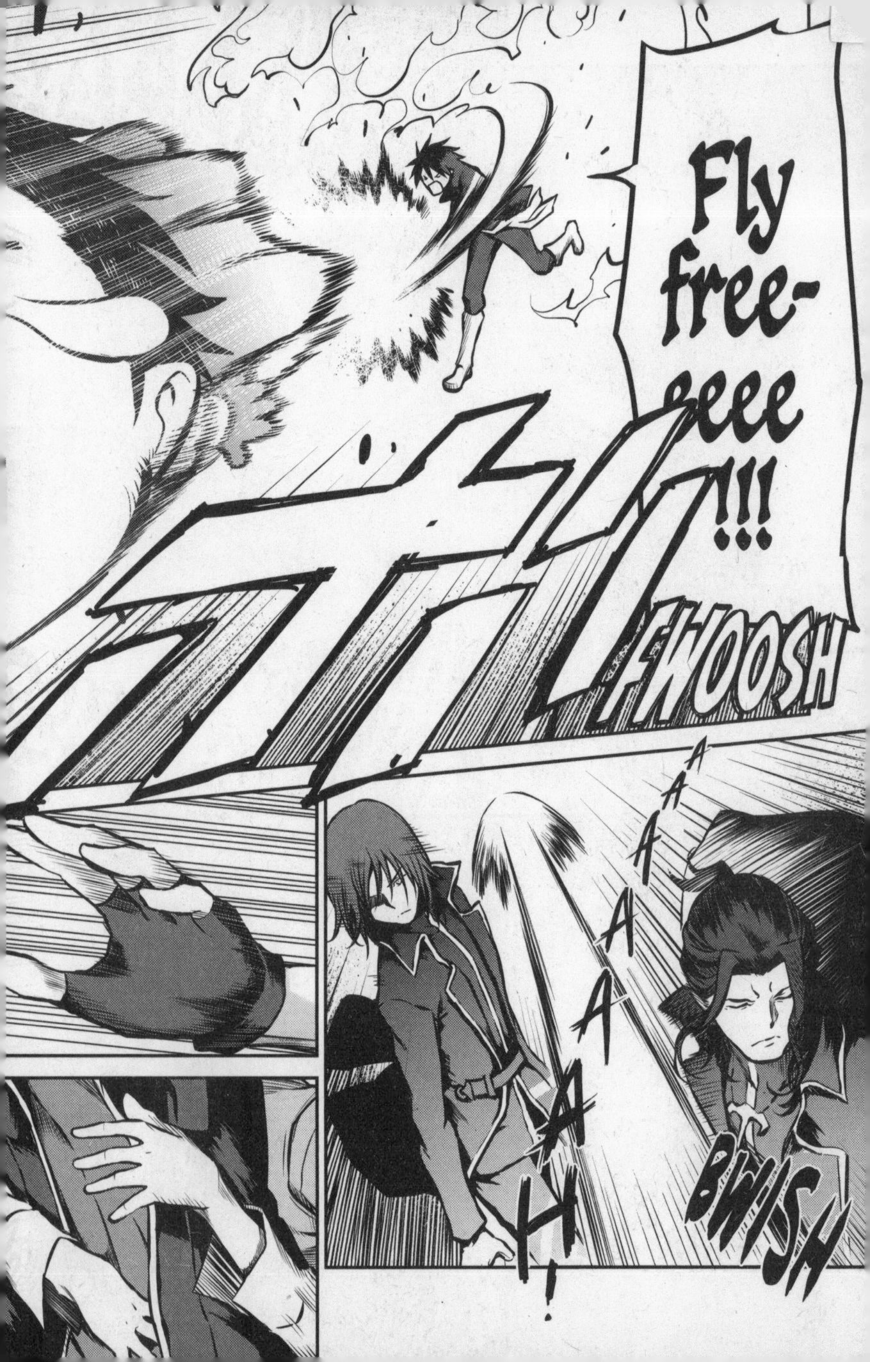
Fly free-eeee!!!
WHOOSH
BWISH
AAAAAAH!

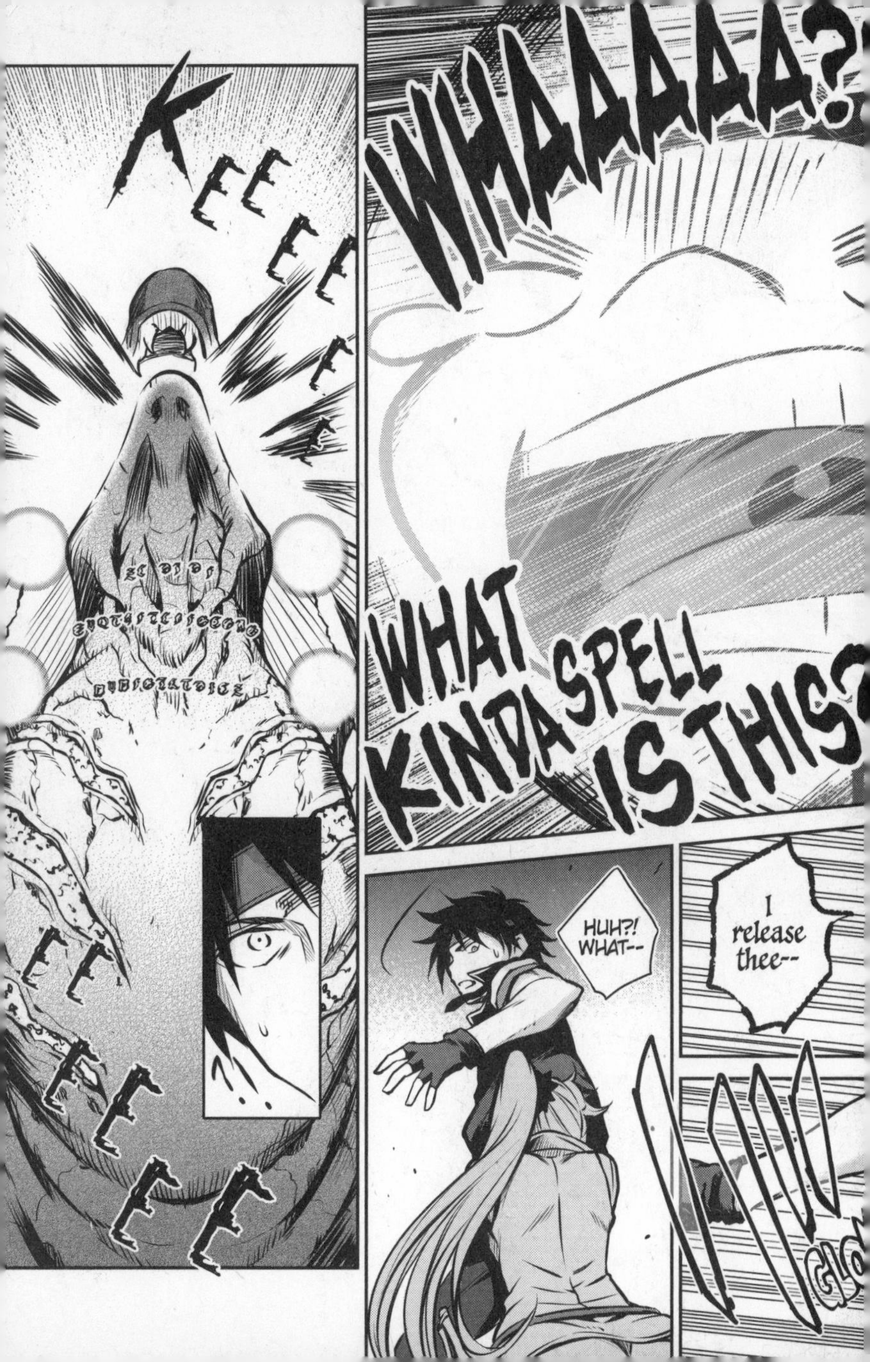
WHAAAAAA
WHAT KINDA SPELL IS THIS
I release thee--
HUH?! WHAT--
KEEEEEEEEEEEEEE

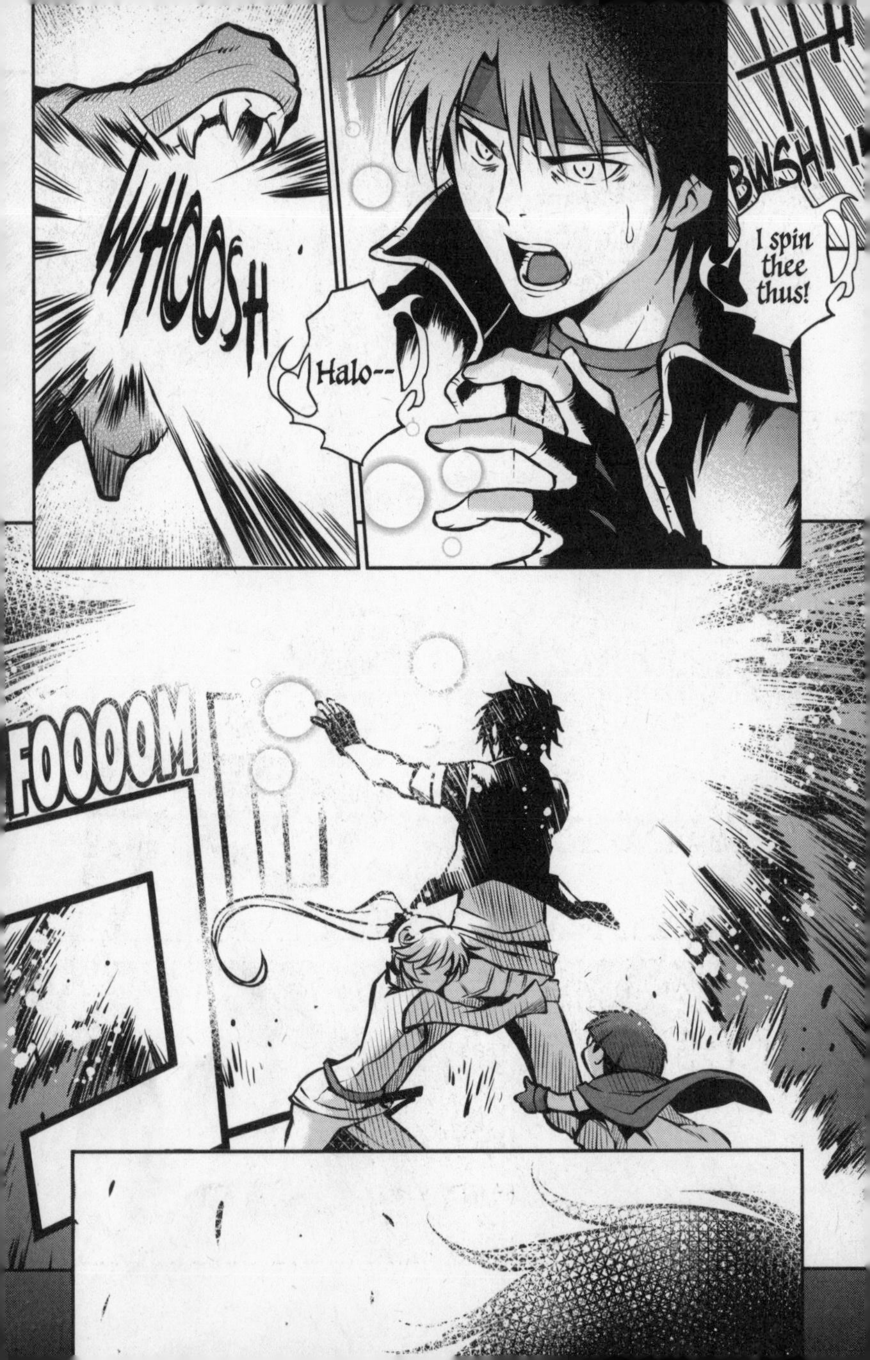
BWSH!!
I spin thee thus!
Halo--
WHOOSH
FOOOM

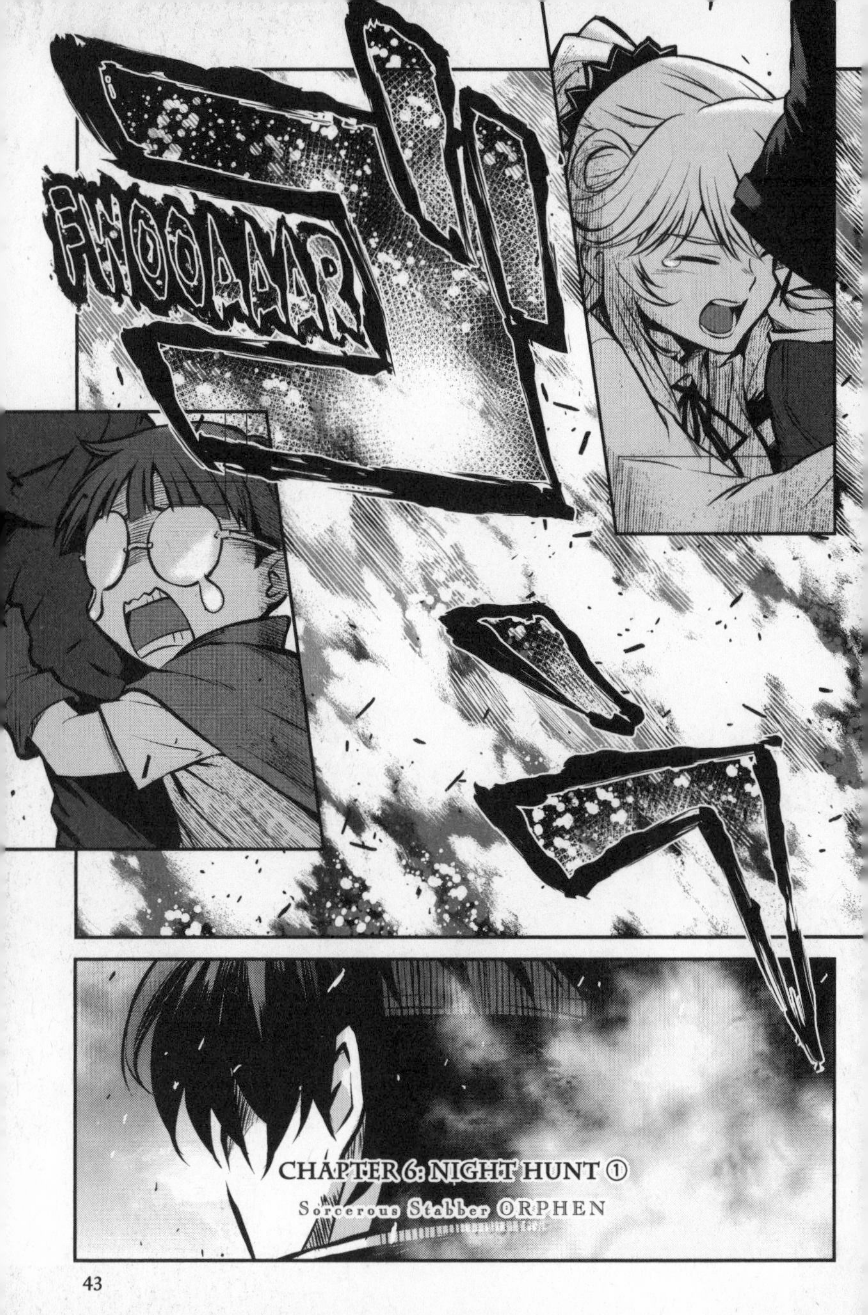
FWOOAAAR
CHAPTER 6: NIGHT HUNT ①
Sorcerous Stabber ORPHEN

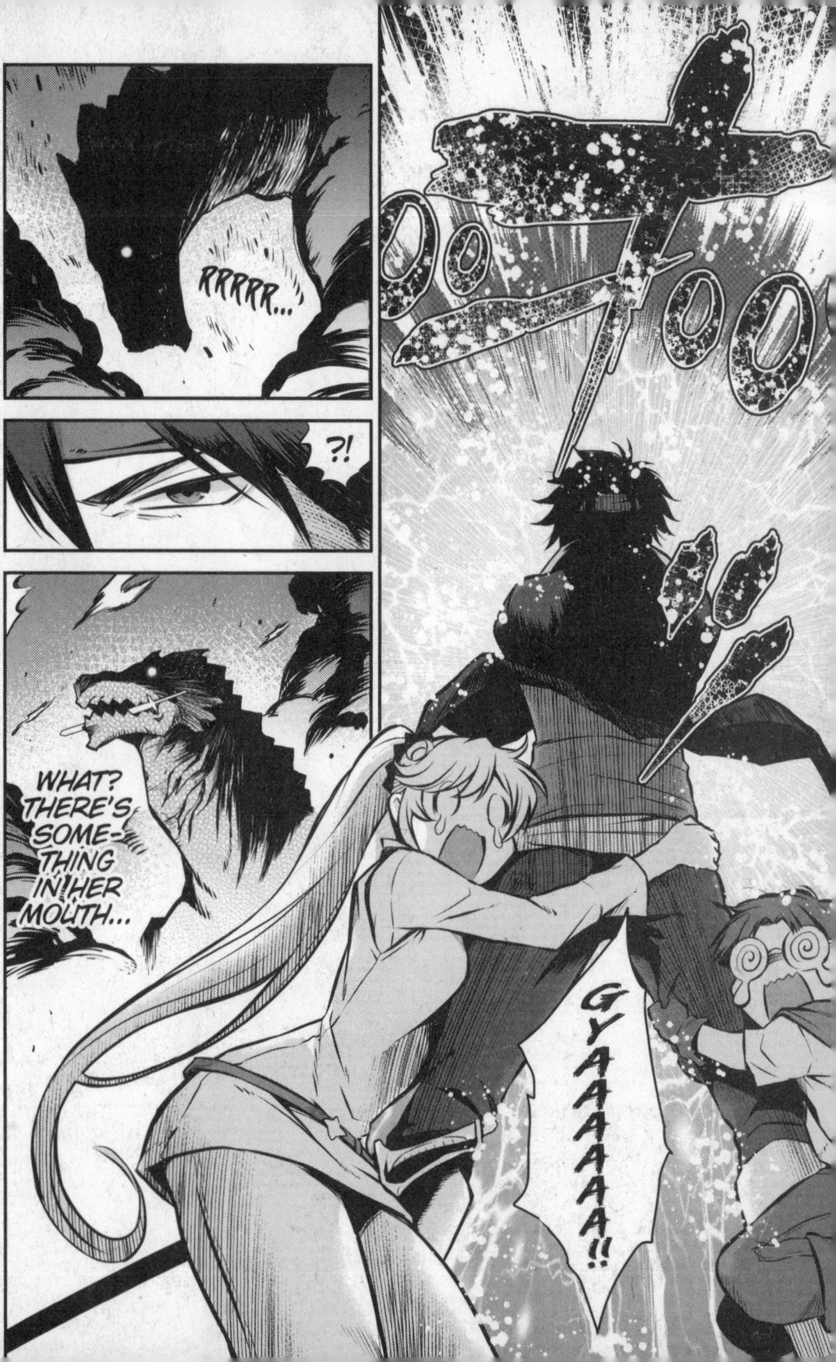
GYAAAAAAA!!
RRRRR...
?!
WHAT? THERE'S SOME-THING IN HER MOUTH...

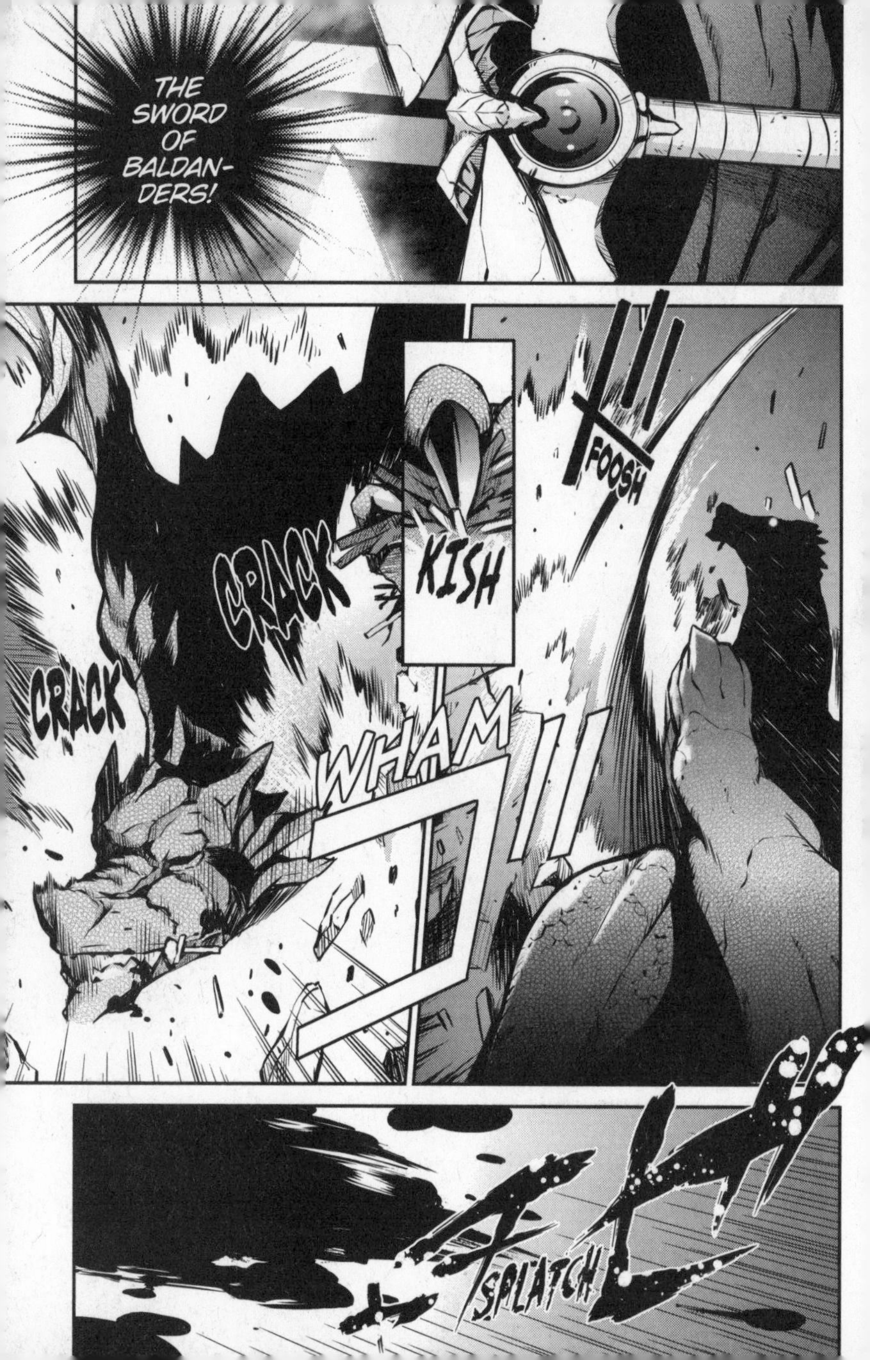
THE SWORD OF BALDAN-DERS!
FOOSH
KISH
CRACK
CRACK
WHAM
SPLATCH

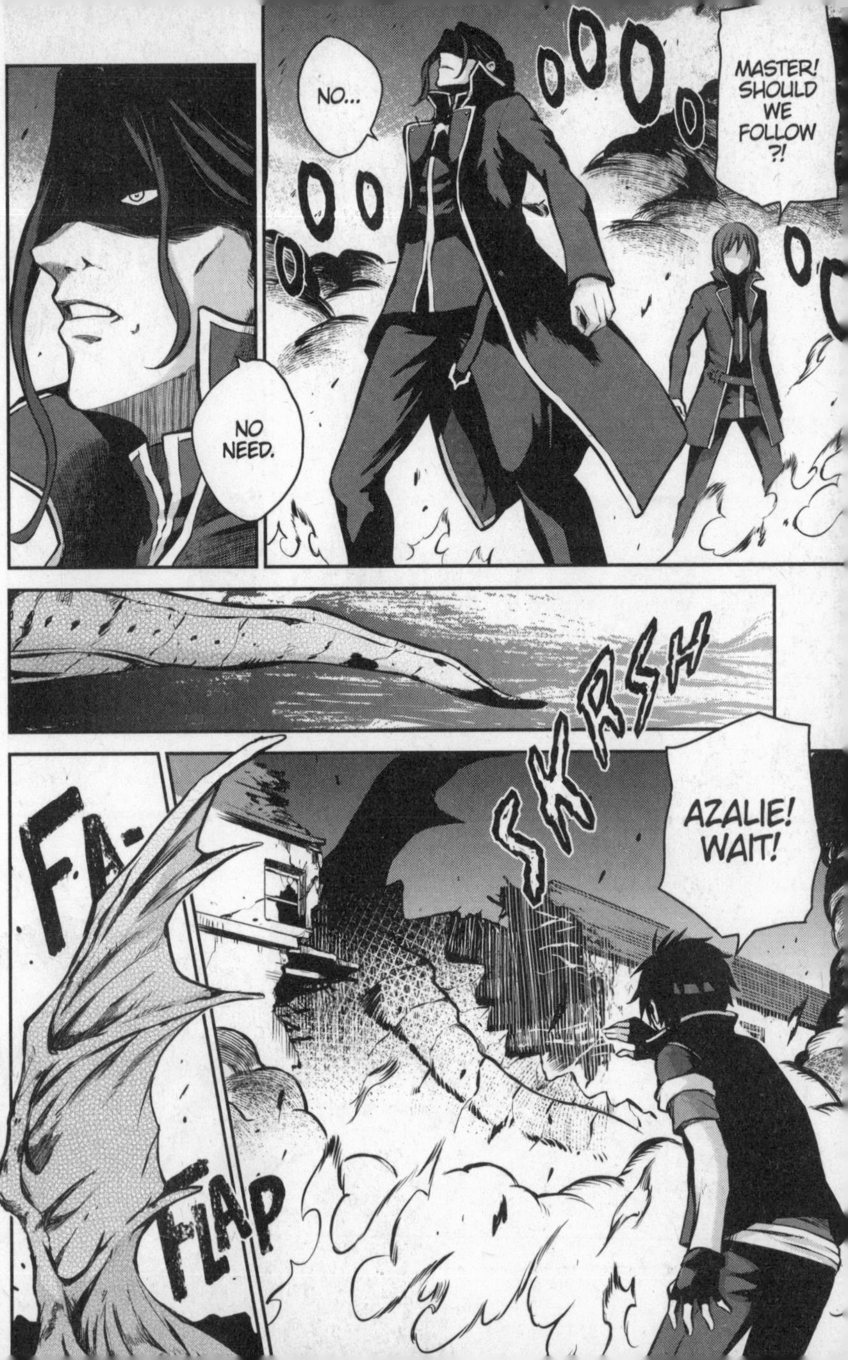
MASTER! SHOULD WE FOLLOW ?!
NO...
NO NEED.
SKRSH
AZALIE! WAIT!
FA-
FLAP

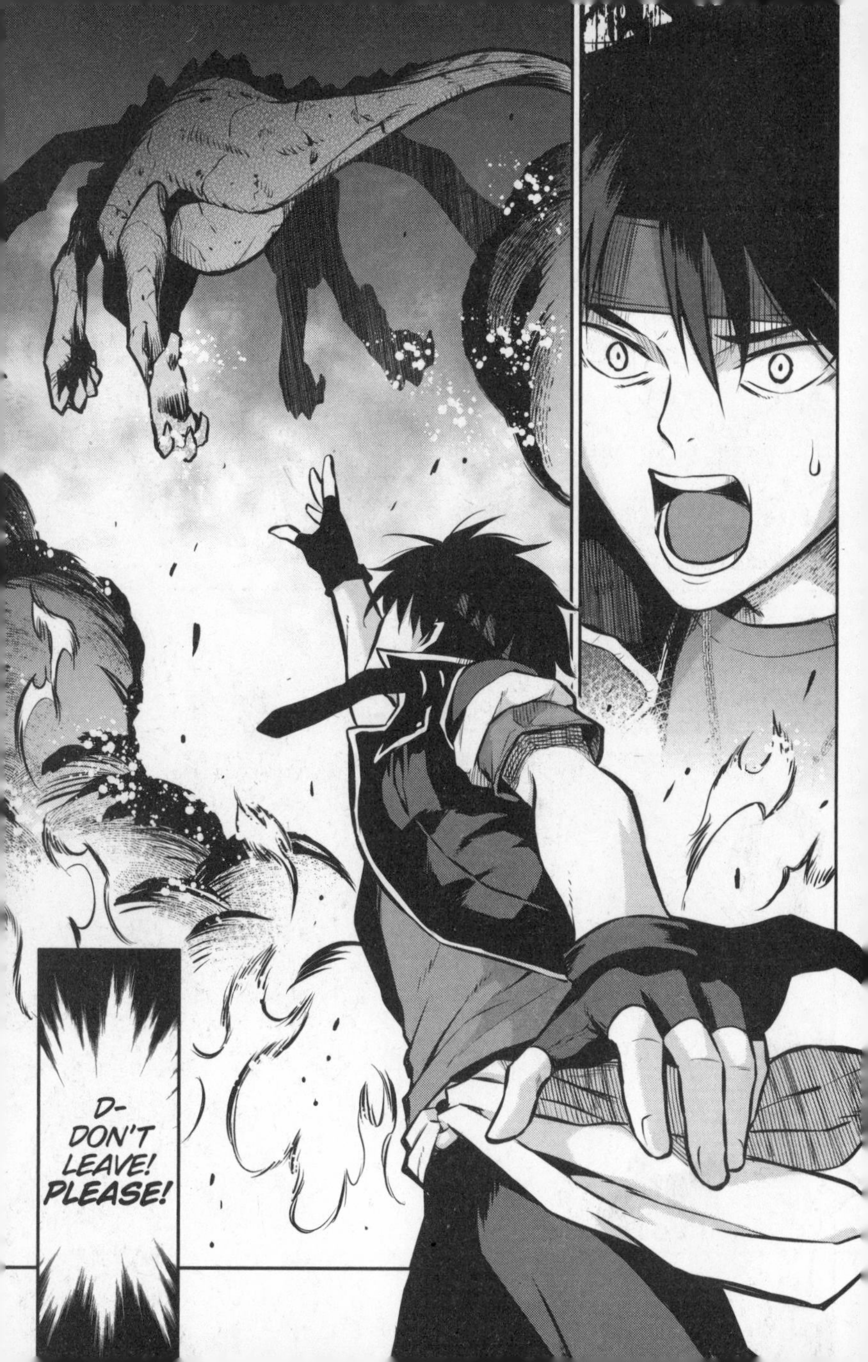
D- DON'T LEAVE! PLEASE!

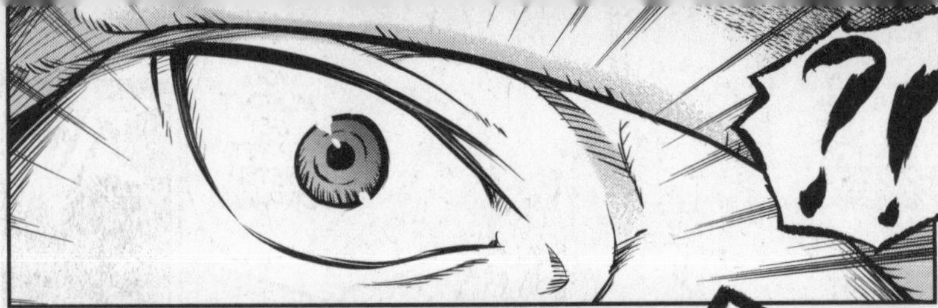
?!

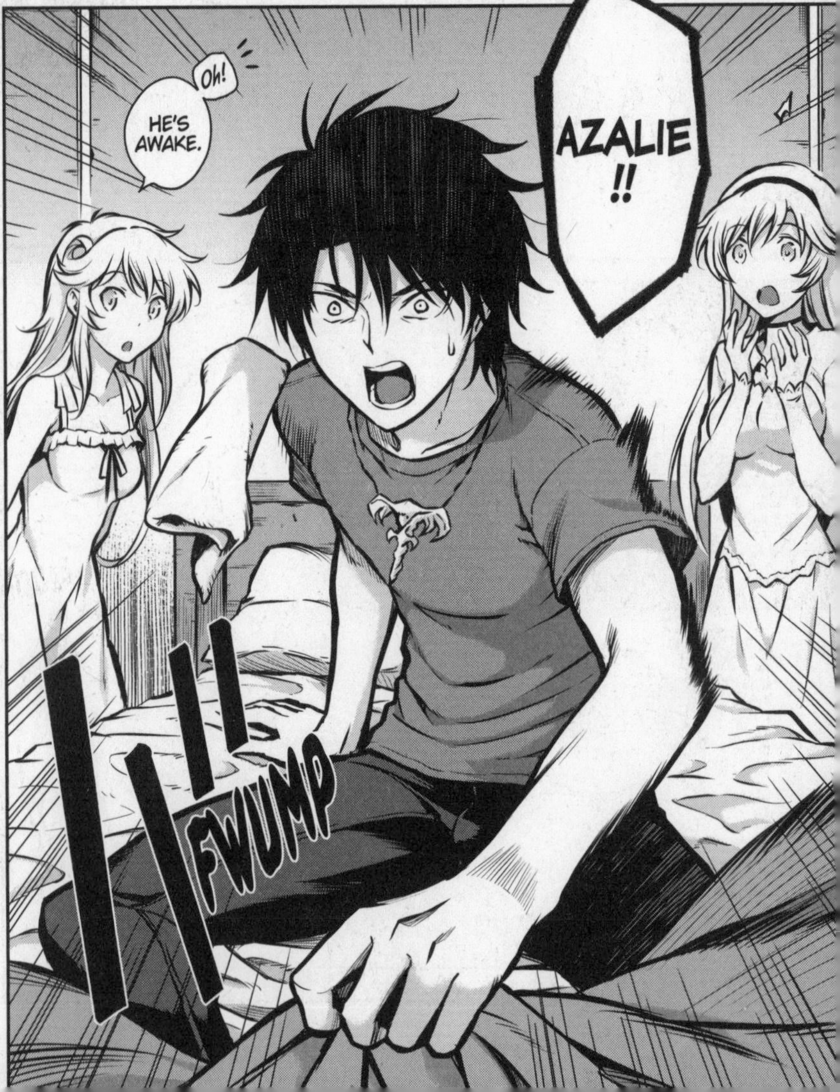
AZALIE !!
Oh!
HE'S AWAKE.
FWUMP

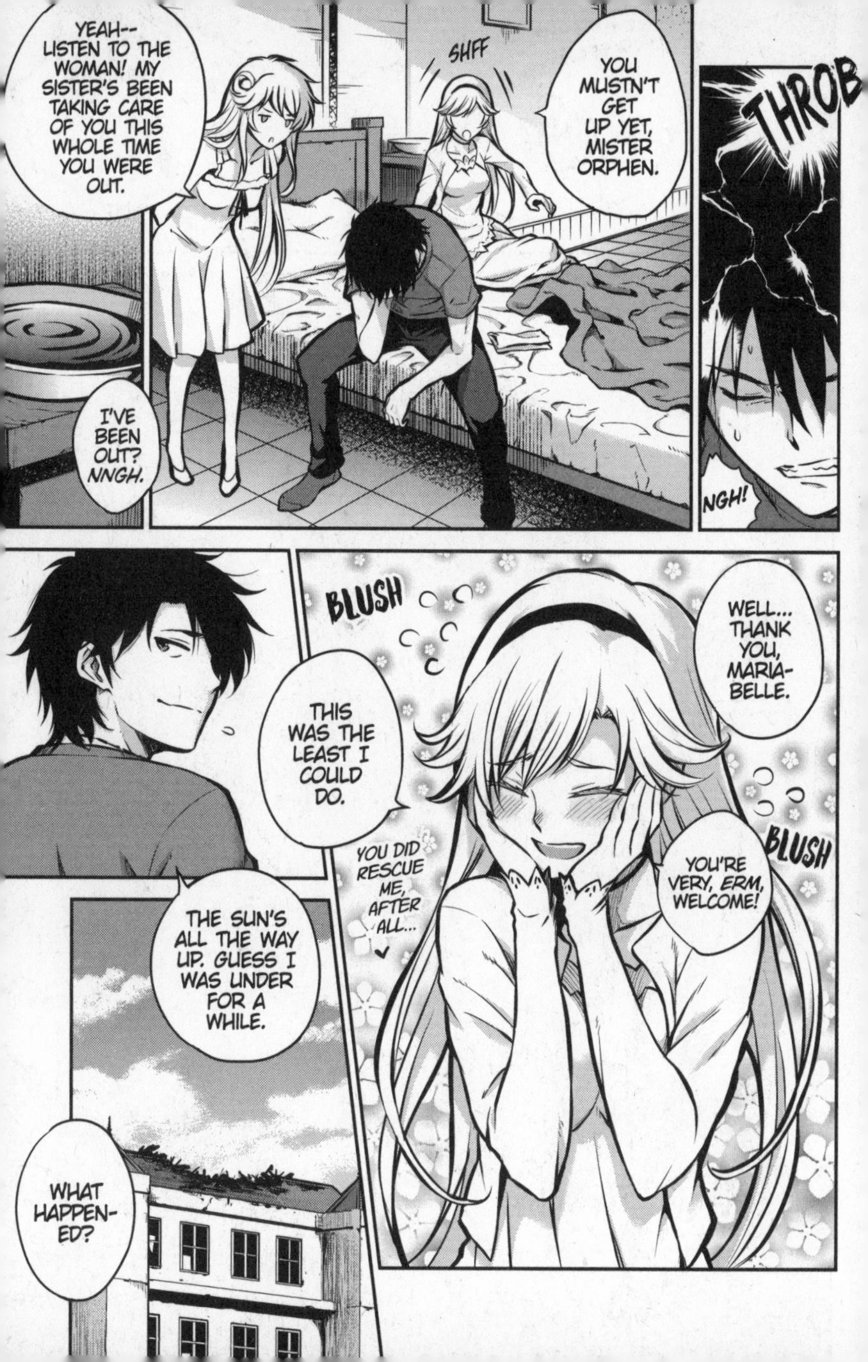
THROB
NGH!
YOU MUSTN'T GET UP YET, MISTER ORPHEN.
SHFF
YEAH-- LISTEN TO THE WOMAN! MY SISTER'S BEEN TAKING CARE OF YOU THIS WHOLE TIME YOU WERE OUT.
I'VE BEEN OUT? NNGH.
WELL... THANK YOU, MARIA-BELLE.
BLUSH
THIS WAS THE LEAST I COULD DO.
BLUSH
YOU'RE VERY, ERM, WELCOME!
YOU DID RESCUE ME, AFTER ALL...
THE SUN'S ALL THE WAY UP. GUESS I WAS UNDER FOR A WHILE.
WHAT HAPPEN-ED?

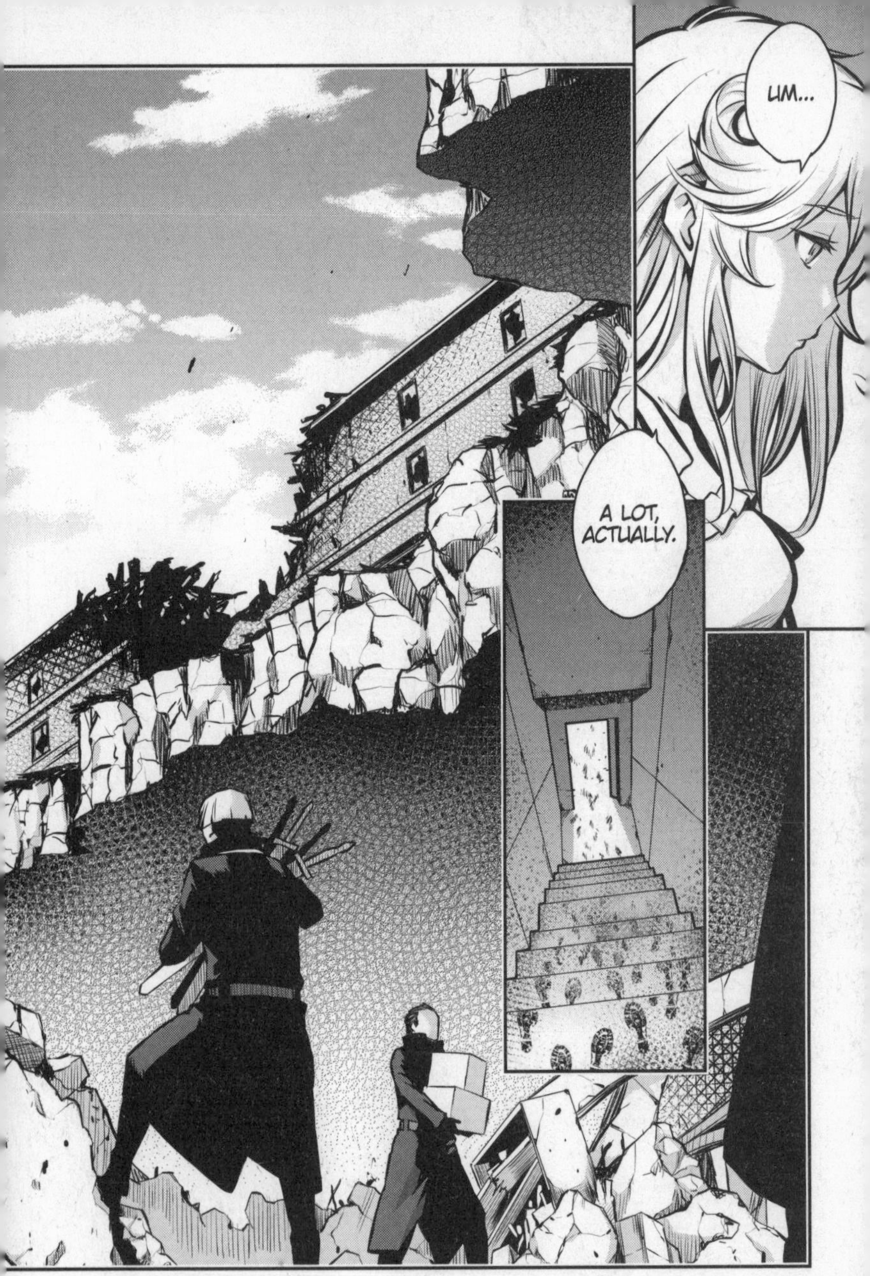
UM...
A LOT, ACTUALLY.

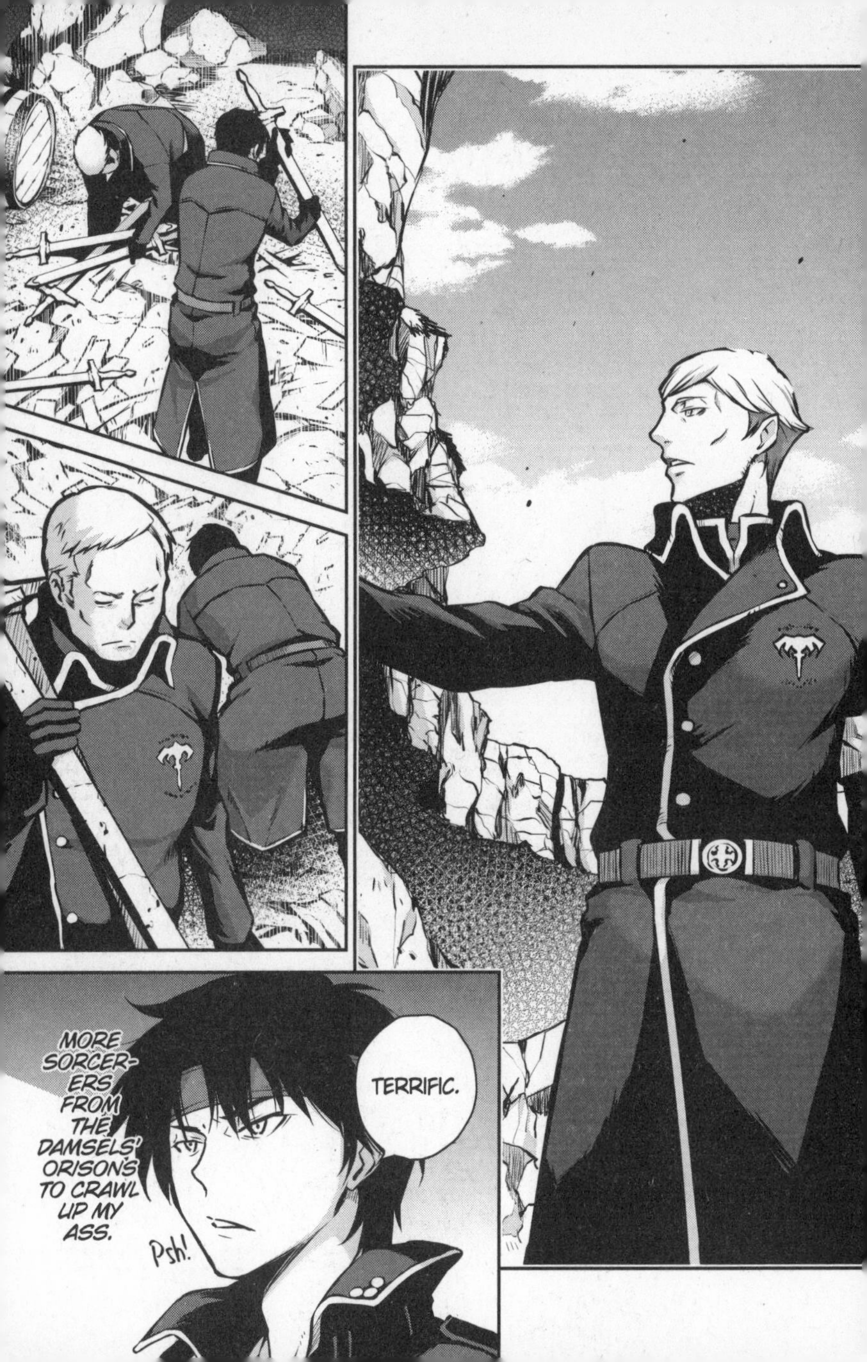
TERRIFIC.
MORE SORCERER-ERS FROM THE DAMSELS' ORISONS TO CRAWL UP MY ASS.
Psh!

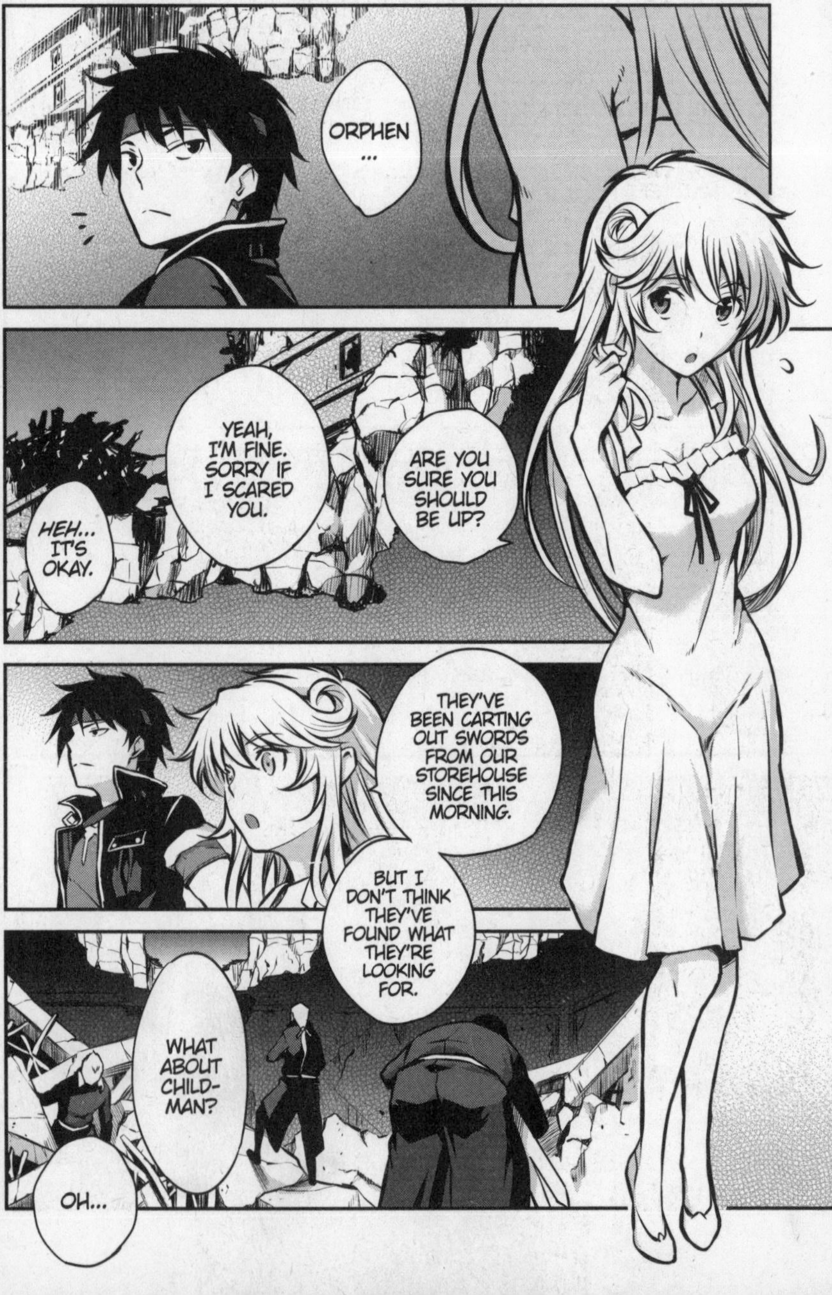
ORPHEN
...
ARE YOU SURE YOU SHOULD BE UP?
YEAH, I'M FINE. SORRY IF I SCARED YOU.
HEH... IT'S OKAY.
THEY'VE BEEN CARTING OUT SWORDS FROM OUR STOREHOUSE SINCE THIS MORNING.
BUT I DON'T THINK THEY'VE FOUND WHAT THEY'RE LOOKING FOR.
WHAT ABOUT CHILD-MAN?
OH...

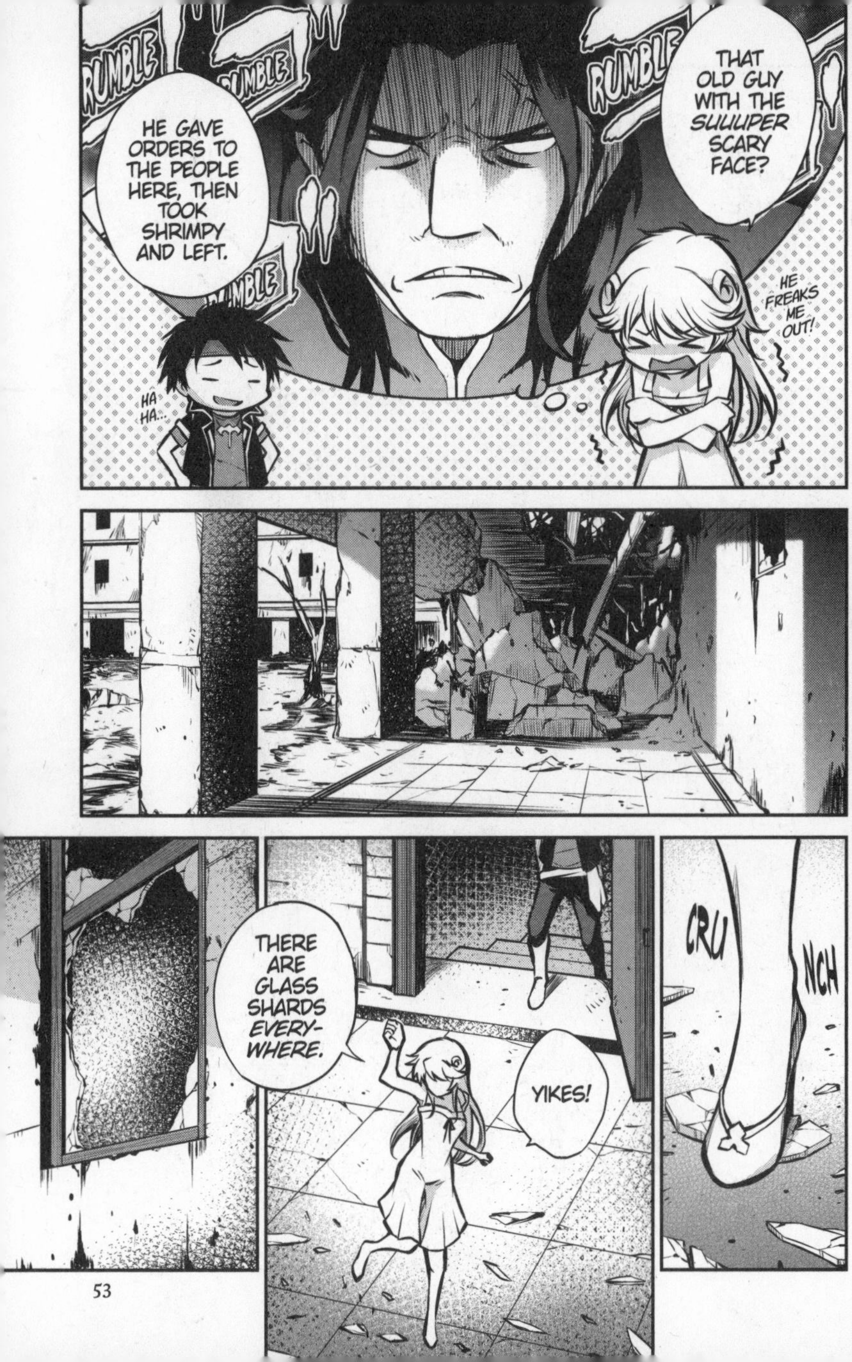
THAT OLD GUY WITH THE SUUUPER SCARY FACE?
RUMBLE
RUMBLE
RUMBLE
RUMBLE
HE GAVE ORDERS TO THE PEOPLE HERE, THEN TOOK SHRIMPY AND LEFT.
HE FREAKS ME OUT!
HA HA...
CRU NCH
YIKES!
THERE ARE GLASS SHARDS EVERY-WHERE.

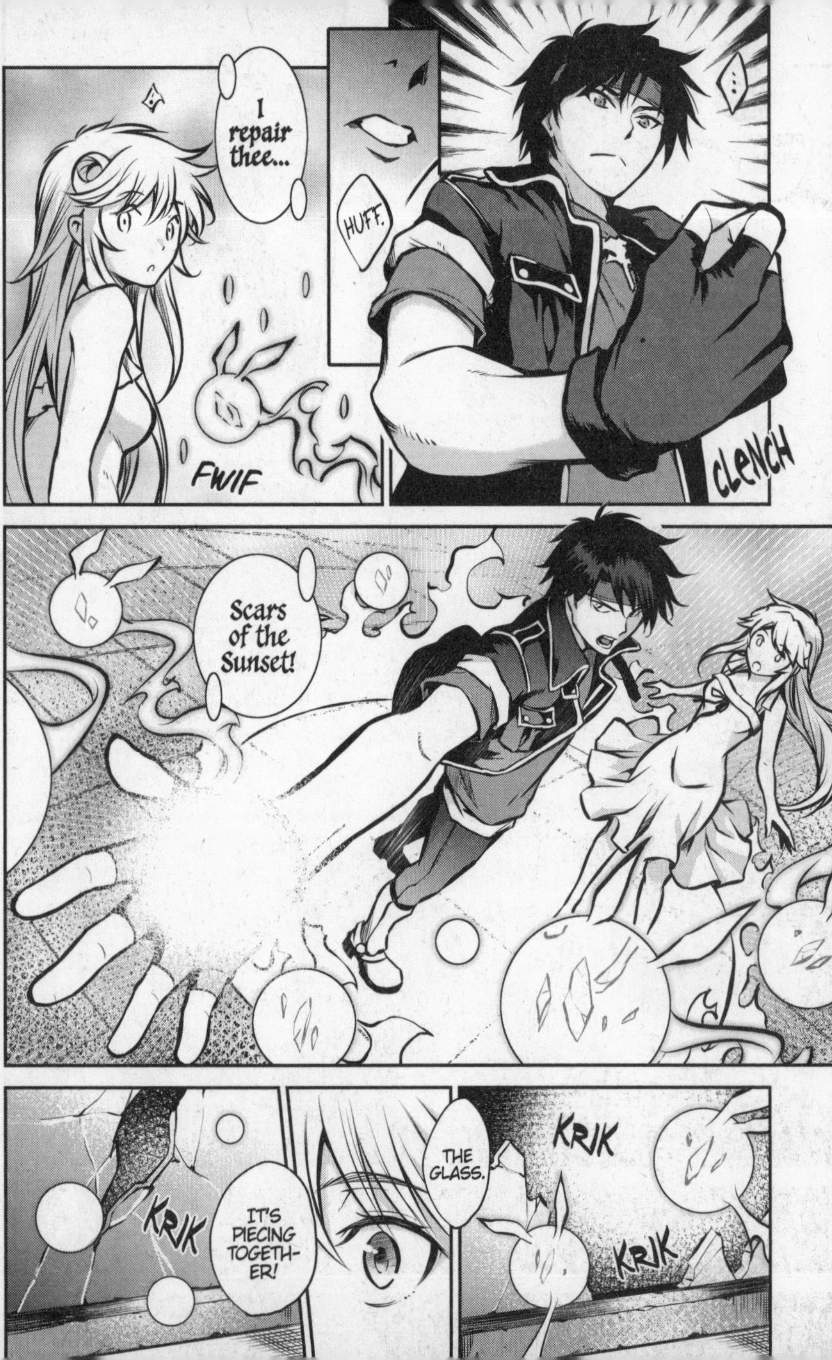
CLENCH
HUFF.
I repair thee...
FWIF
Scars of the Sunset!
KRIK
KRIK
THE GLASS.
IT'S PIECING TOGETH-ER!
KRIK

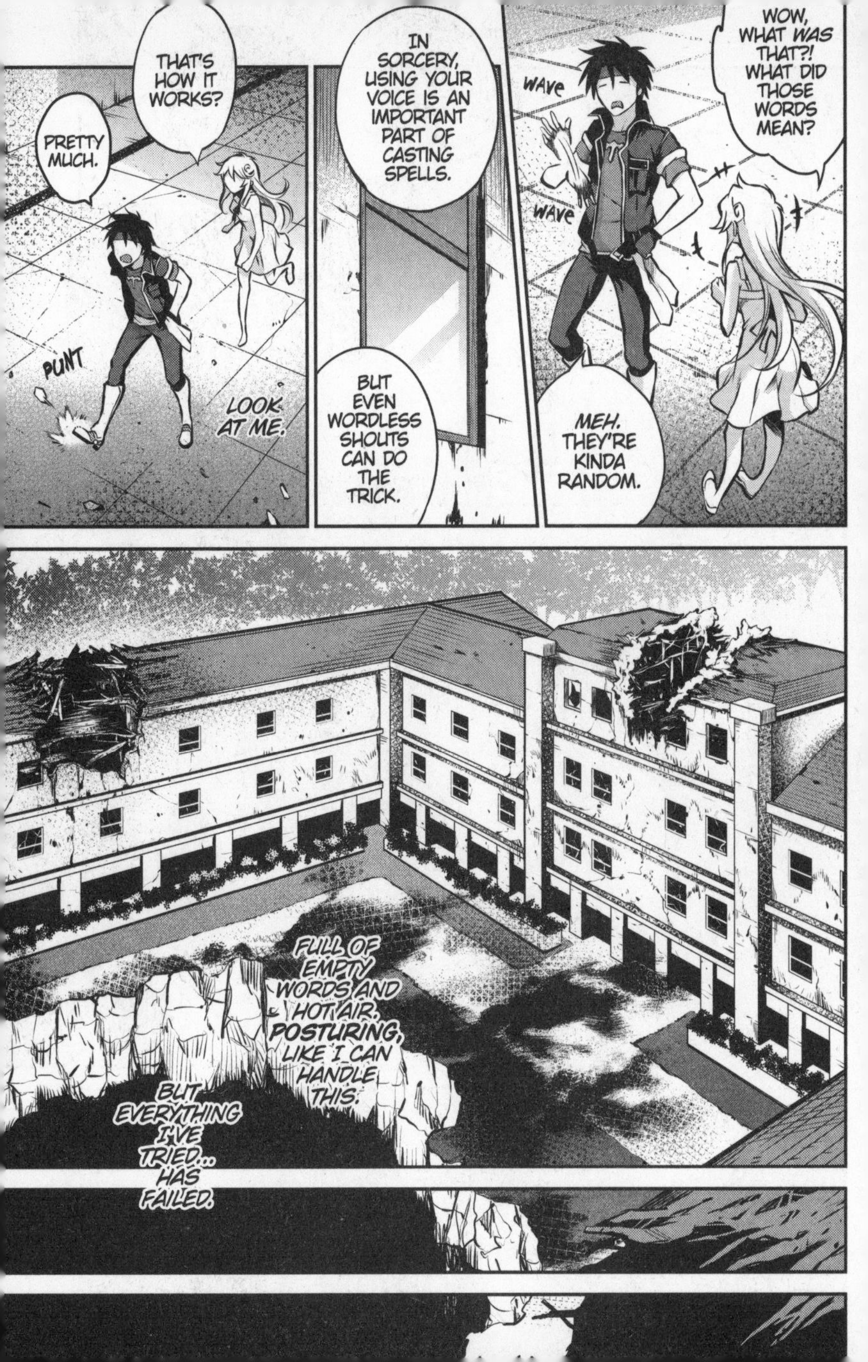
WOW, WHAT WAS THAT?! WHAT DID THOSE WORDS MEAN?
WAVE
WAVE
MEH. THEY'RE KINDA RANDOM.
IN SORCERY, USING YOUR VOICE IS AN IMPORTANT PART OF CASTING SPELLS.
BUT EVEN WORDLESS SHOUTS CAN DO THE TRICK.
THAT'S HOW IT WORKS?
PRETTY MUCH.
PUNT
LOOK AT ME.
FULL OF EMPTY WORDS AND HOT AIR. POSTURING, LIKE I CAN HANDLE THIS.
BUT EVERYTHING I'VE TRIED... HAS FAILED.

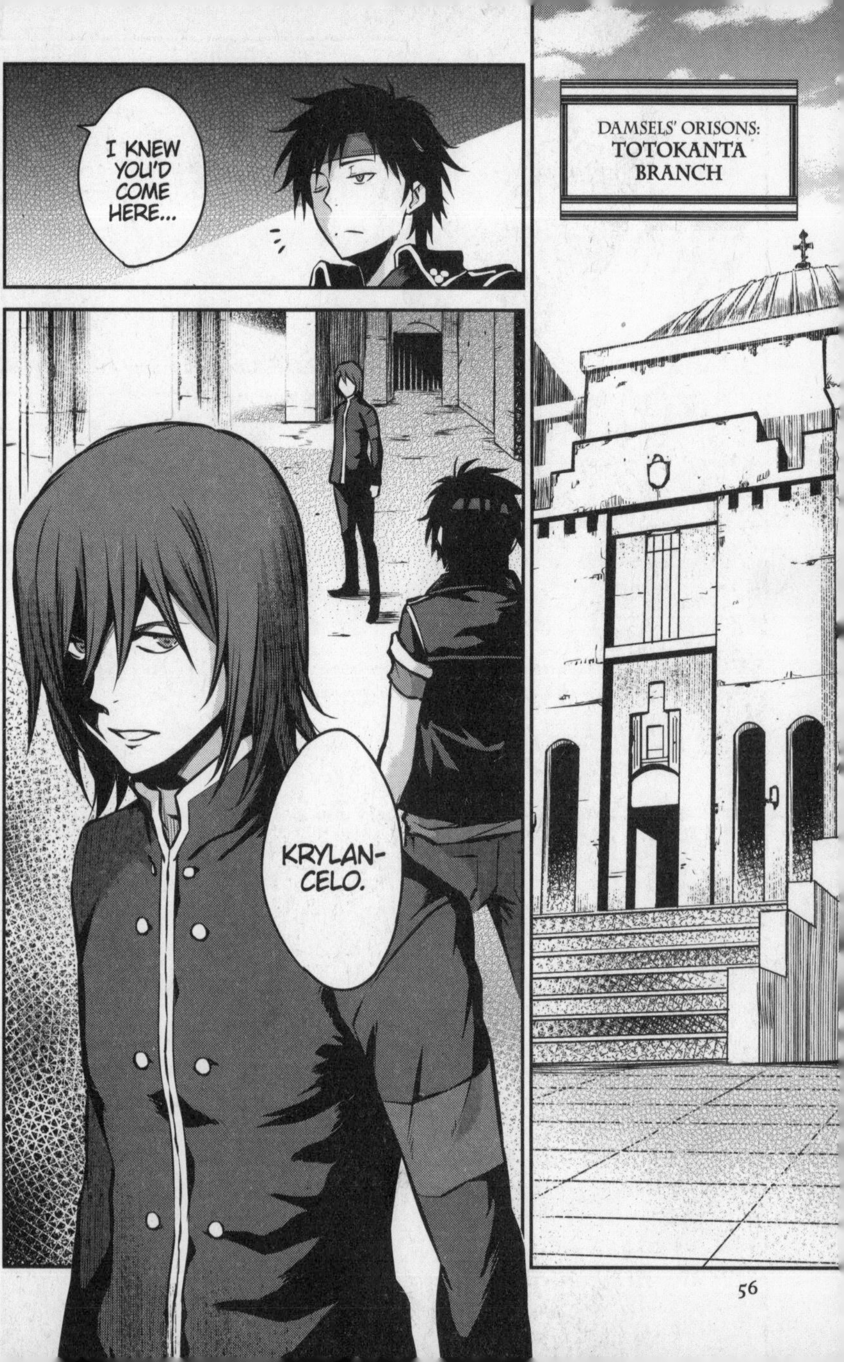
DAMSELS' ORISONS: TOTOKANTA BRANCH
I KNEW YOU'D COME HERE...
KRYLAN-CELO.

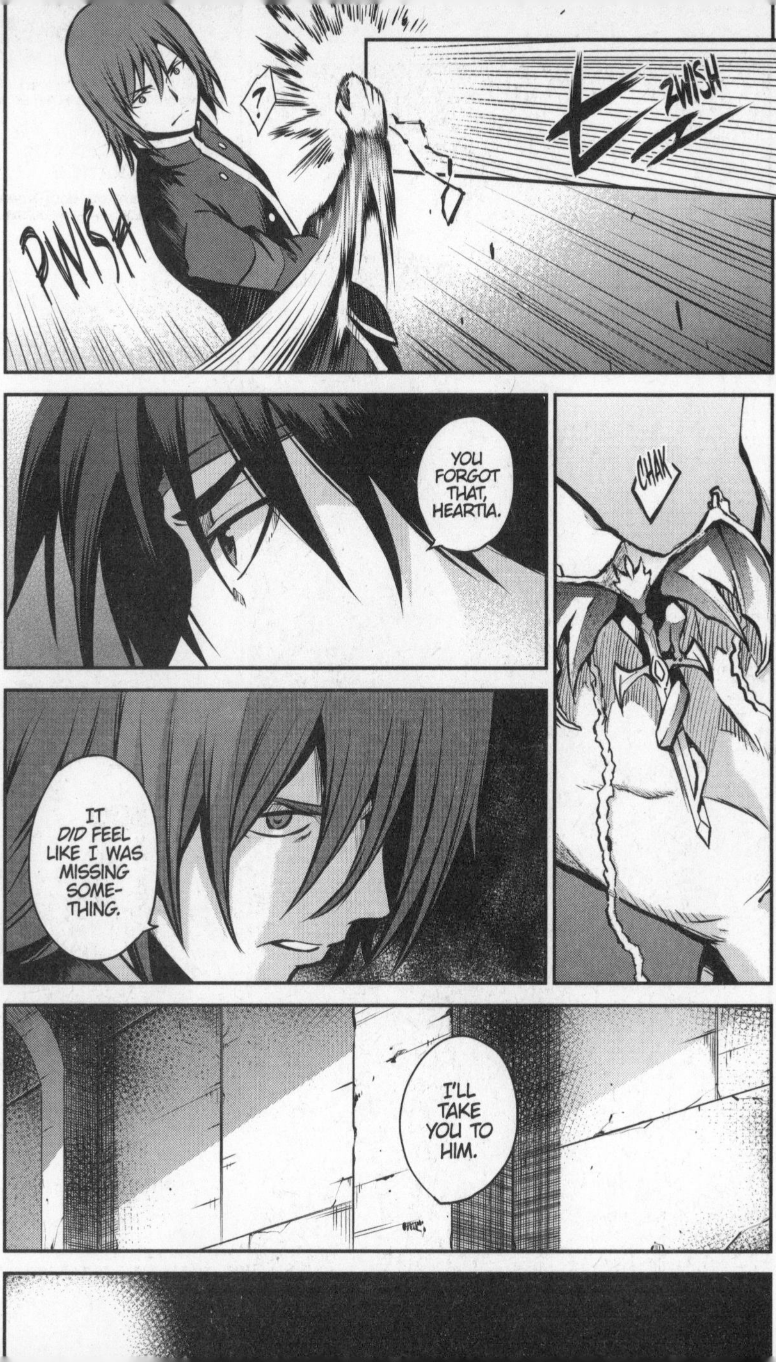
ZWISH
?
PWISH
CHAK
YOU FORGOT THAT, HEARTIA.
IT *DID* FEEL LIKE I WAS MISSING SOME-THING.
I'LL TAKE YOU TO HIM.

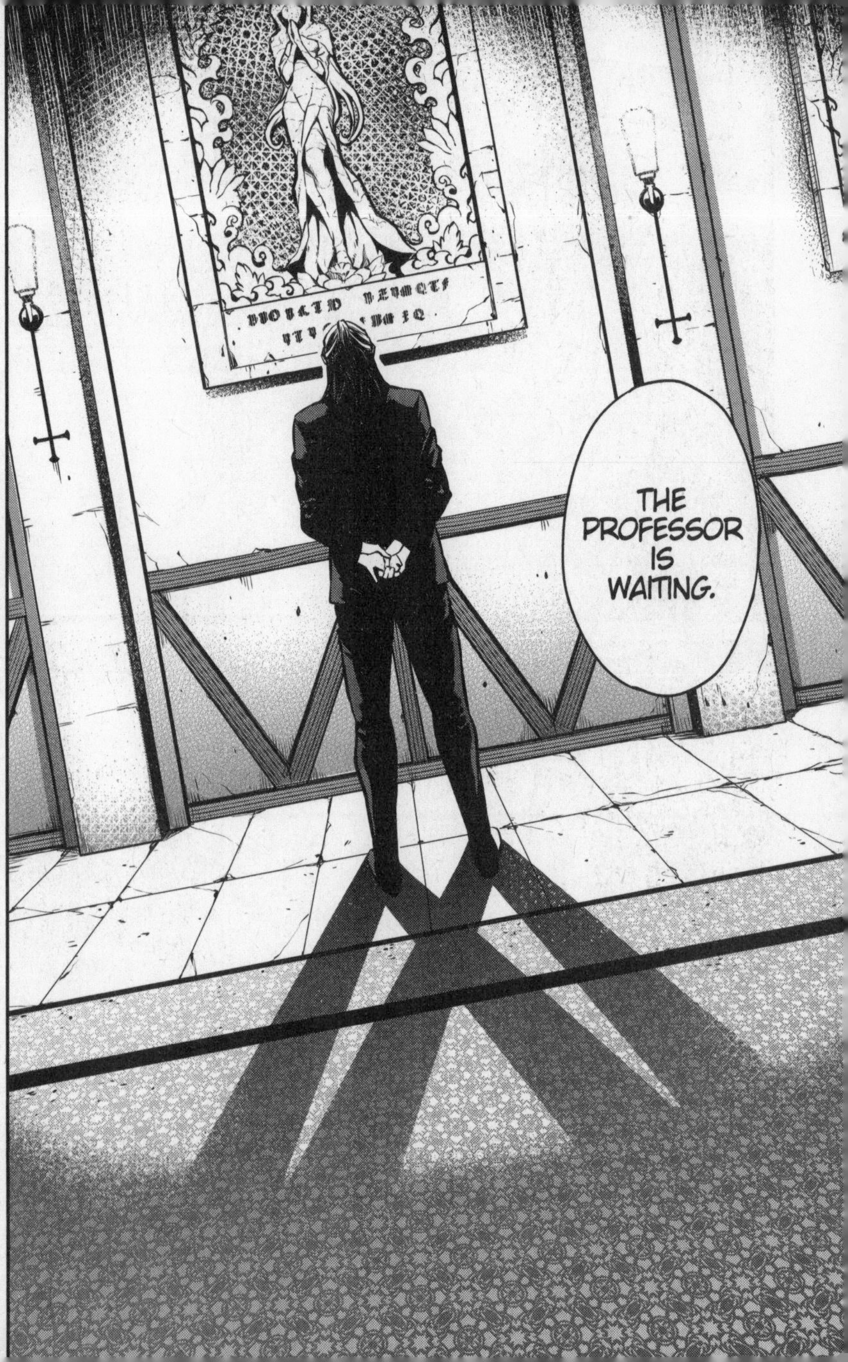
THE PROFESSOR IS WAITING.

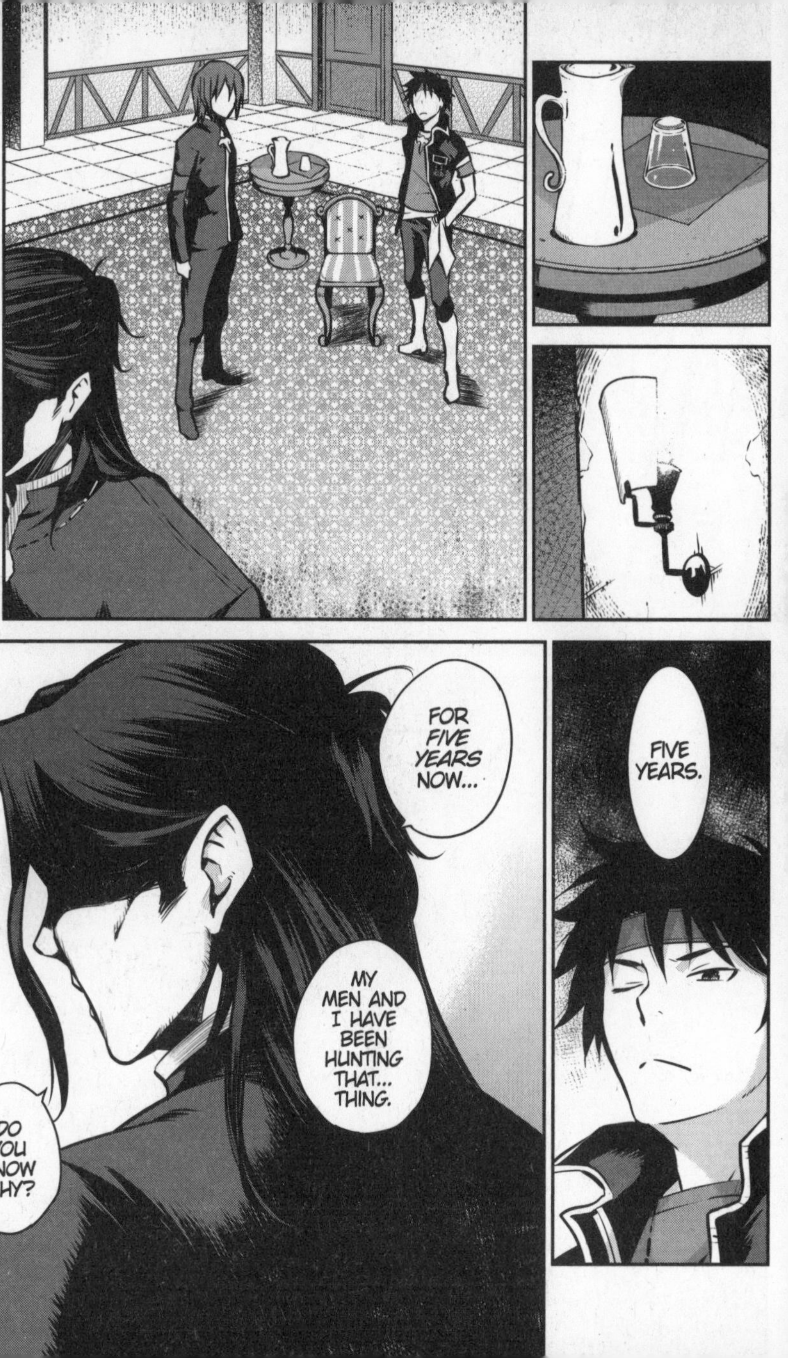
FIVE YEARS.
FOR FIVE YEARS NOW...
MY MEN AND I HAVE BEEN HUNTING THAT... THING.
DO YOU KNOW WHY?

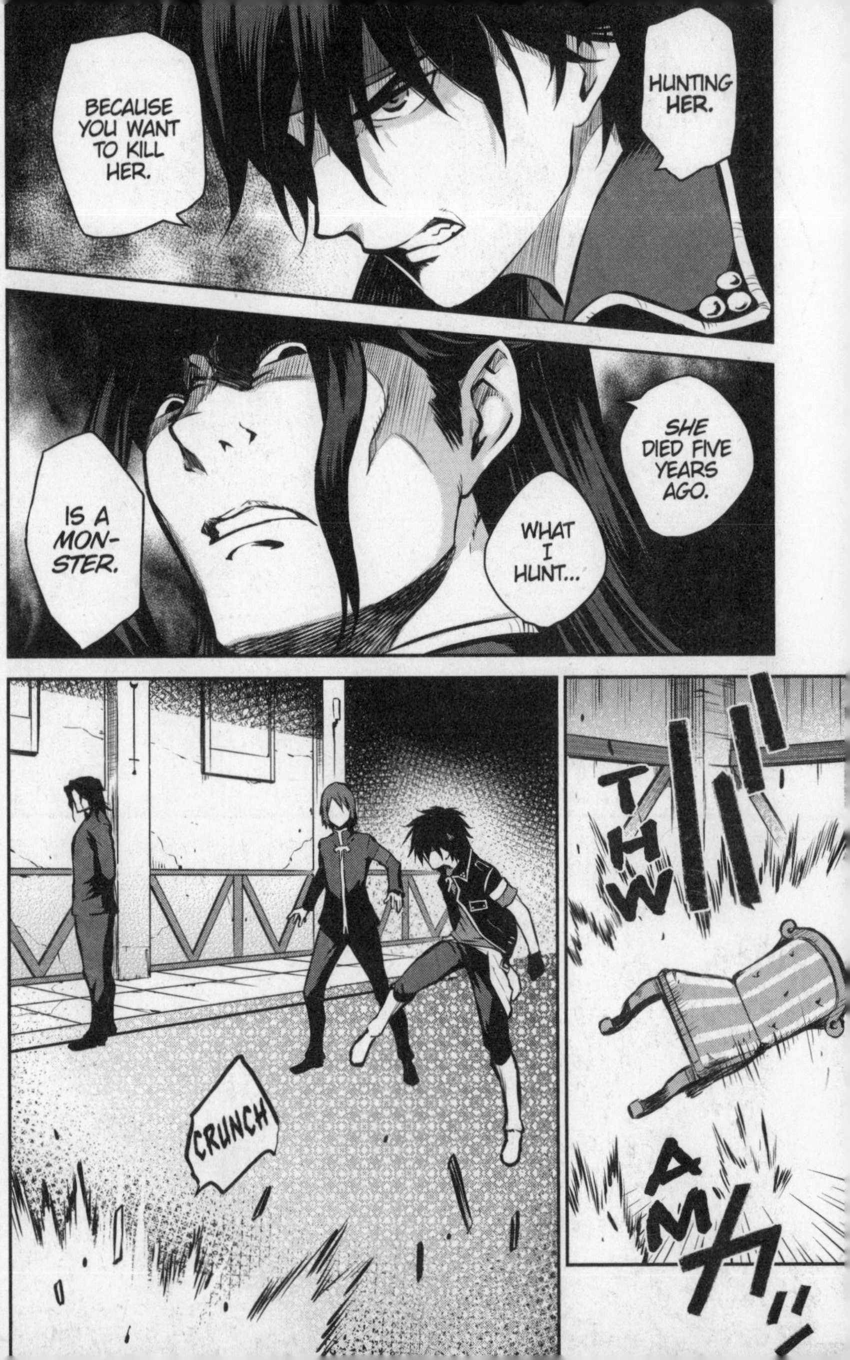
HUNTING HER.
BECAUSE YOU WANT TO KILL HER.
SHE DIED FIVE YEARS AGO.
WHAT I HUNT...
IS A MONSTER.
THW
AM
CRUNCH

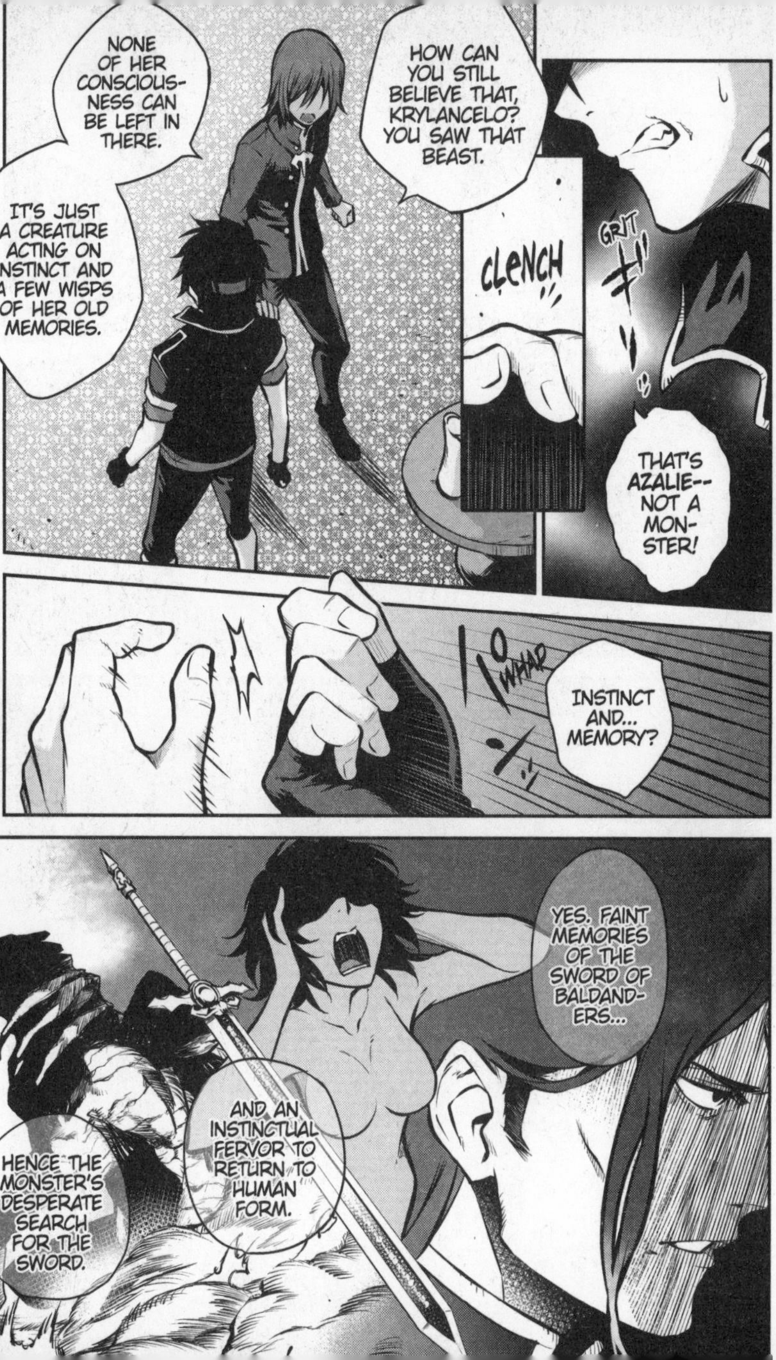
GRIT
THAT'S AZALIE-- NOT A MONSTER!
CLENCH
HOW CAN YOU STILL BELIEVE THAT, KRYLANCELO? YOU SAW THAT BEAST.
NONE OF HER CONSCIOUS-NESS CAN BE LEFT IN THERE.
IT'S JUST A CREATURE ACTING ON INSTINCT AND A FEW WISPS OF HER OLD MEMORIES.
WHAP
INSTINCT AND... MEMORY?
YES. FAINT MEMORIES OF THE SWORD OF BALDAND-ERS...
AND AN INSTINCTUAL FERVOR TO RETURN TO HUMAN FORM.
HENCE THE MONSTER'S DESPERATE SEARCH FOR THE SWORD.

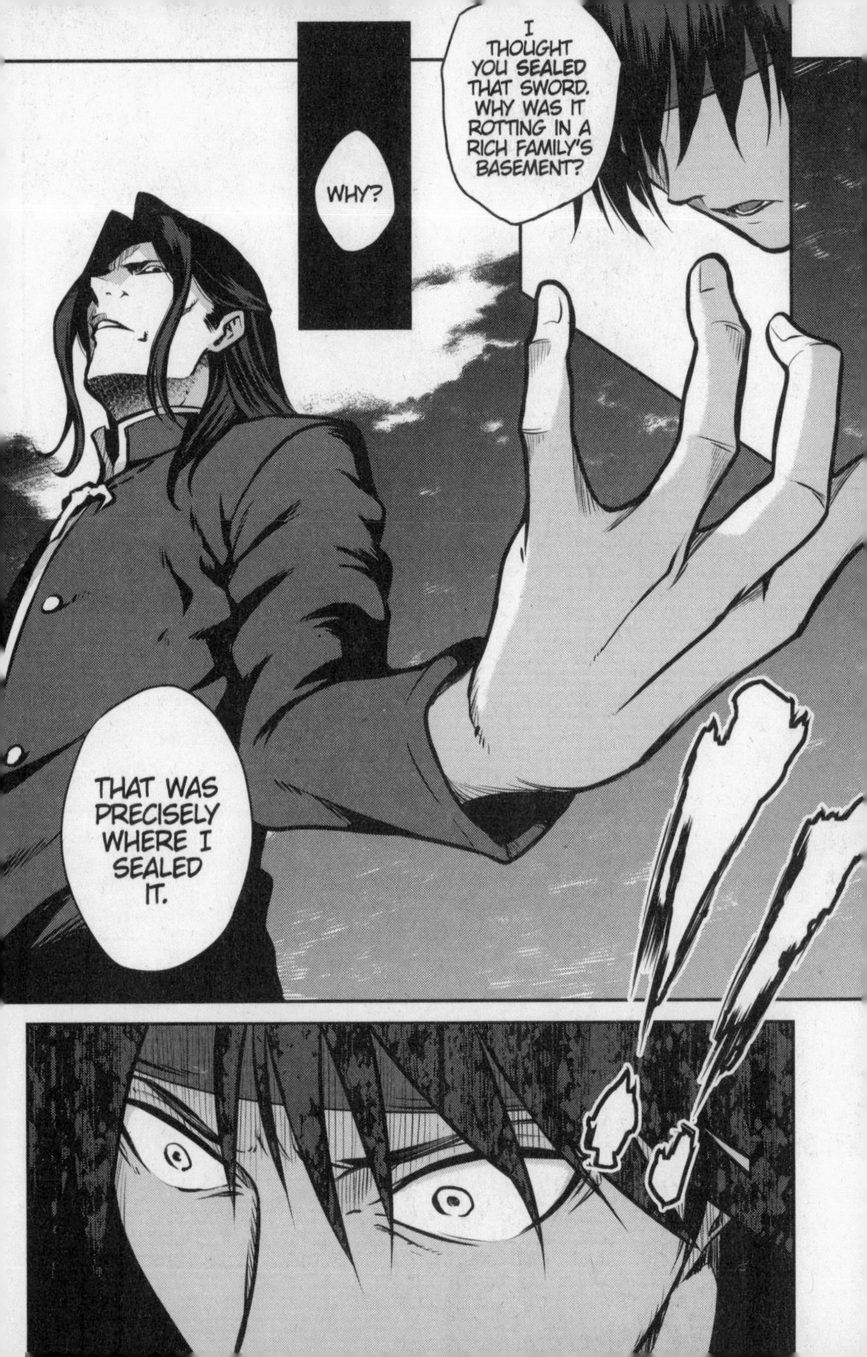
I THOUGHT YOU SEALED THAT SWORD. WHY WAS IT ROTTING IN A RICH FAMILY'S BASEMENT?
WHY?
THAT WAS PRECISELY WHERE I SEALED IT.

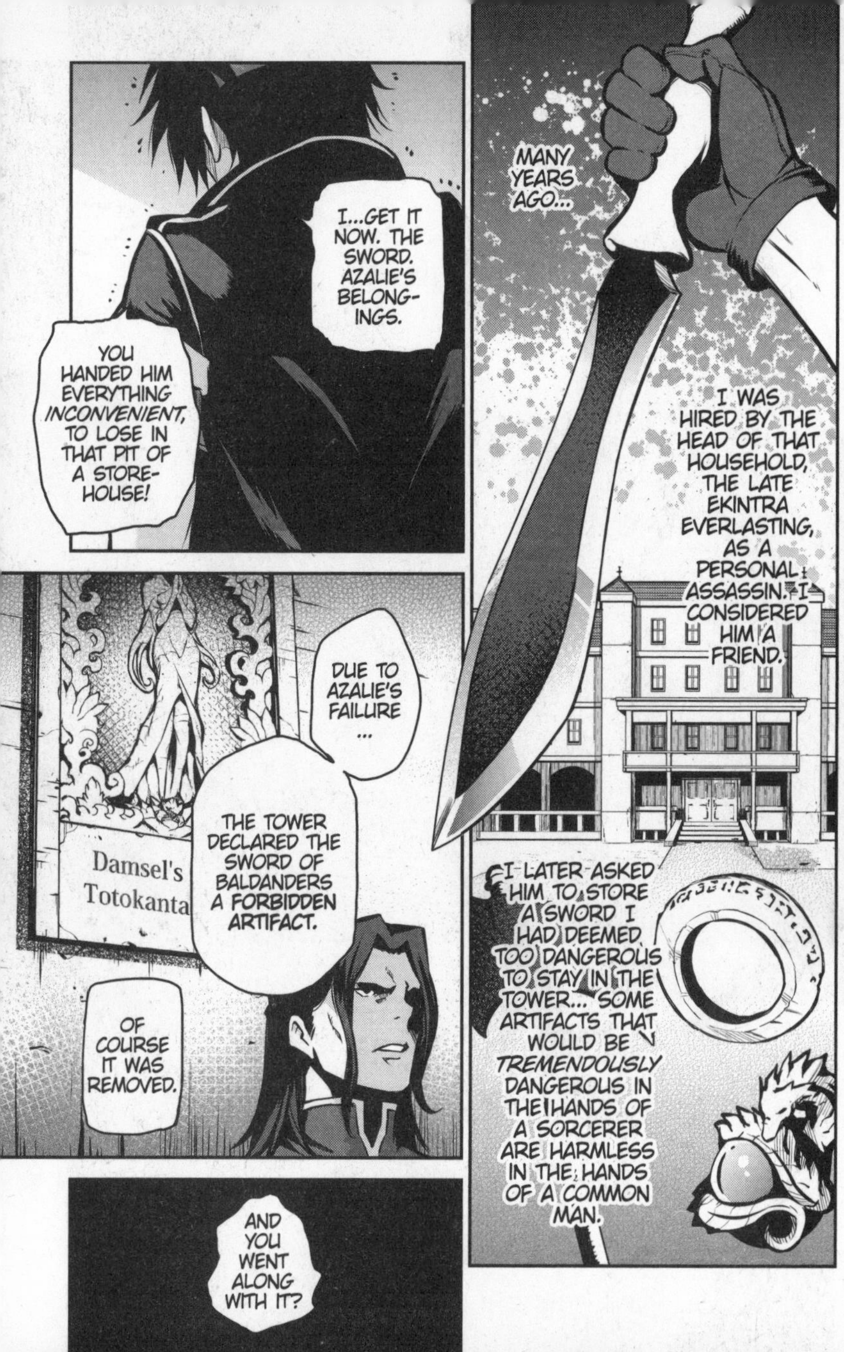
MANY YEARS AGO...
I WAS HIRED BY THE HEAD OF THAT HOUSEHOLD, THE LATE EKINTRA EVERLASTING, AS A PERSONAL ASSASSIN. I CONSIDERED HIM A FRIEND.
I LATER ASKED HIM TO STORE A SWORD I HAD DEEMED TOO DANGEROUS TO STAY IN THE TOWER... SOME ARTIFACTS THAT WOULD BE *TREMENDOUSLY* DANGEROUS IN THE HANDS OF A SORCERER ARE HARMLESS IN THE HANDS OF A COMMON MAN.
I...GET IT NOW. THE SWORD. AZALIE'S BELONG-INGS.
YOU HANDED HIM EVERYTHING *INCONVENIENT,* TO LOSE IN THAT PIT OF A STORE-HOUSE!
Damsel's Totokanta
DUE TO AZALIE'S FAILURE ...
THE TOWER DECLARED THE SWORD OF BALDANDERS A FORBIDDEN ARTIFACT.
OF COURSE IT WAS REMOVED.
AND YOU WENT ALONG WITH IT?

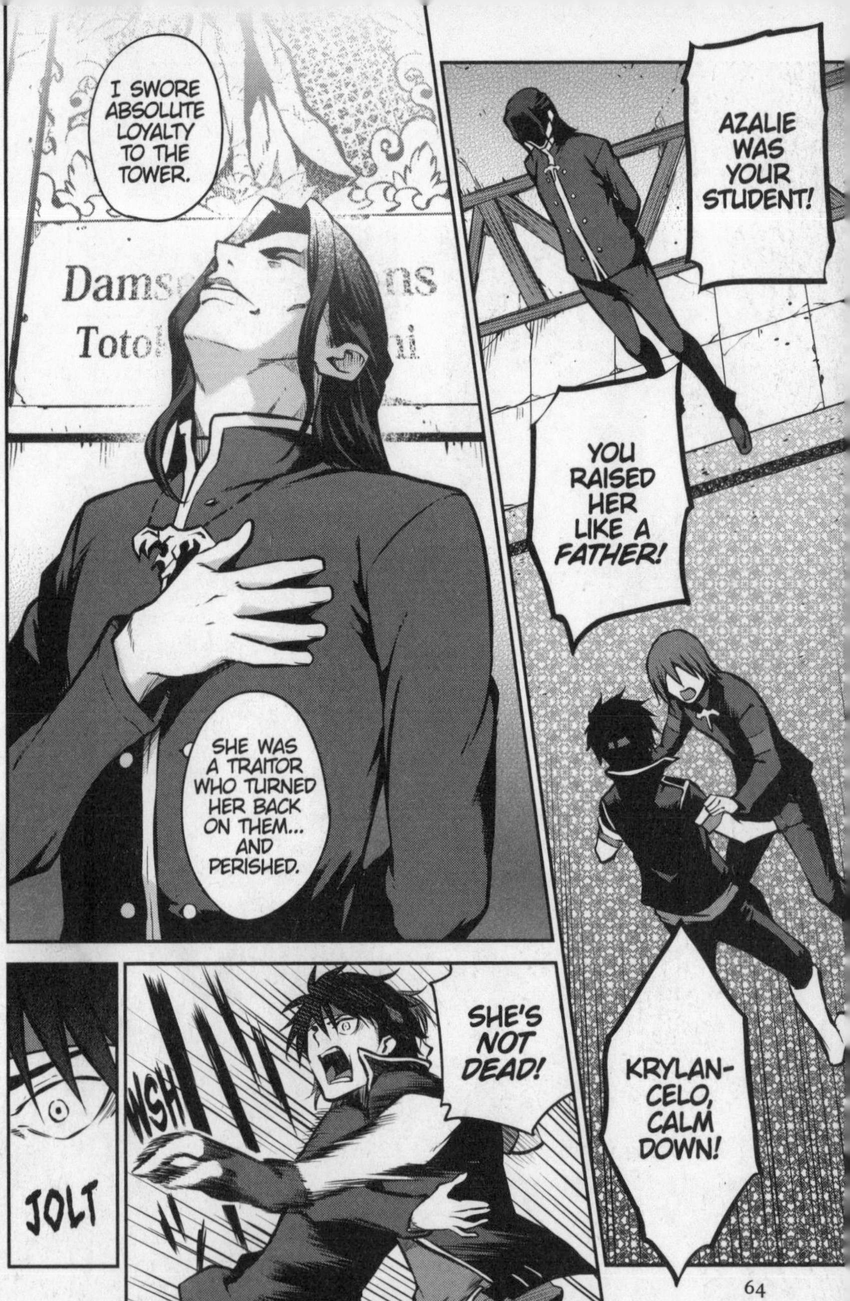
AZALIE WAS YOUR STUDENT!
YOU RAISED HER LIKE A *FATHER!*
KRYLAN-CELO, CALM DOWN!
I SWORE ABSOLUTE LOYALTY TO THE TOWER.
SHE WAS A TRAITOR WHO TURNED HER BACK ON THEM... AND PERISHED.
SHE'S *NOT* DEAD!
WSH
JOLT

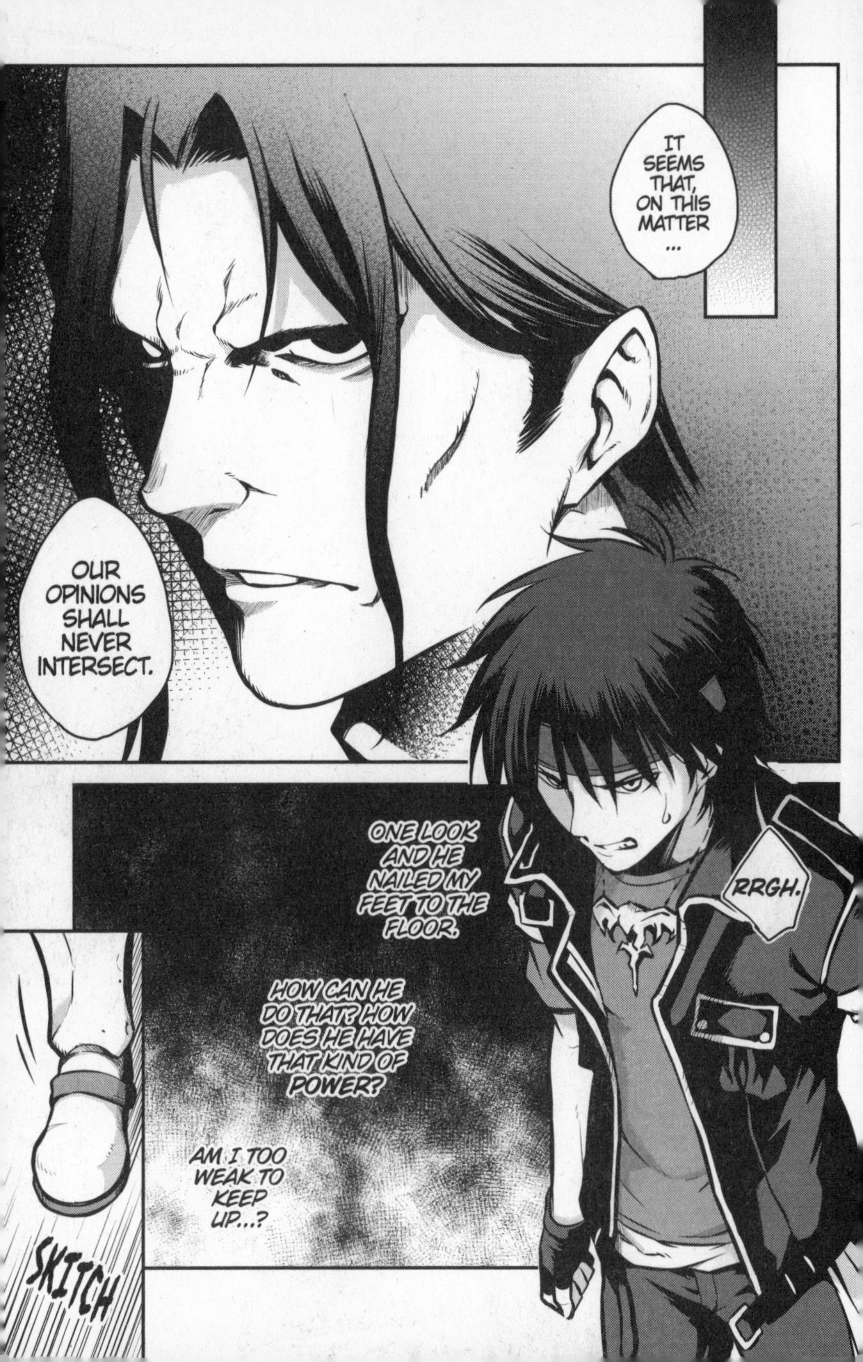
IT SEEMS THAT, ON THIS MATTER...
OUR OPINIONS SHALL NEVER INTERSECT.
RRGH.
ONE LOOK AND HE NAILED MY FEET TO THE FLOOR.
HOW CAN HE DO THAT? HOW DOES HE HAVE THAT KIND OF POWER?
AM I TOO WEAK TO KEEP UP...?
SKITCH

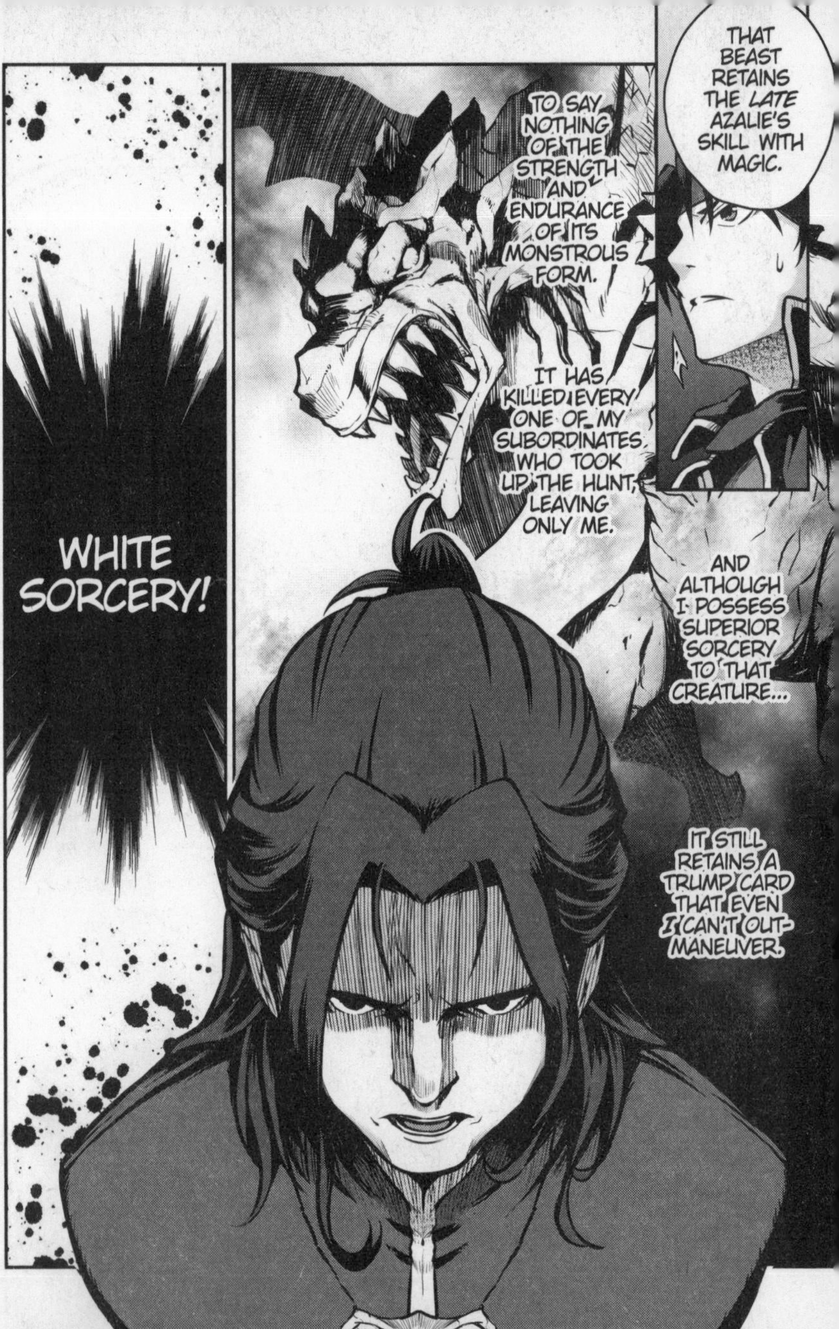
THAT BEAST RETAINS THE *LATE* AZALIE'S SKILL WITH MAGIC.
TO SAY NOTHING OF THE STRENGTH AND ENDURANCE OF ITS MONSTROUS FORM.
IT HAS KILLED EVERY ONE OF MY SUBORDINATES WHO TOOK UP THE HUNT, LEAVING ONLY ME.
AND ALTHOUGH I POSSESS SUPERIOR SORCERY TO THAT CREATURE...
IT STILL RETAINS A TRUMP CARD THAT EVEN I CAN'T OUT-MANEUVER.
WHITE SORCERY!

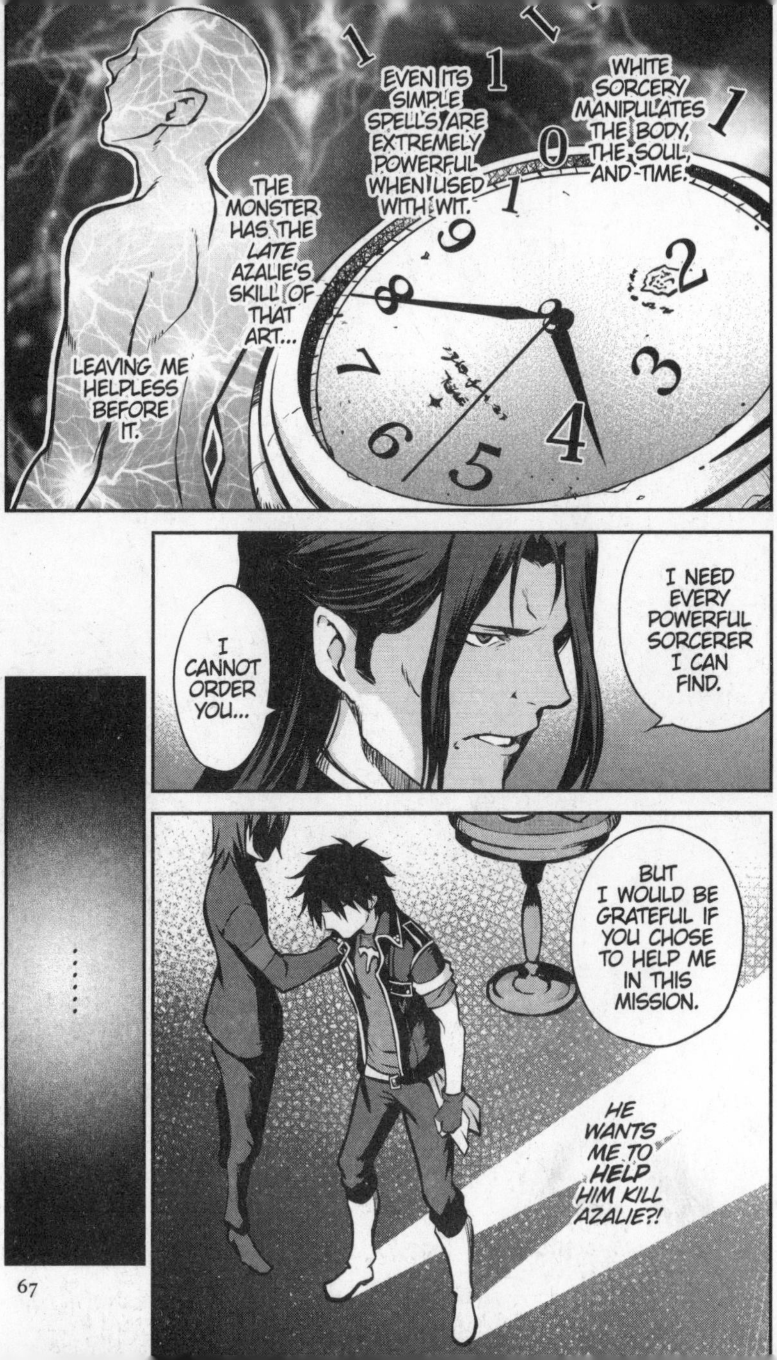
WHITE SORCERY MANIPULATES THE BODY, THE SOUL, AND TIME.
EVEN ITS SIMPLE SPELLS ARE EXTREMELY POWERFUL WHEN USED WITH WIT.
THE MONSTER HAS THE LATE AZALIE'S SKILL OF THAT ART...
LEAVING ME HELPLESS BEFORE IT.
I NEED EVERY POWERFUL SORCERER I CAN FIND.
I CANNOT ORDER YOU...
BUT I WOULD BE GRATEFUL IF YOU CHOSE TO HELP ME IN THIS MISSION.
HE WANTS ME TO HELP HIM KILL AZALIE?!
......

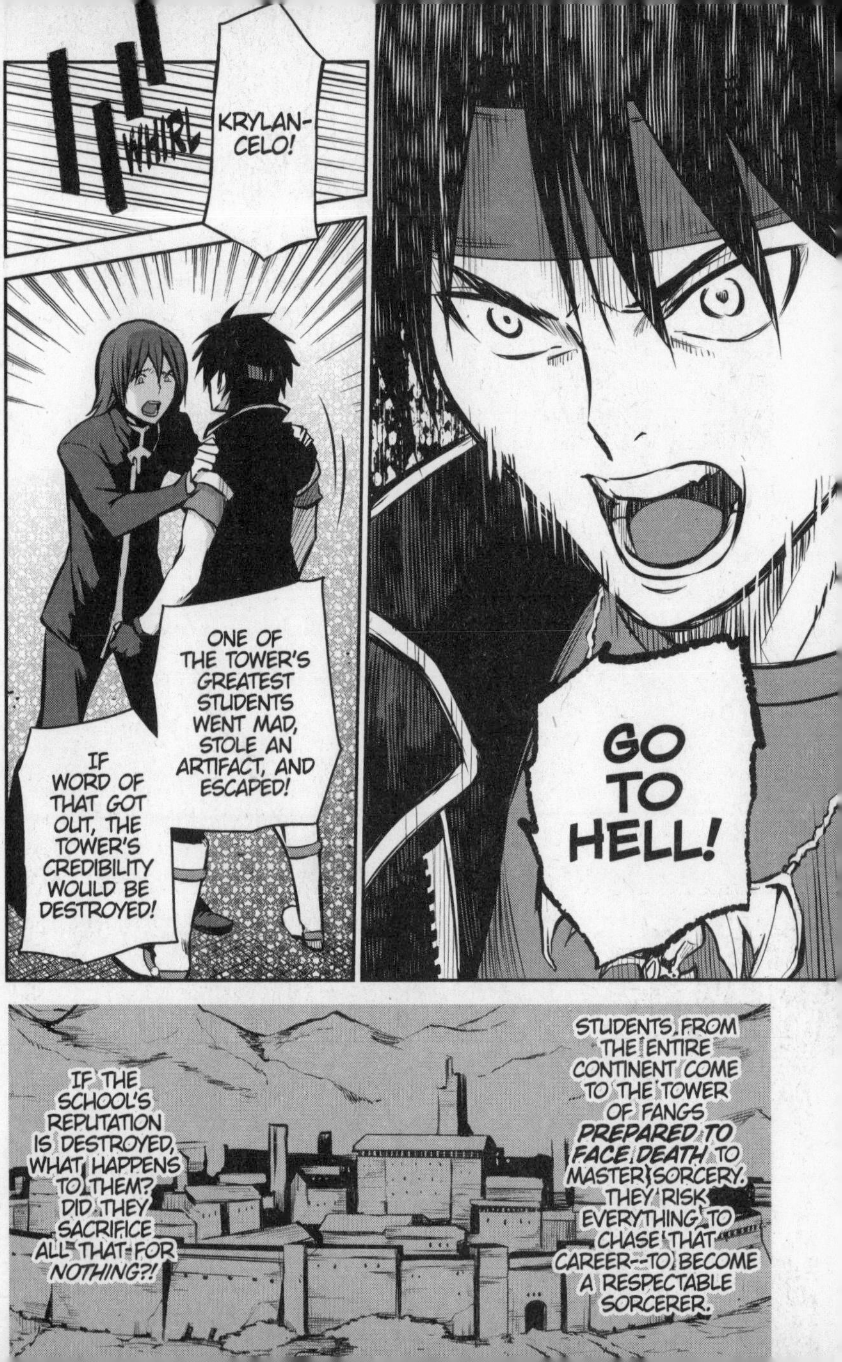
GO TO HELL!
WHIRL
KRYLAN-CELO!
ONE OF THE TOWER'S GREATEST STUDENTS WENT MAD, STOLE AN ARTIFACT, AND ESCAPED!
IF WORD OF THAT GOT OUT, THE TOWER'S CREDIBILITY WOULD BE DESTROYED!
STUDENTS FROM THE ENTIRE CONTINENT COME TO THE TOWER OF FANGS *PREPARED TO FACE DEATH* TO MASTER SORCERY. THEY RISK EVERYTHING TO CHASE THAT CAREER--TO BECOME A RESPECTABLE SORCERER.
IF THE SCHOOL'S REPUTATION IS DESTROYED, WHAT HAPPENS TO THEM? DID THEY SACRIFICE ALL THAT FOR *NOTHING*?!

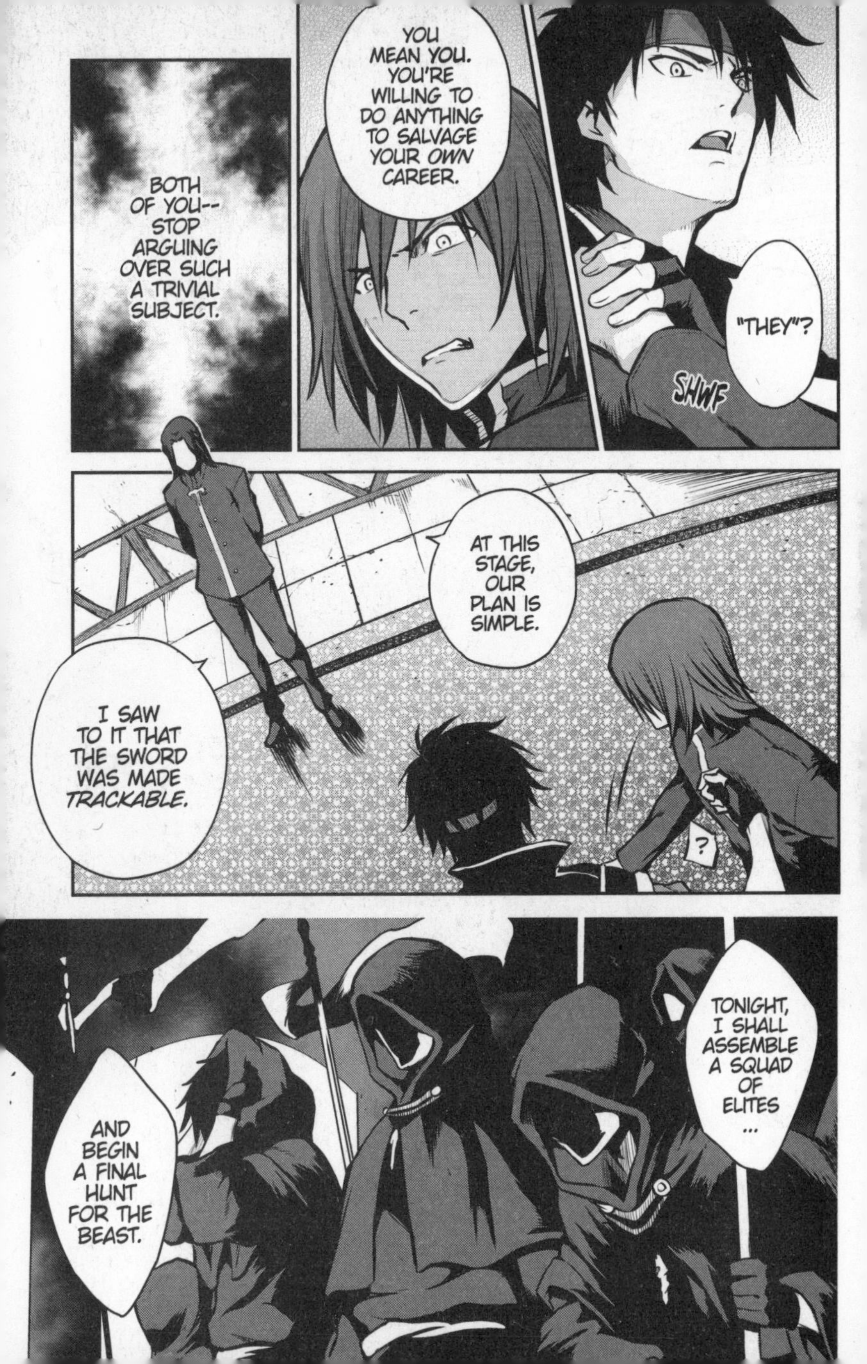
"THEY"?
SHWF
YOU MEAN YOU. YOU'RE WILLING TO DO ANYTHING TO SALVAGE YOUR *OWN* CAREER.
BOTH OF YOU-- STOP ARGUING OVER SUCH A TRIVIAL SUBJECT.
AT THIS STAGE, OUR PLAN IS SIMPLE.
?
I SAW TO IT THAT THE SWORD WAS MADE *TRACKABLE.*
TONIGHT, I SHALL ASSEMBLE A SQUAD OF ELITES ...
AND BEGIN A FINAL HUNT FOR THE BEAST.

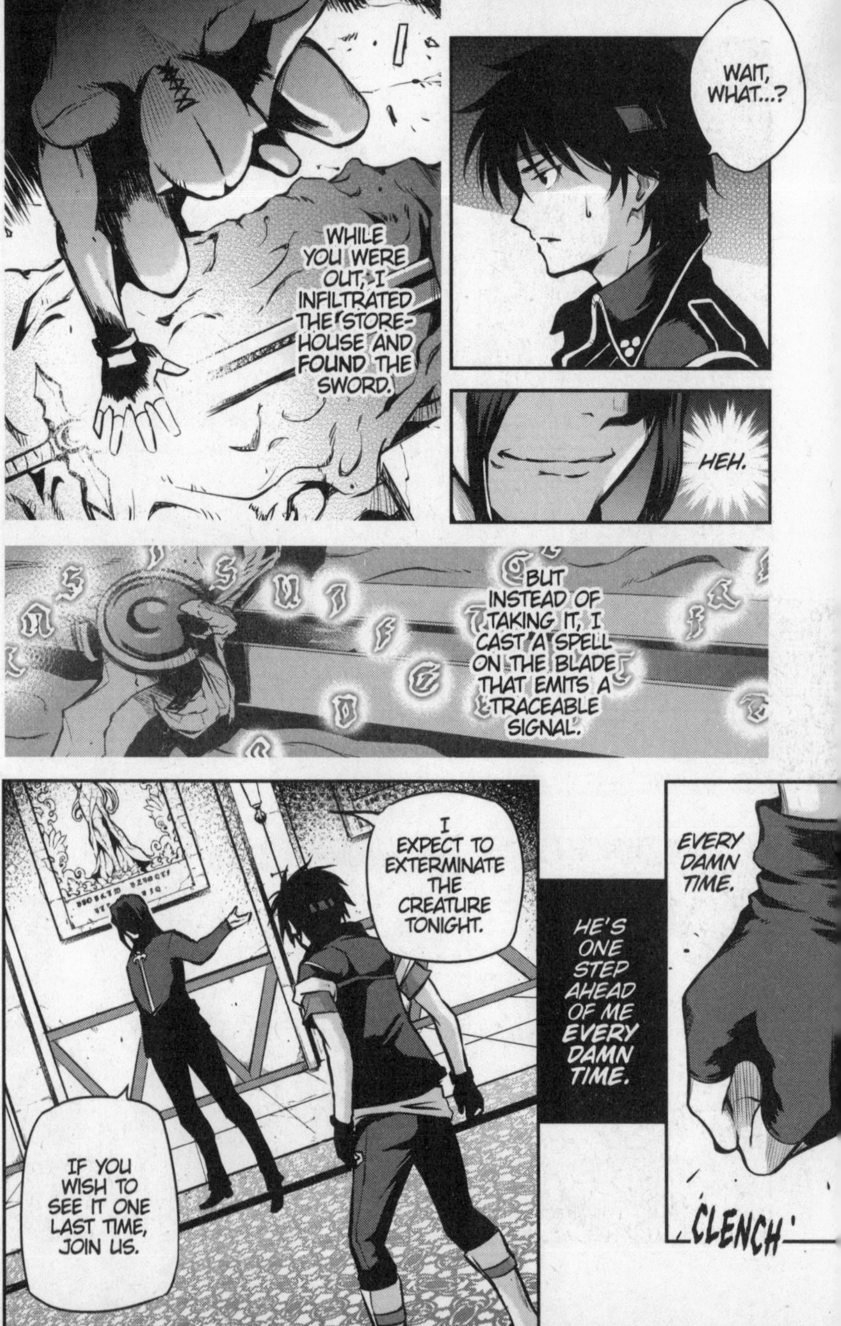
WAIT, WHAT...?
HEH.
WHILE YOU WERE OUT, I INFILTRATED THE STORE-HOUSE AND FOUND THE SWORD.
BUT INSTEAD OF TAKING IT, I CAST A SPELL ON THE BLADE THAT EMITS A TRACEABLE SIGNAL.
EVERY DAMN TIME.
CLENCH
HE'S ONE STEP AHEAD OF ME EVERY DAMN TIME.
I EXPECT TO EXTERMINATE THE CREATURE TONIGHT.
IF YOU WISH TO SEE IT ONE LAST TIME, JOIN US.

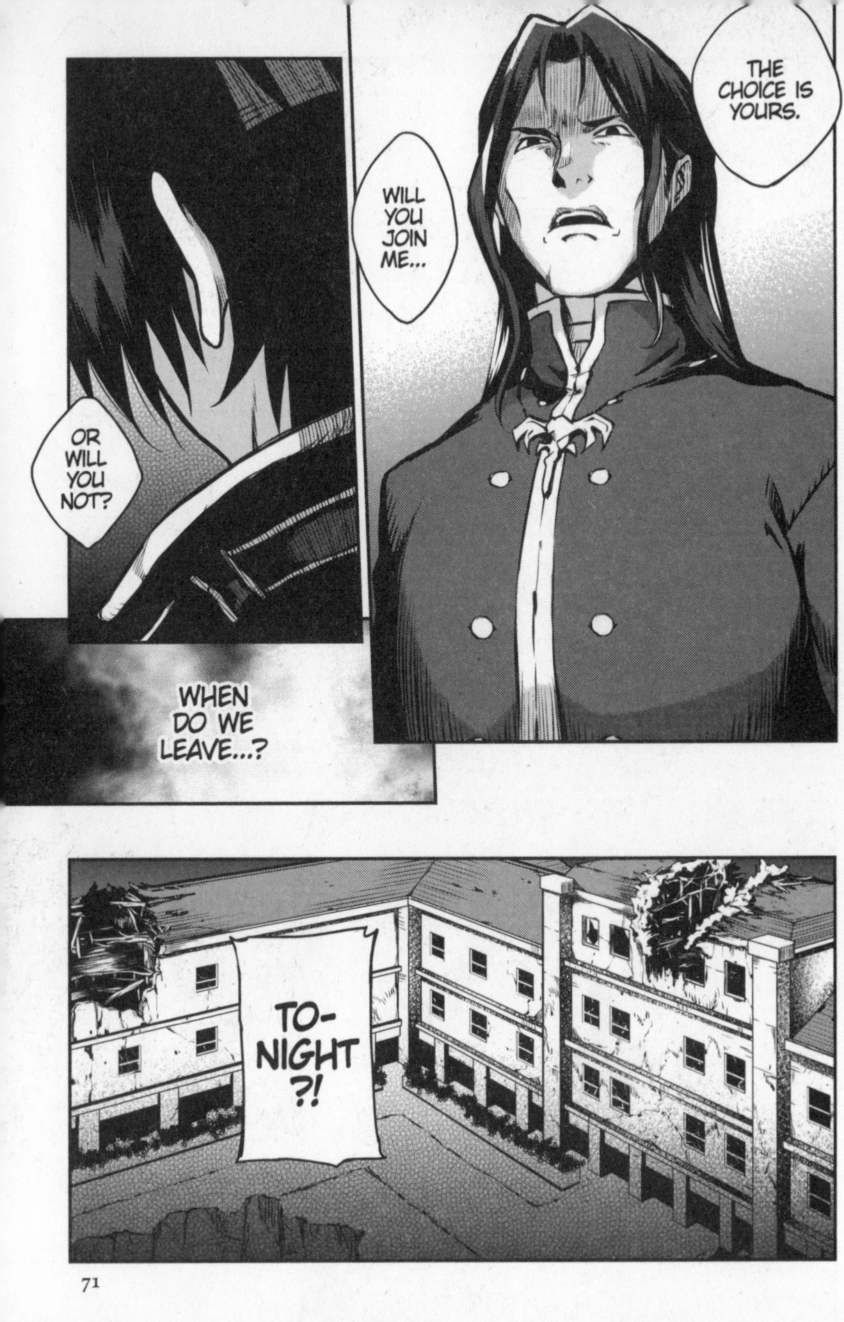
THE CHOICE IS YOURS.
WILL YOU JOIN ME...
OR WILL YOU NOT?
WHEN DO WE LEAVE...?
TO-NIGHT?!

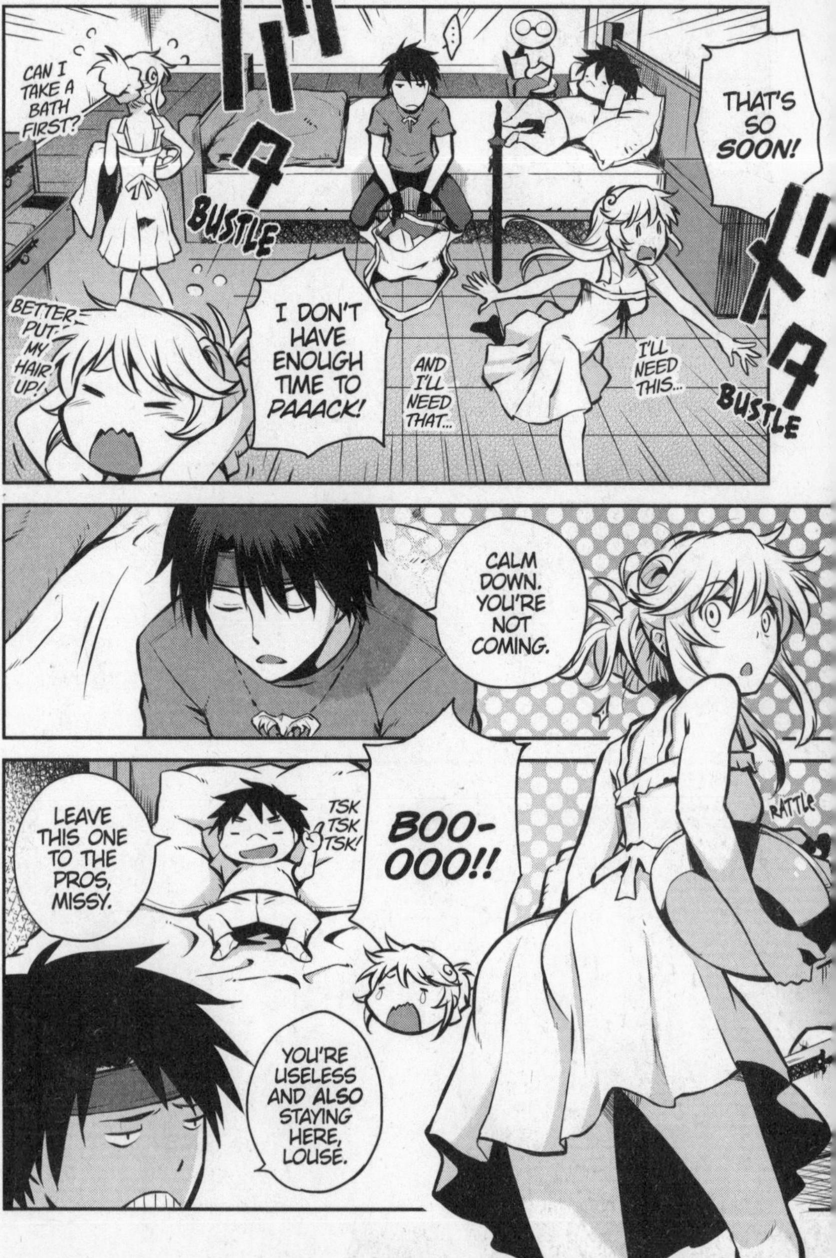
THAT'S SO SOON!
ドタ
BUSTLE
I'LL NEED THIS...
AND I'LL NEED THAT...
I DON'T HAVE ENOUGH TIME TO PAAACK!
ドタ
BUSTLE
CAN I TAKE A BATH FIRST?
BETTER PUT MY HAIR UP!
CALM DOWN. YOU'RE NOT COMING.
RATTLE
BOO-OOO!!
TSK TSK TSK!
LEAVE THIS ONE TO THE PROS, MISSY.
YOU'RE USELESS AND ALSO STAYING HERE, LOUISE.

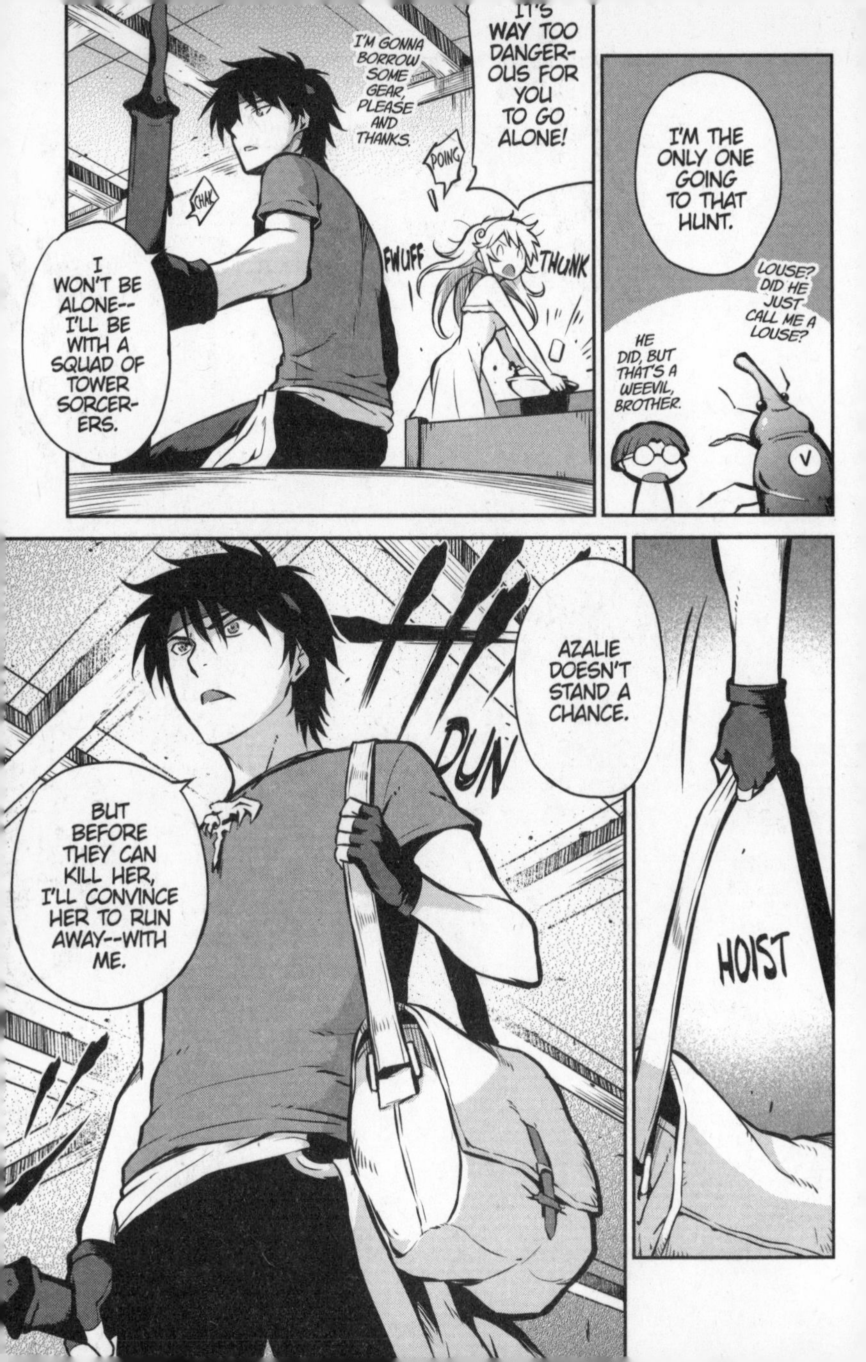
I'M THE ONLY ONE GOING TO THAT HUNT.
LOUSE? DID HE JUST CALL ME A LOUSE?
HE DID, BUT THAT'S A WEEVIL, BROTHER.
IT'S WAY TOO DANGER-OUS FOR YOU TO GO ALONE!
I'M GONNA BORROW SOME GEAR, PLEASE AND THANKS.
POING
THUNK
FWUFF
CHAK
I WON'T BE ALONE--I'LL BE WITH A SQUAD OF TOWER SORCERER-ERS.
HOIST
AZALIE DOESN'T STAND A CHANCE.
DUN
BUT BEFORE THEY CAN KILL HER, I'LL CONVINCE HER TO RUN AWAY--WITH ME.

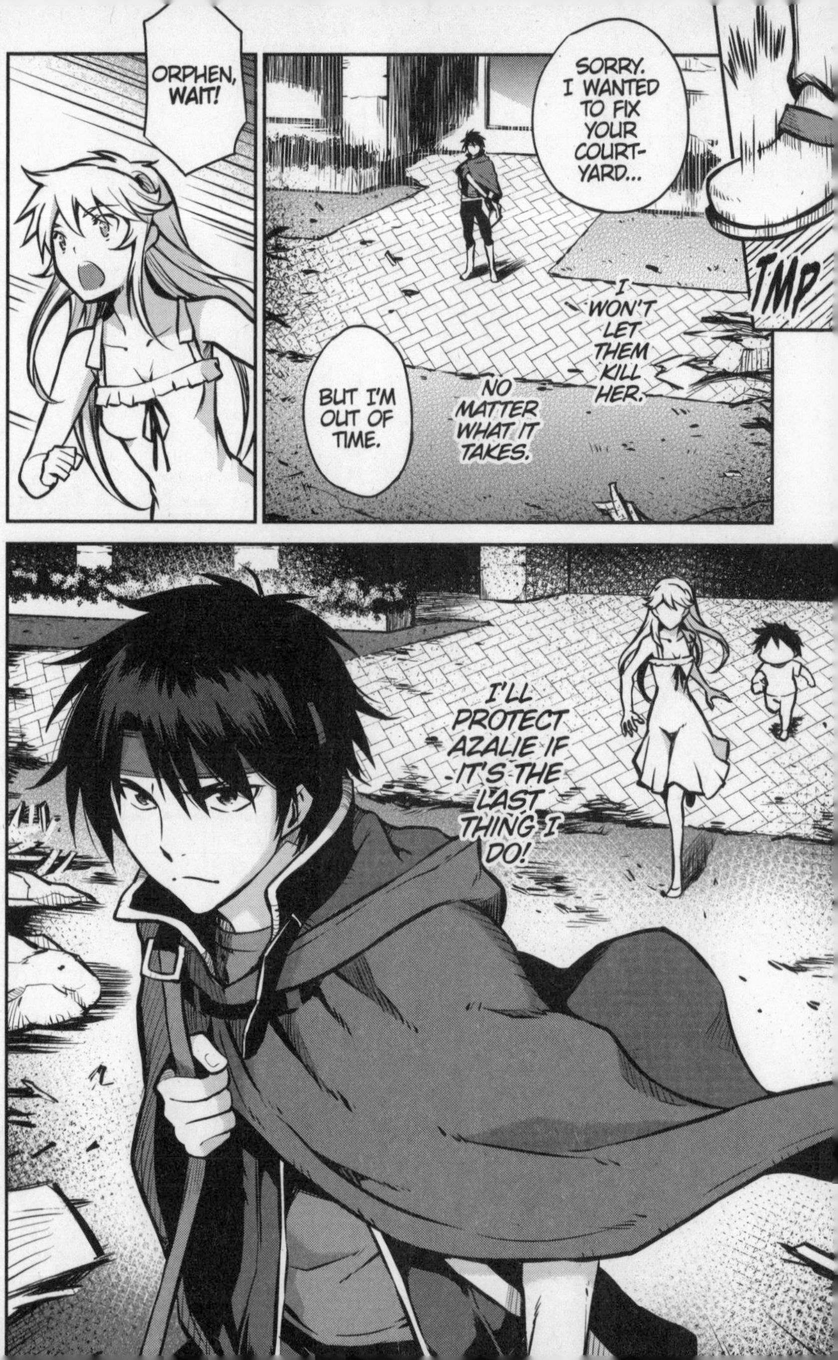
SORRY. I WANTED TO FIX YOUR COURTYARD...
TMP
I WON'T LET THEM KILL HER.
NO MATTER WHAT IT TAKES.
BUT I'M OUT OF TIME.
ORPHEN, WAIT!
I'LL PROTECT AZALIE IF IT'S THE LAST THING I DO!

Sorcerous Stabber ORPHEN

CHARACTER DESIGNS ③: VOLKAN & DORTIN

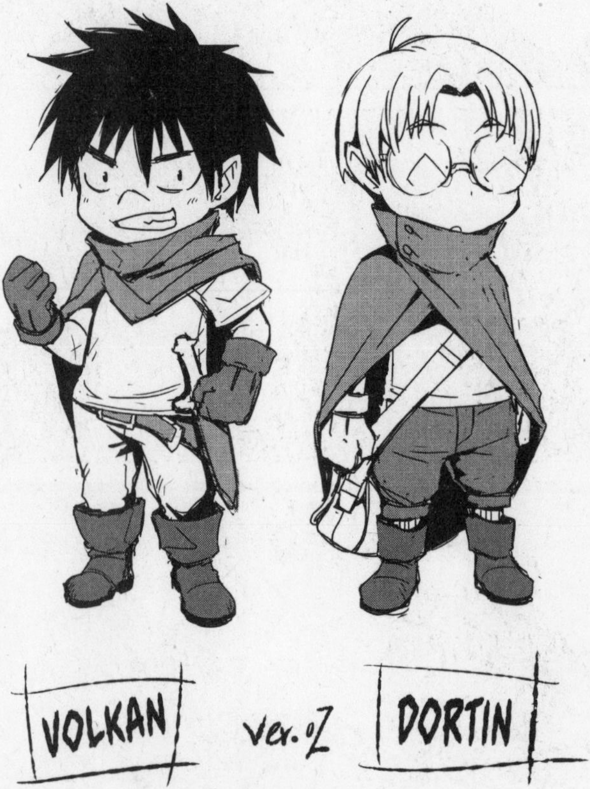
VOLKAN
ver. 02
DORTIN

CHAPTER 7: NIGHT HUNT ②

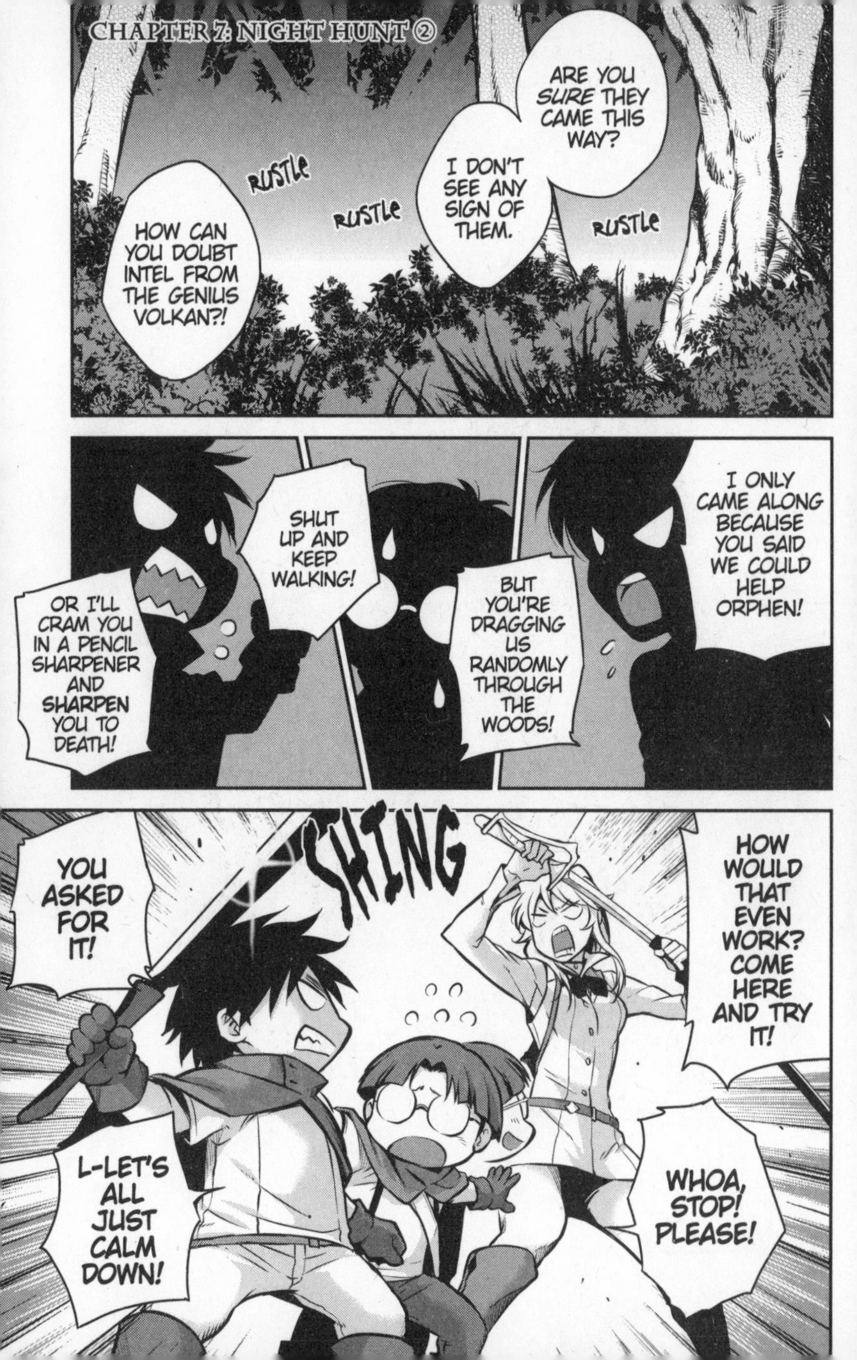

ARE YOU SURE THEY CAME THIS WAY?
I DON'T SEE ANY SIGN OF THEM.
RUSTLE
RUSTLE
RUSTLE
HOW CAN YOU DOUBT INTEL FROM THE GENIUS VOLKAN?!
I ONLY CAME ALONG BECAUSE YOU SAID WE COULD HELP ORPHEN!
BUT YOU'RE DRAGGING US RANDOMLY THROUGH THE WOODS!
SHUT UP AND KEEP WALKING!
OR I'LL CRAM YOU IN A PENCIL SHARPENER AND SHARPEN YOU TO DEATH!
HOW WOULD THAT EVEN WORK? COME HERE AND TRY IT!
SHING
YOU ASKED FOR IT!
WHOA, STOP! PLEASE!
L-LET'S ALL JUST CALM DOWN!

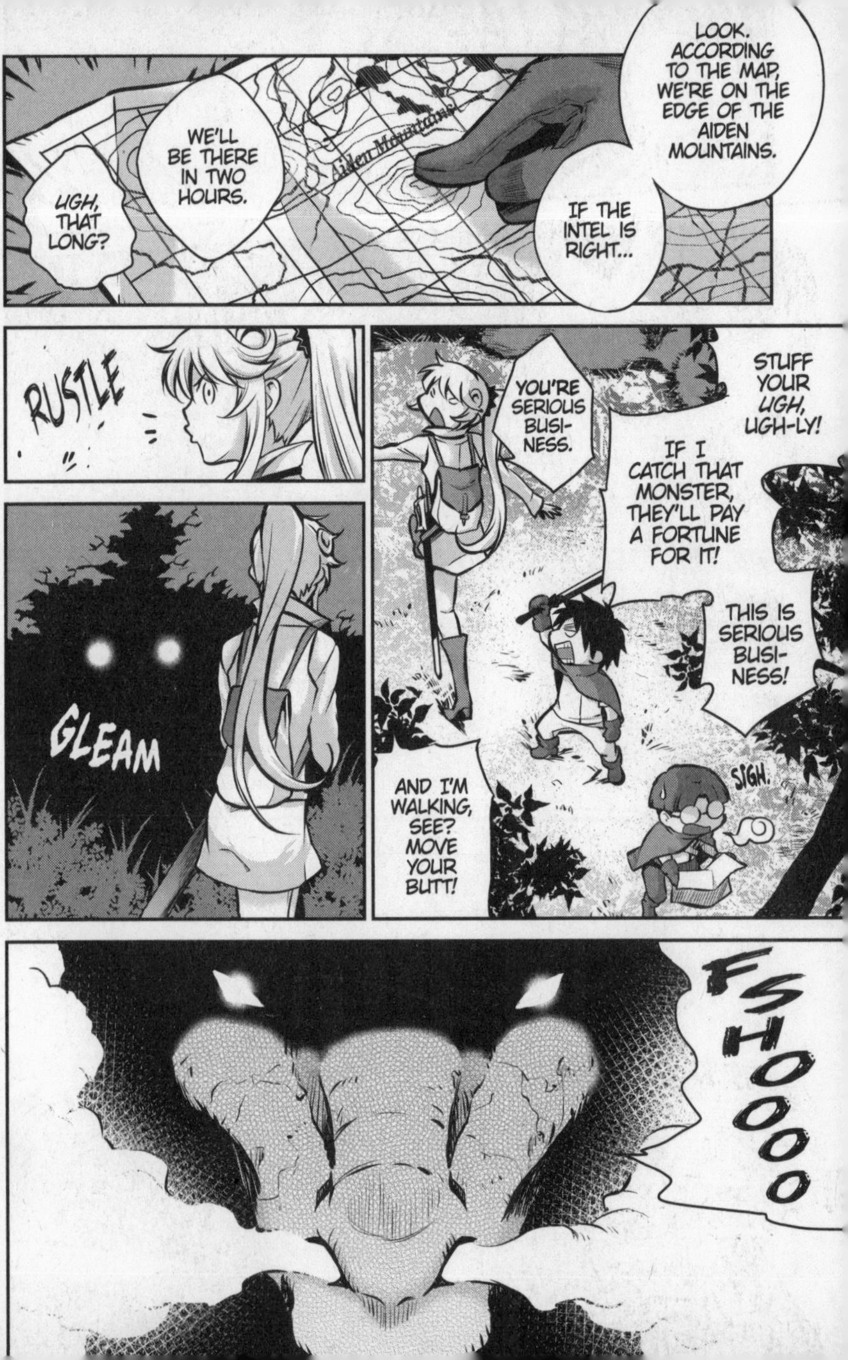
LOOK. ACCORDING TO THE MAP, WE'RE ON THE EDGE OF THE AIDEN MOUNTAINS.
Aiden Mountains
IF THE INTEL IS RIGHT...
WE'LL BE THERE IN TWO HOURS.
UGH, THAT LONG?
STUFF YOUR UGH, UGH-LY!
IF I CATCH THAT MONSTER, THEY'LL PAY A FORTUNE FOR IT!
THIS IS SERIOUS BUSI-NESS!
YOU'RE SERIOUS BUSI-NESS.
SIGH.
AND I'M WALKING, SEE? MOVE YOUR BUTT!
RUSTLE
GLEAM
FSHOOOO

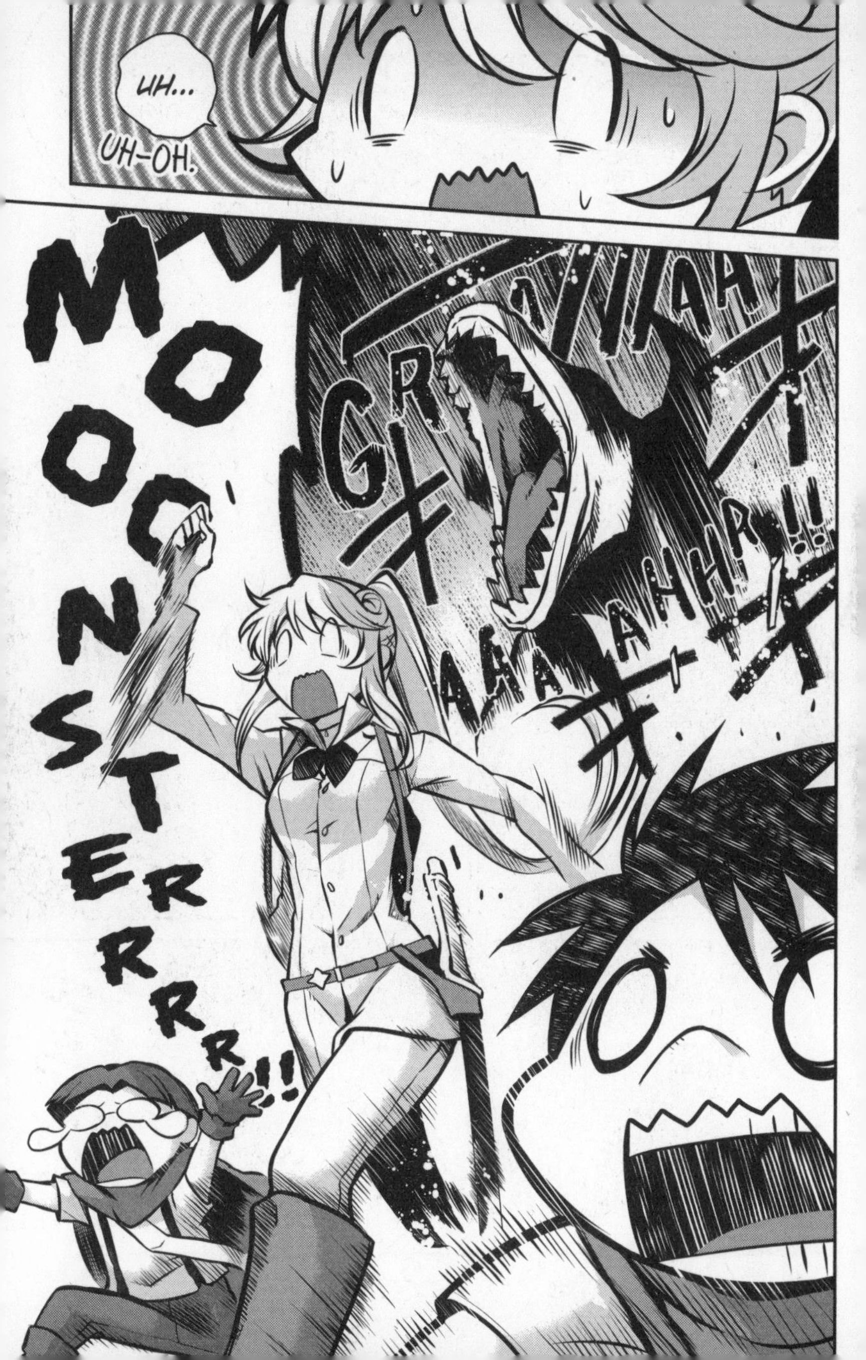
UH...
UH-OH.
GRAAAAAAAAHHR!!
MOOONSTERRRR!!!

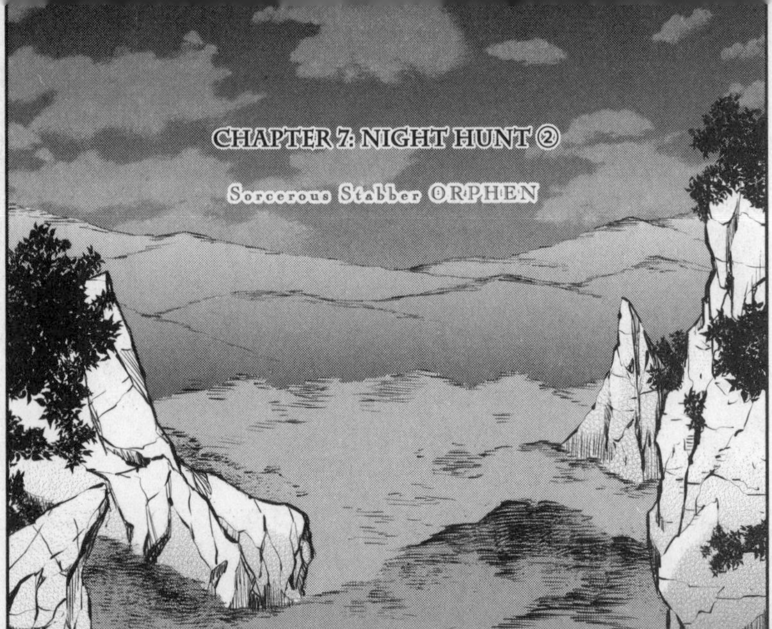
CHAPTER 7: NIGHT HUNT ②
Sorcerous Stabber ORPHEN
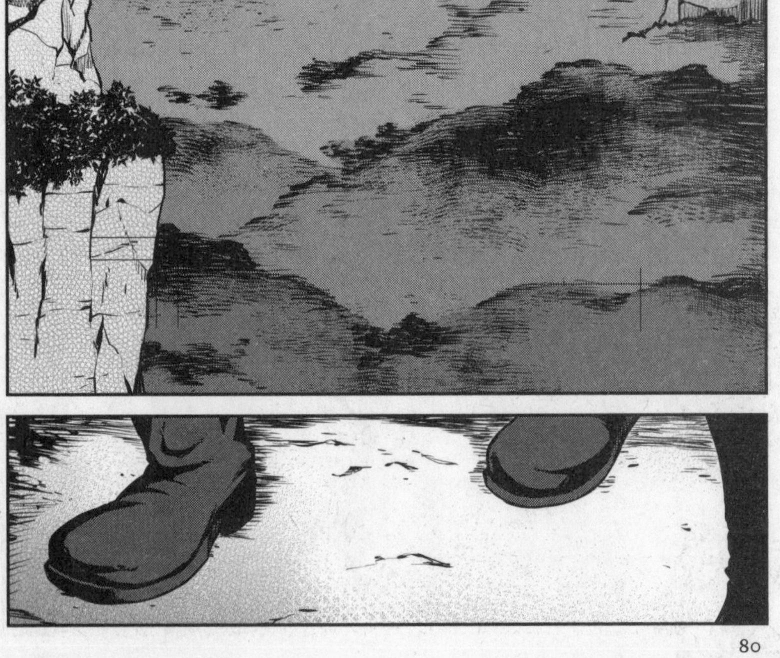

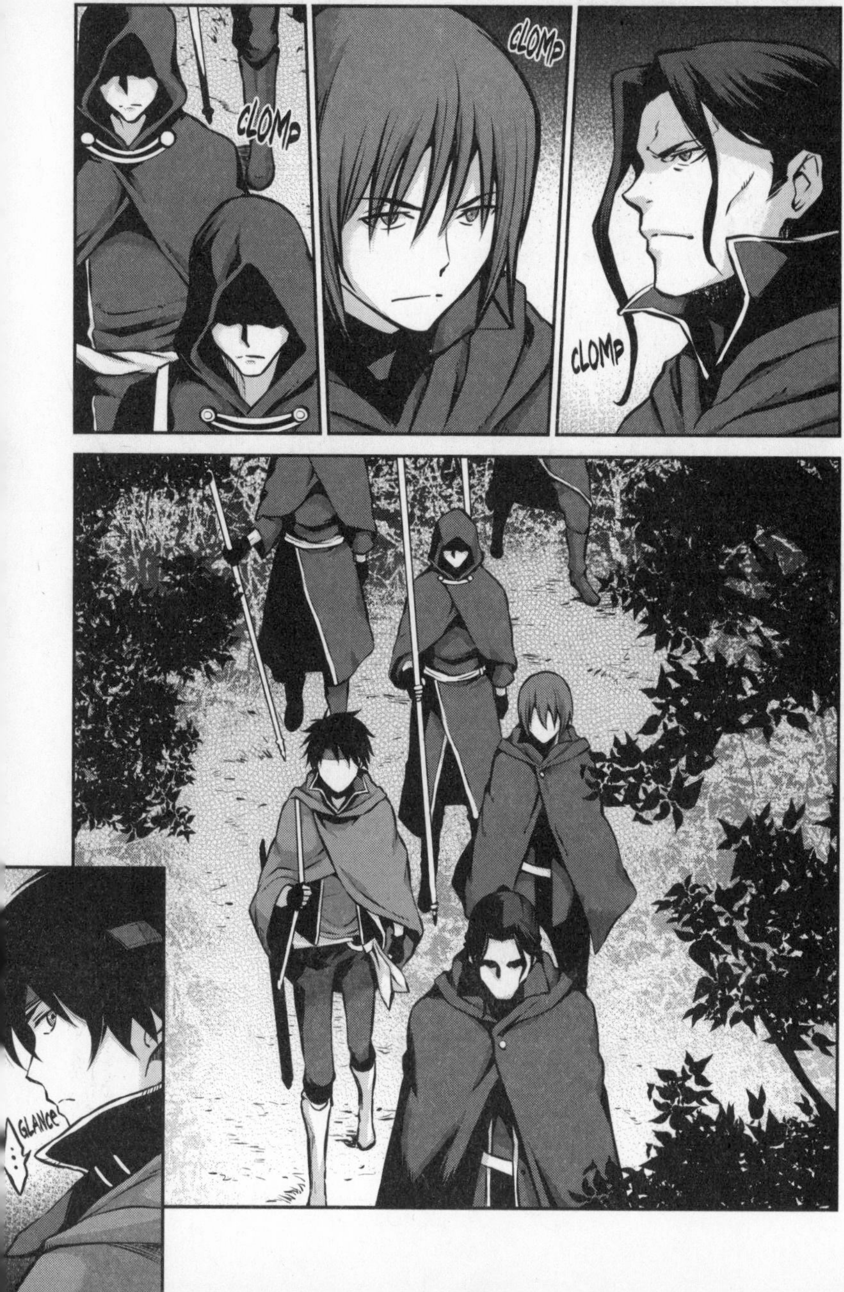
CLOMP
CLOMP
CLOMP
GLANCE
...

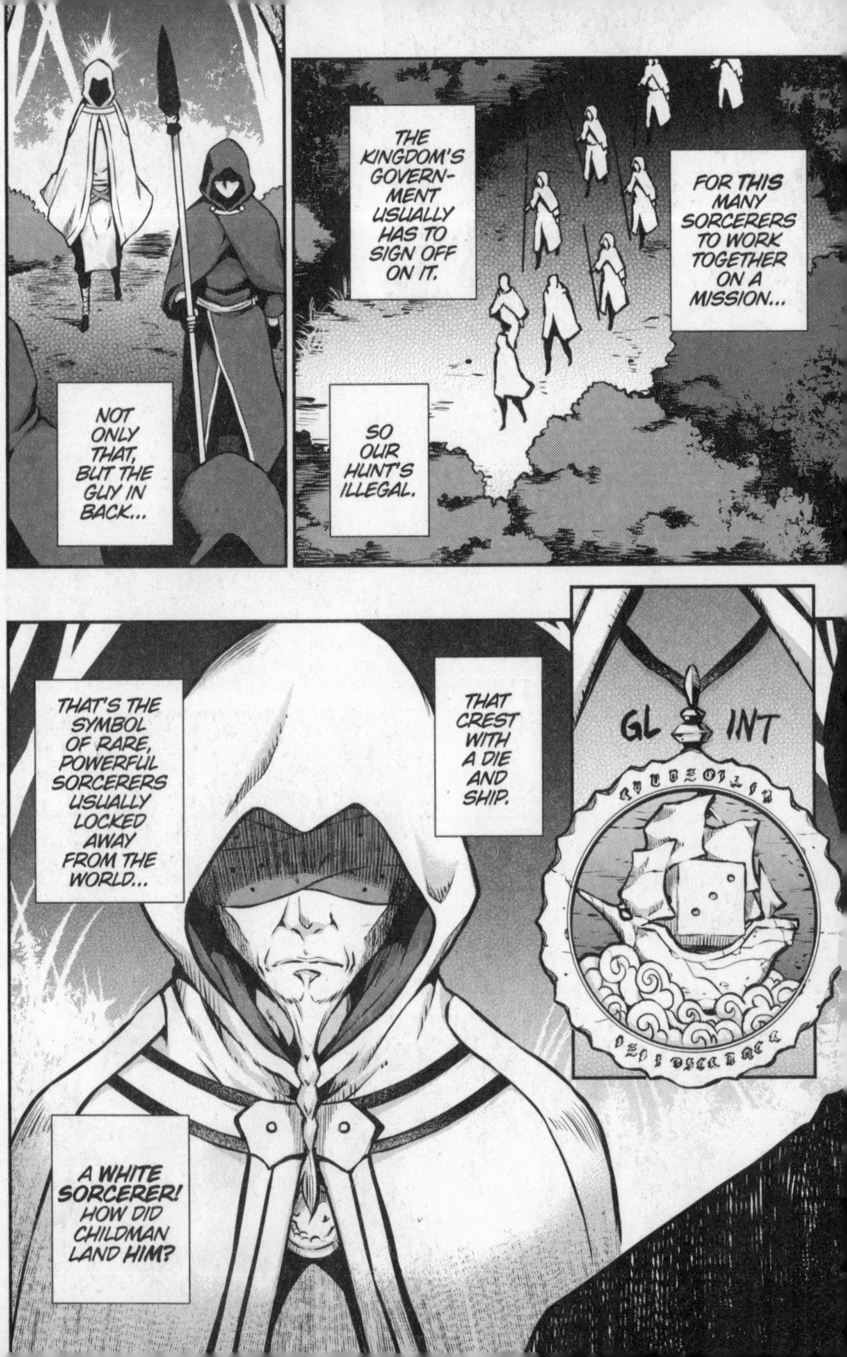
FOR THIS MANY SORCERERS TO WORK TOGETHER ON A MISSION...
THE KINGDOM'S GOVERN-MENT USUALLY HAS TO SIGN OFF ON IT.
SO OUR HUNT'S ILLEGAL.
NOT ONLY THAT, BUT THE GUY IN BACK...
GL INT
THAT CREST WITH A DIE AND SHIP.
THAT'S THE SYMBOL OF RARE, POWERFUL SORCERERS USUALLY LOCKED AWAY FROM THE WORLD...
A WHITE SORCERER! HOW DID CHILDMAN LAND HIM?

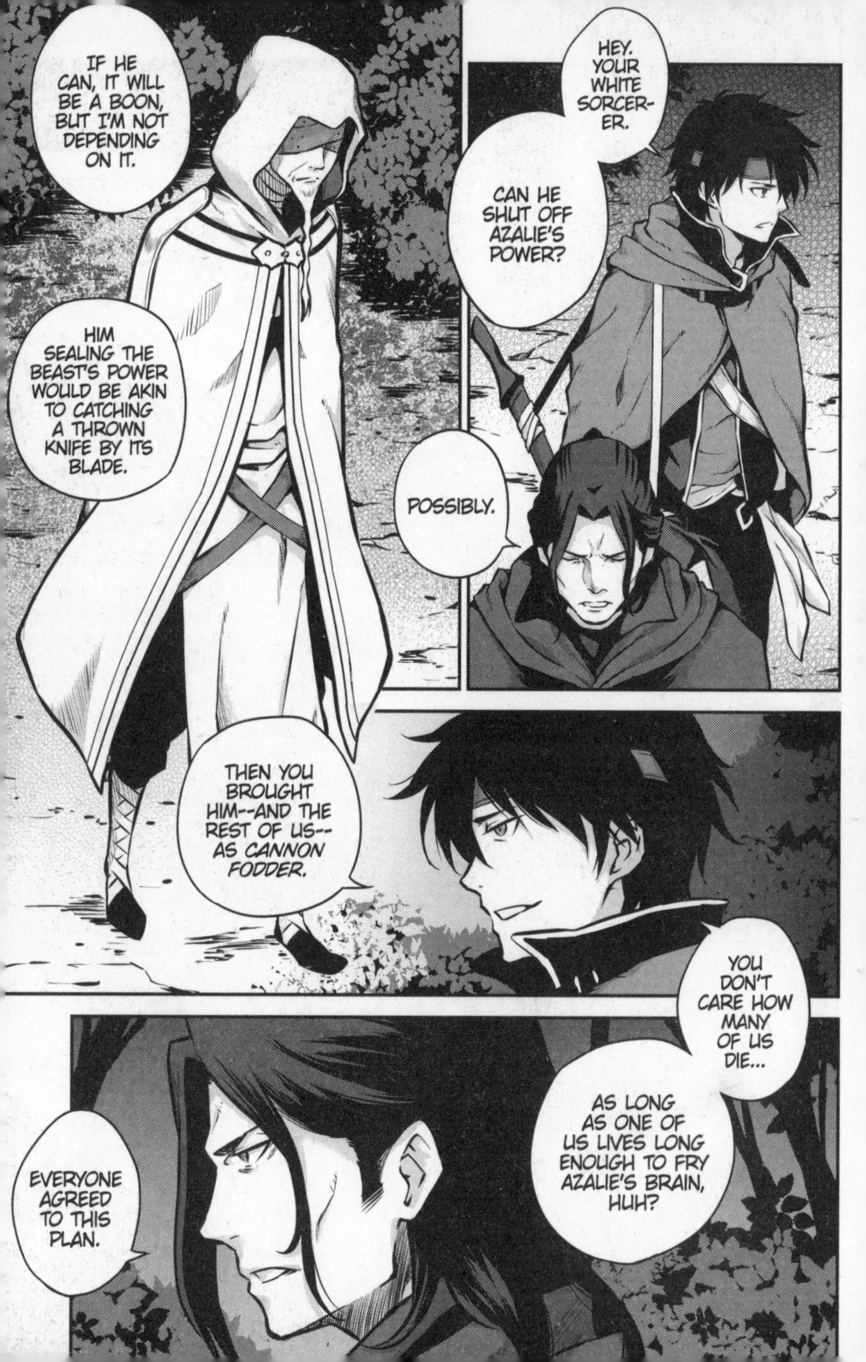
HEY. YOUR WHITE SORCERER.
CAN HE SHUT OFF AZALIE'S POWER?
POSSIBLY.
IF HE CAN, IT WILL BE A BOON, BUT I'M NOT DEPENDING ON IT.
HIM SEALING THE BEAST'S POWER WOULD BE AKIN TO CATCHING A THROWN KNIFE BY ITS BLADE.
THEN YOU BROUGHT HIM--AND THE REST OF US--AS *CANNON FODDER*.
YOU DON'T CARE HOW MANY OF US DIE...
AS LONG AS ONE OF US LIVES LONG ENOUGH TO FRY AZALIE'S BRAIN, HUH?
EVERYONE AGREED TO THIS PLAN.

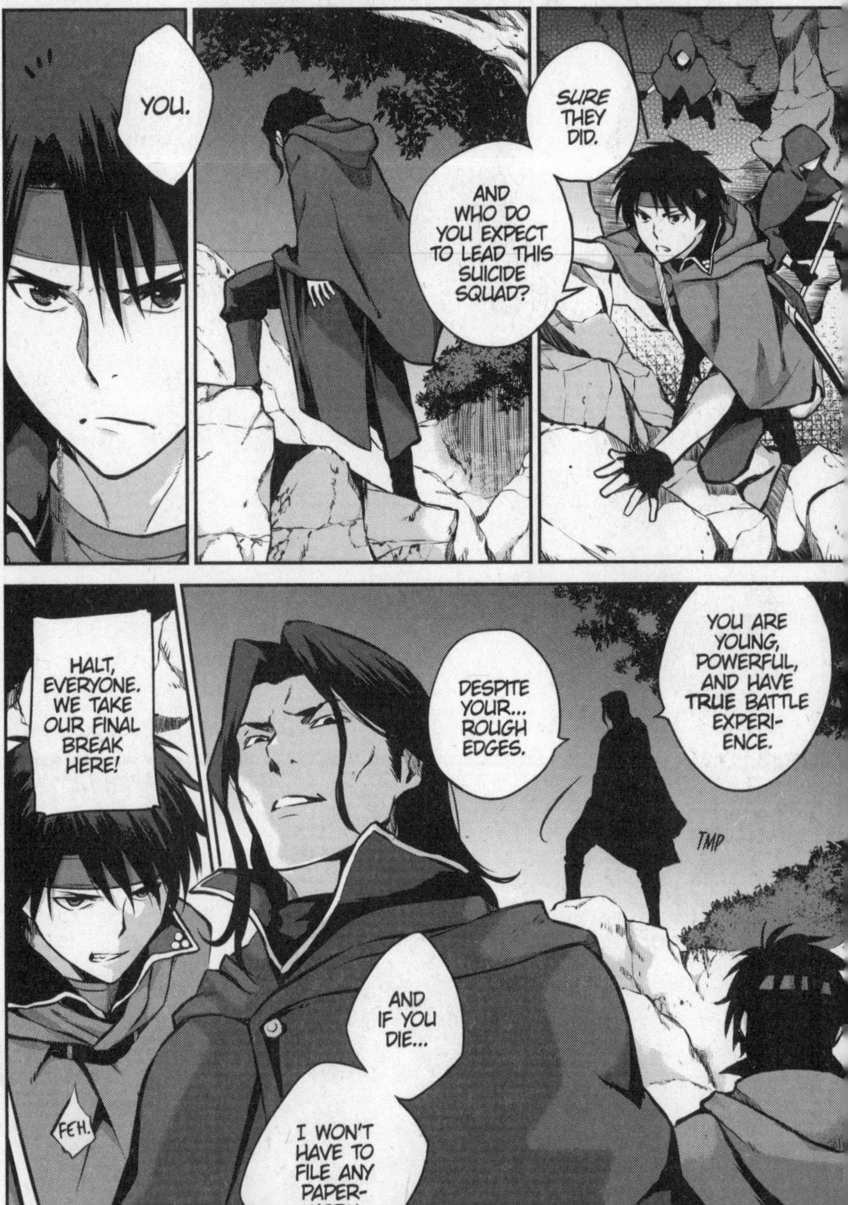
SURE THEY DID.
AND WHO DO YOU EXPECT TO LEAD THIS SUICIDE SQUAD?
YOU.
YOU ARE YOUNG, POWERFUL, AND HAVE TRUE BATTLE EXPERI-ENCE.
DESPITE YOUR... ROUGH EDGES.
HALT, EVERYONE. WE TAKE OUR FINAL BREAK HERE!
TMP
AND IF YOU DIE...
I WON'T HAVE TO FILE ANY PAPER-WORK.
FEH.

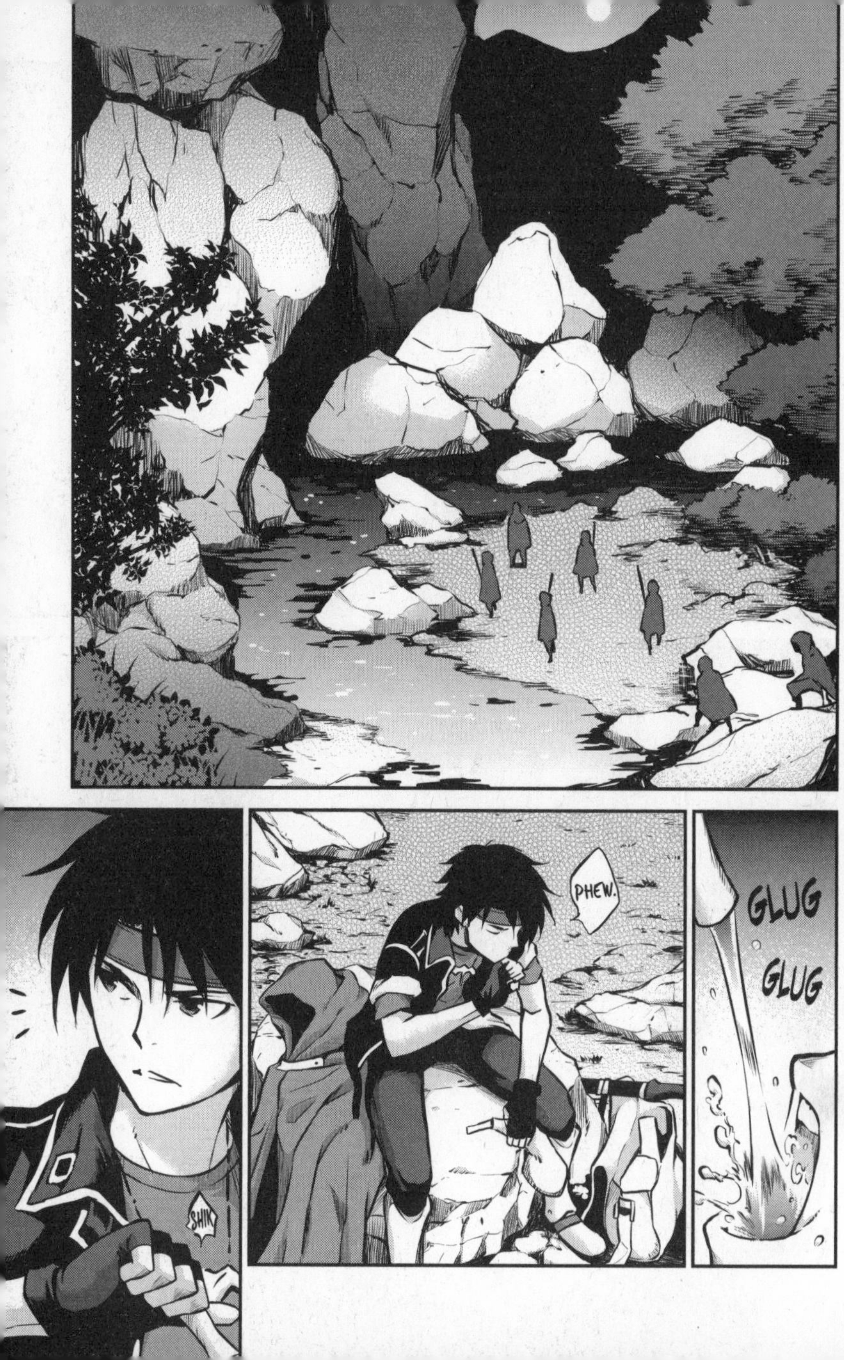
GLUG
GLUG
PHEW.
SHIK

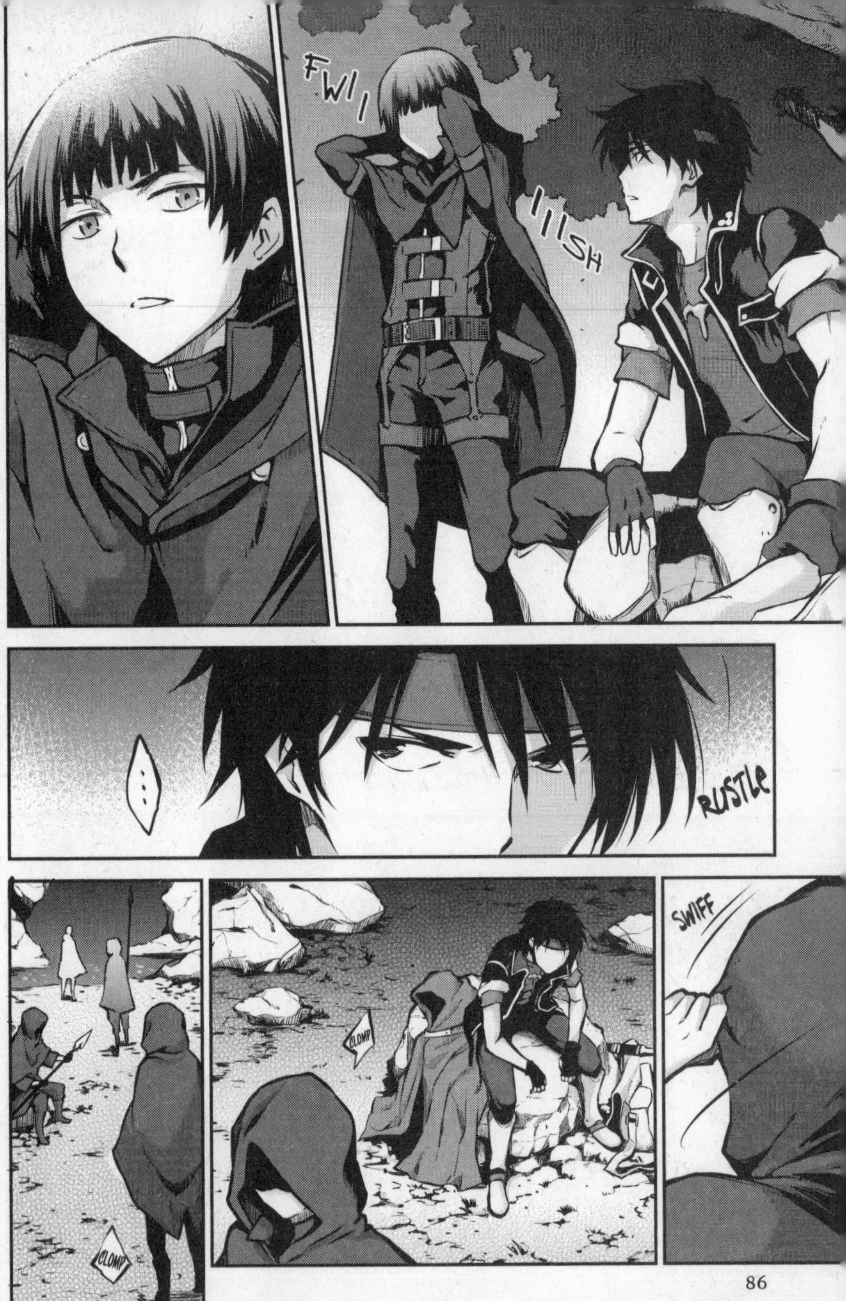
FWI I
IIISH
...
RUSTLE
SWIFF
CLOMP
CLOMP

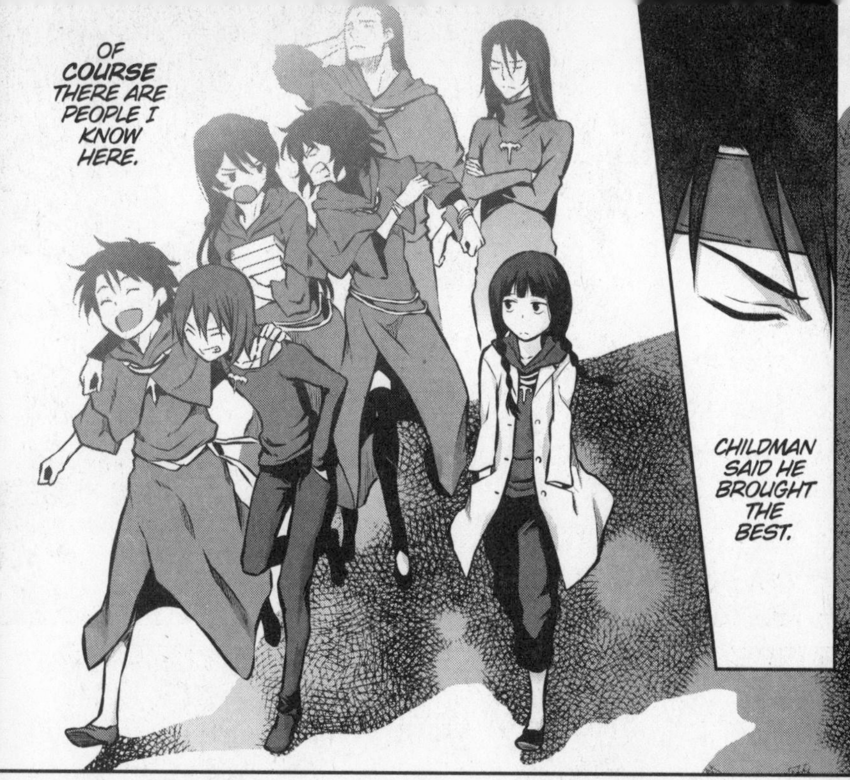
OF COURSE THERE ARE PEOPLE I KNOW HERE.
CHILDMAN SAID HE BROUGHT THE BEST.

BUT...

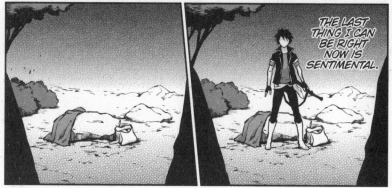

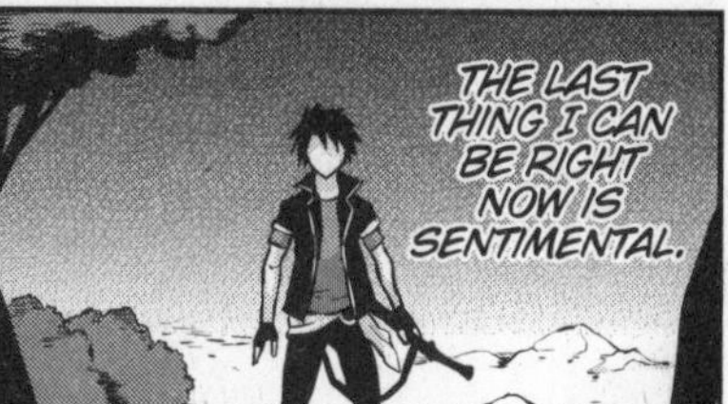
THE LAST THING I CAN BE RIGHT NOW IS SENTIMENTAL.

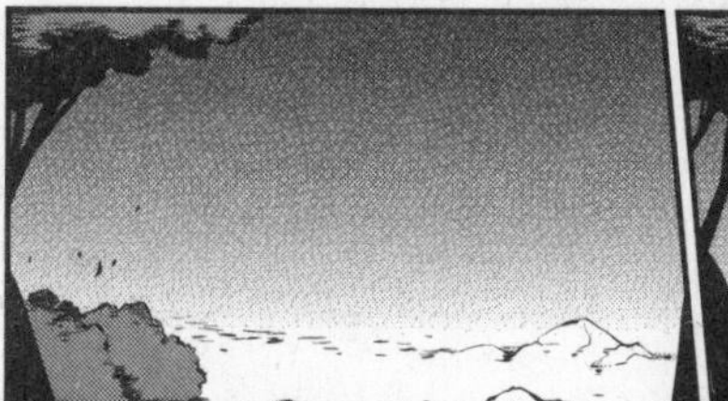

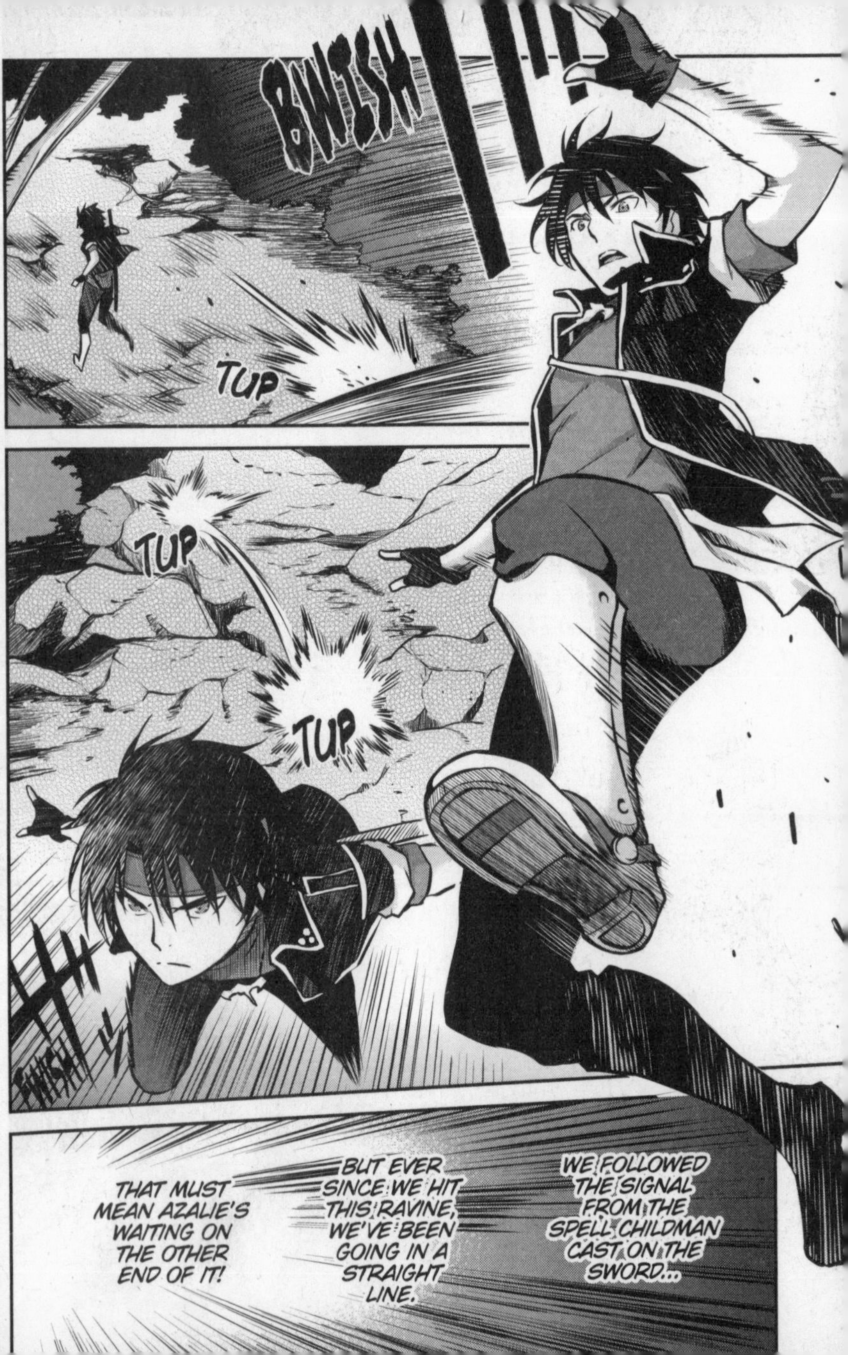
BWISH
TUP
TUP
TUP
FWISH
WE FOLLOWED THE SIGNAL FROM THE SPELL CHILDMAN CAST ON THE SWORD...
BUT EVER SINCE WE HIT THIS RAVINE, WE'VE BEEN GOING IN A STRAIGHT LINE.
THAT MUST MEAN AZALIE'S WAITING ON THE OTHER END OF IT!

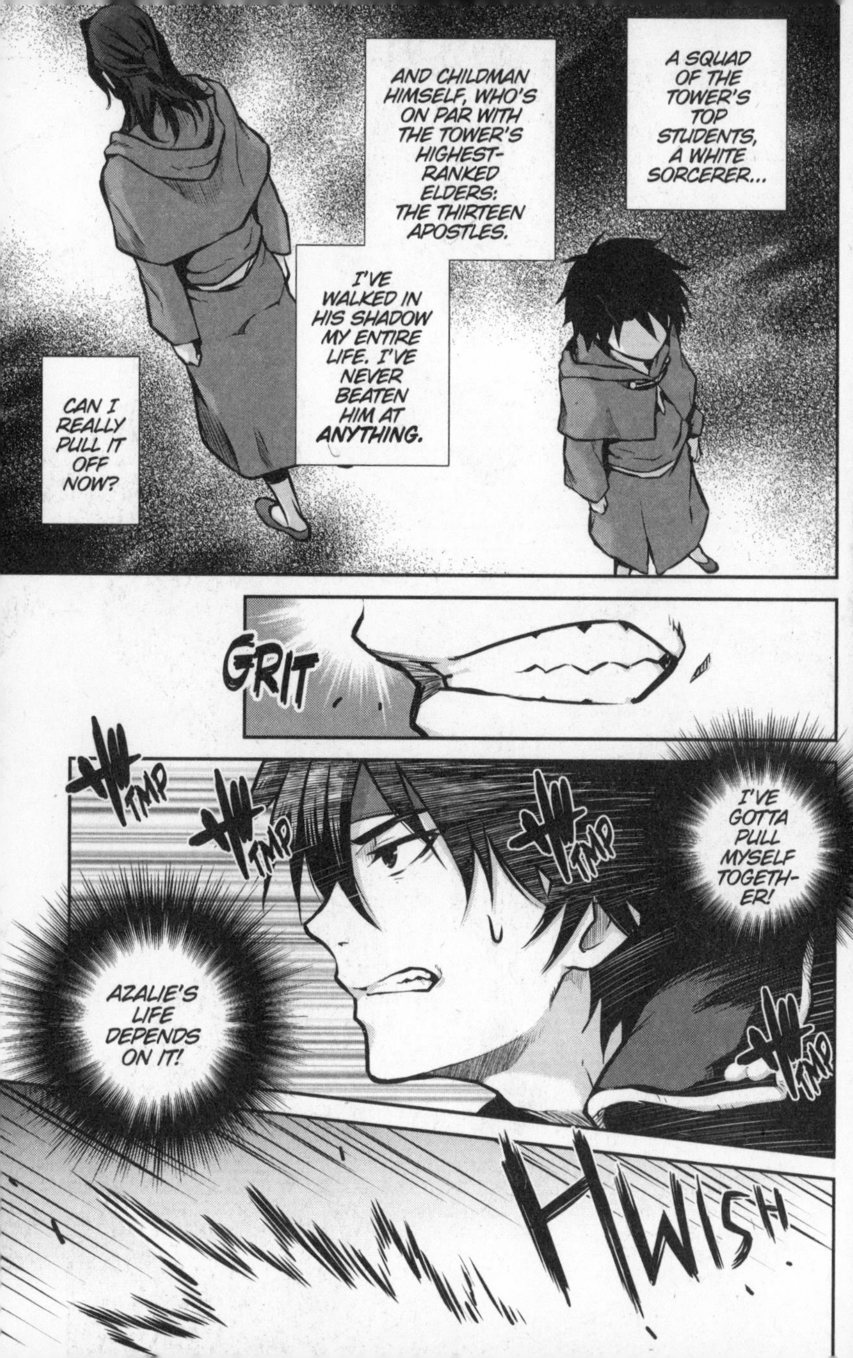
A SQUAD OF THE TOWER'S TOP STUDENTS, A WHITE SORCERER...
AND CHILDMAN HIMSELF, WHO'S ON PAR WITH THE TOWER'S HIGHEST-RANKED ELDERS: THE THIRTEEN APOSTLES.
I'VE WALKED IN HIS SHADOW MY ENTIRE LIFE. I'VE NEVER BEATEN HIM AT ANYTHING.
CAN I REALLY PULL IT OFF NOW?
GRIT
I'VE GOTTA PULL MYSELF TOGETHER!
TMP
TMP
TMP
TMP
TMP
AZALIE'S LIFE DEPENDS ON IT!
HWISH

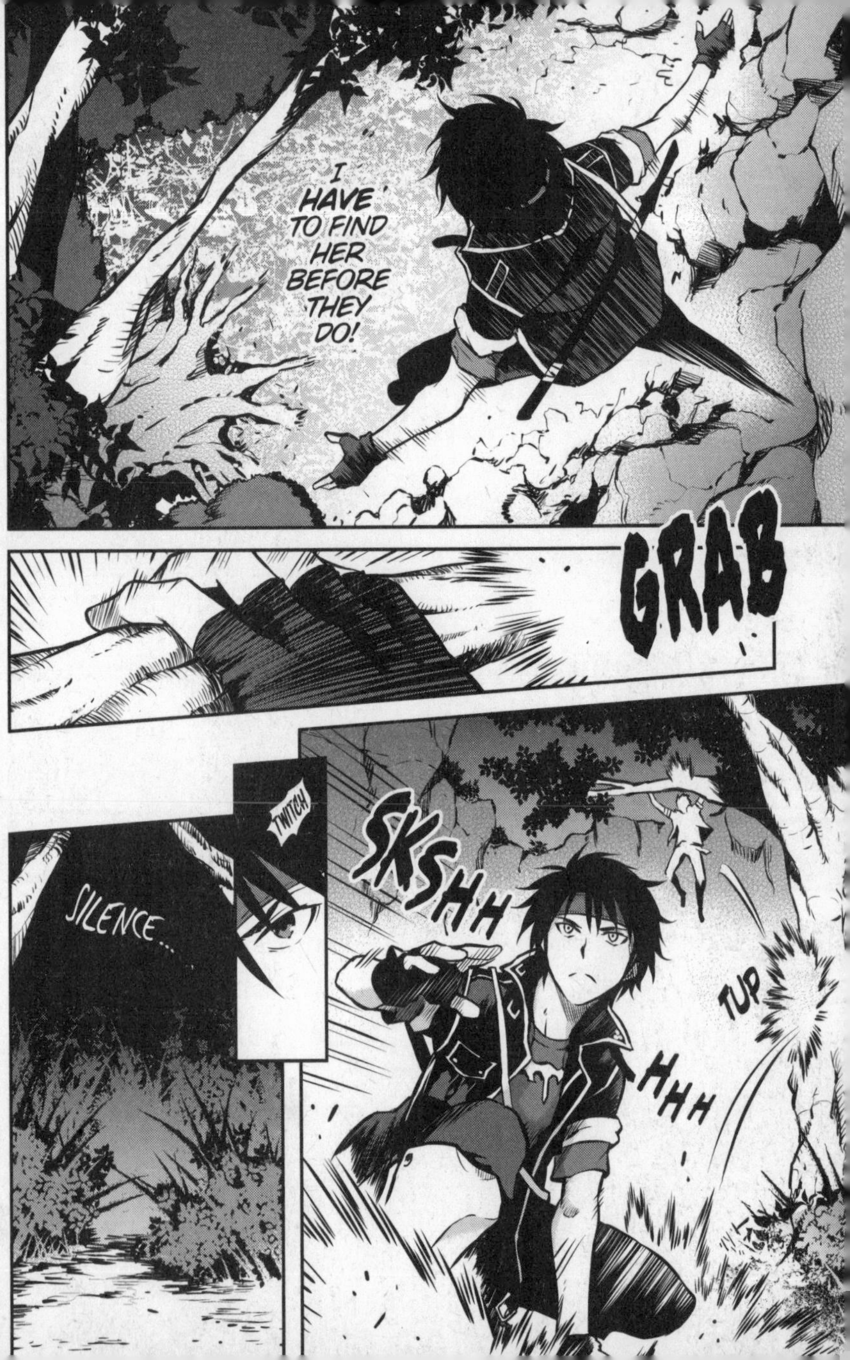
I HAVE TO FIND HER BEFORE THEY DO!
GRAB
SKSHHH
TUP
HHH
TWITCH
SILENCE...

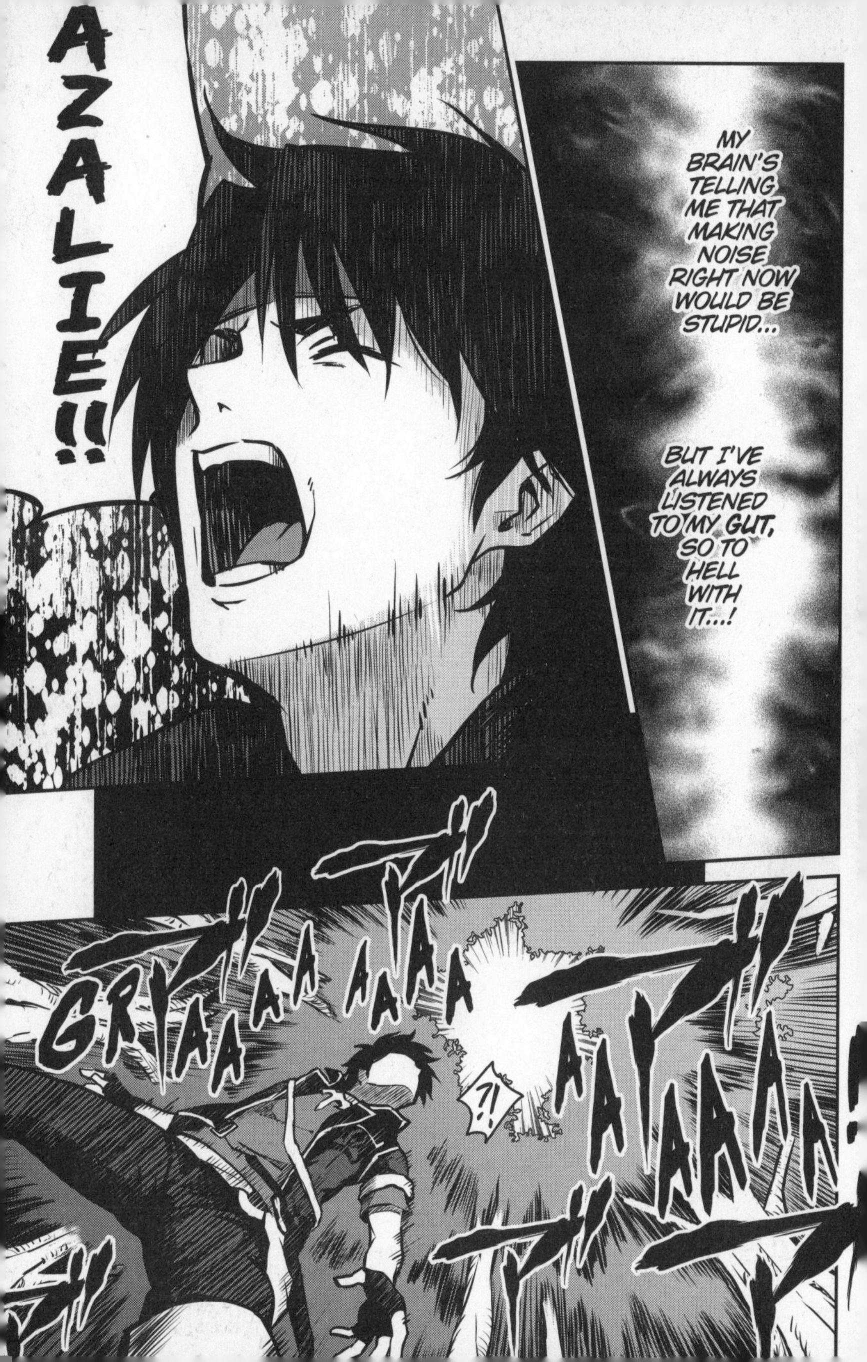
MY BRAIN'S TELLING ME THAT MAKING NOISE RIGHT NOW WOULD BE STUPID...
BUT I'VE ALWAYS LISTENED TO MY GUT, SO TO HELL WITH IT...!
AZALIE!!
AAYAAAAA!!
GRYAAAAAAAAA
?!

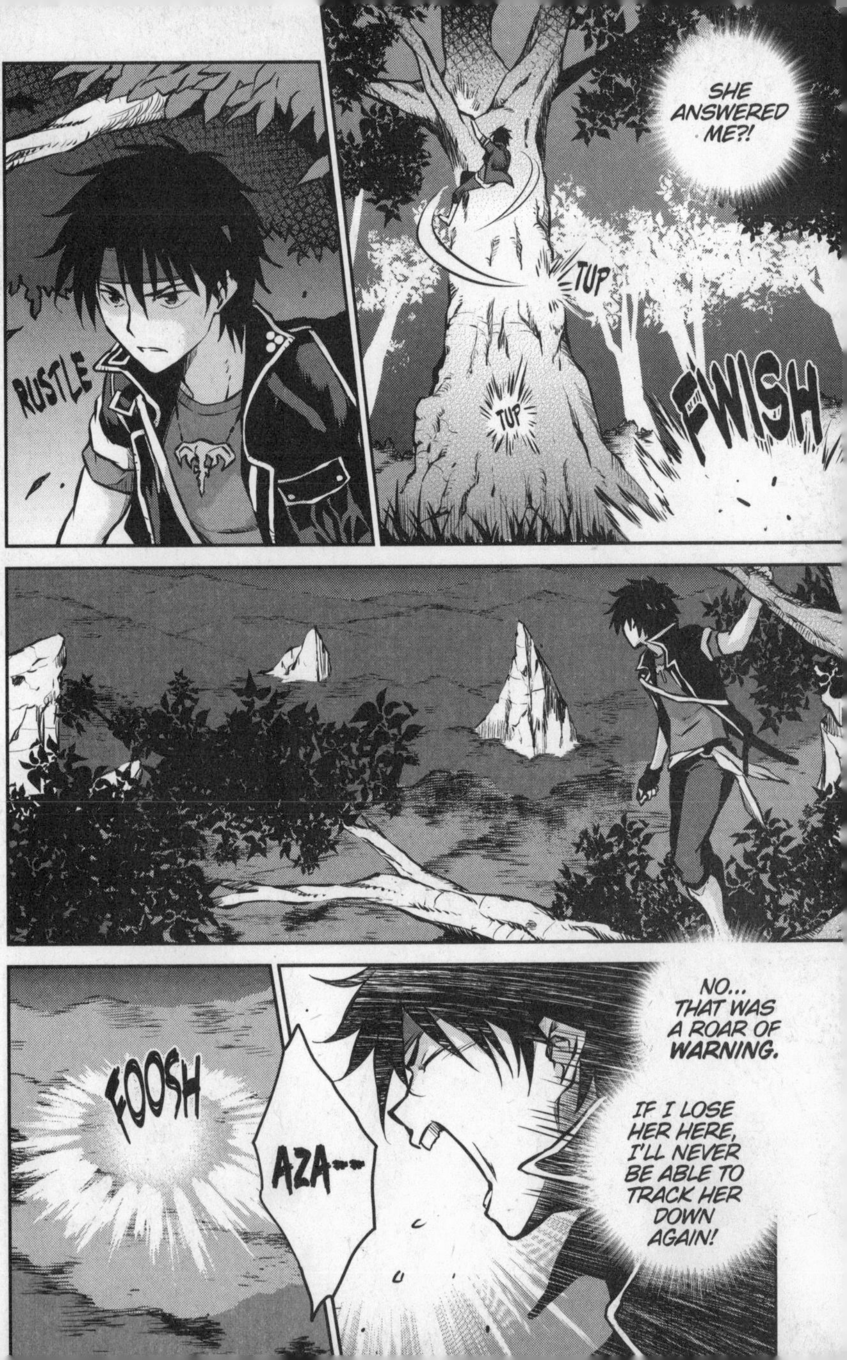
SHE ANSWERED ME?!
TUP
TUP
FWISH
RUSTLE
NO... THAT WAS A ROAR OF WARNING.
IF I LOSE HER HERE, I'LL NEVER BE ABLE TO TRACK HER DOWN AGAIN!
AZA--
FOOSH

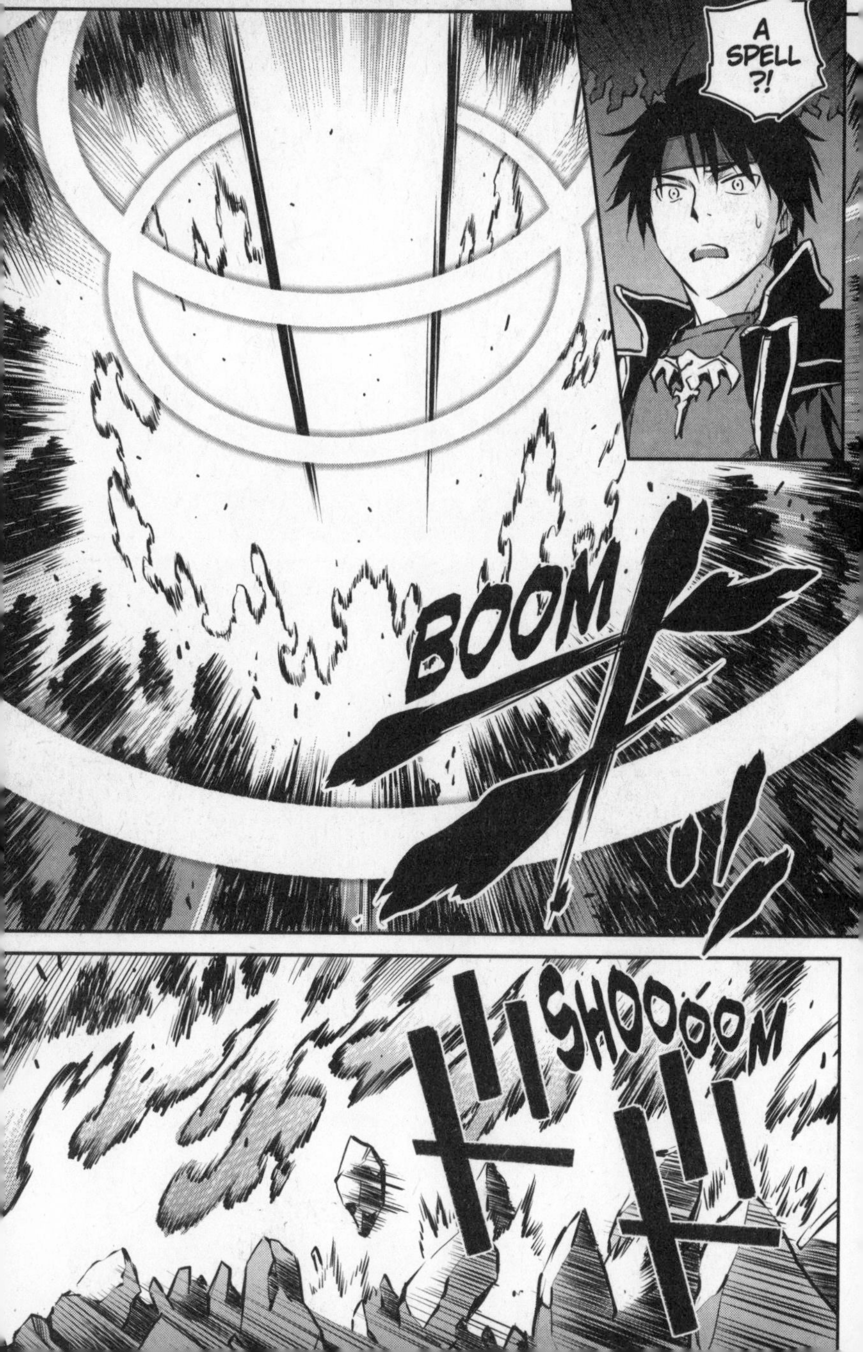
A SPELL ?!
BOOM
SHOOOOM

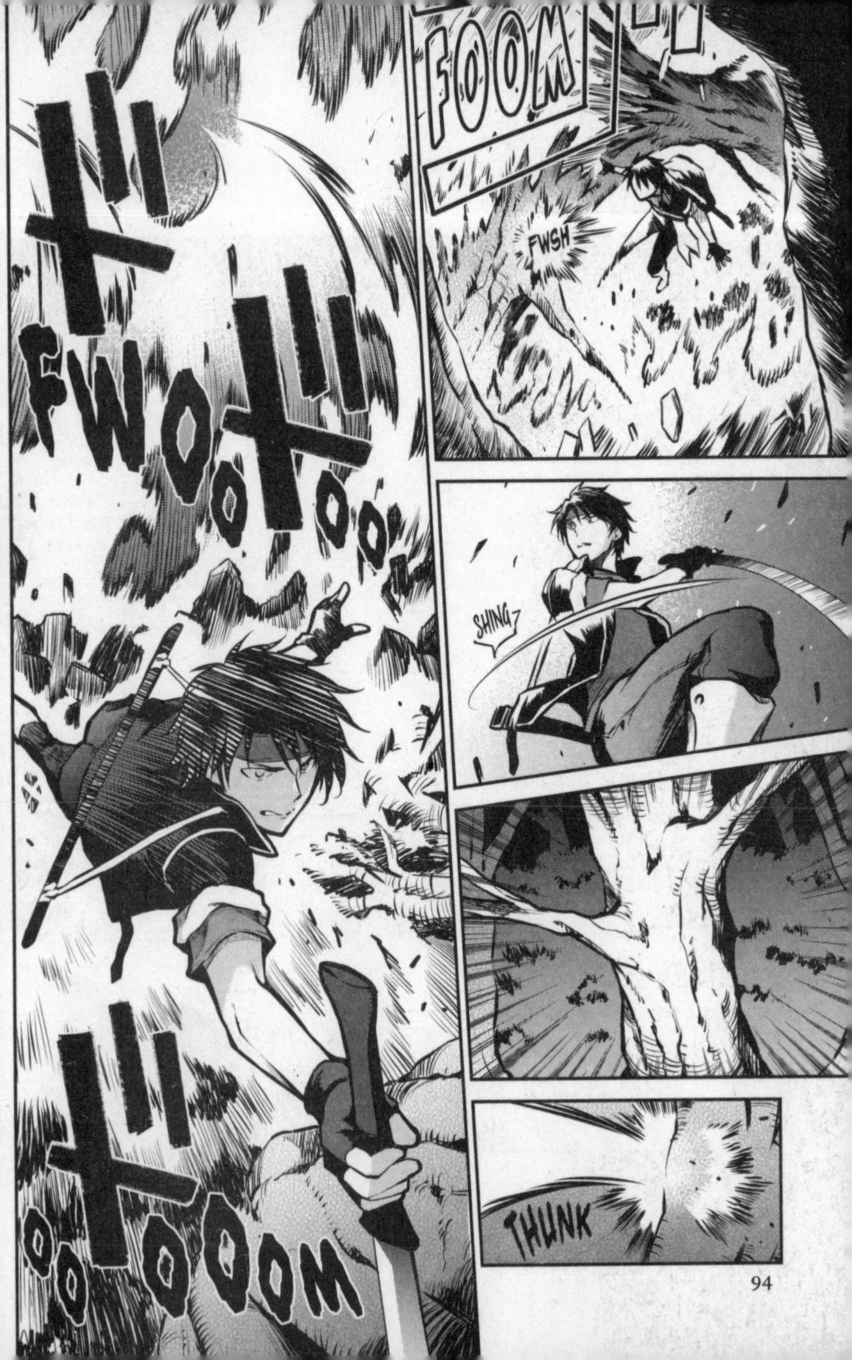
FOOM
FWSH
SHING
THUNK
FWOOOOO
OOOOOM

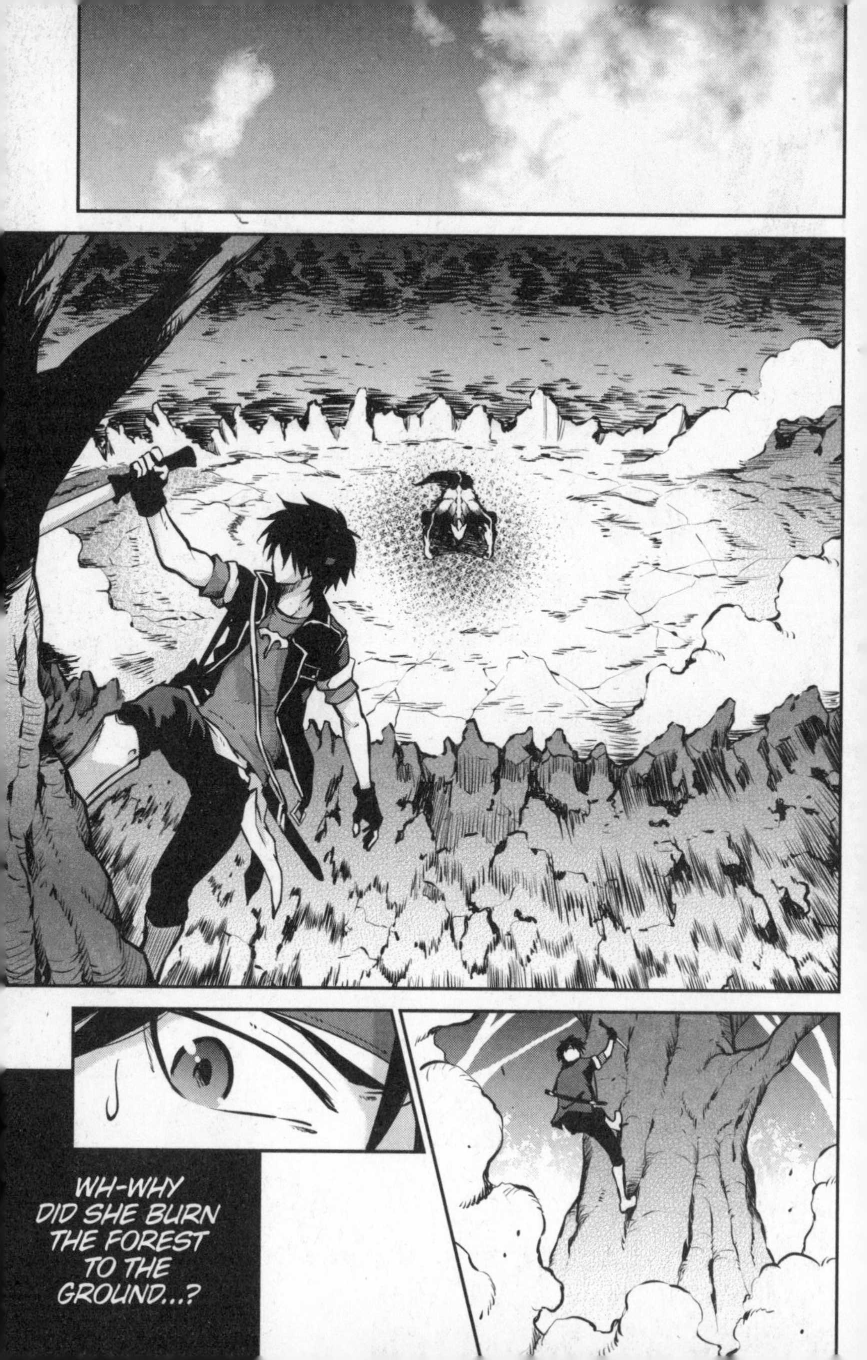
WH-WHY DID SHE BURN THE FOREST TO THE GROUND...?

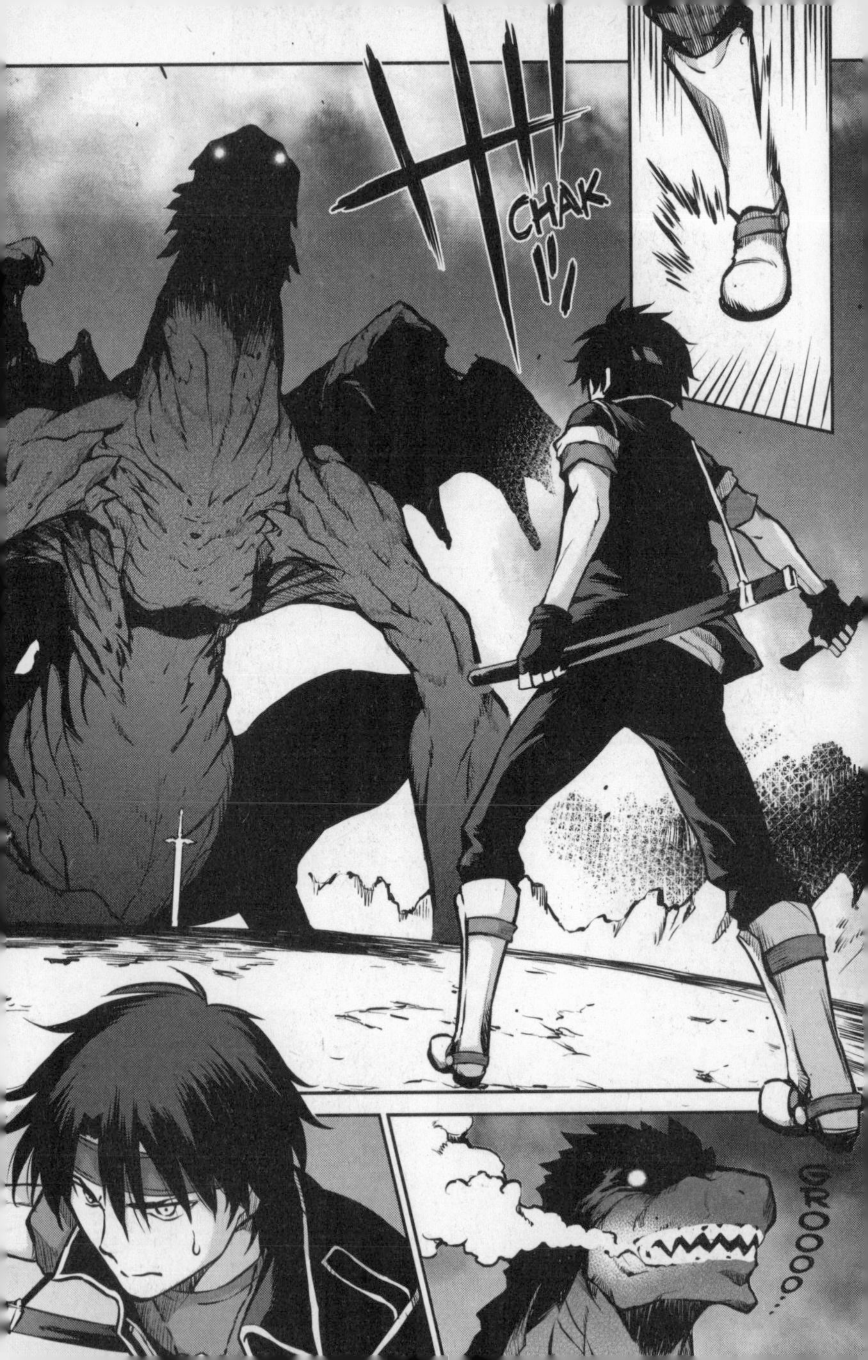
CHAK
GROOOOO...

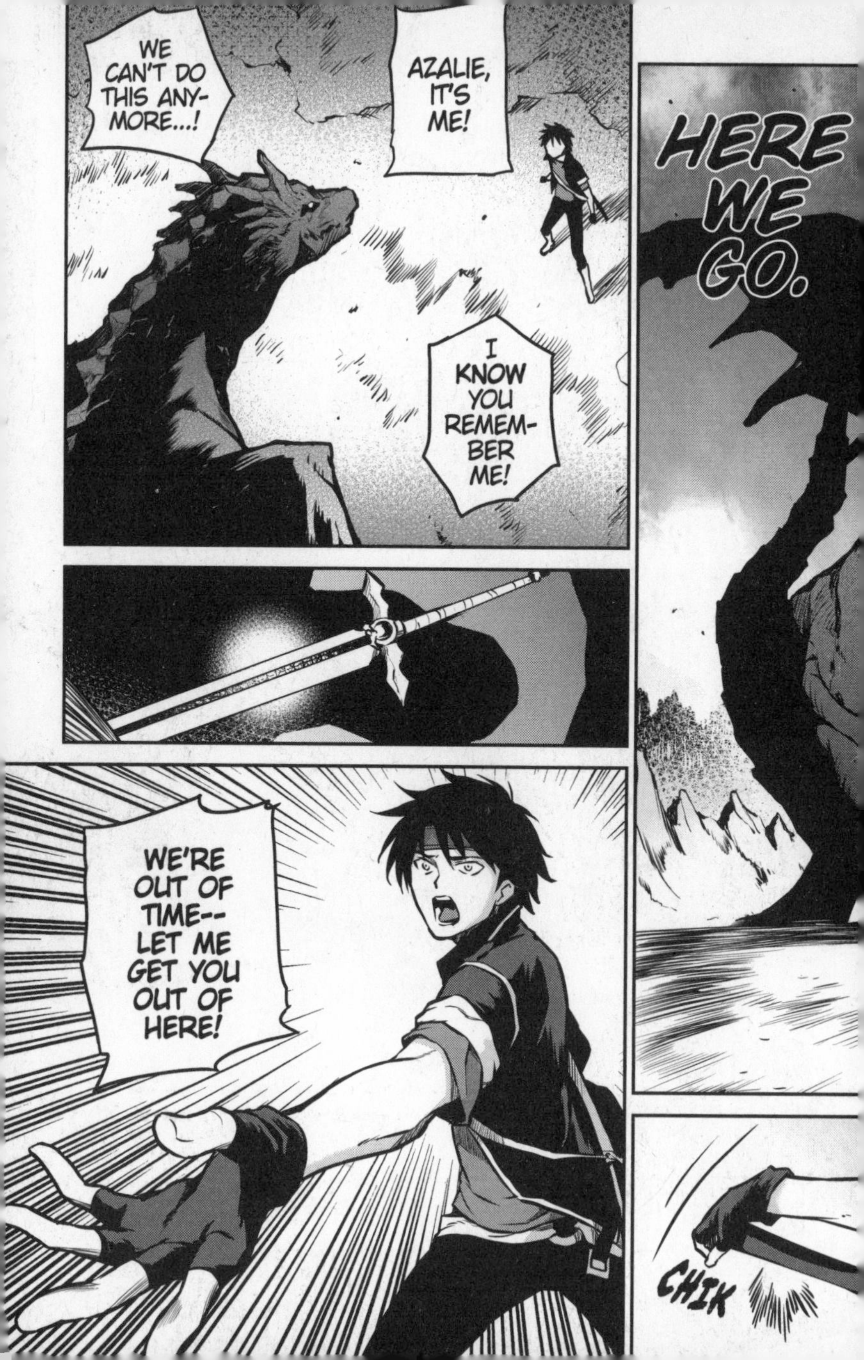
HERE WE GO.
AZALIE, IT'S ME!
WE CAN'T DO THIS ANY-MORE...!
I KNOW YOU REMEMBER ME!
CHIK
WE'RE OUT OF TIME-- LET ME GET YOU OUT OF HERE!

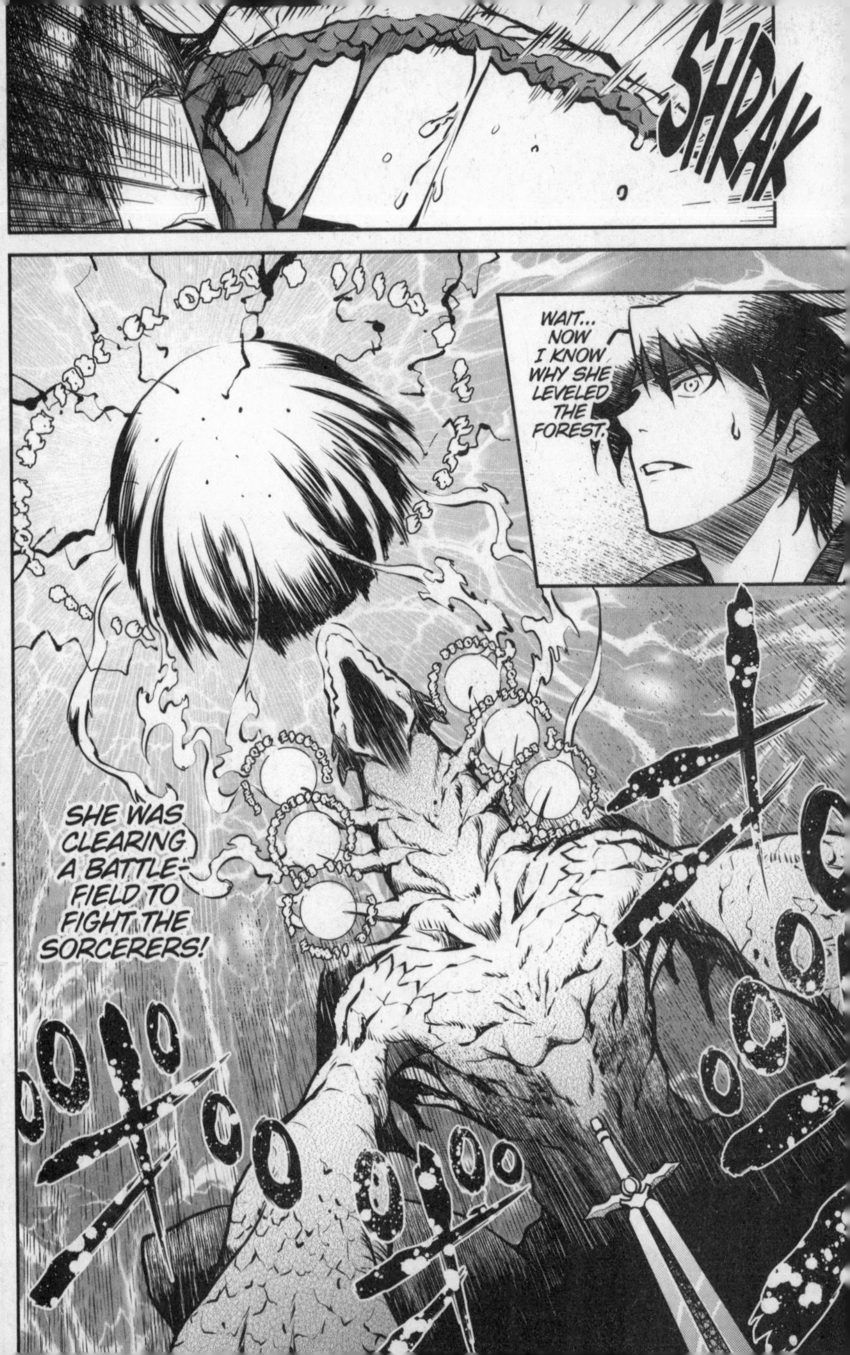
SHRAK
WAIT... NOW I KNOW WHY SHE LEVELED THE FOREST.
SHE WAS CLEARING A BATTLE-FIELD TO FIGHT THE SORCERERS!

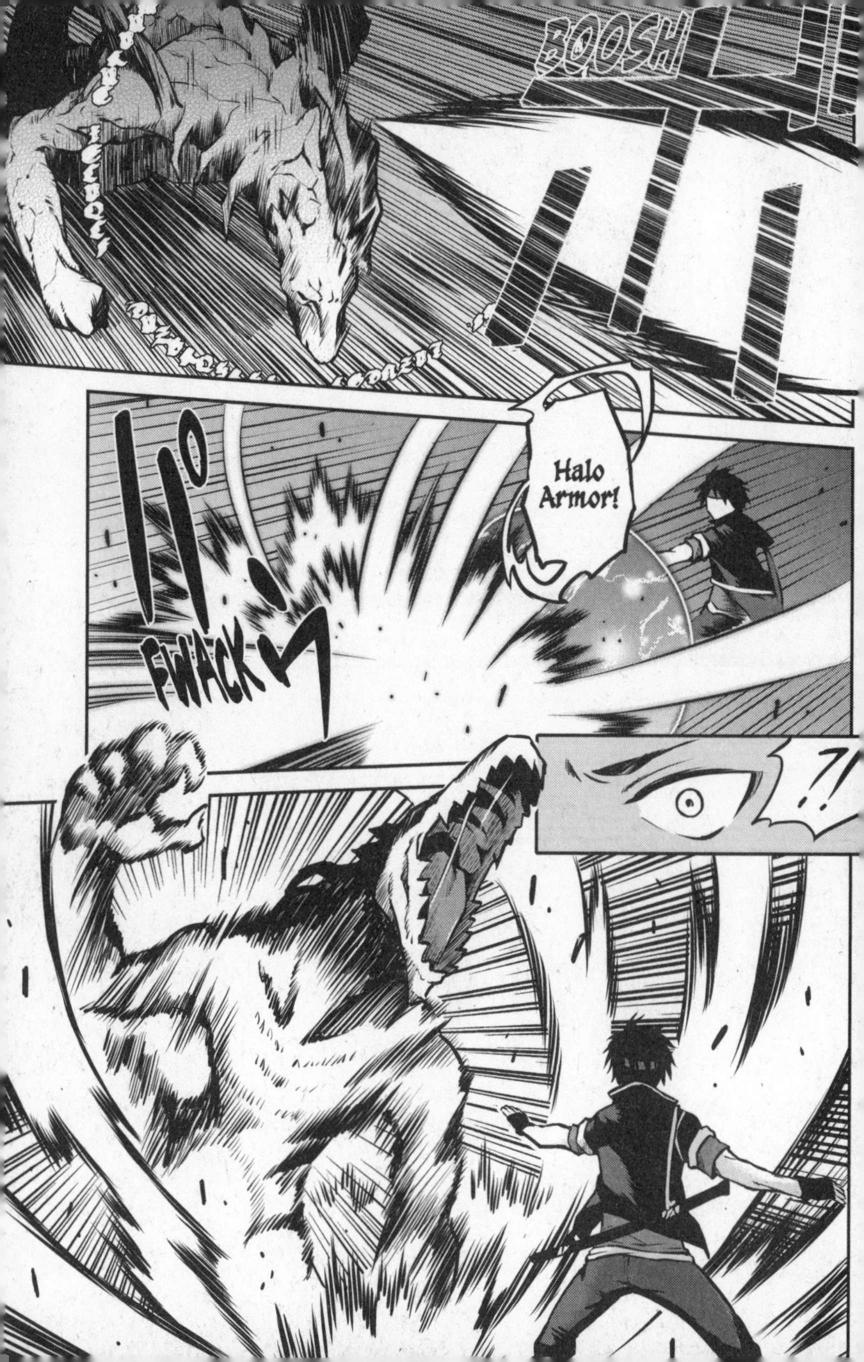
BOOSH!
Halo Armor!
FWACK
?!

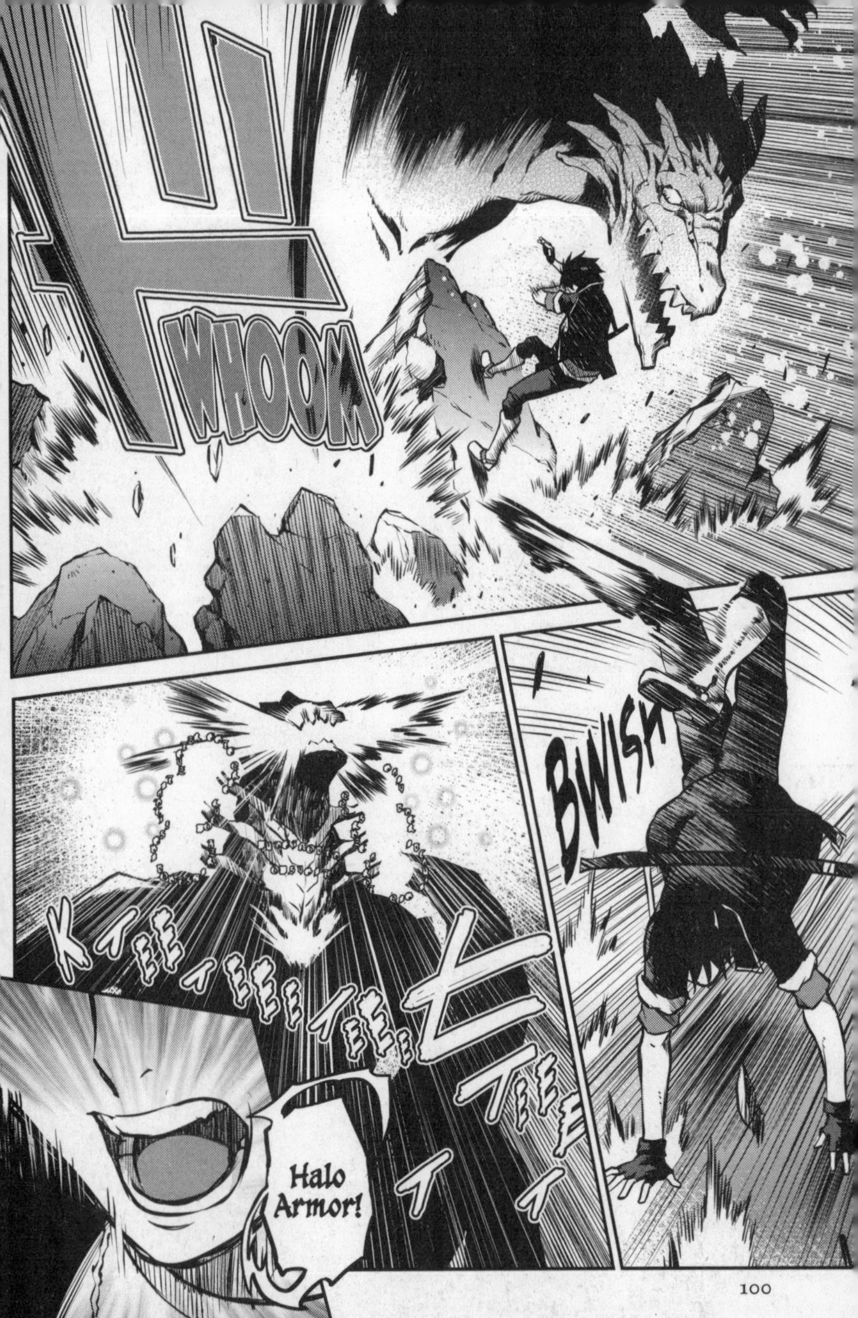
WHOOM
BWISH
Halo Armor!

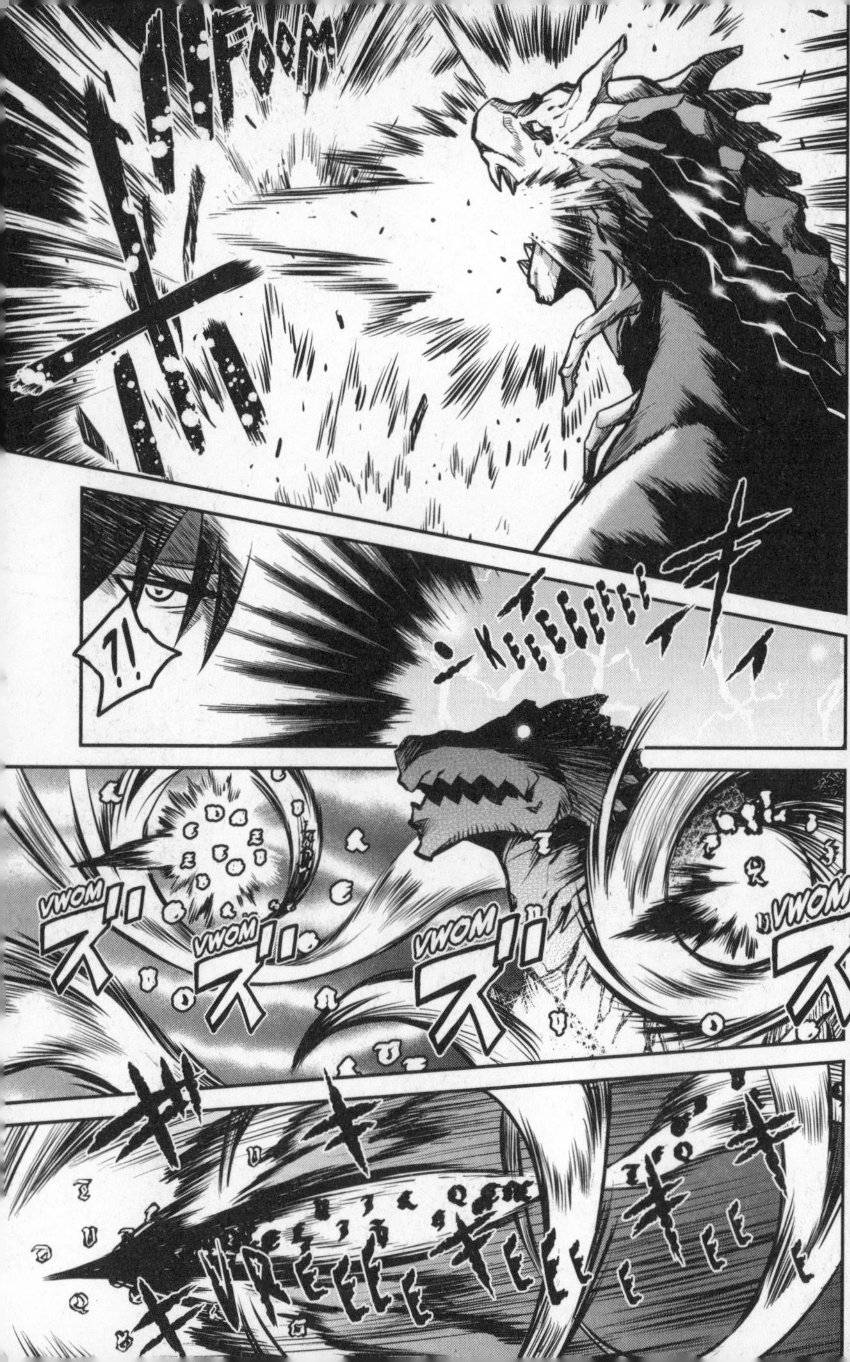
FOOM
KEEEEEEEE
?!
VWOM
VWOM
VWOM
VWOM
VREEEEEEEEEEEEEE

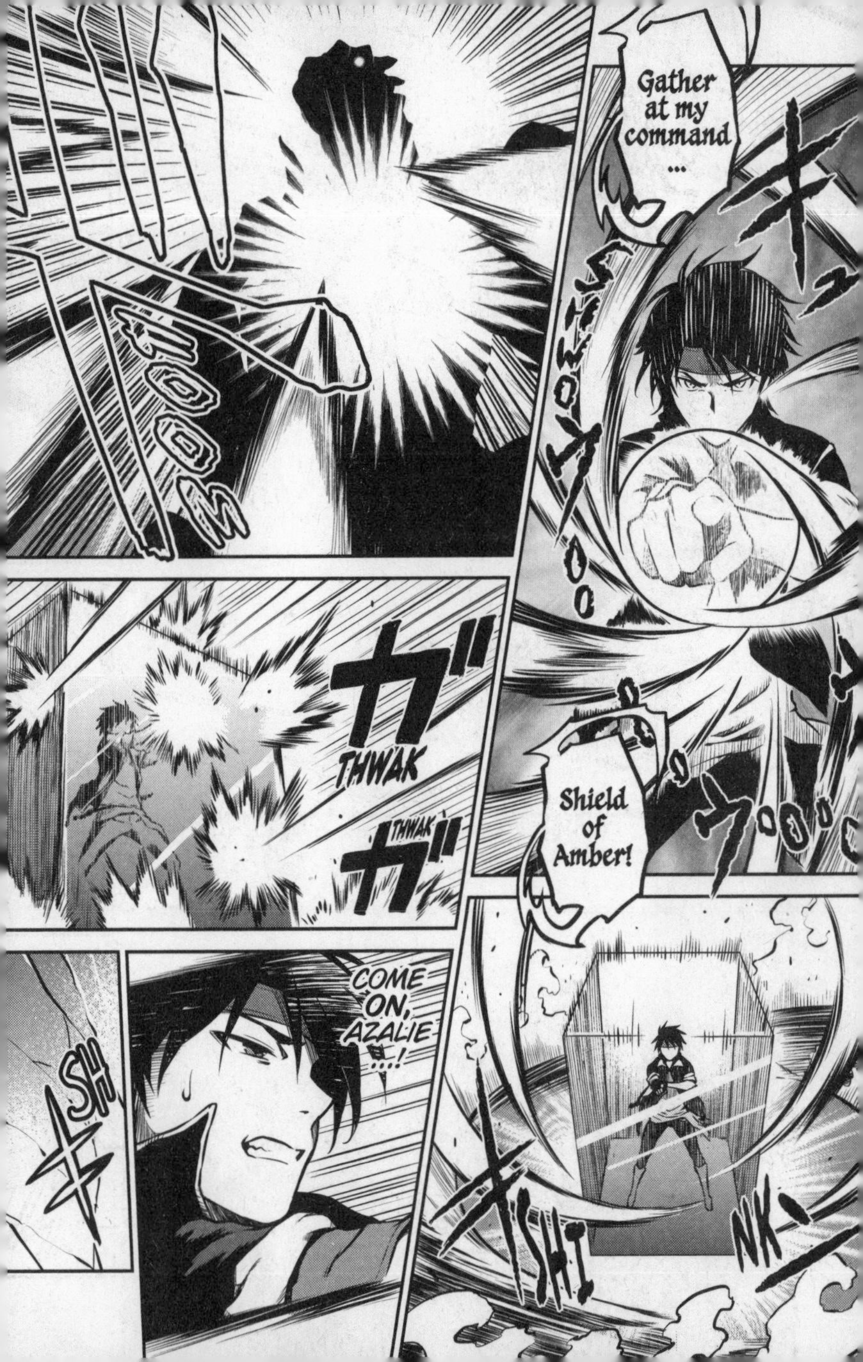
Gather at my command ...
Shield of Amber!
THWAK
THWAK
SHI
NK
COME ON, AZALIE...!
SH

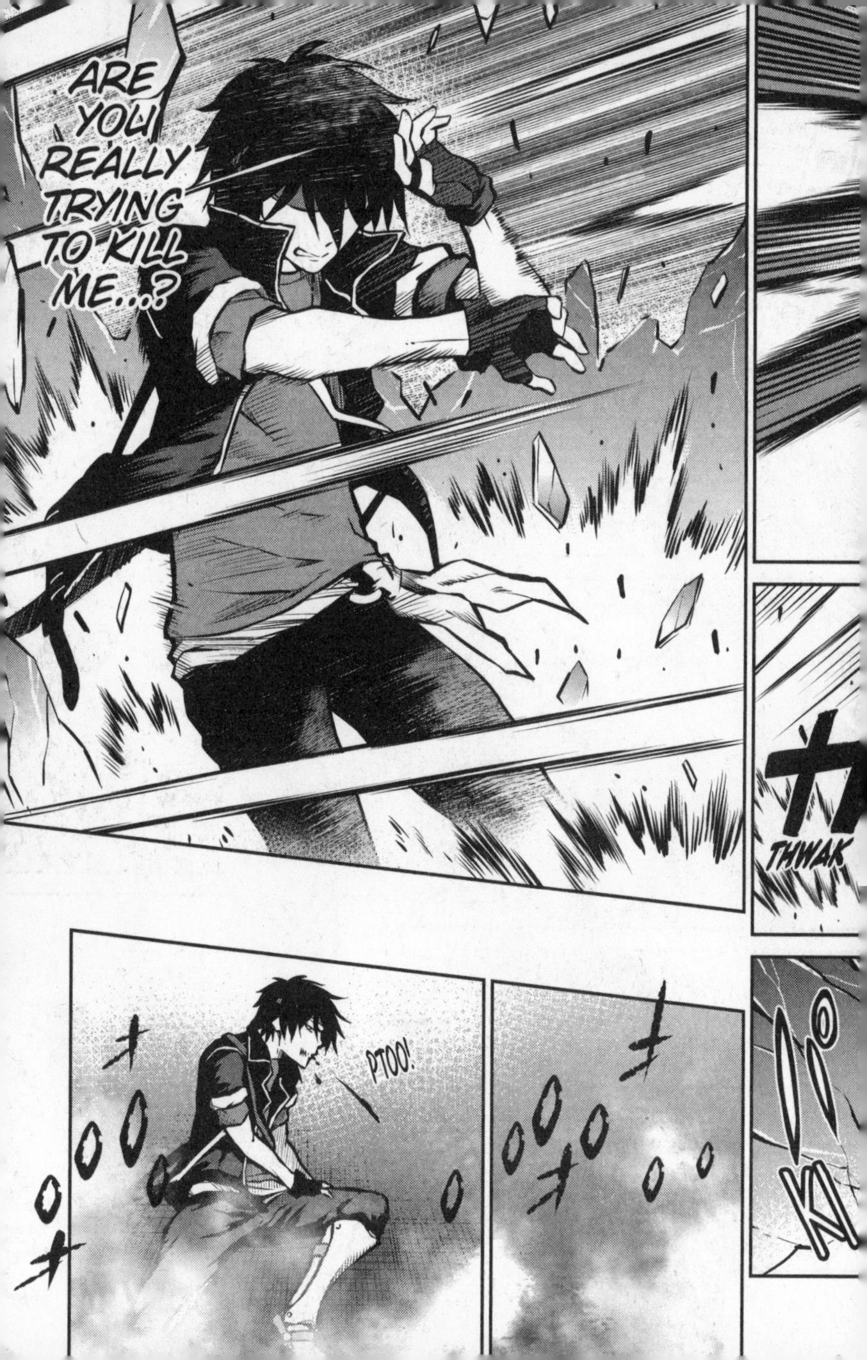
THWAK
ARE YOU REALLY TRYING TO KILL ME...?
PTOO!

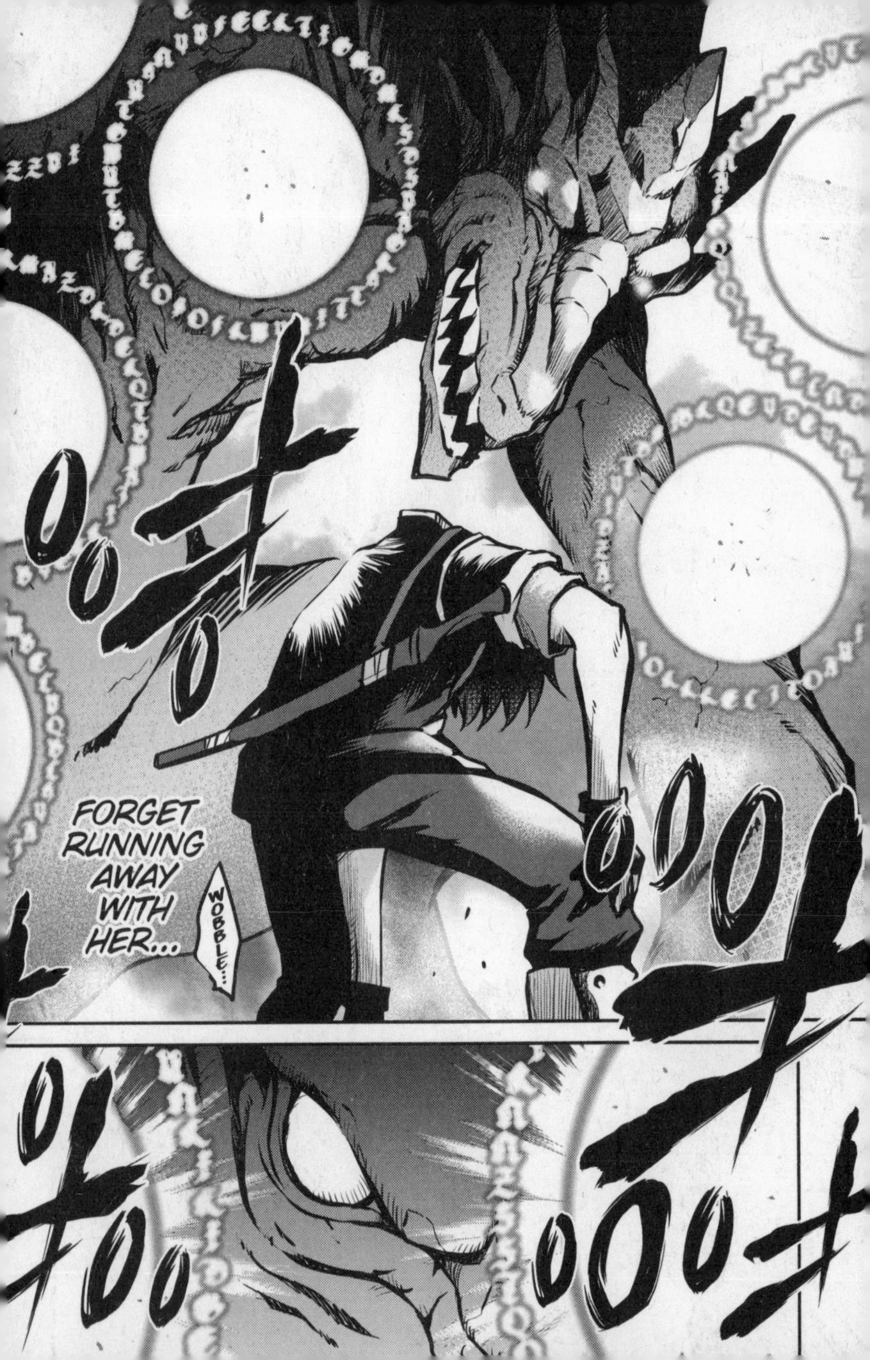
FORGET RUNNING AWAY WITH HER...
WOBBLE...

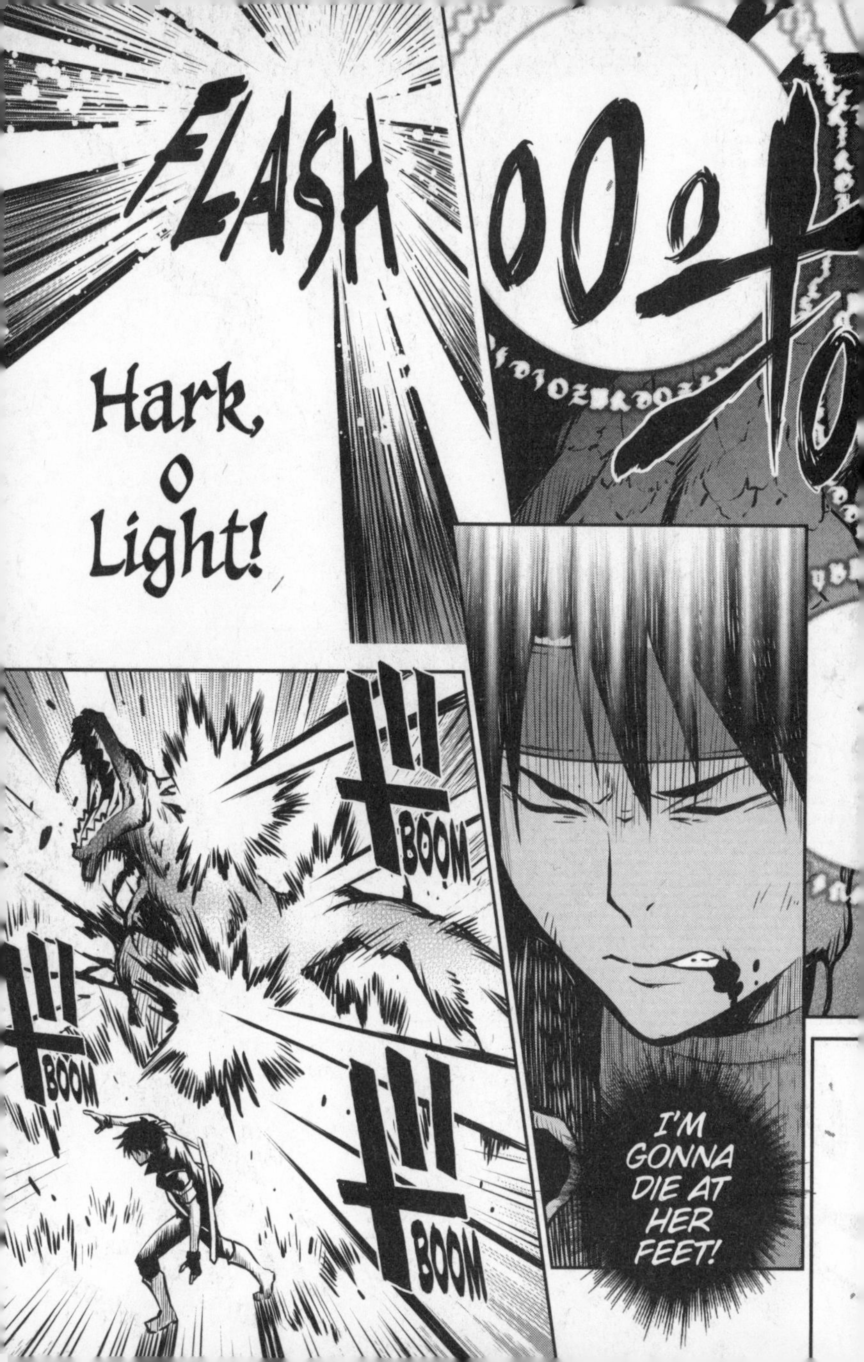
FLASH
Hark, O Light!
I'M GONNA DIE AT HER FEET!
BOOM
BOOM
BOOM

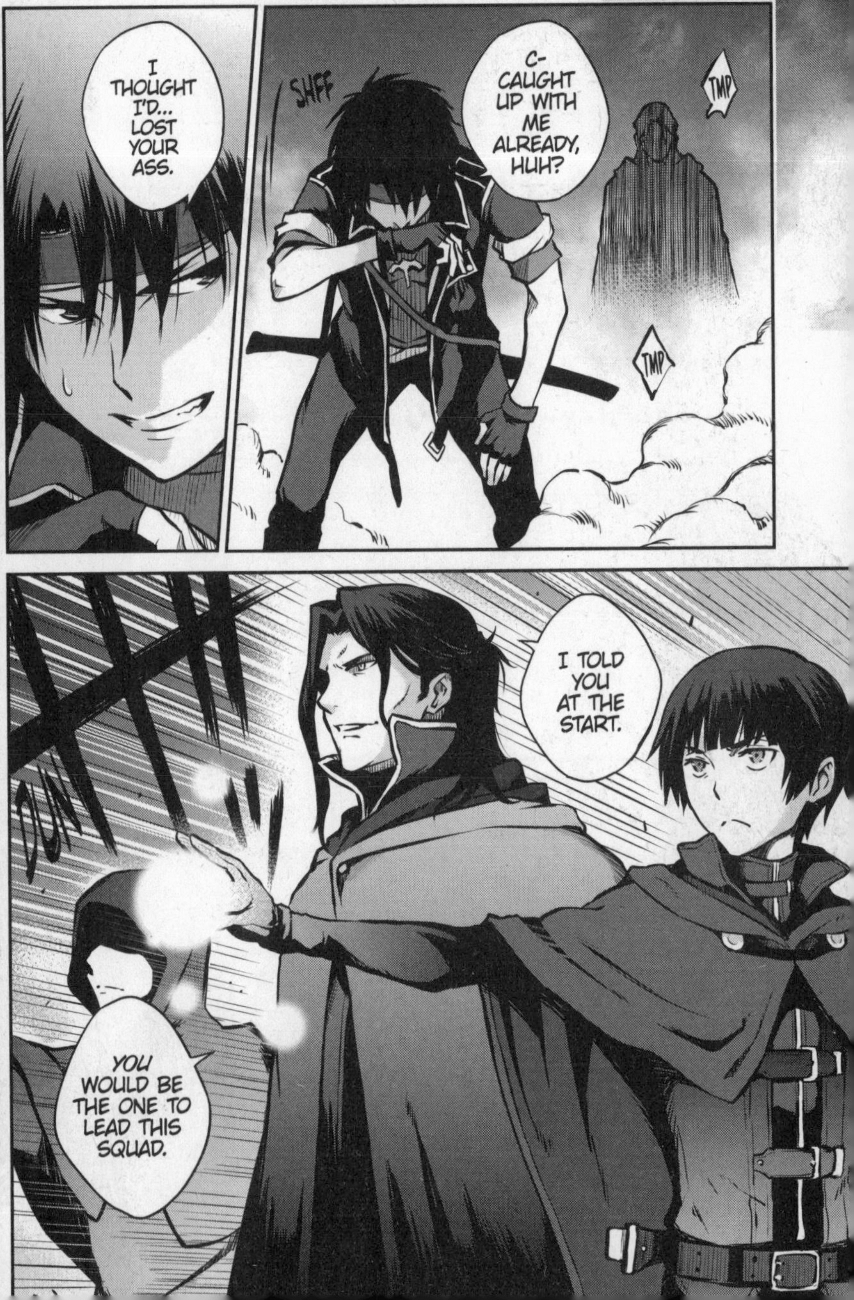
TMP
C-CAUGHT UP WITH ME ALREADY, HUH?
SHFF
TMP
I THOUGHT I'D... LOST YOUR ASS.
I TOLD YOU AT THE START.
DUN
YOU WOULD BE THE ONE TO LEAD THIS SQUAD.

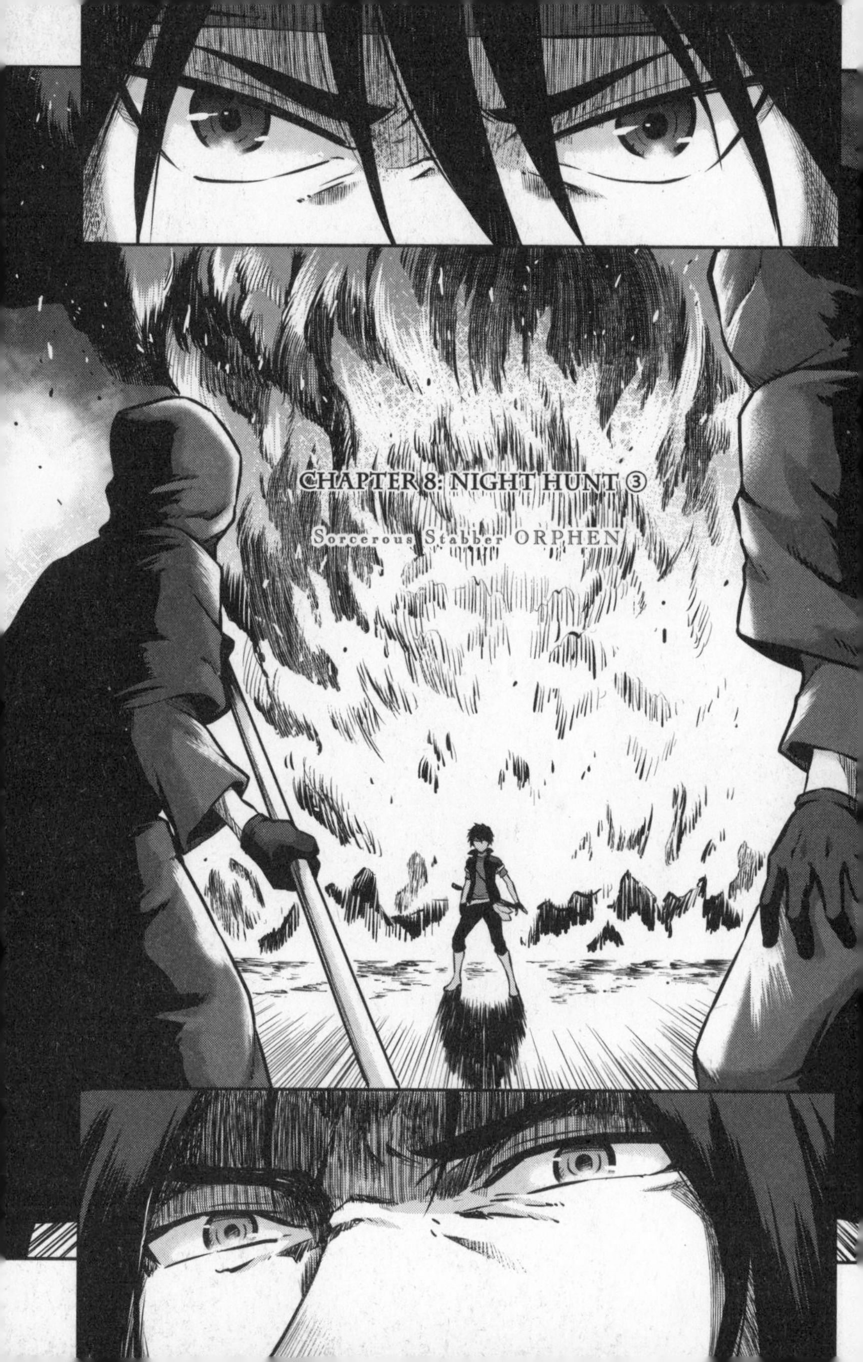
CHAPTER 8: NIGHT HUNT ③
Sorcerous Stabber ORPHEN

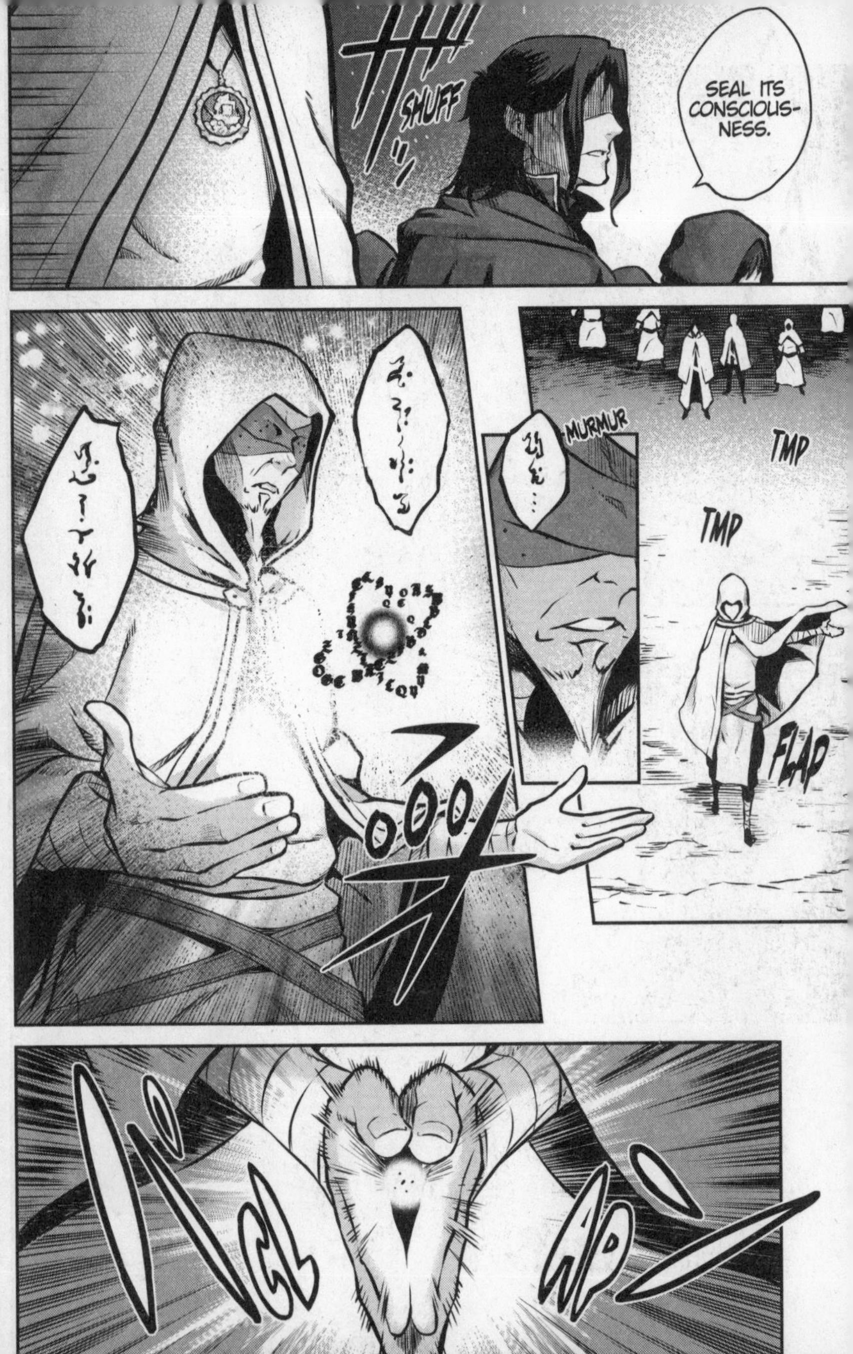
SEAL ITS CONSCIOUS-NESS.
SHUFF
TMP
TMP
FLAP
MURMUR

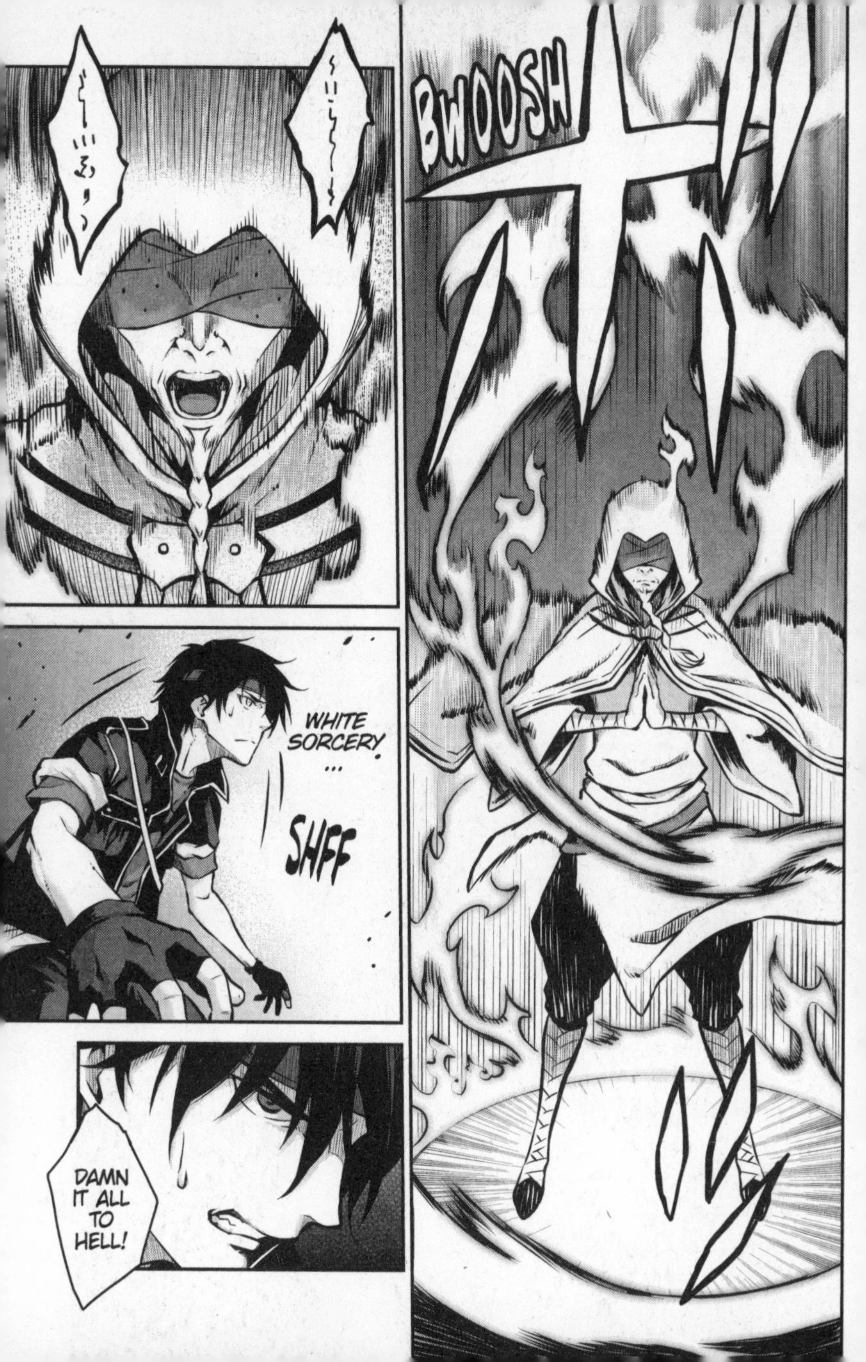
BWOOSH
WHITE SORCERY...
SHFF
DAMN IT ALL TO HELL!

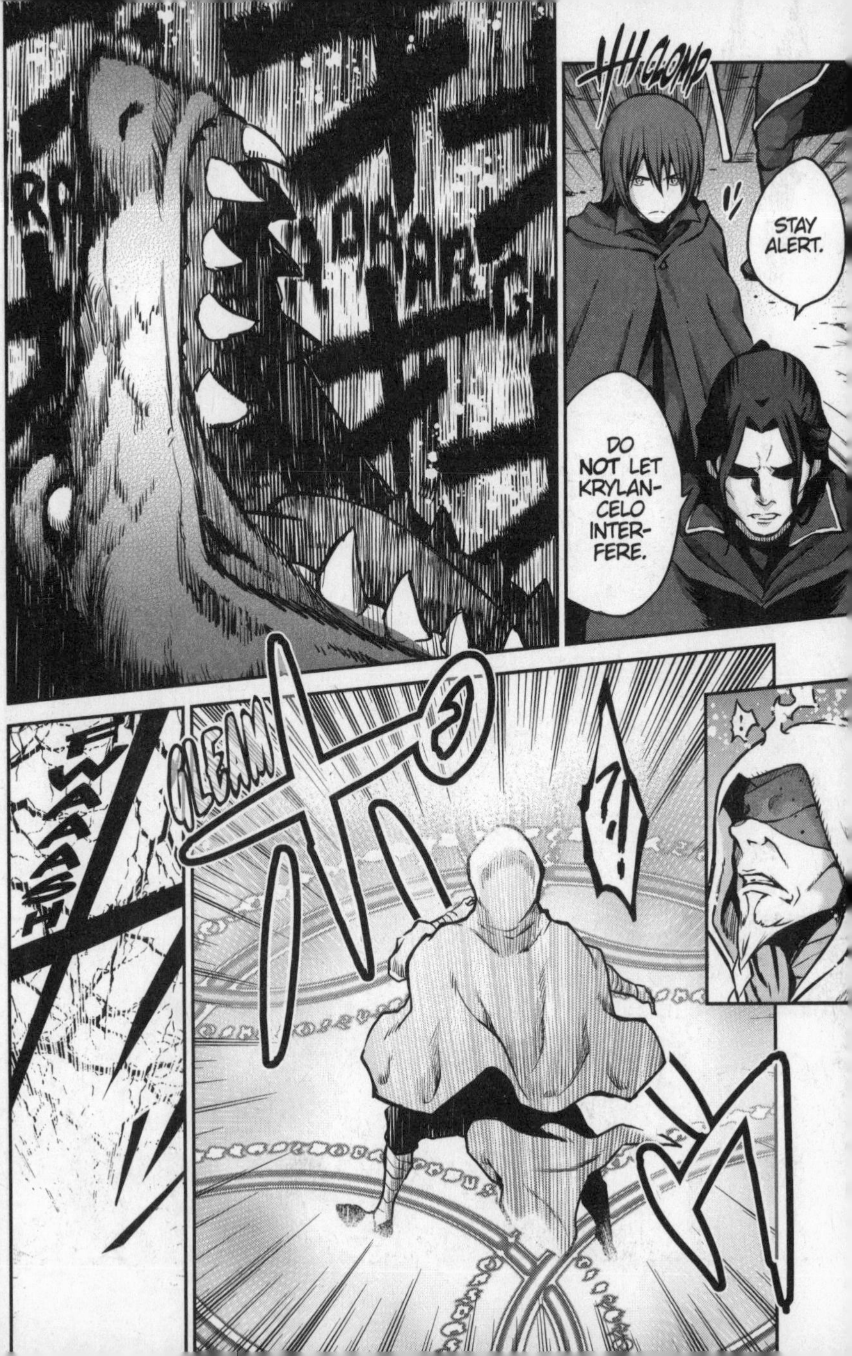
CLOMP
STAY ALERT.
DO NOT LET KRYLANCELO INTERFERE.
!
GLEAM
?!
FWAAASH

HAGH!

FWOOM

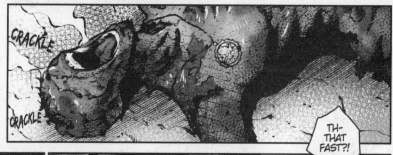

CRACKLE

CRACKLE

TH-THAT FAST?!

HOOO...

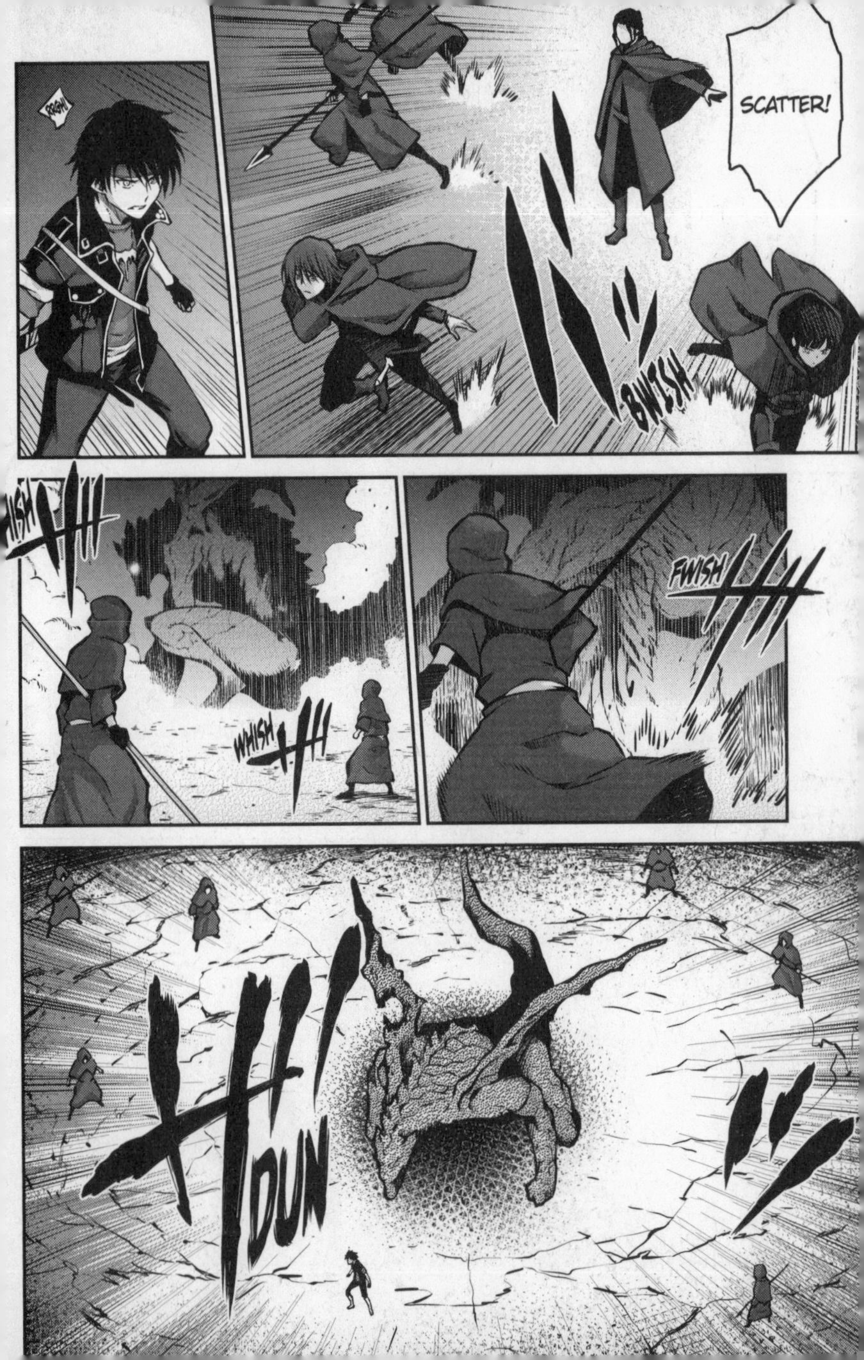
SCATTER!
BWISH
RRGH!
FWISH
WHISH
DUN

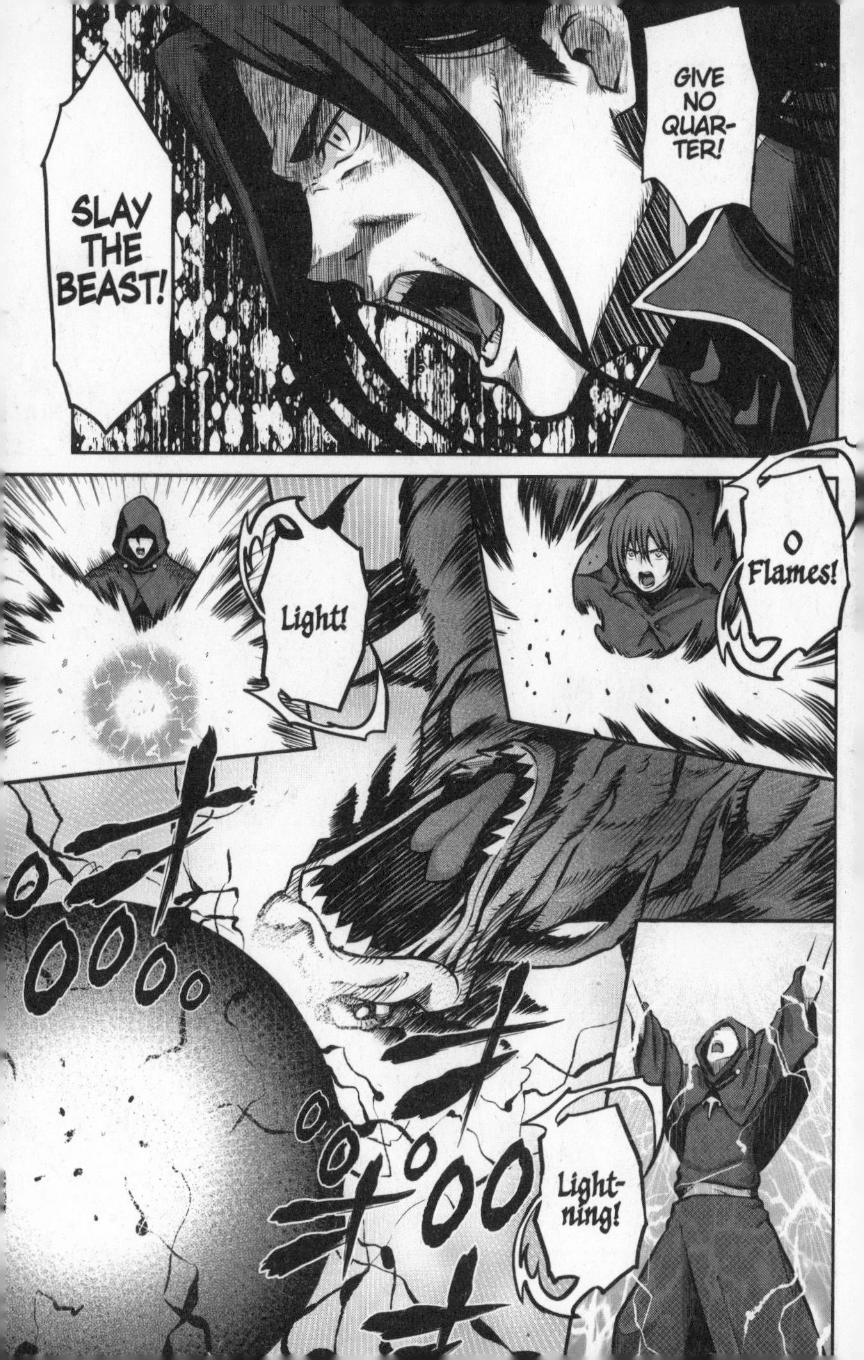
GIVE NO QUAR-TER!
SLAY THE BEAST!
O Flames!
Light!
Light-ning!

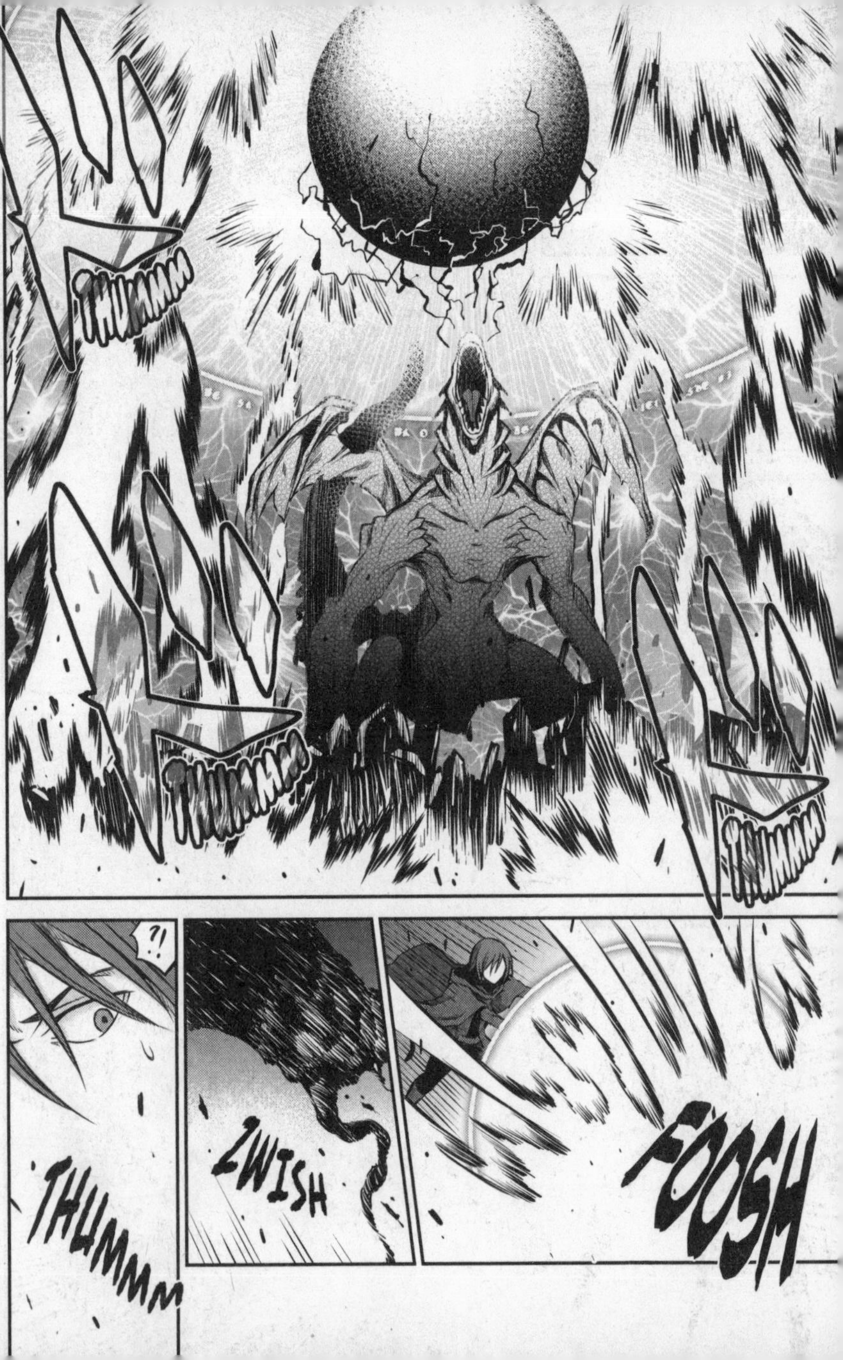
THUMMM
THUMMM
THUMMM
FOOSH
ZWISH
?!
THUMMM

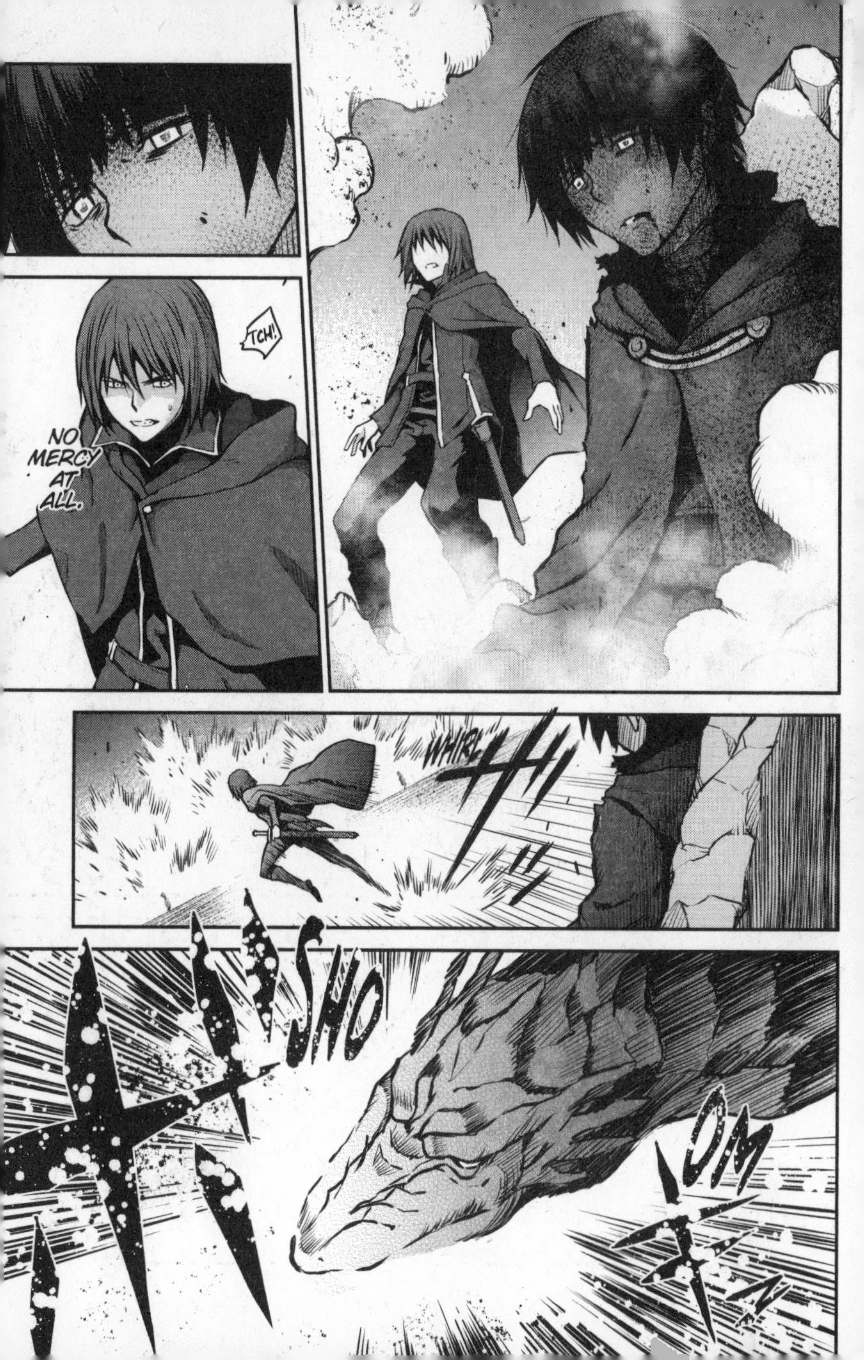
TCH!
NO MERCY AT ALL.
WHIRL
SHO
OM

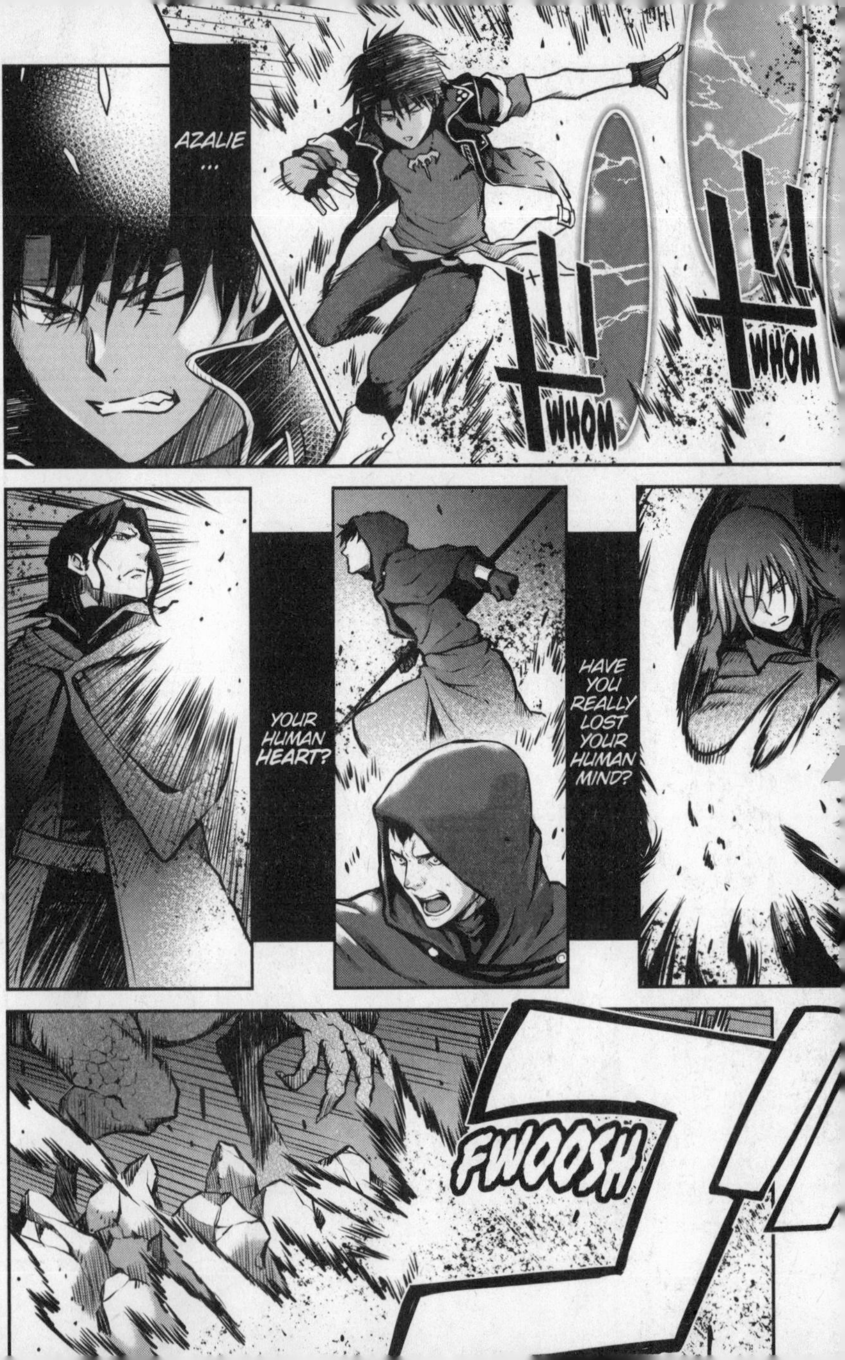
WHOM
WHOM
AZALIE ...
HAVE YOU REALLY LOST YOUR HUMAN MIND?
YOUR HUMAN HEART?
FWOOSH

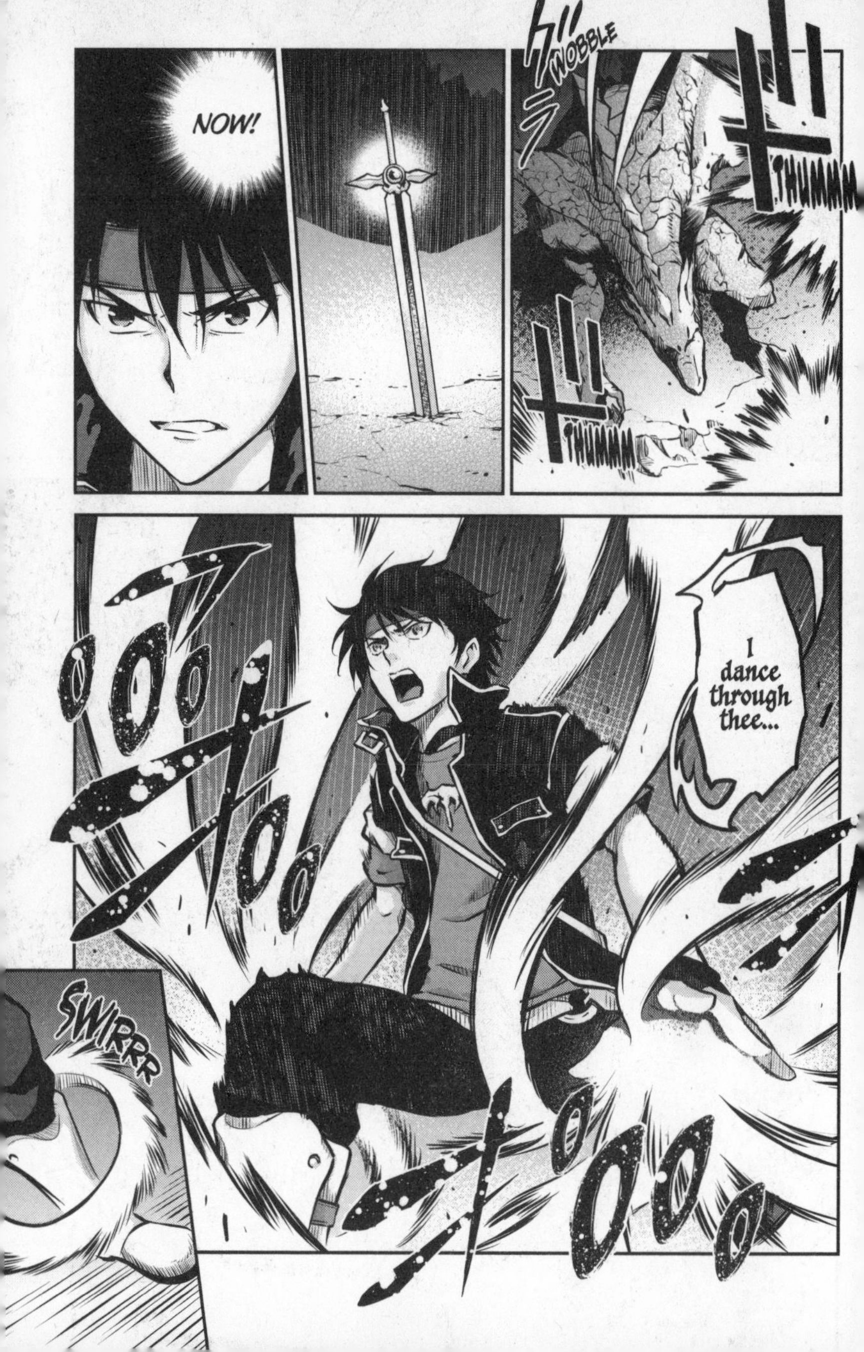
WOBBLE
THUMMMM
THUMMM
NOW!
I dance through thee...
SWIRRR

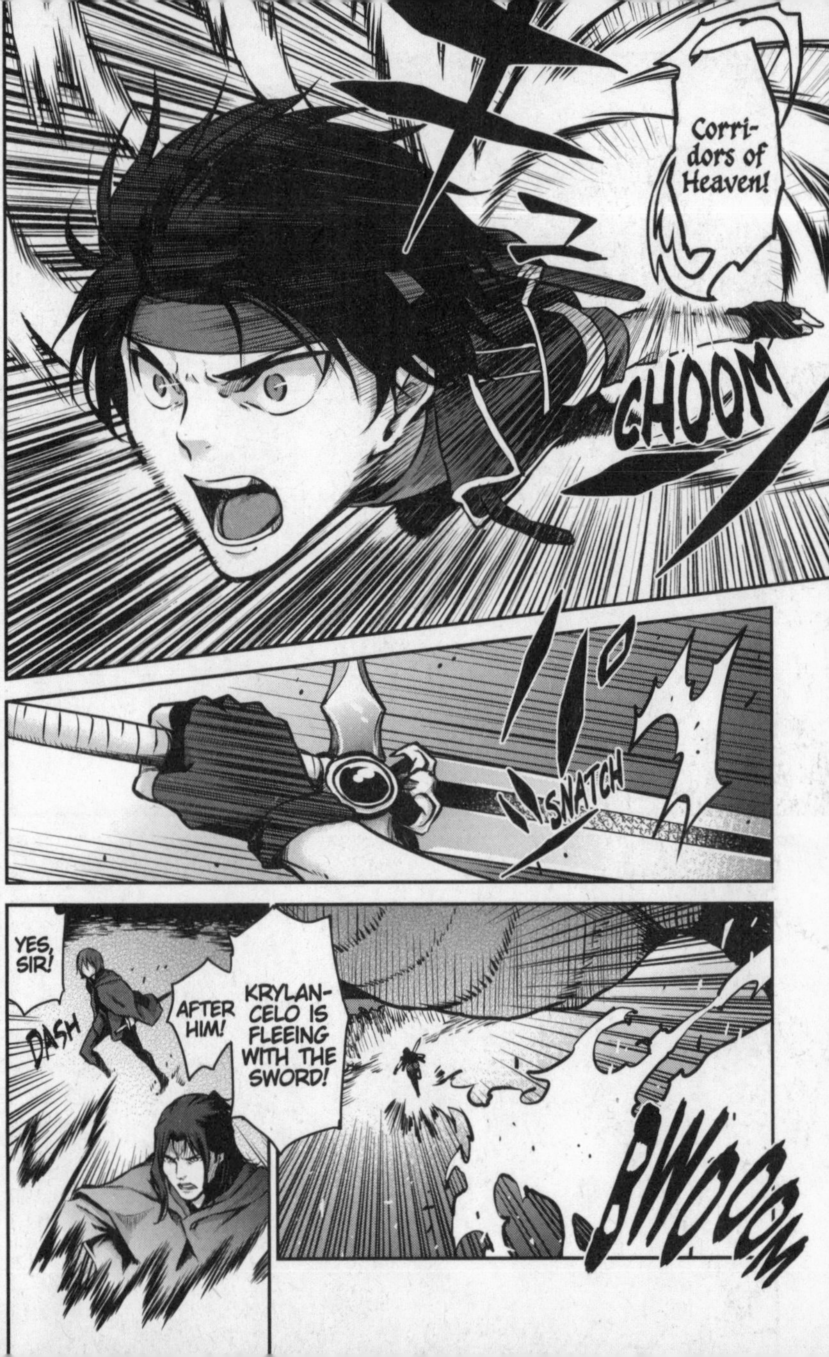
Corri-dors of Heaven!
CHOOM
SNATCH
KRYLAN-CELO IS FLEEING WITH THE SWORD!
AFTER HIM!
YES, SIR!
DASH
BWOOOM

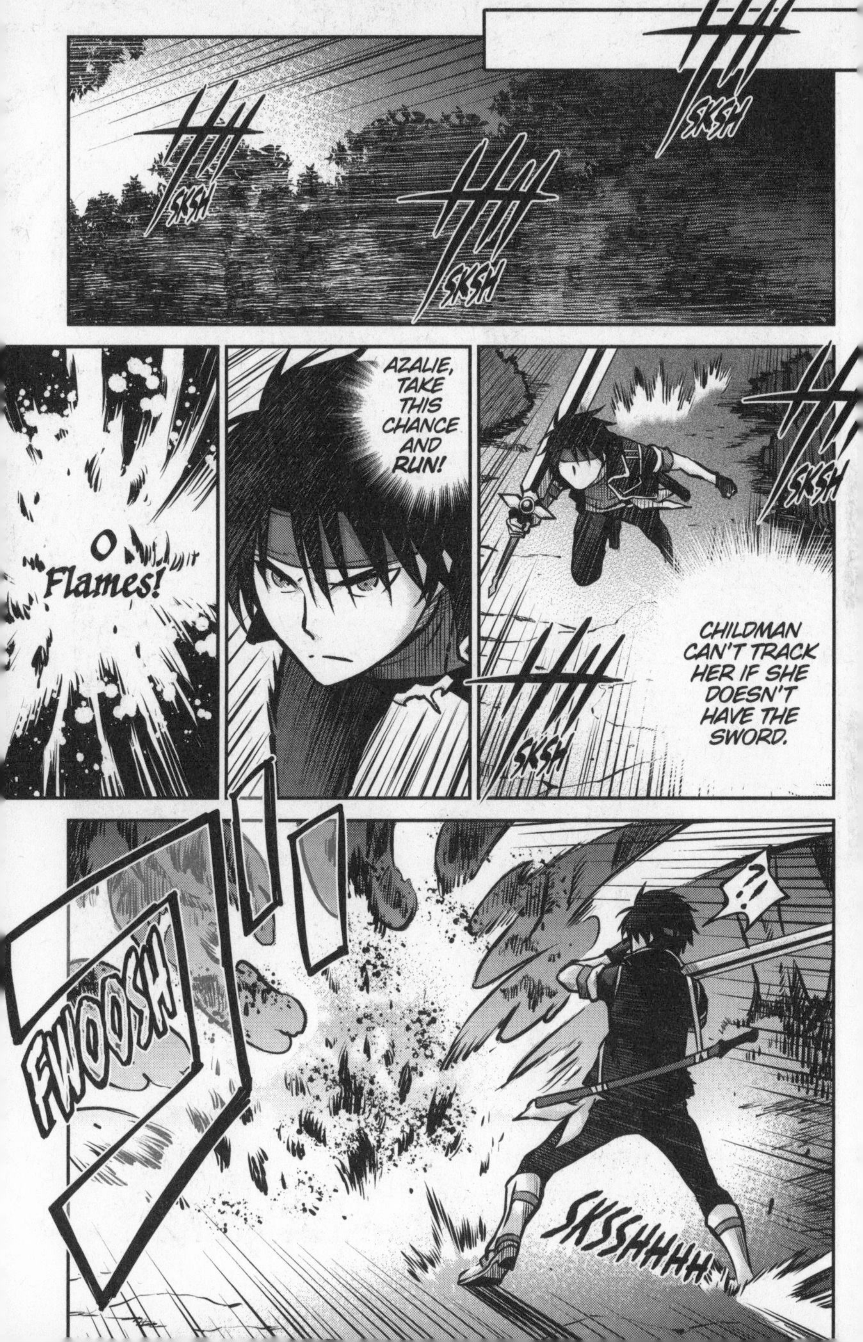
SKSH
SKSH
SKSH
SKSH
CHILDMAN CAN'T TRACK HER IF SHE DOESN'T HAVE THE SWORD.
SKSH
AZALIE, TAKE THIS CHANCE AND RUN!
O Flames!
?!
FWOOSH
SKSSHHHH

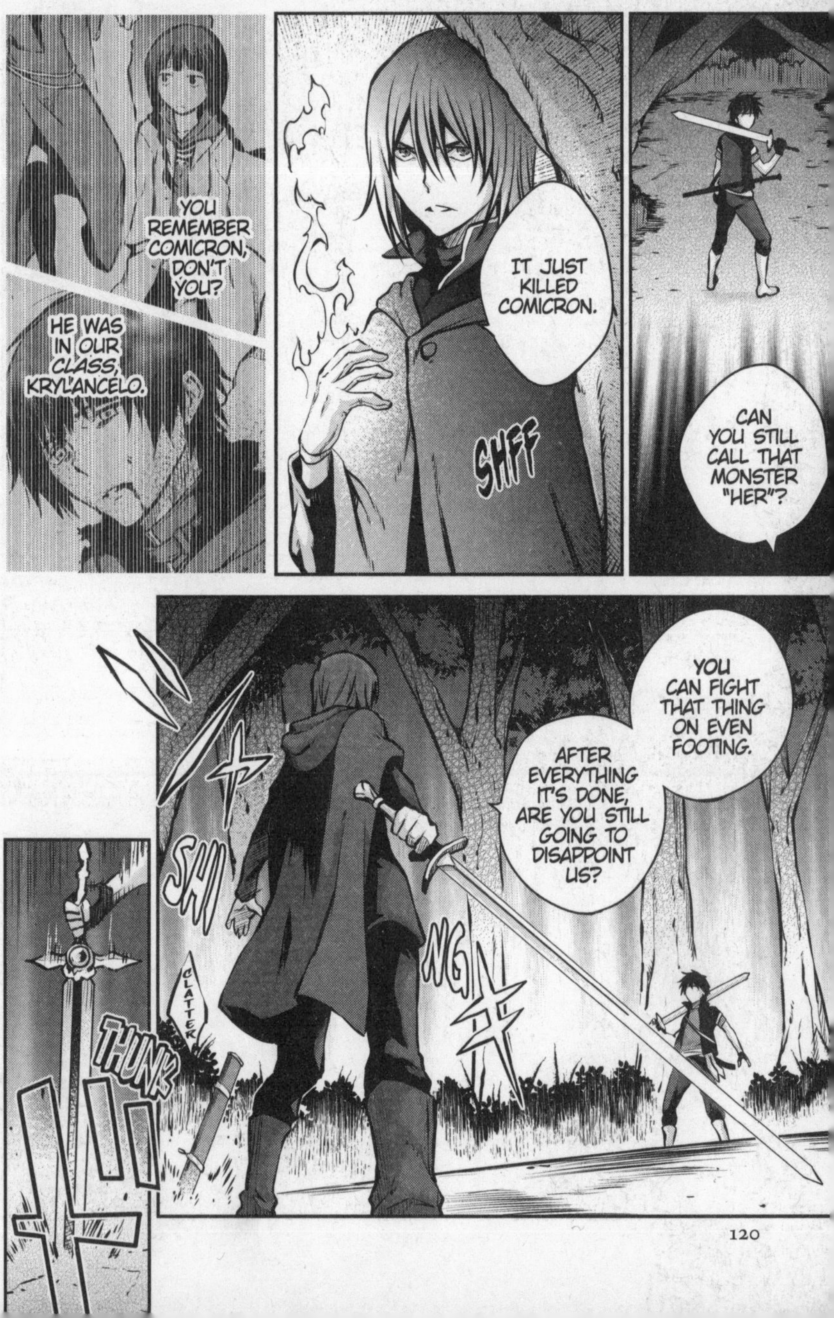

CAN YOU STILL CALL THAT MONSTER "HER"?
IT JUST KILLED COMICRON.
SHFF
YOU REMEMBER COMICRON, DON'T YOU?
HE WAS IN OUR CLASS, KRYL'ANCELO.
YOU CAN FIGHT THAT THING ON EVEN FOOTING.
AFTER EVERYTHING IT'S DONE, ARE YOU STILL GOING TO DISAPPOINT US?
SHIING
CLATTER
THUNK

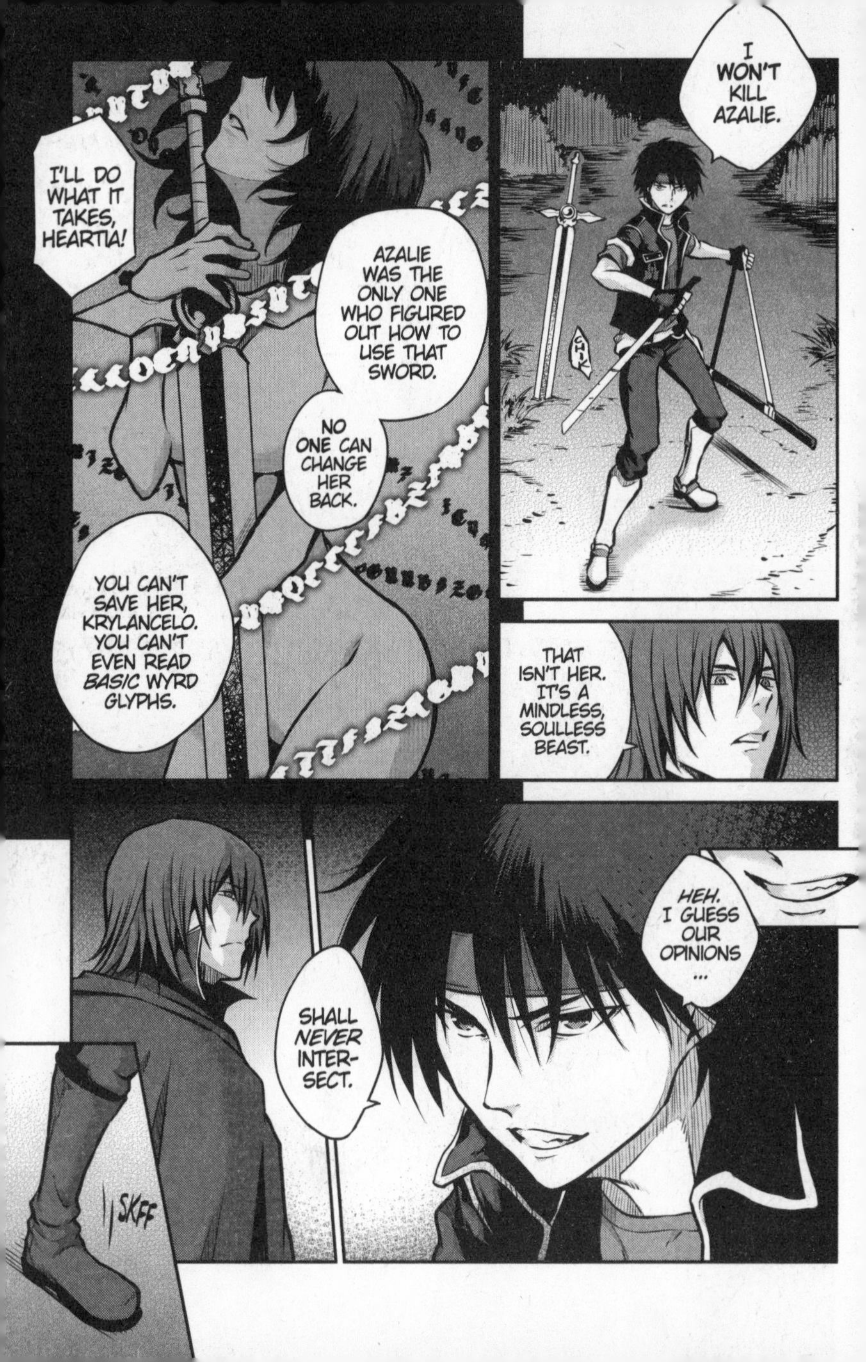
I WON'T KILL AZALIE.
CHIK
THAT ISN'T HER. IT'S A MINDLESS, SOULLESS BEAST.
I'LL DO WHAT IT TAKES, HEARTIA!
AZALIE WAS THE ONLY ONE WHO FIGURED OUT HOW TO USE THAT SWORD.
NO ONE CAN CHANGE HER BACK.
YOU CAN'T SAVE HER, KRYLANCELO. YOU CAN'T EVEN READ *BASIC* WYRD GLYPHS.
HEH. I GUESS OUR OPINIONS ...
SHALL *NEVER* INTER-SECT.
SKFF

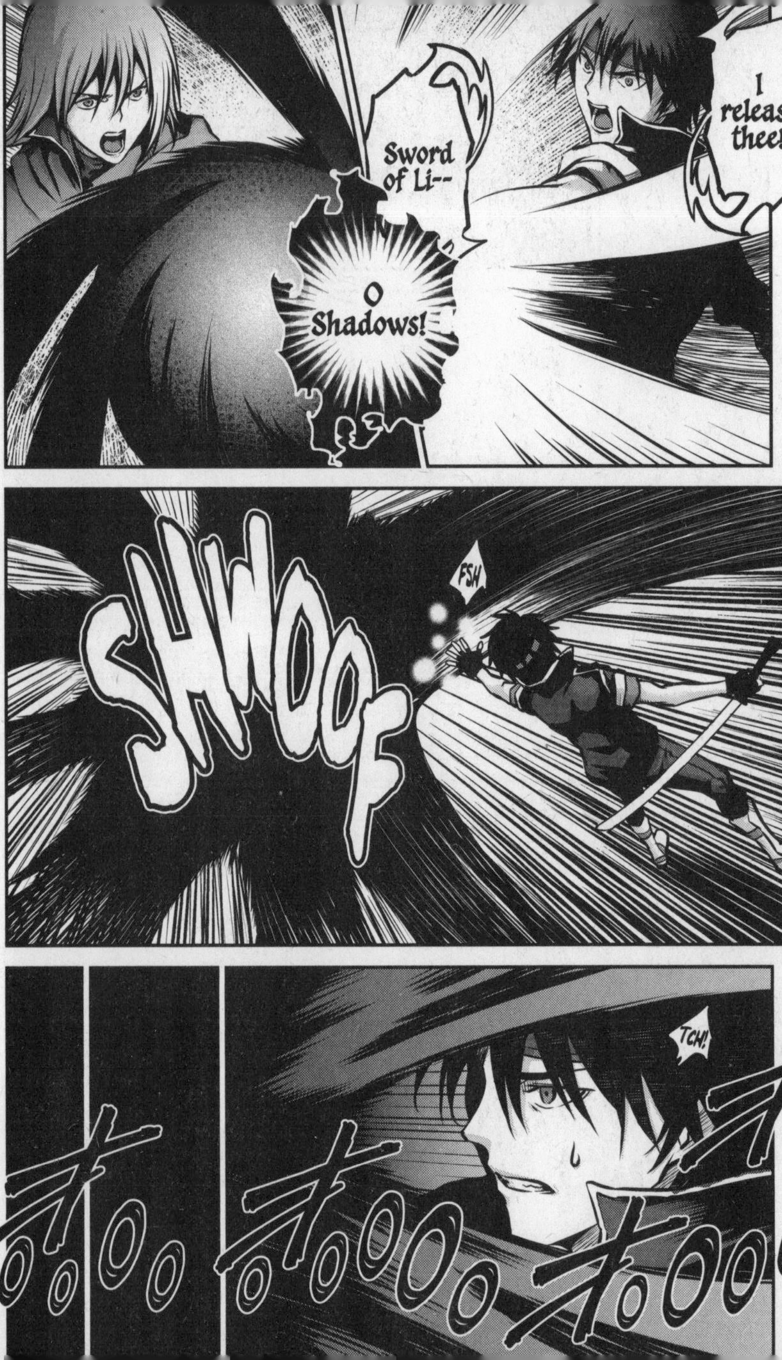
I release thee!
Sword of Li--
O Shadows!
SHWOOF
FSH
TCH!

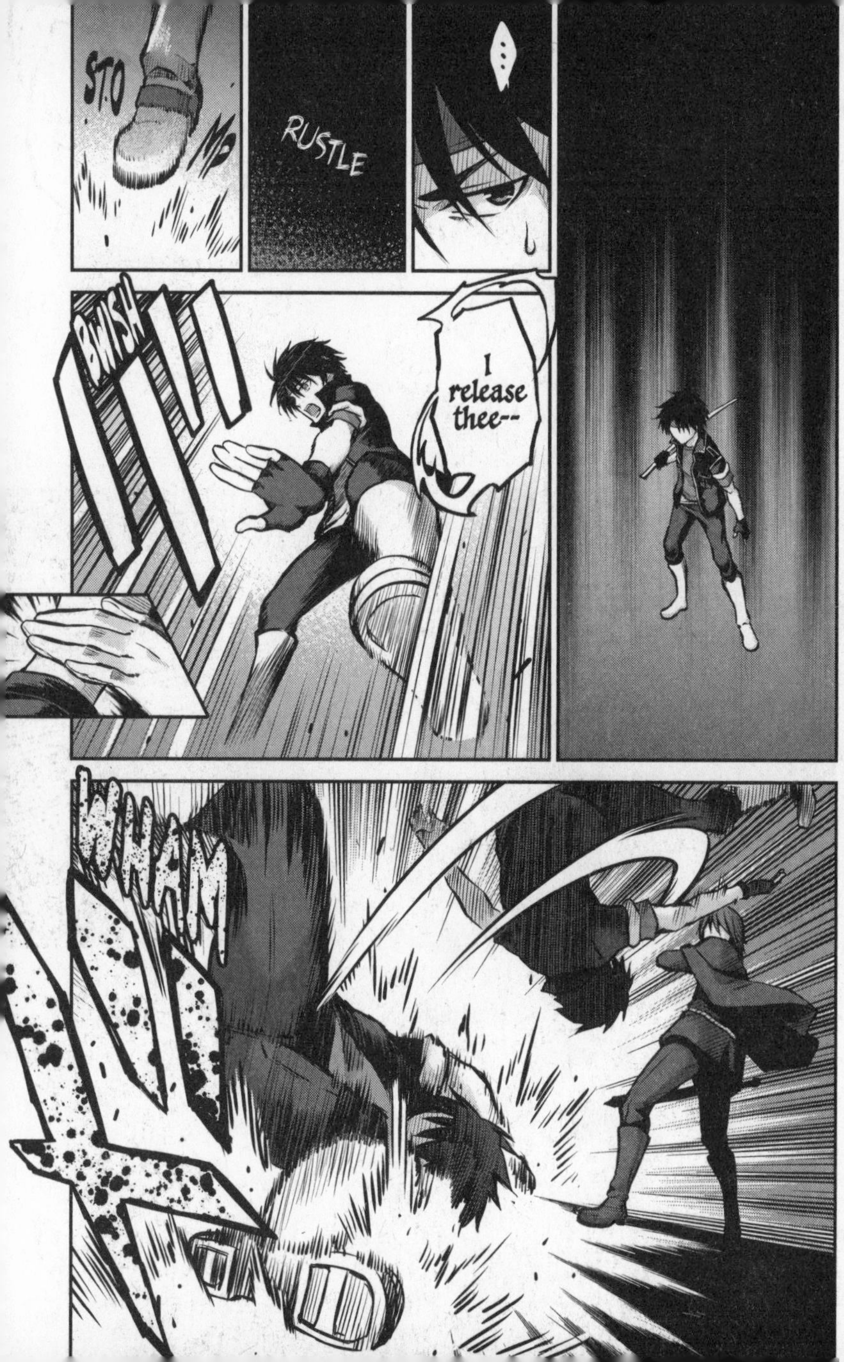

...
RUSTLE
STOMP
I release thee--
BWISH
WHAM

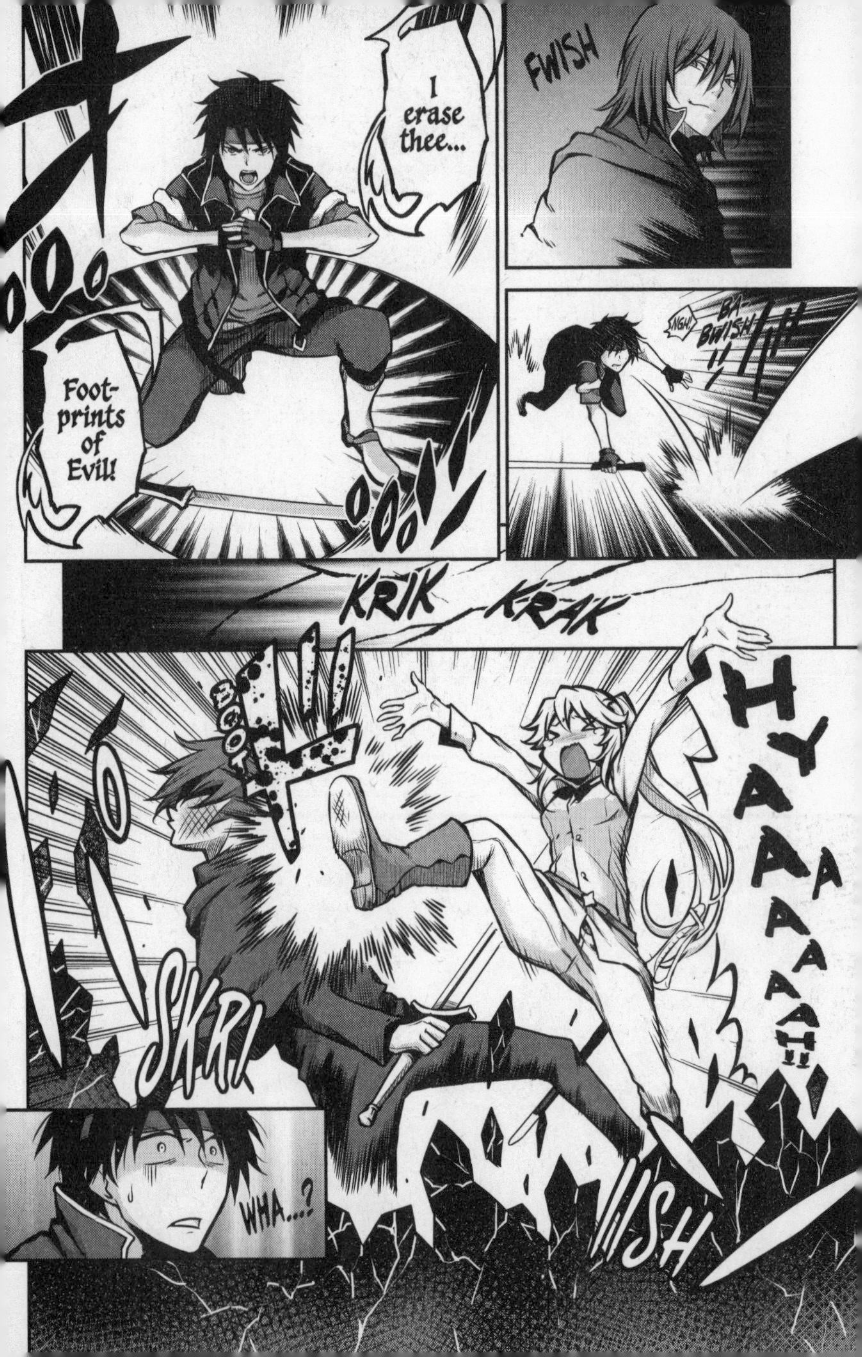
FWISH
NGH
BA-BWISH!!
I erase thee...
Foot-prints of Evil!
KRIK
KRAK
HYAAAAAAAAH!!
BOOT
SKRI
ISH
WHA...?

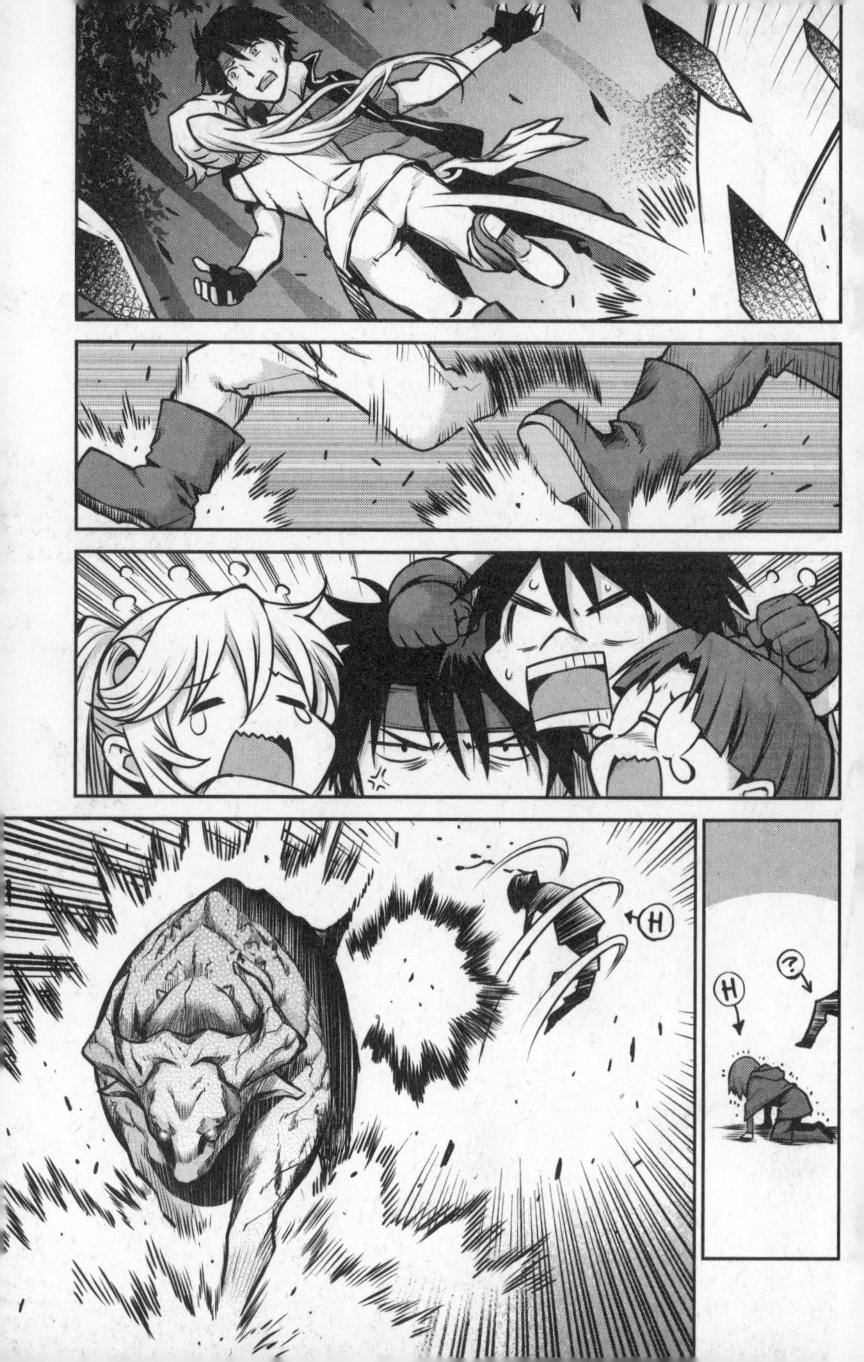

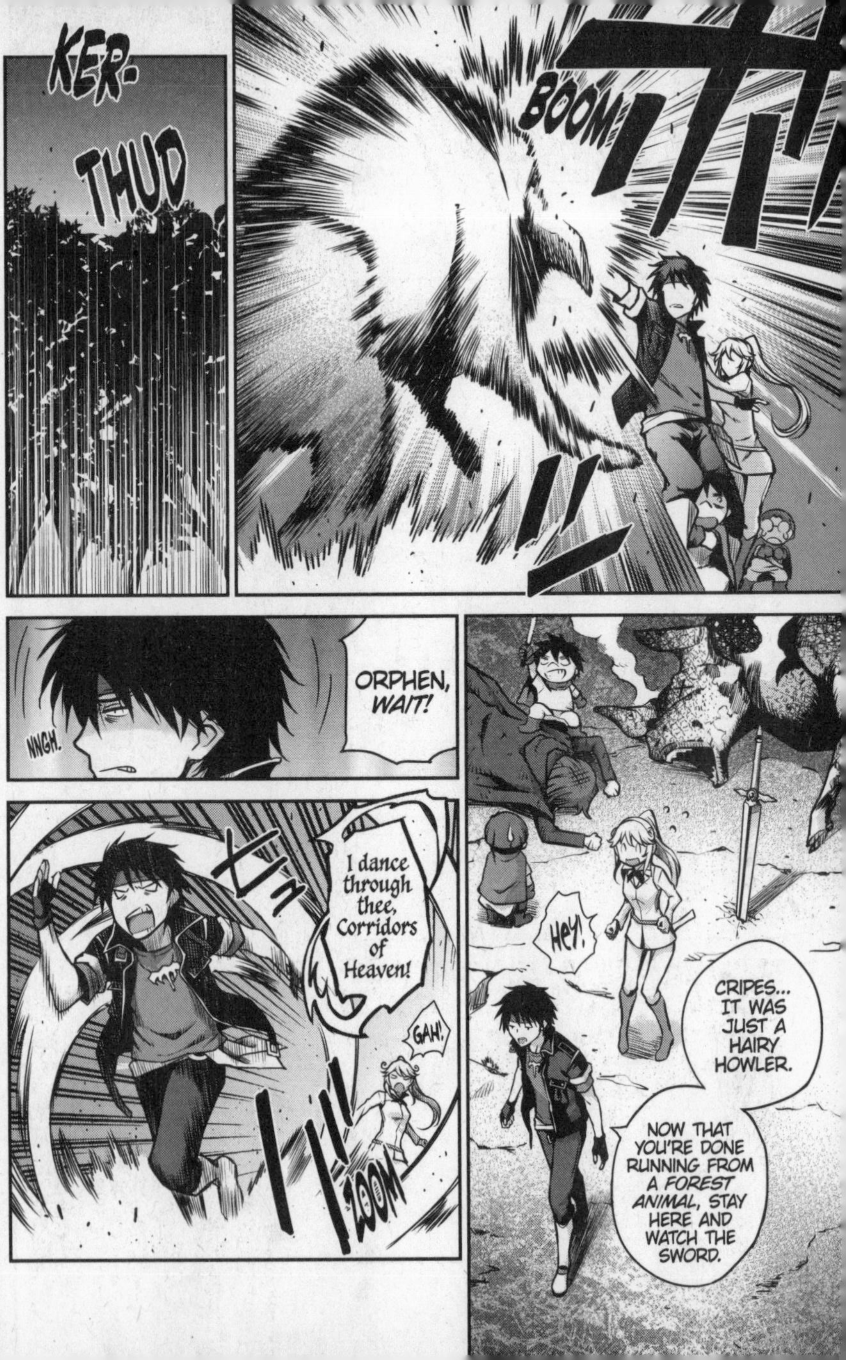
BOOM
KER-
THUD
Hey!
CRIPES... IT WAS JUST A HAIRY HOWLER.
NOW THAT YOU'RE DONE RUNNING FROM A *FOREST ANIMAL*, STAY HERE AND WATCH THE SWORD.
ORPHEN, *WAIT!*
NNGH.
I dance through thee, Corridors of Heaven!
GAH!
ZOOM

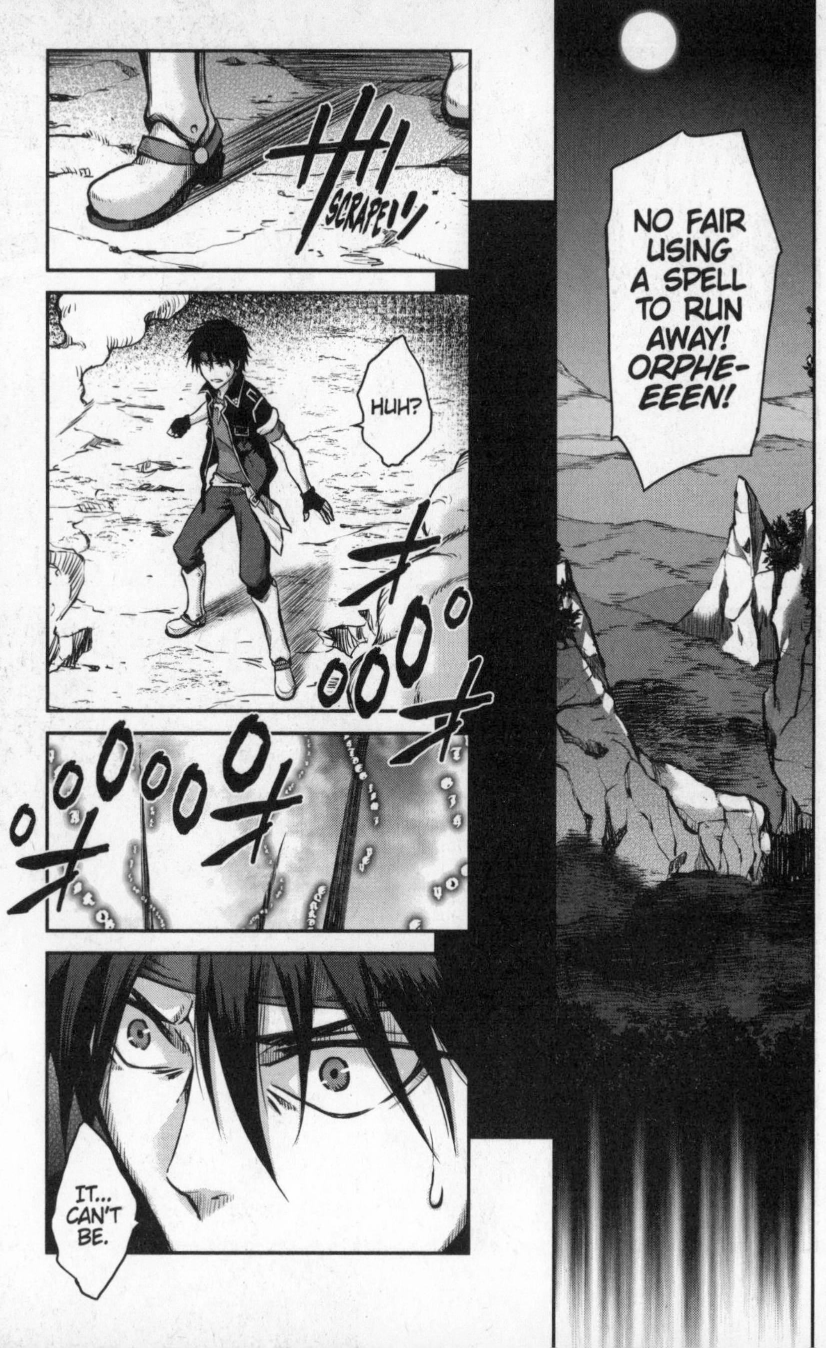
NO FAIR USING A SPELL TO RUN AWAY! ORPHE-EEEN!
SCRAPE
HUH?
IT... CAN'T BE.

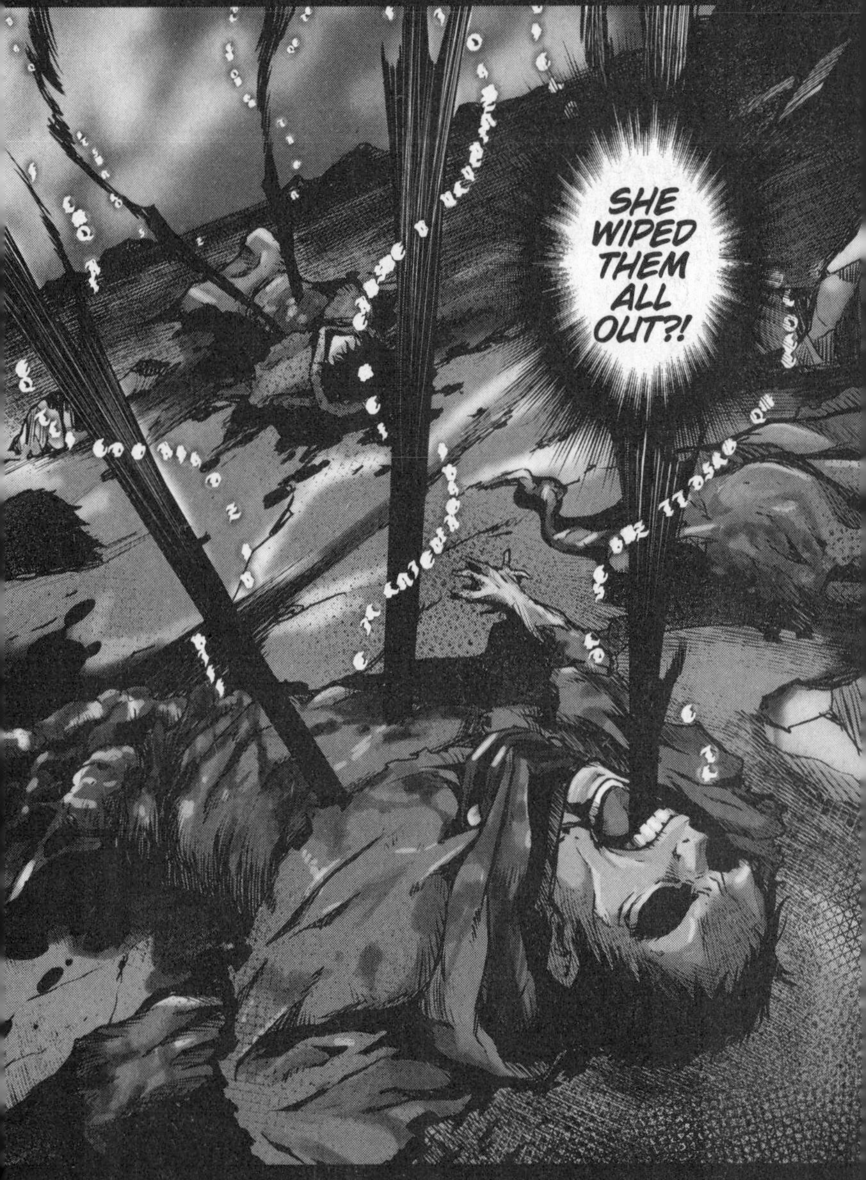
SHE WIPED THEM ALL OUT?!

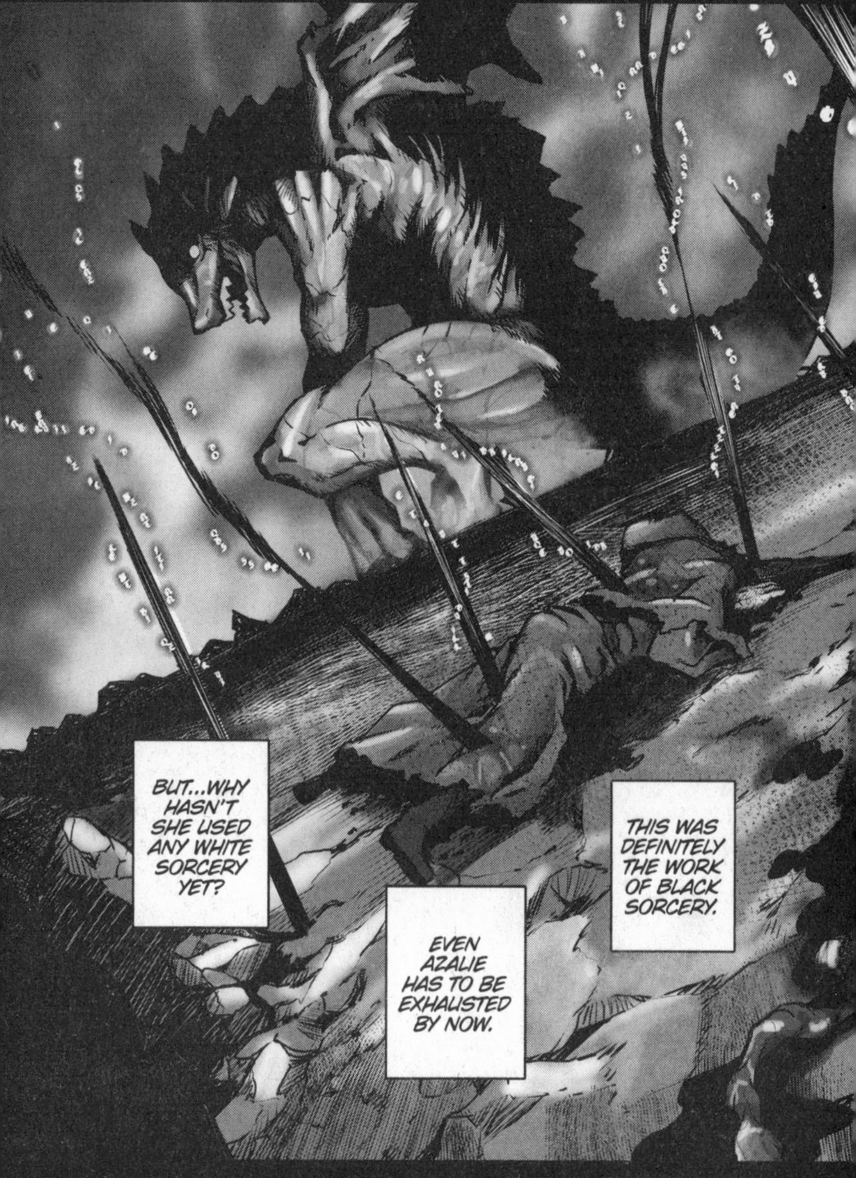
THIS WAS DEFINITELY THE WORK OF BLACK SORCERY.
EVEN AZALIE HAS TO BE EXHAUSTED BY NOW.
BUT...WHY HASN'T SHE USED ANY WHITE SORCERY YET?

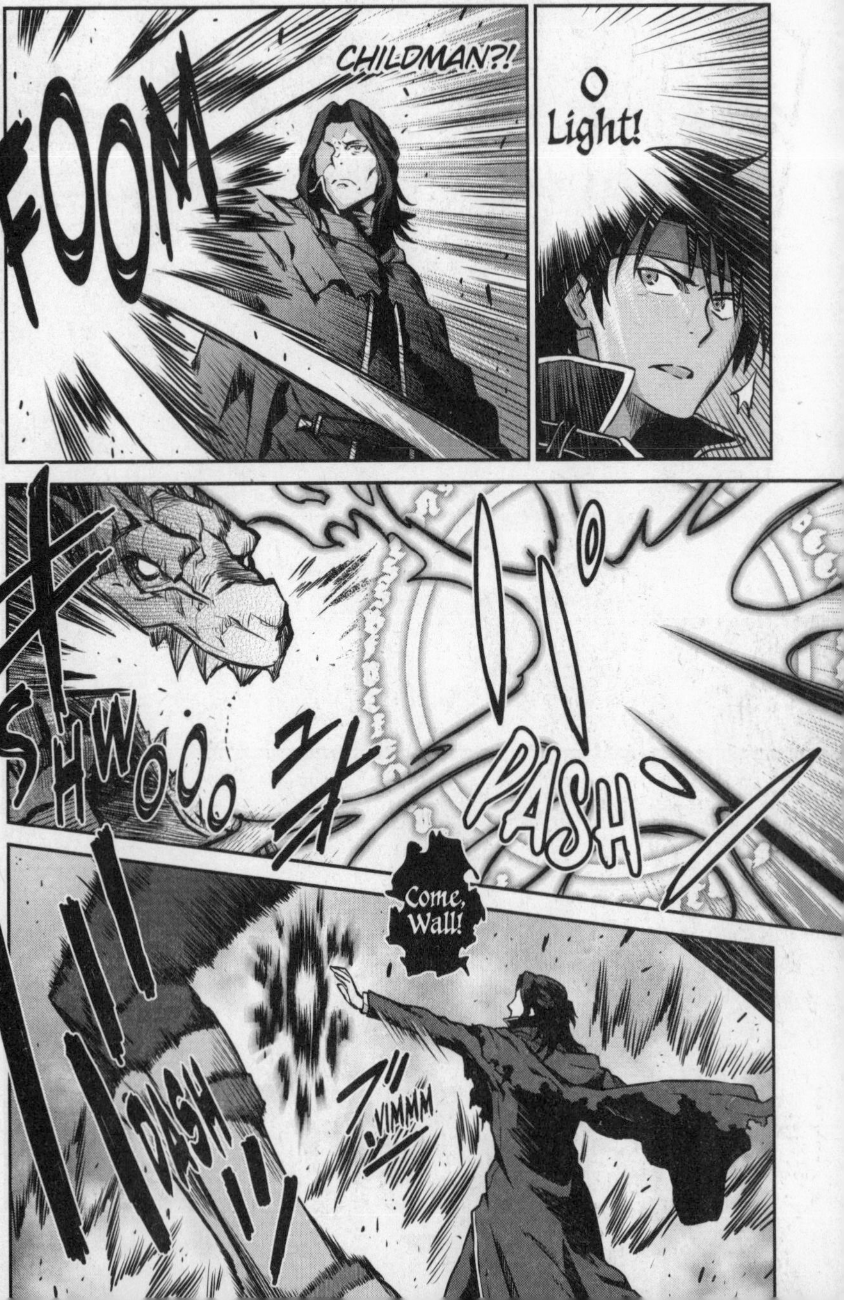
O Light!
CHILDMAN?!
FOOM
PASH
SHWOOO
Come, Wall!
VIMMM
DASH

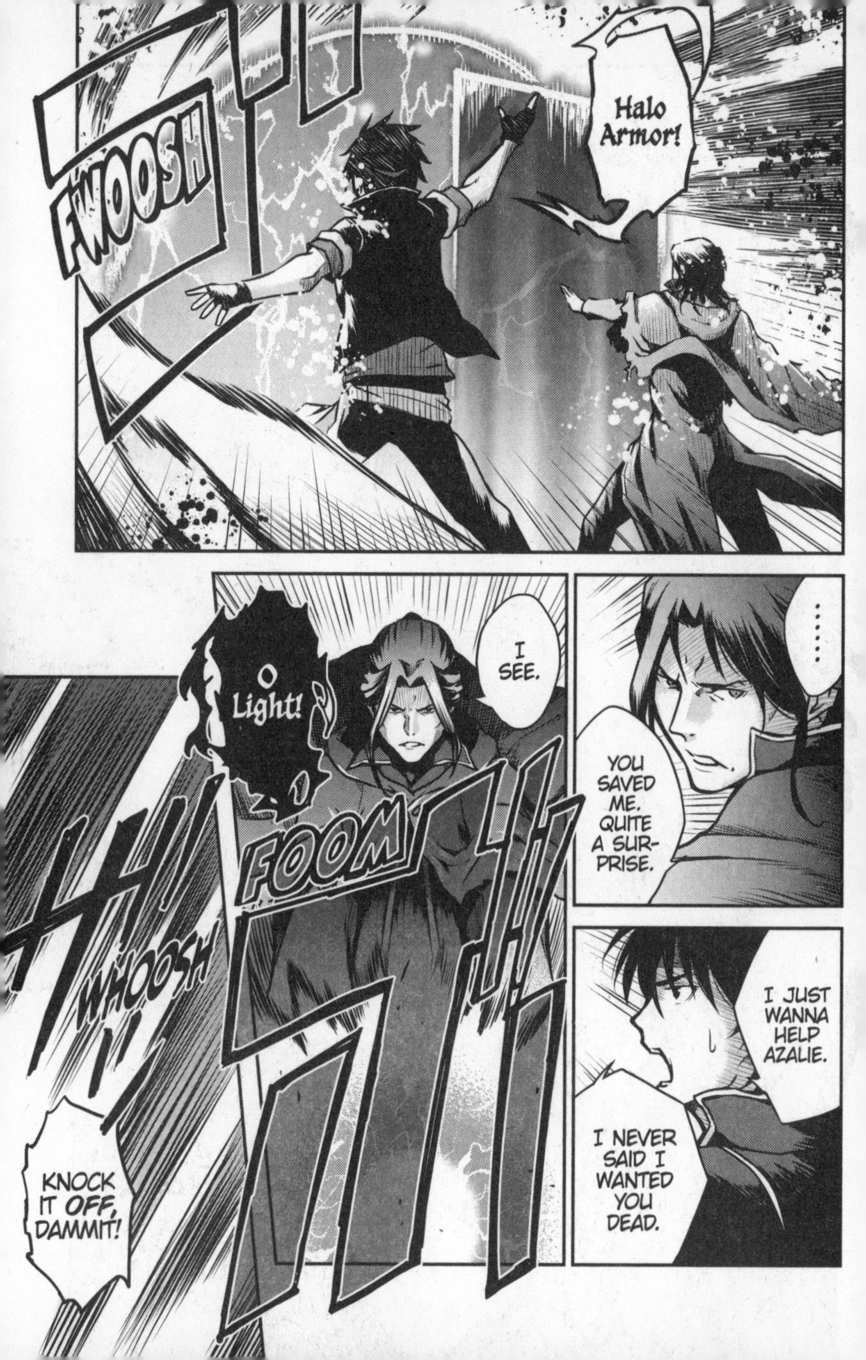
Halo Armor!
FWOOSH
......
YOU SAVED ME. QUITE A SUR-PRISE.
I JUST WANNA HELP AZALIE.
I NEVER SAID I WANTED YOU DEAD.
I SEE.
O Light!
FOOM
WHOOSH
KNOCK IT OFF, DAMMIT!

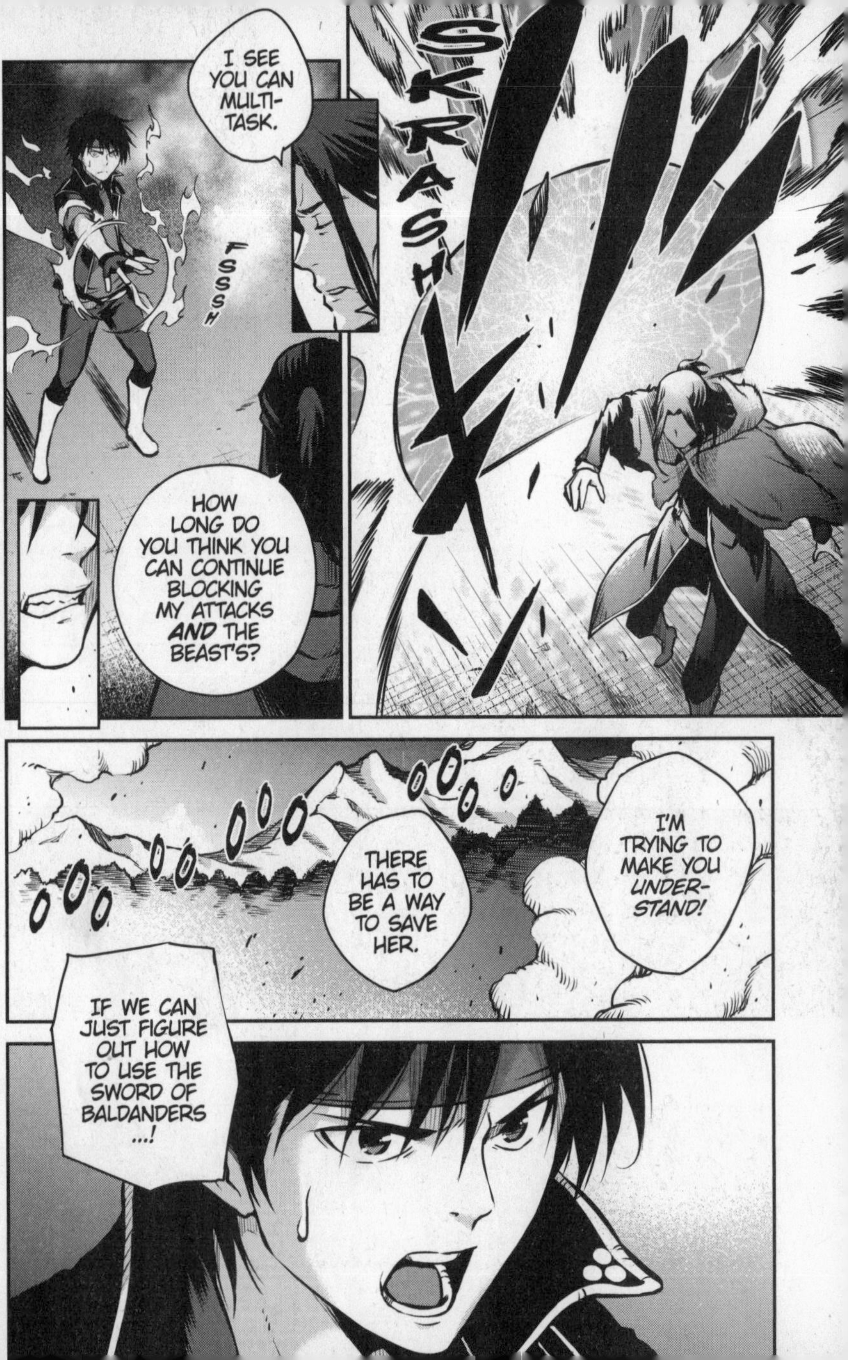
SKRASH
I SEE YOU CAN MULTI-TASK.
FSSSH
HOW LONG DO YOU THINK YOU CAN CONTINUE BLOCKING MY ATTACKS *AND* THE BEAST'S?
I'M TRYING TO MAKE YOU UNDERSTAND!
THERE HAS TO BE A WAY TO SAVE HER.
IF WE CAN JUST FIGURE OUT HOW TO USE THE SWORD OF BALDANDERS ...!

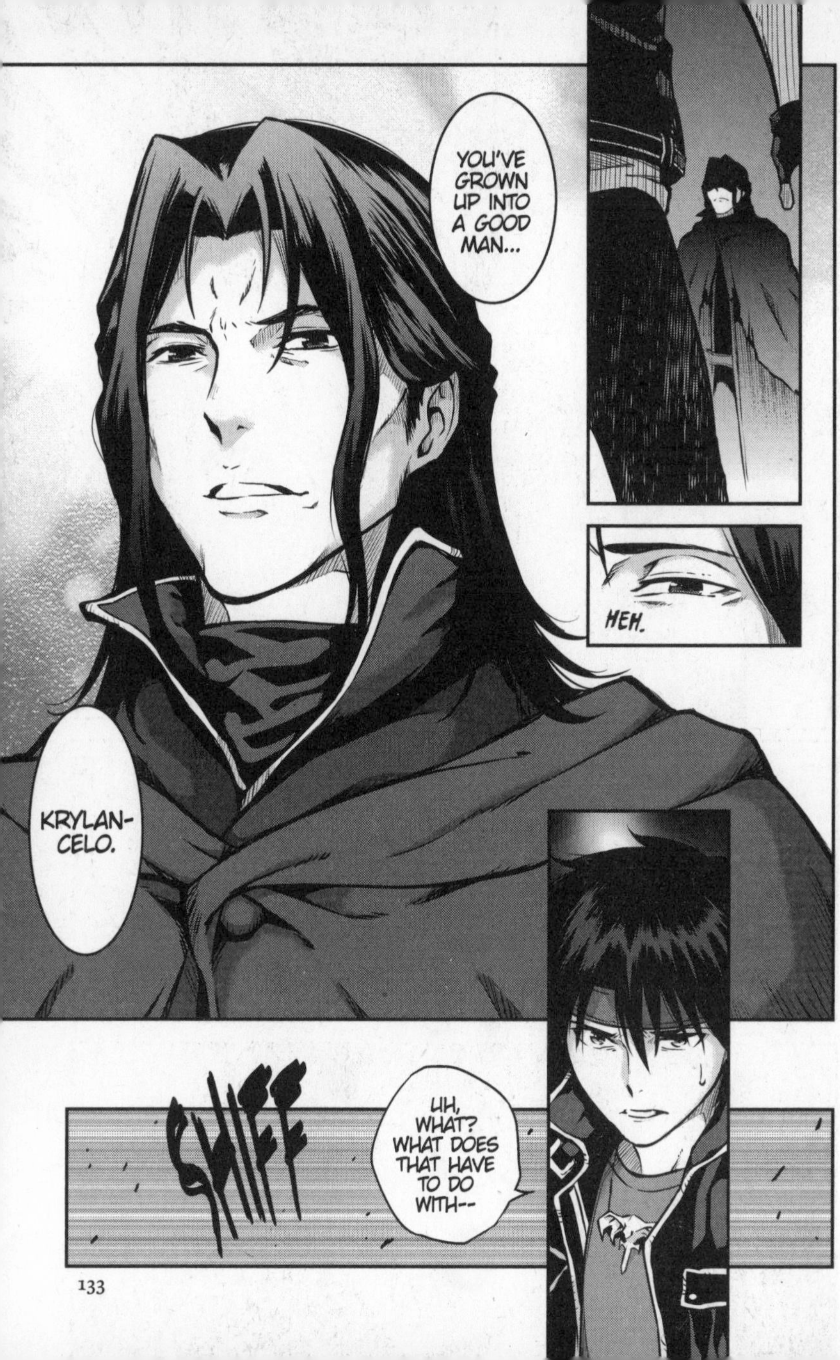
HEH.
YOU'VE GROWN UP INTO A GOOD MAN...
KRYLAN-CELO.
UH, WHAT? WHAT DOES THAT HAVE TO DO WITH--
SHIFF

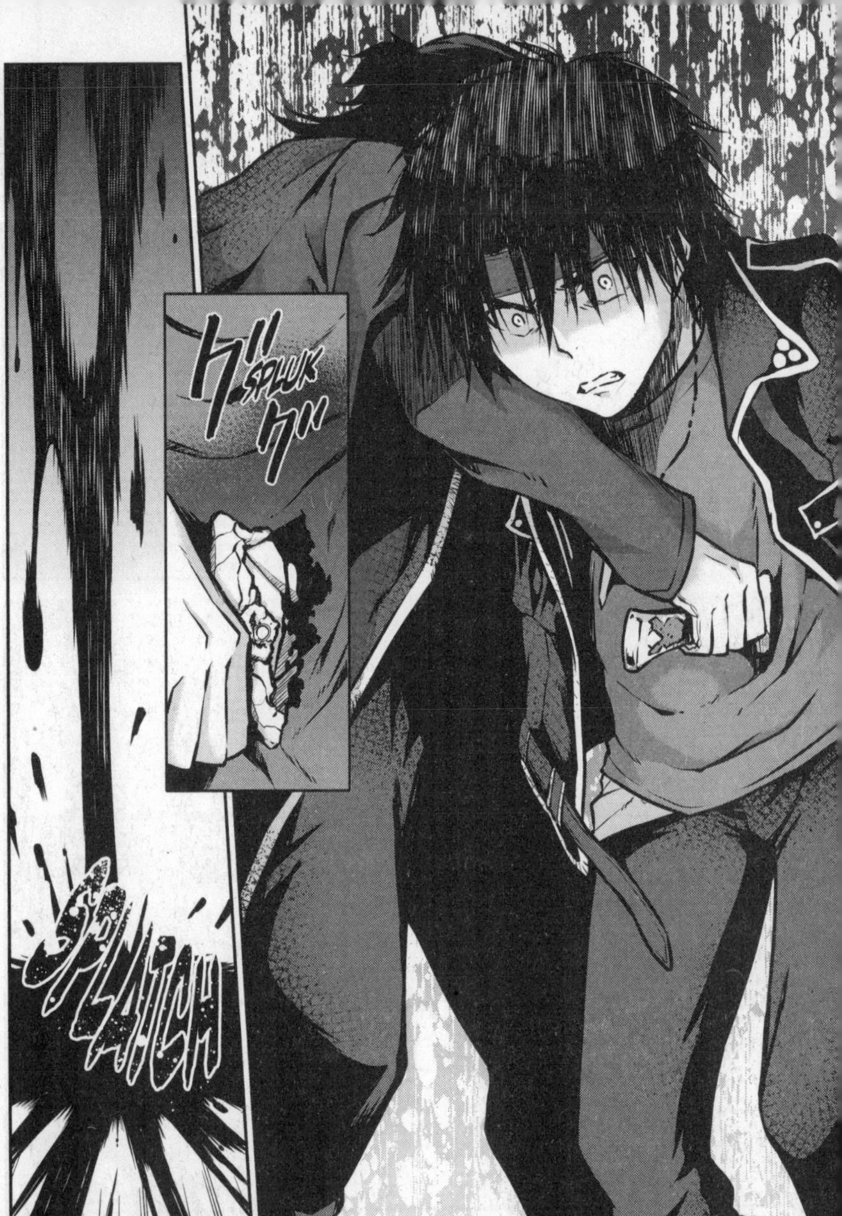
SPLUK
SPLATCH

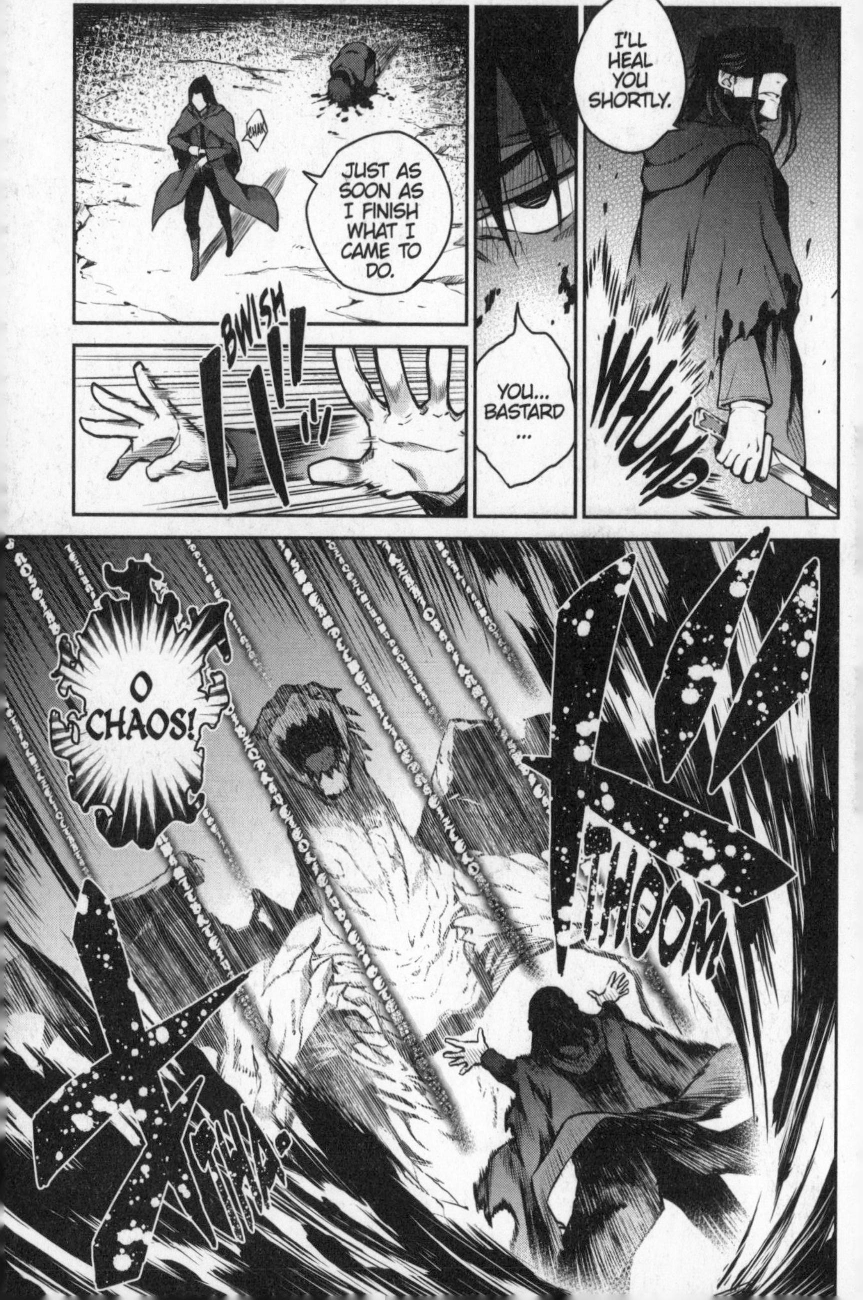
I'LL HEAL YOU SHORTLY.
WHUMP
YOU... BASTARD...
CHAK
JUST AS SOON AS I FINISH WHAT I CAME TO DO.
BWISH
THOOM!
O CHAOS!

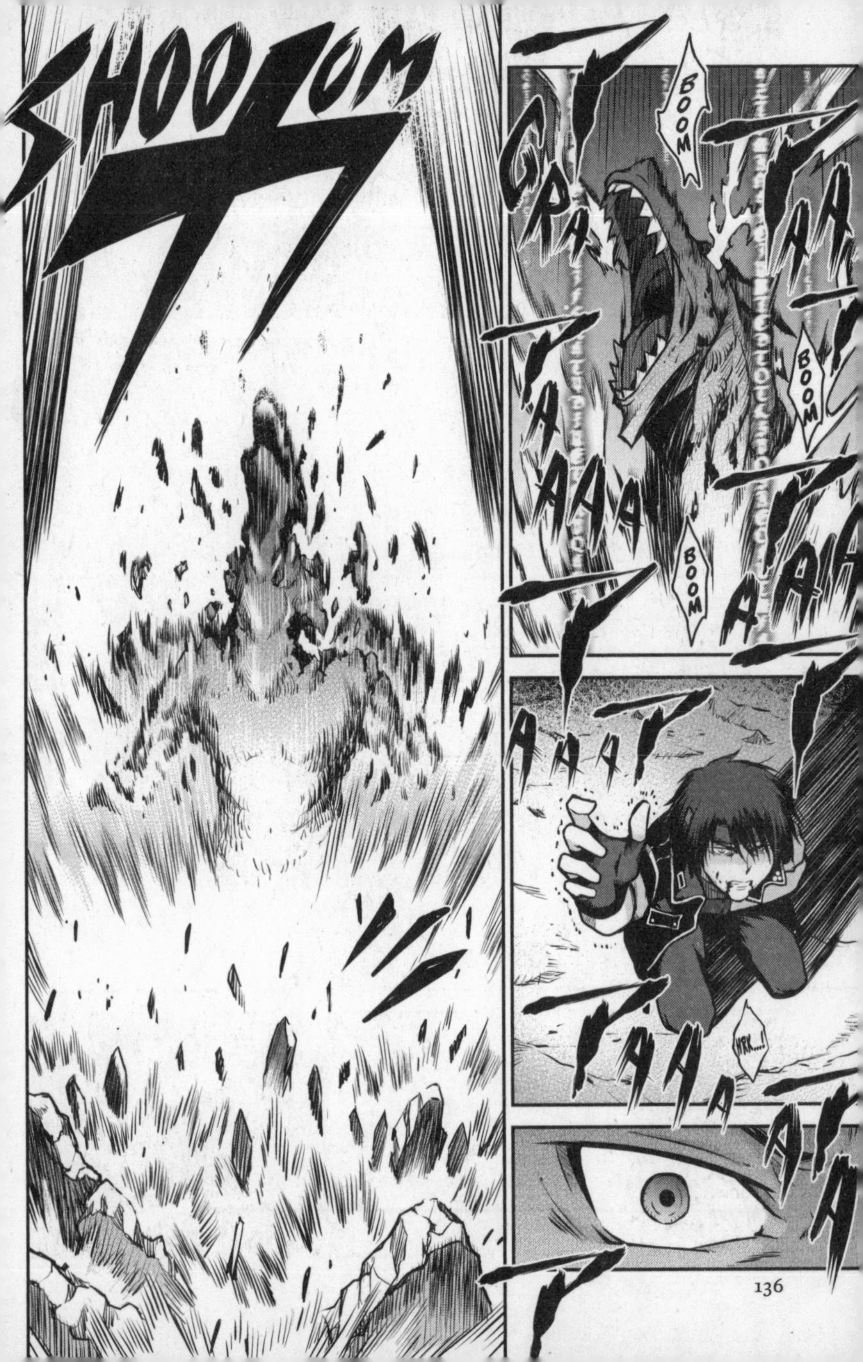
GRAAAAAAAAAAAAAAAAAAAAAAAA!!
BOOM
BOOM
BOOM
HRK...!
SHOOZOM

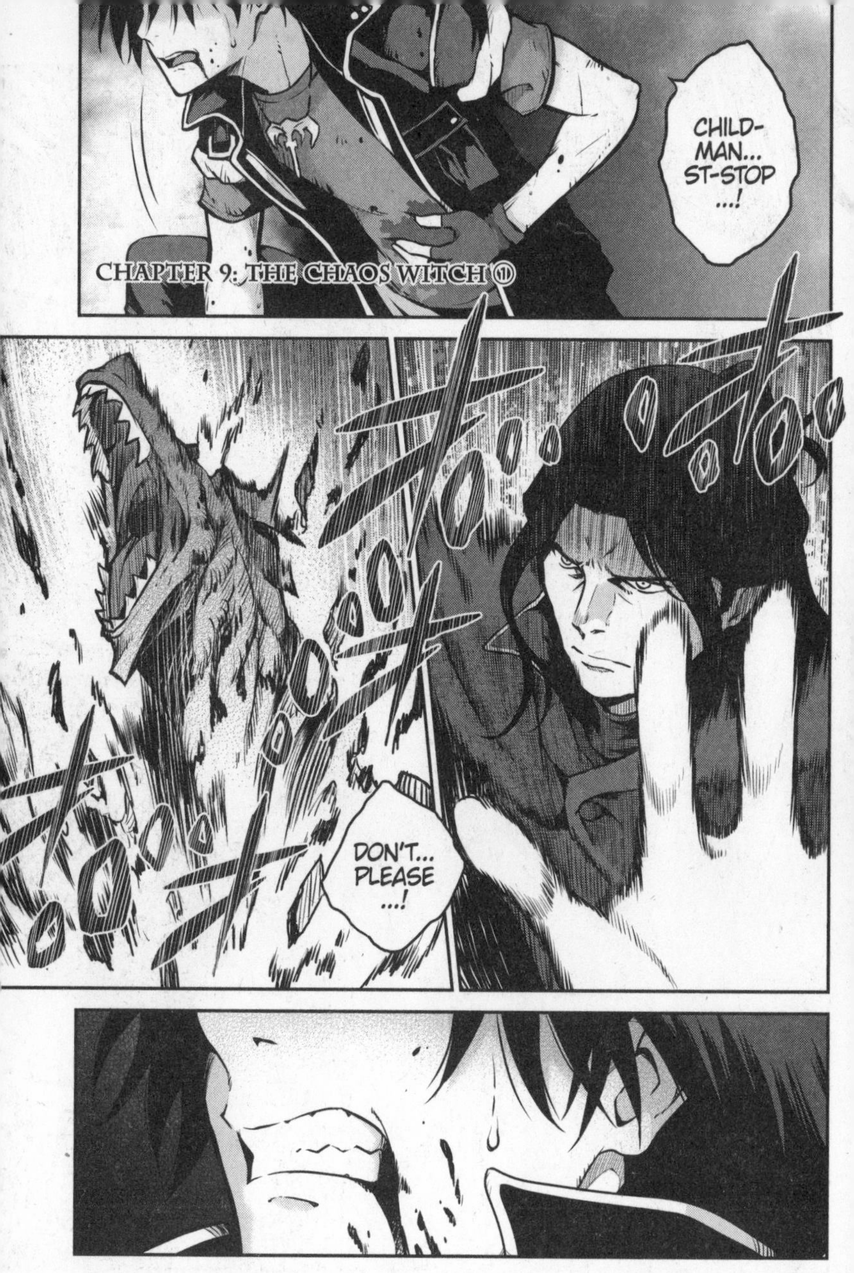
CHAPTER 9: THE CHAOS WITCH ⑪
CHILD-MAN... ST-STOP ...!
DON'T... PLEASE ...!

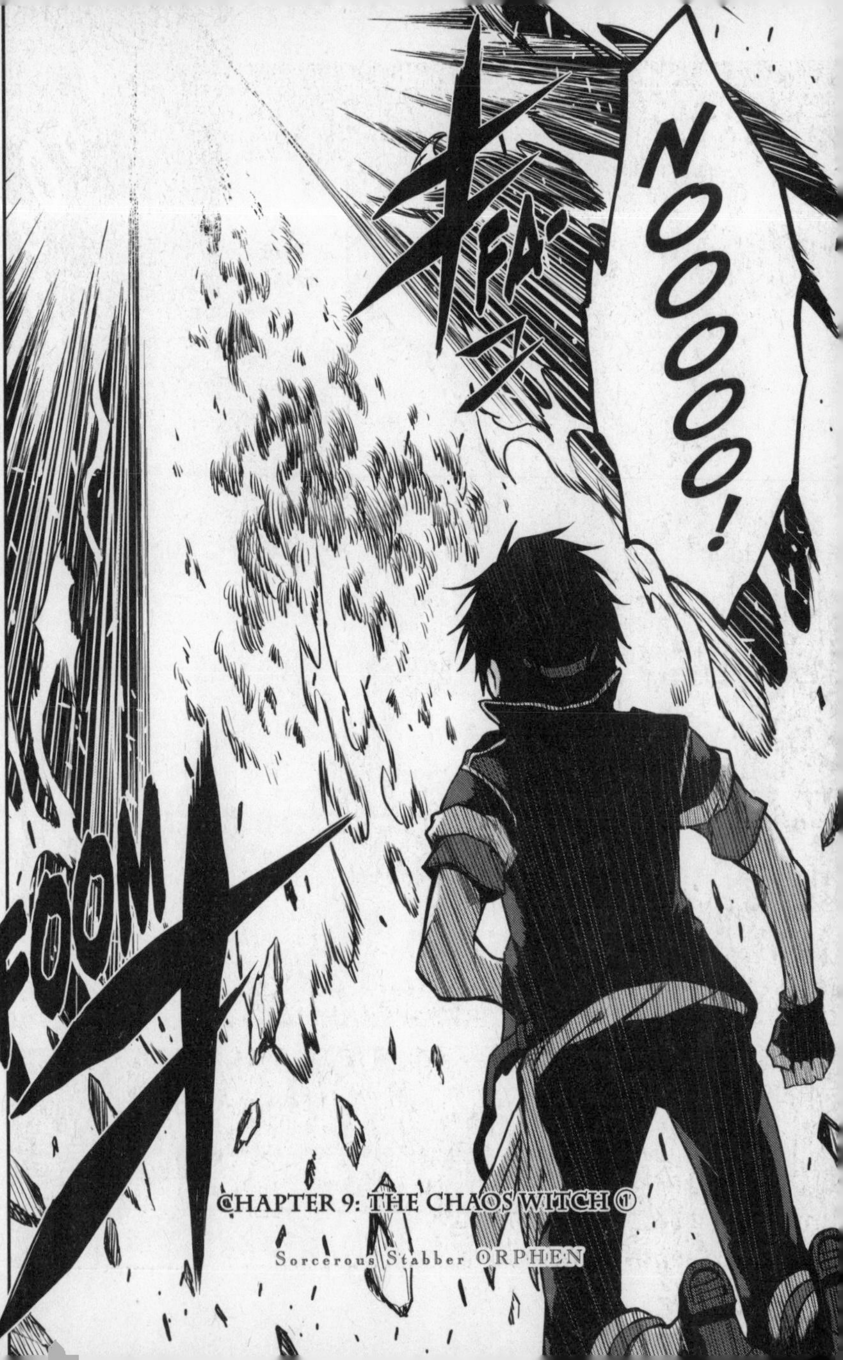
NOOOOO!
FA'
FOOM
CHAPTER 9: THE CHAOS WITCH ①
Sorcerous Stabber ORPHEN

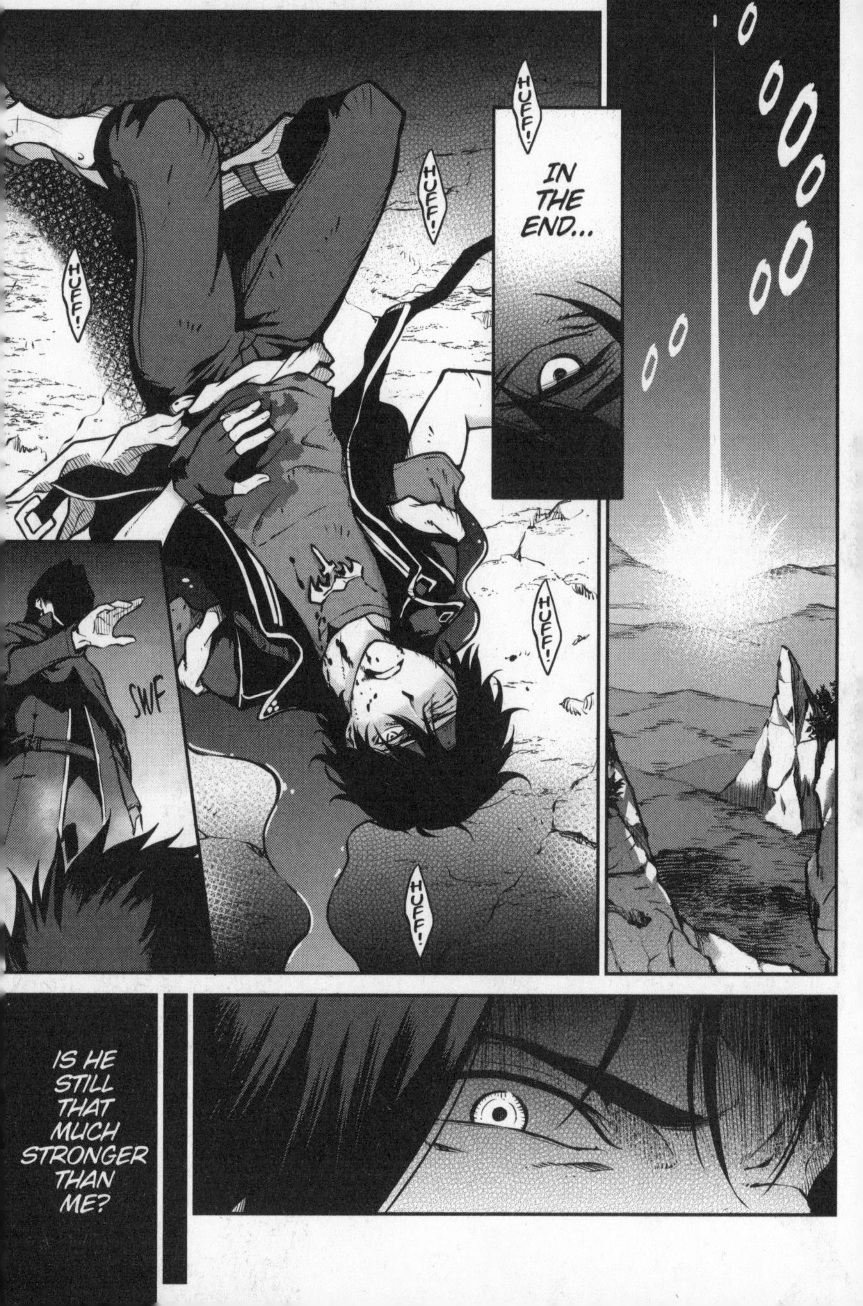
IN THE END...
HUFF!
HUFF!
HUFF!
SWF
HUFF!
HUFF!
IS HE STILL THAT MUCH STRONGER THAN ME?

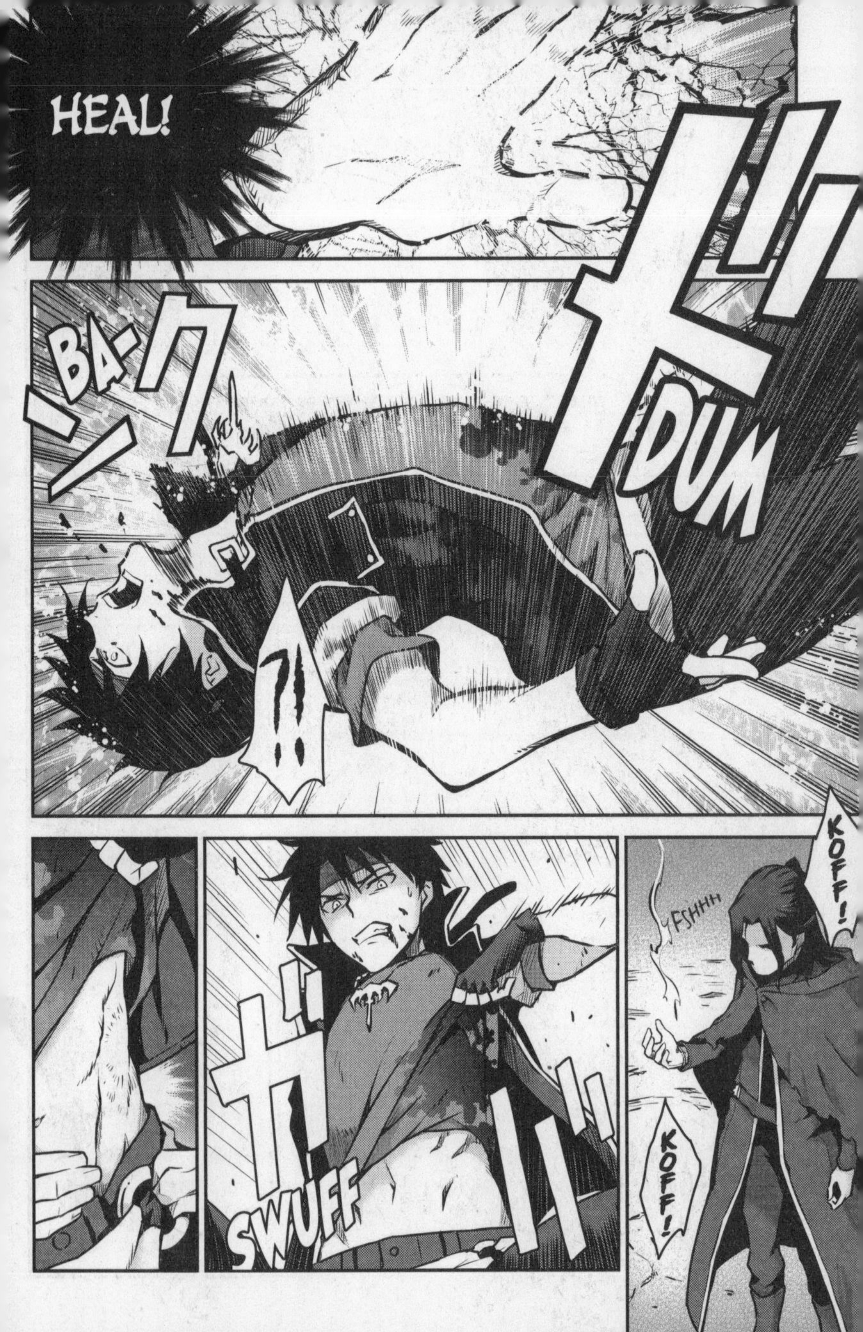
HEAL!
DUM
BA-
?!
KOFF!
FSHHH
KOFF!
SWUFF

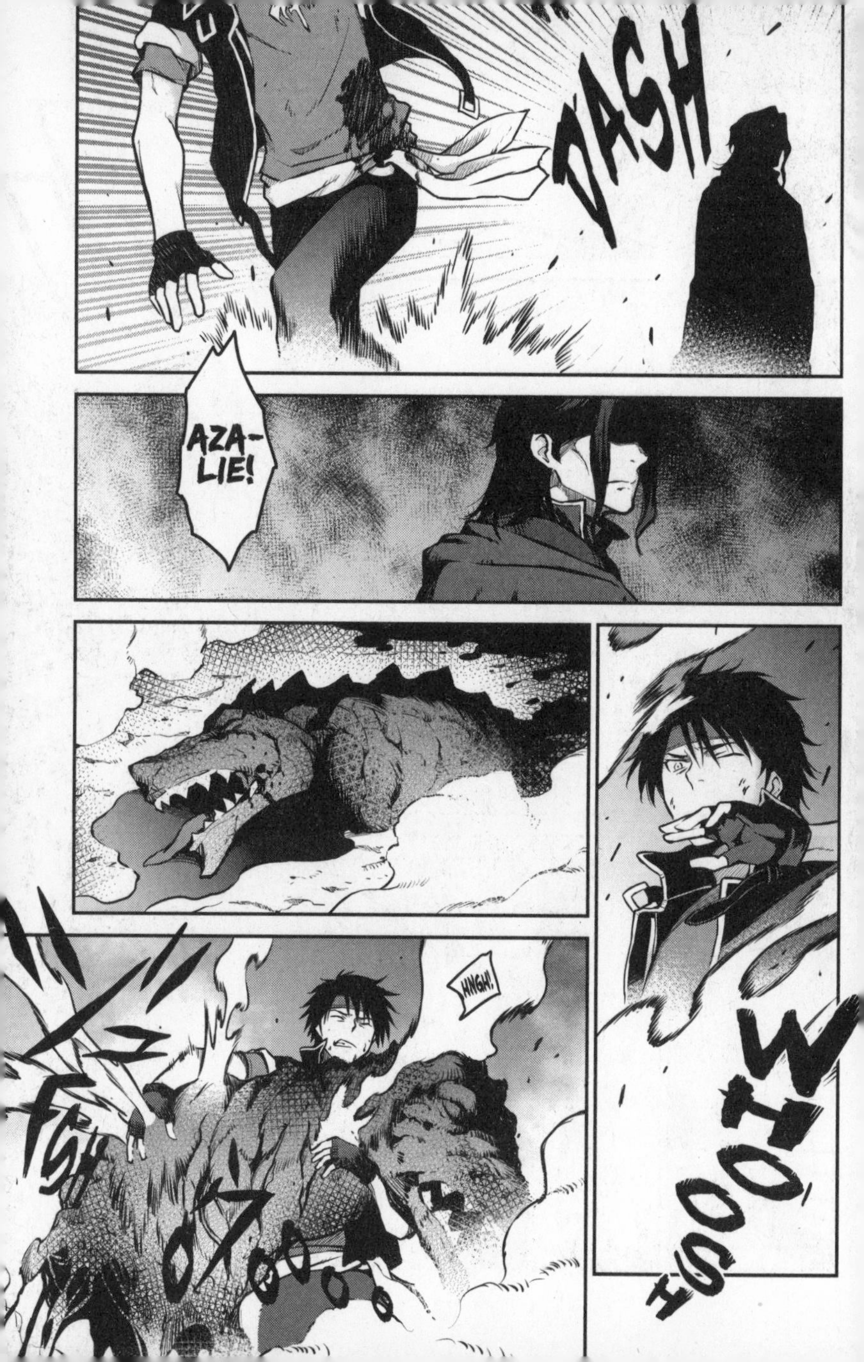
DASH
AZA-
LIE!
WHOOSH
HNGH!
FSH

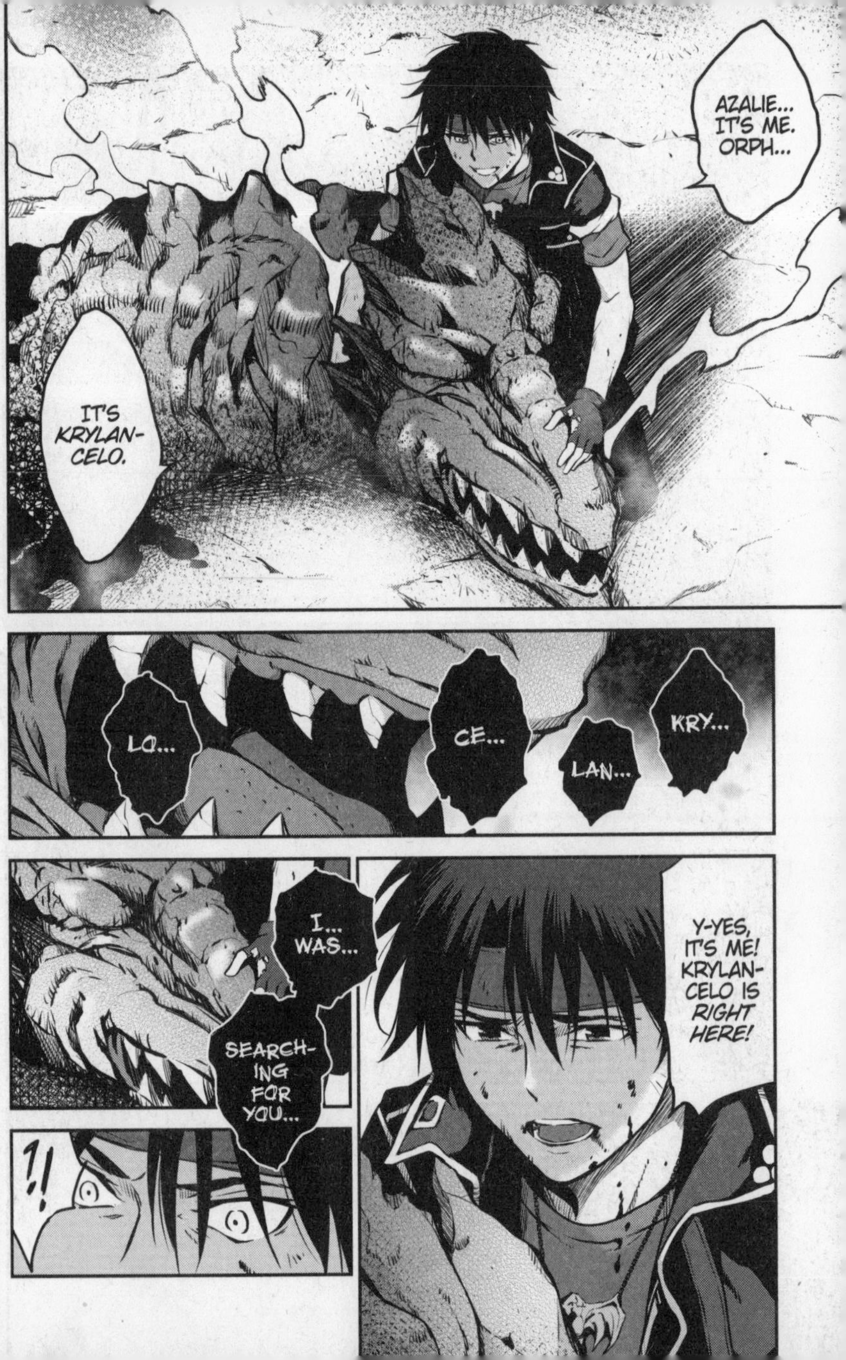
AZALIE... IT'S ME. ORPH...
IT'S KRYLAN-CELO.
KRY...
LAN...
CE...
LO...
Y-YES, IT'S ME! KRYLAN-CELO IS *RIGHT HERE!*
I... WAS...
SEARCH-ING FOR YOU...
?!

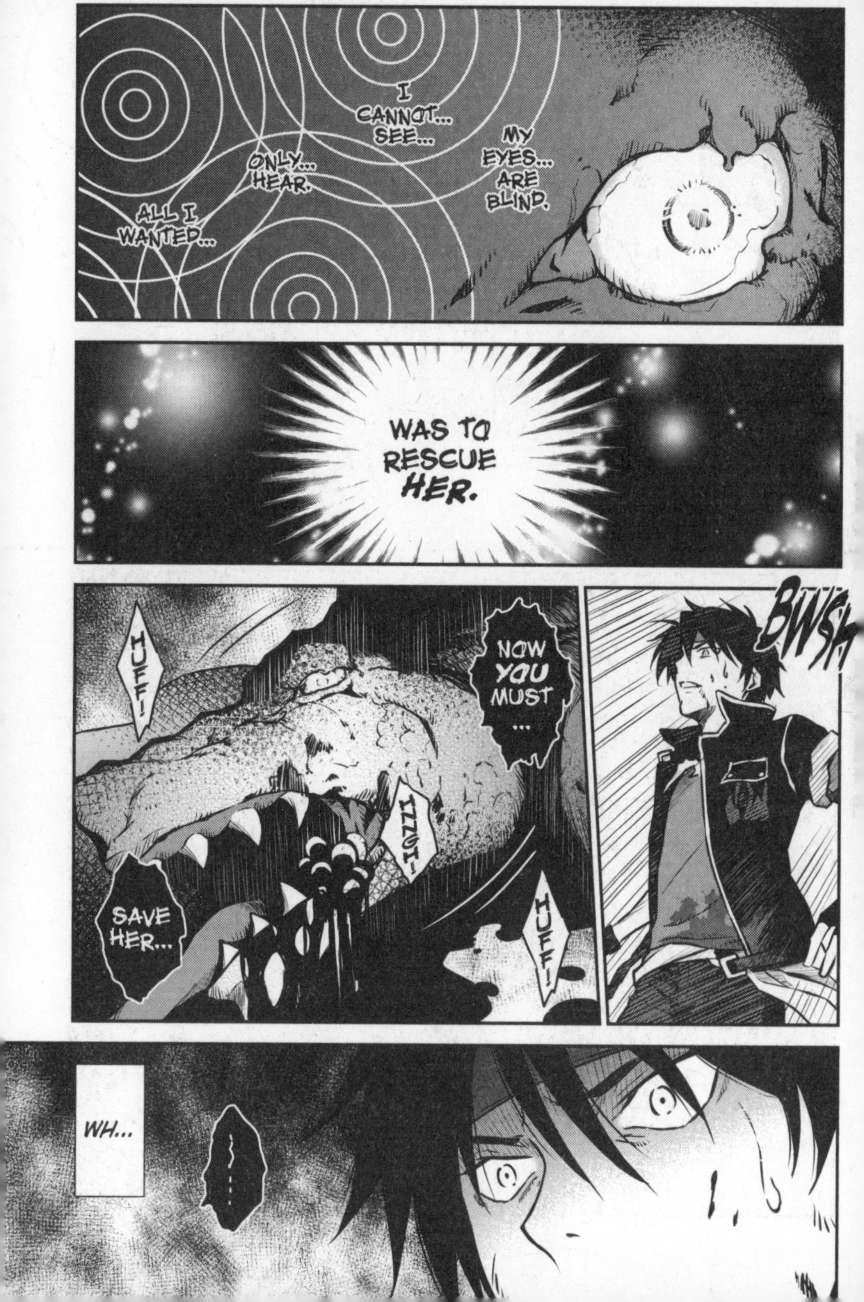
MY EYES... ARE BLIND.
I CANNOT... SEE...
ONLY... HEAR.
ALL I WANTED...
WAS TO RESCUE HER.
BWSH
NOW YOU MUST ...
HUFF!
INNGH!
HUFF!
SAVE HER...
!?......
WH...

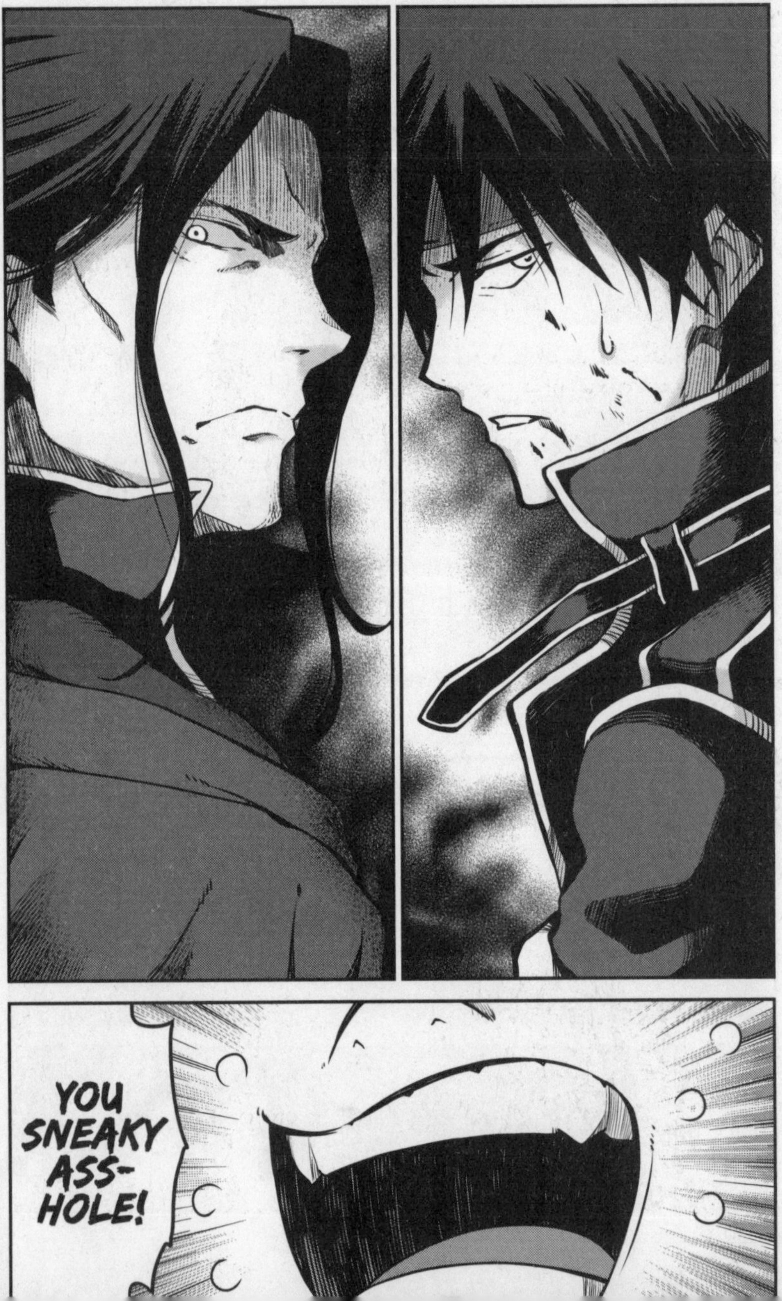
YOU SNEAKY ASS-HOLE!

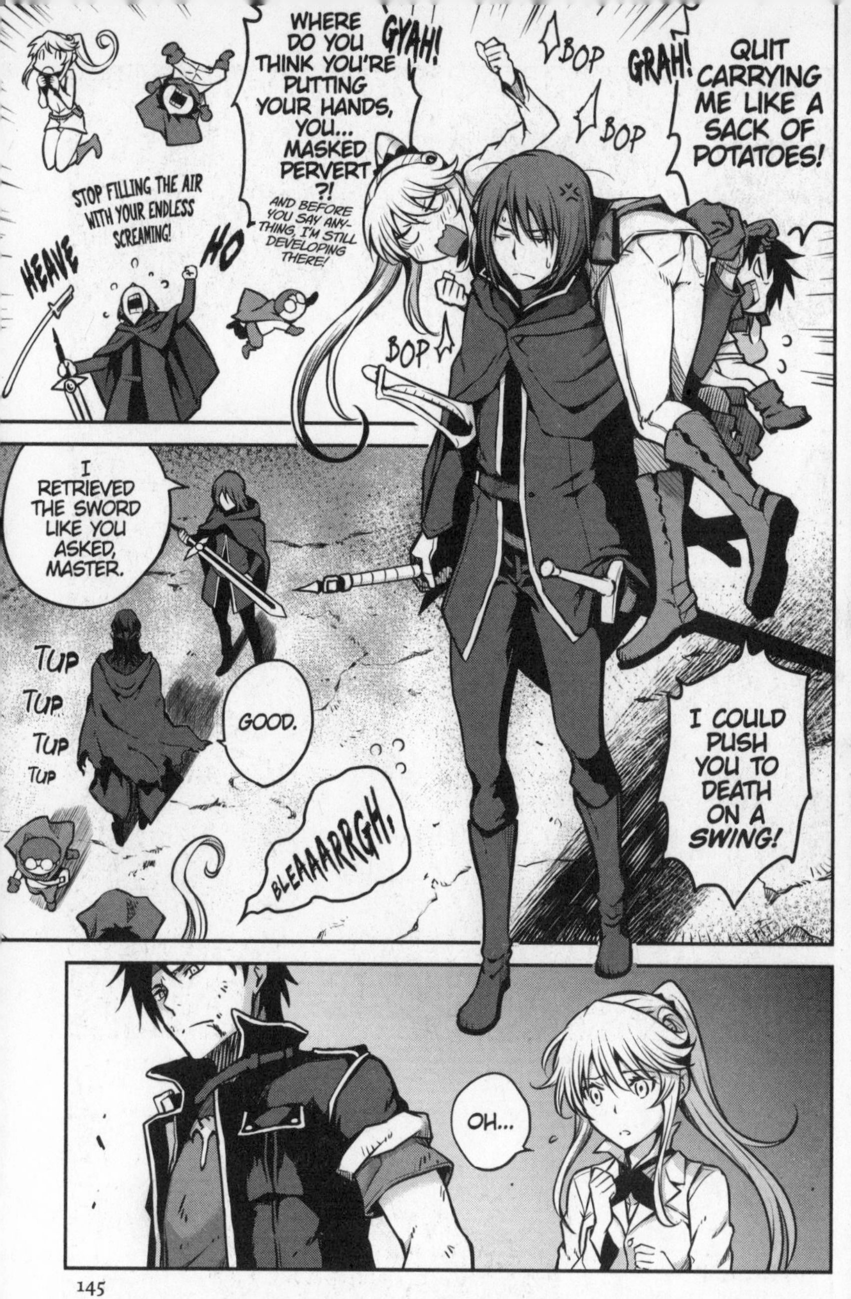
QUIT CARRYING ME LIKE A SACK OF POTATOES!
GRAH!
BOP
BOP
GYAH!
WHERE DO YOU THINK YOU'RE PUTTING YOUR HANDS, YOU... MASKED PERVERT ?!
AND BEFORE YOU SAY ANY-THING, I'M STILL DEVELOPING THERE!
HO
STOP FILLING THE AIR WITH YOUR ENDLESS SCREAMING!
HEAVE
I COULD PUSH YOU TO DEATH ON A SWING!
BOP
I RETRIEVED THE SWORD LIKE YOU ASKED, MASTER.
GOOD.
BLEAAARRGH,
TUP
TUP
TUP
TUP
OH...

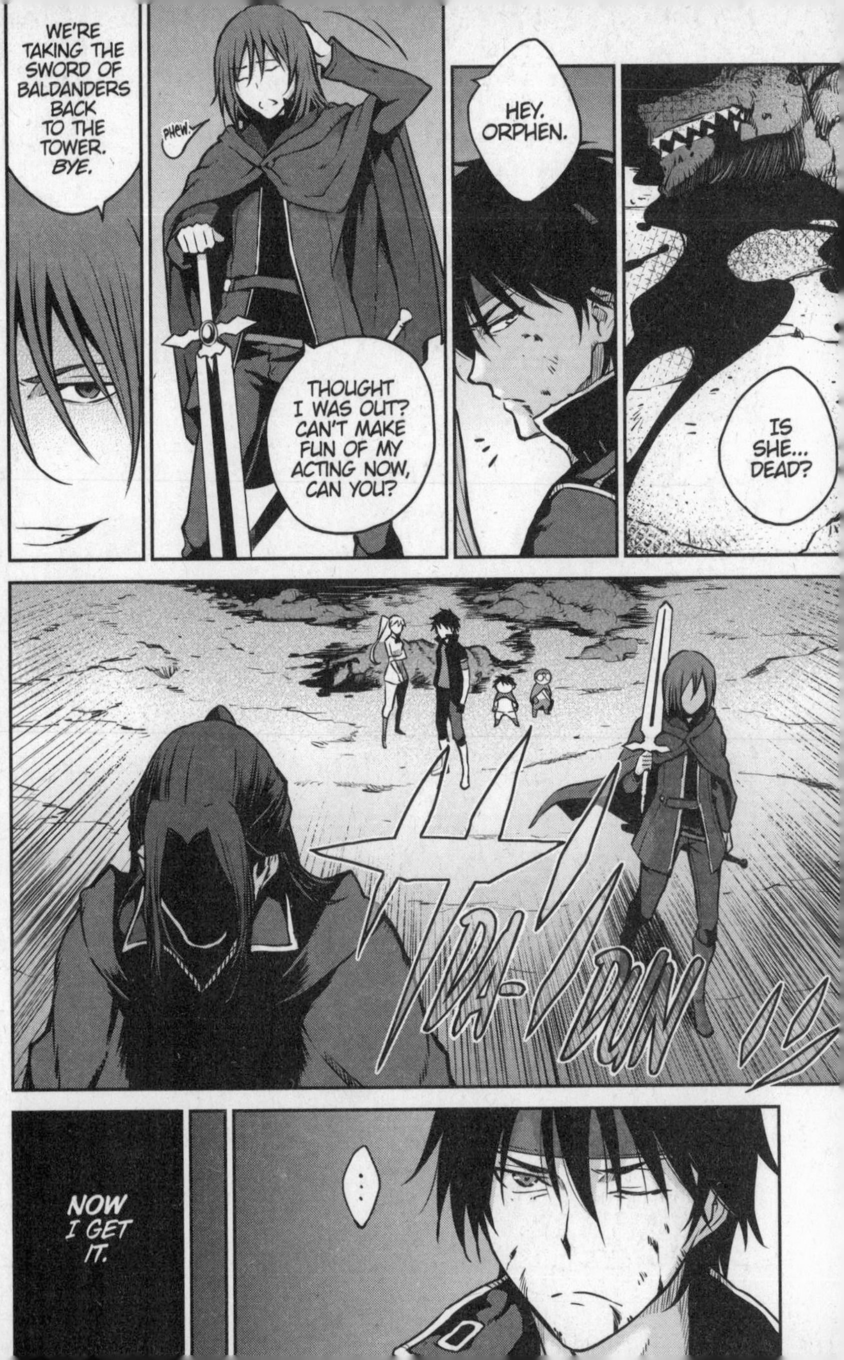
IS SHE... DEAD?
HEY. ORPHEN.
PHEW.
THOUGHT I WAS OUT? CAN'T MAKE FUN OF MY ACTING NOW, CAN YOU?
WE'RE TAKING THE SWORD OF BALDANDERS BACK TO THE TOWER. BYE.
...
NOW I GET IT.

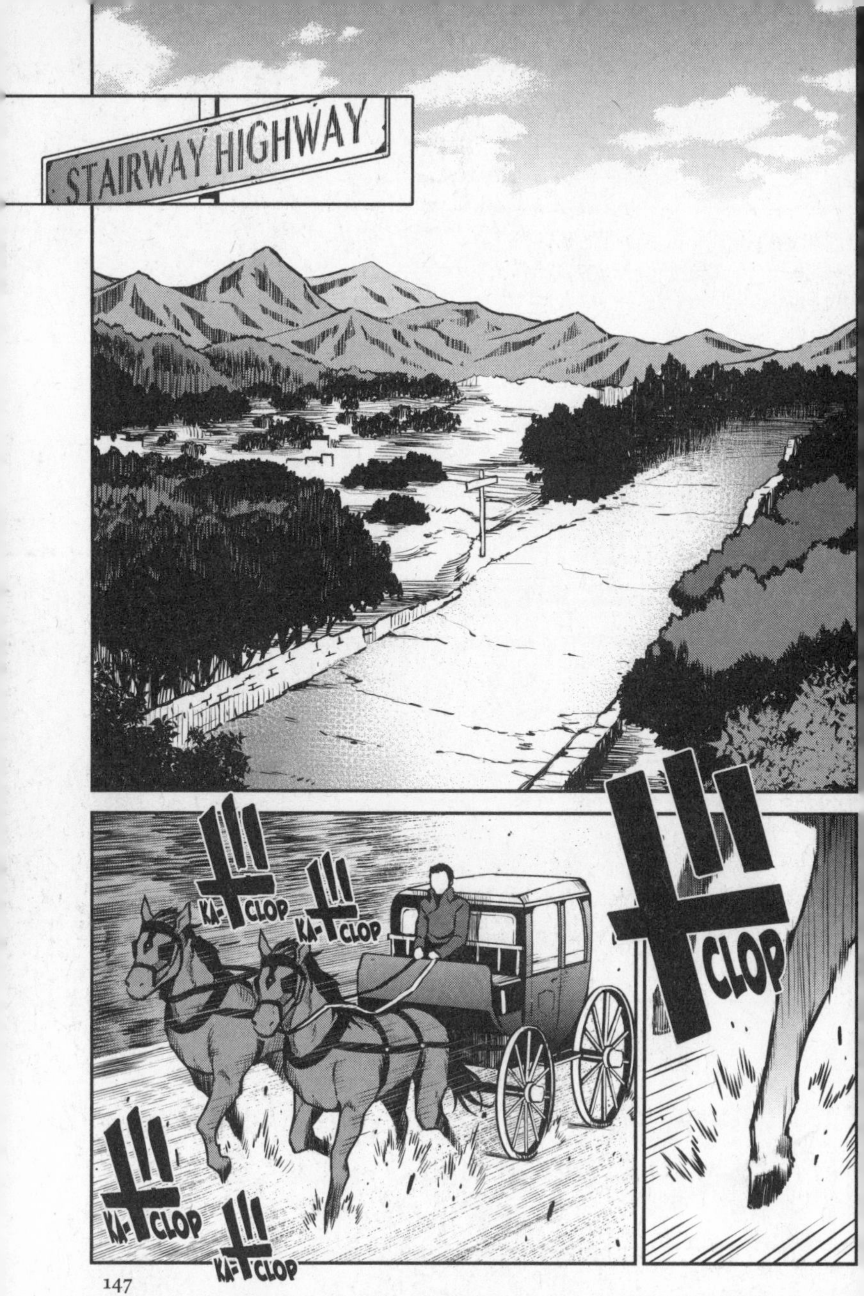
STAIRWAY HIGHWAY
CLOP
KA-CLOP
KA-CLOP
KA-CLOP
KA-CLOP

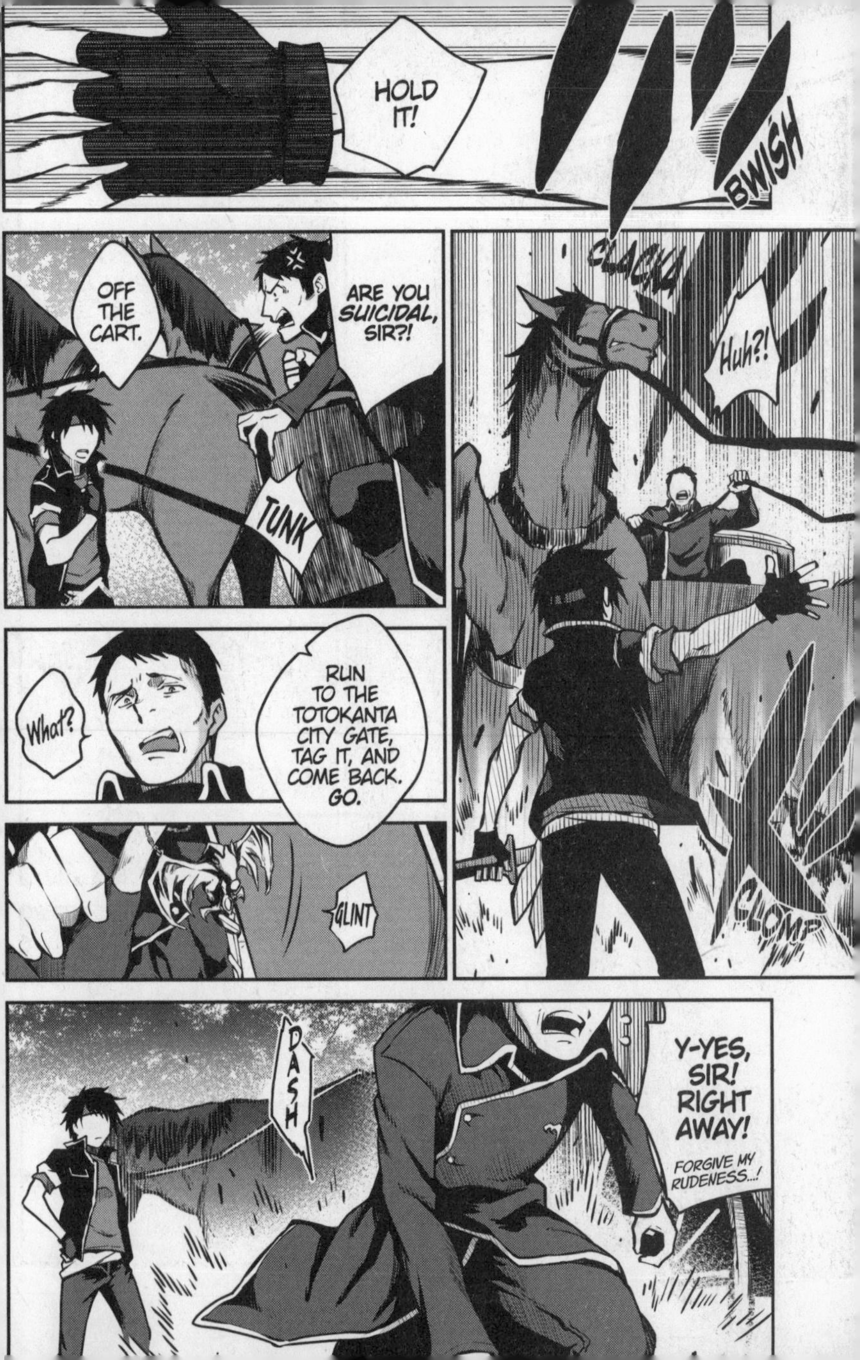
BWISH
HOLD IT!
CLACK
Huh?!
CLOMP
ARE YOU SUICIDAL, SIR?!
OFF THE CART.
TUNK
RUN TO THE TOTOKANTA CITY GATE, TAG IT, AND COME BACK. GO.
What?
GLINT
Y-YES, SIR! RIGHT AWAY!
FORGIVE MY RUDENESS...!
DASH

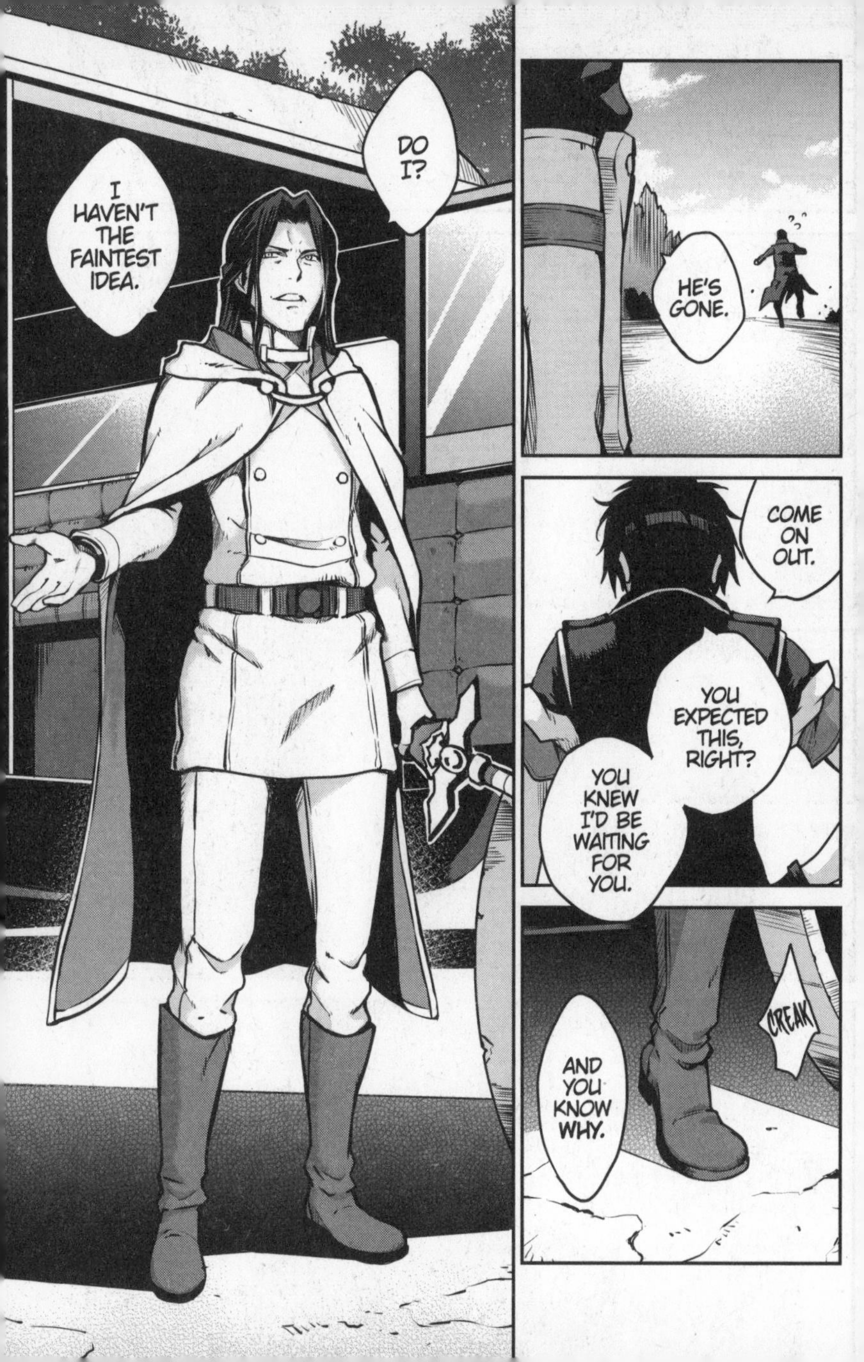
HE'S GONE.
COME ON OUT.
YOU EXPECTED THIS, RIGHT?
YOU KNEW I'D BE WAITING FOR YOU.
CREAK
AND YOU KNOW WHY.
DO I?
I HAVEN'T THE FAINTEST IDEA.

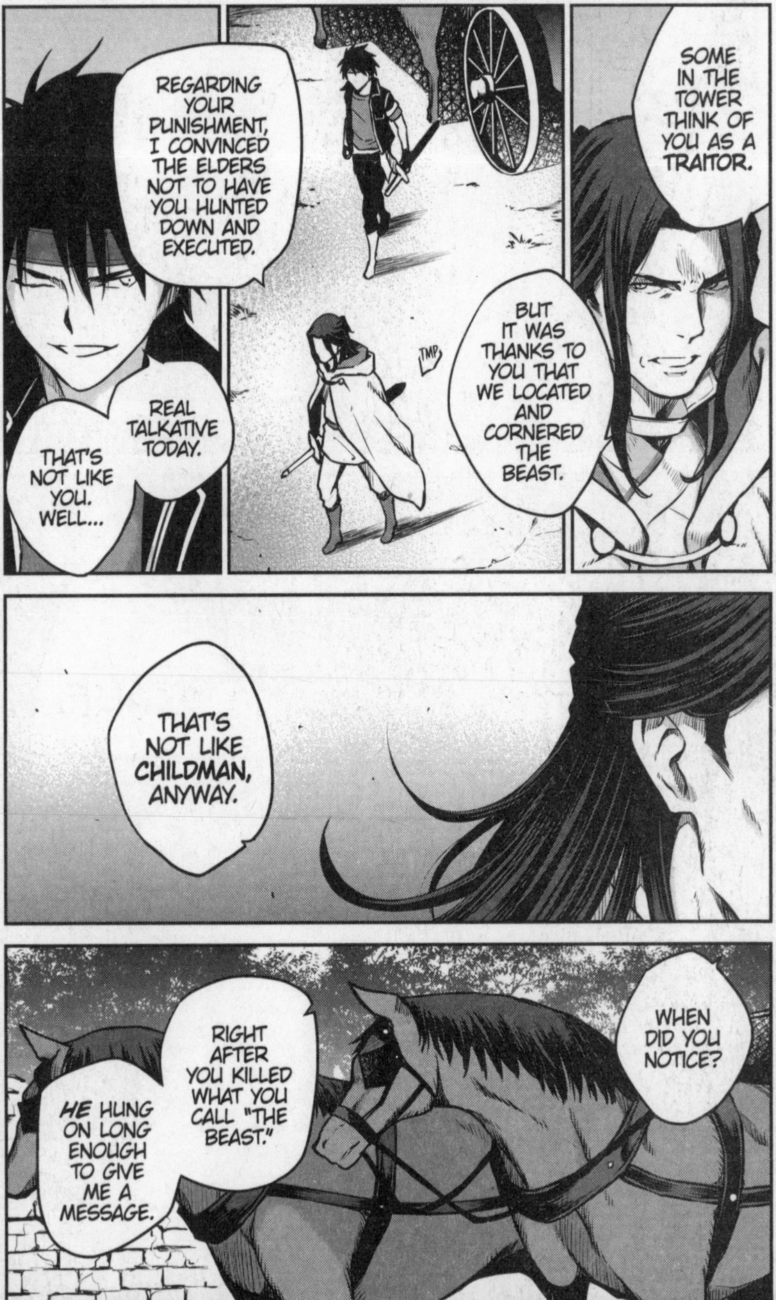
SOME IN THE TOWER THINK OF YOU AS A TRAITOR.
BUT IT WAS THANKS TO YOU THAT WE LOCATED AND CORNERED THE BEAST.
REGARDING YOUR PUNISHMENT, I CONVINCED THE ELDERS NOT TO HAVE YOU HUNTED DOWN AND EXECUTED.
TMP
REAL TALKATIVE TODAY.
THAT'S NOT LIKE YOU. WELL...
THAT'S NOT LIKE **CHILDMAN,** ANYWAY.
WHEN DID YOU NOTICE?
RIGHT AFTER YOU KILLED WHAT YOU CALL "THE BEAST."
HE HUNG ON LONG ENOUGH TO GIVE ME A MESSAGE.

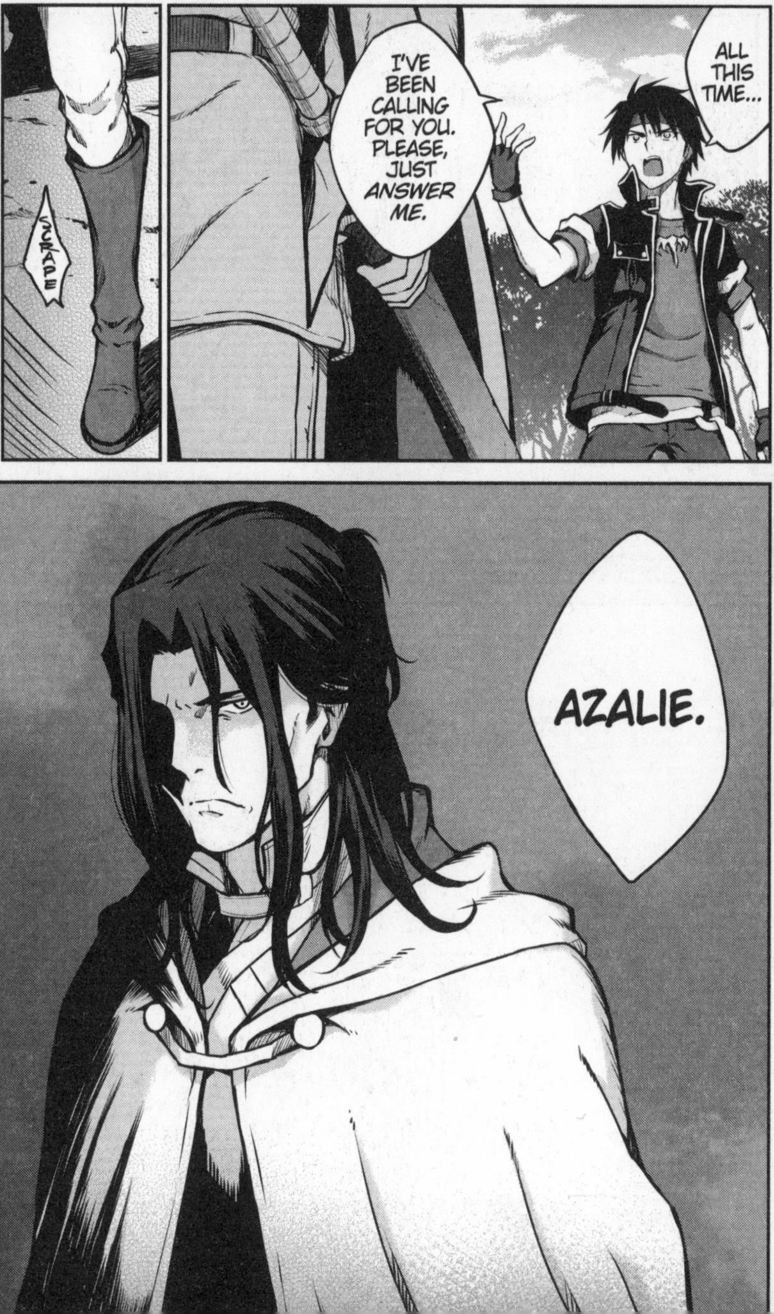
ALL THIS TIME...
I'VE BEEN CALLING FOR YOU. PLEASE, JUST ANSWER ME.
SCRAPE
AZALIE.

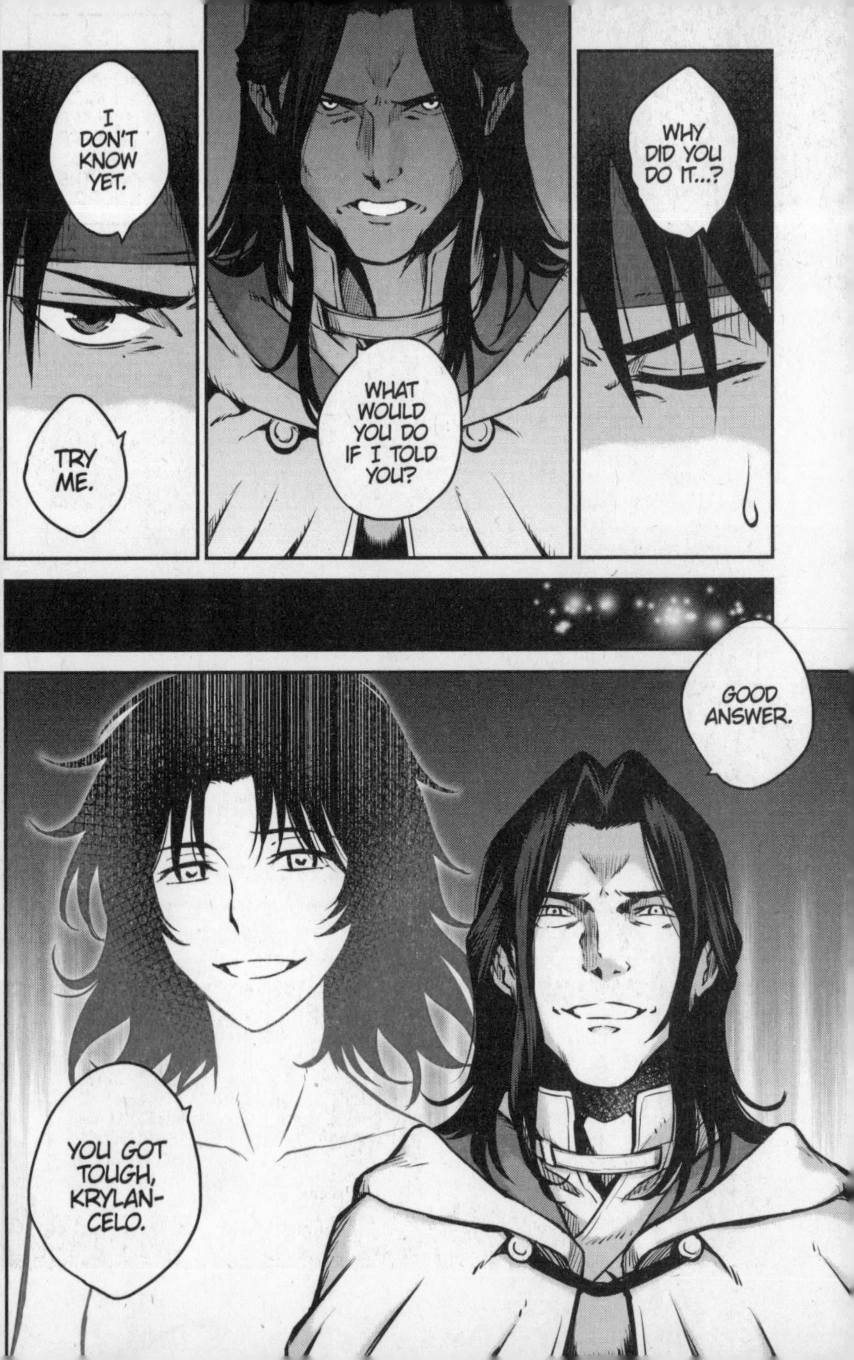
WHY DID YOU DO IT...?
WHAT WOULD YOU DO IF I TOLD YOU?
I DON'T KNOW YET.
TRY ME.
GOOD ANSWER.
YOU GOT TOUGH, KRYLAN-CELO.

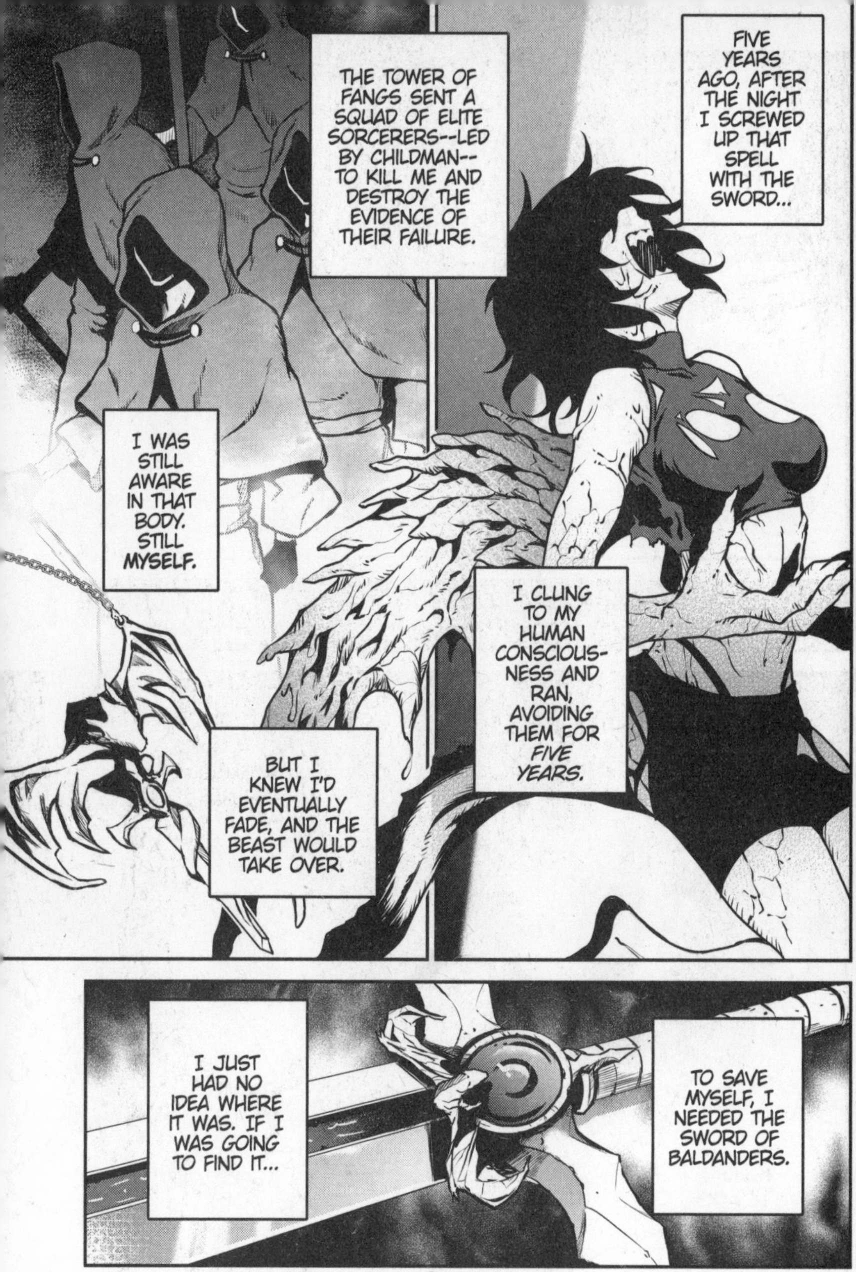
FIVE YEARS AGO, AFTER THE NIGHT I SCREWED UP THAT SPELL WITH THE SWORD...
THE TOWER OF FANGS SENT A SQUAD OF ELITE SORCERERS--LED BY CHILDMAN--TO KILL ME AND DESTROY THE EVIDENCE OF THEIR FAILURE.
I WAS STILL AWARE IN THAT BODY. STILL MYSELF.
I CLUNG TO MY HUMAN CONSCIOUSNESS AND RAN, AVOIDING THEM FOR *FIVE YEARS.*
BUT I KNEW I'D EVENTUALLY FADE, AND THE BEAST WOULD TAKE OVER.
TO SAVE MYSELF, I NEEDED THE SWORD OF BALDANDERS.
I JUST HAD NO IDEA WHERE IT WAS. IF I WAS GOING TO FIND IT...

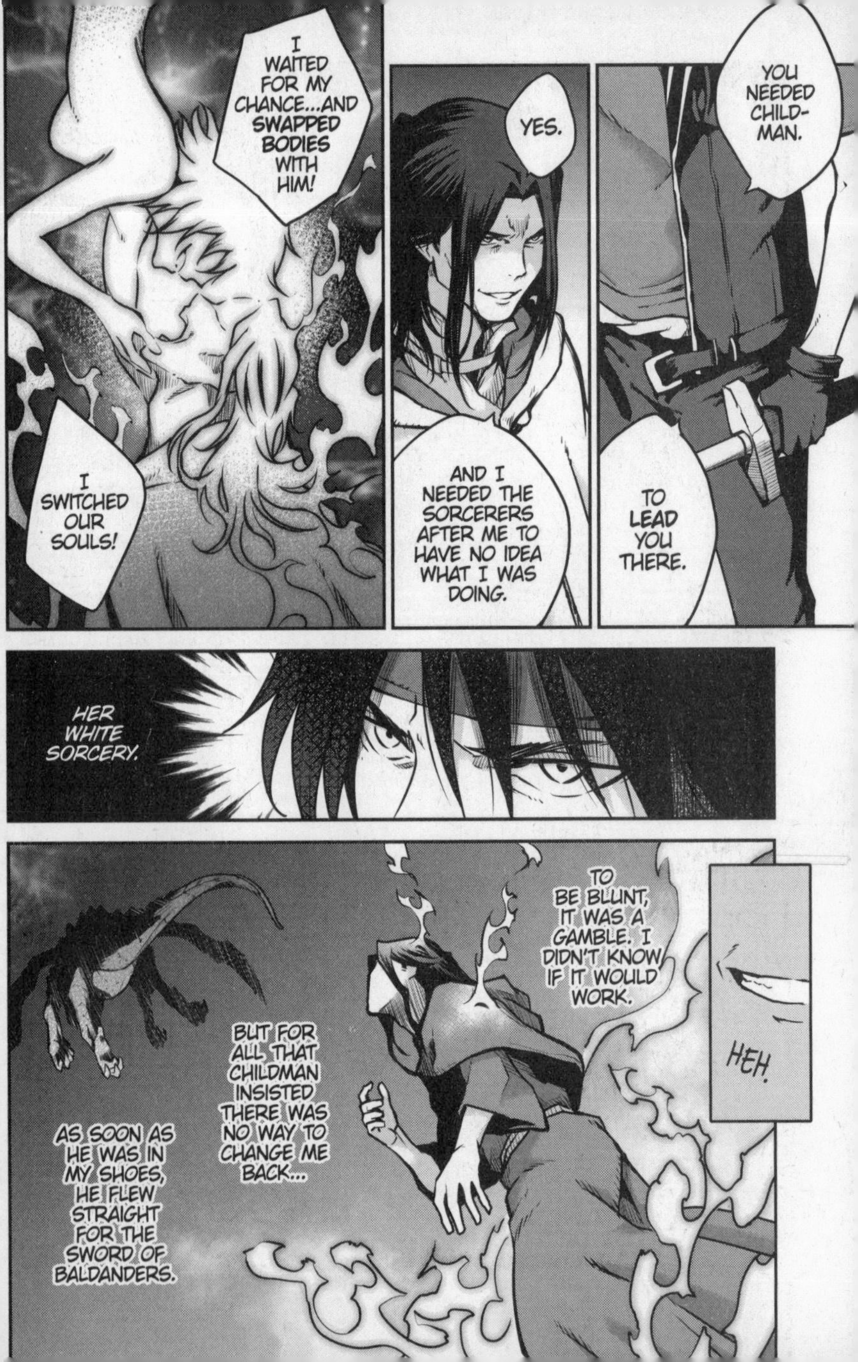
YOU NEEDED CHILD-MAN.
TO LEAD YOU THERE.
YES.
AND I NEEDED THE SORCERERS AFTER ME TO HAVE NO IDEA WHAT I WAS DOING.
I WAITED FOR MY CHANCE...AND SWAPPED BODIES WITH HIM!
I SWITCHED OUR SOULS!
HER WHITE SORCERY.
HEH.
TO BE BLUNT, IT WAS A GAMBLE. I DIDN'T KNOW IF IT WOULD WORK.
BUT FOR ALL THAT CHILDMAN INSISTED THERE WAS NO WAY TO CHANGE ME BACK...
AS SOON AS HE WAS IN MY SHOES, HE FLEW STRAIGHT FOR THE SWORD OF BALDANDERS.

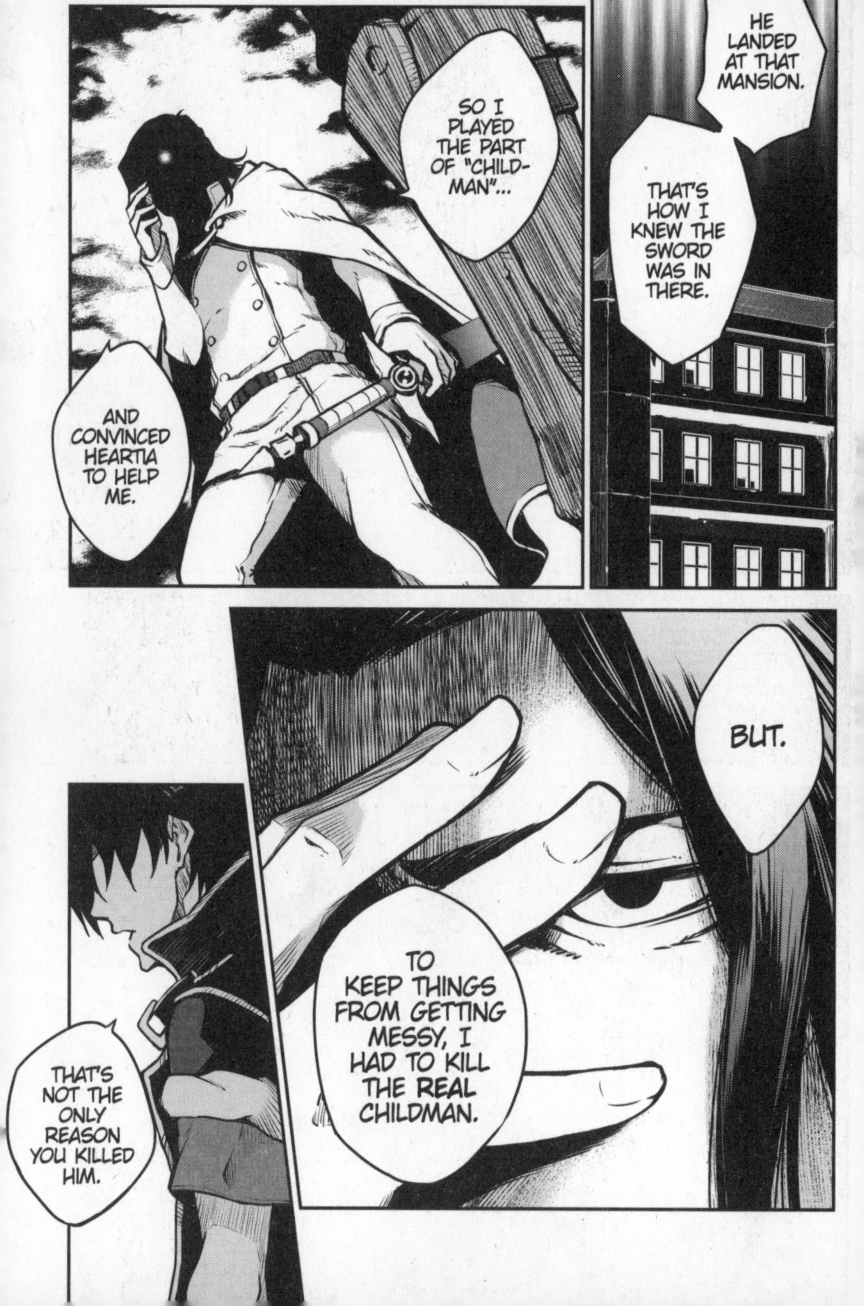
HE LANDED AT THAT MANSION.
THAT'S HOW I KNEW THE SWORD WAS IN THERE.
SO I PLAYED THE PART OF "CHILD-MAN"...
AND CONVINCED HEARTIA TO HELP ME.
BUT.
TO KEEP THINGS FROM GETTING MESSY, I HAD TO KILL THE REAL CHILDMAN.
THAT'S NOT THE ONLY REASON YOU KILLED HIM.

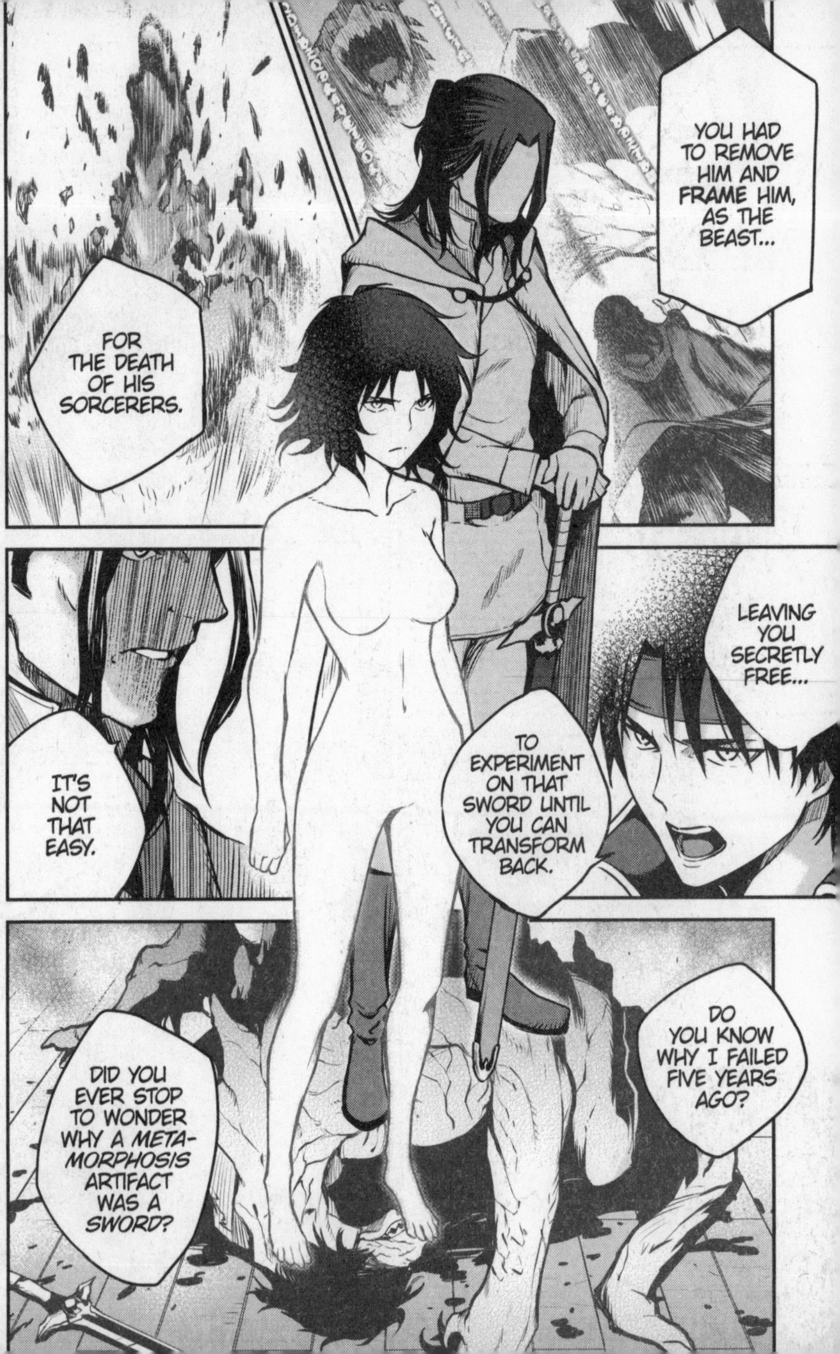
YOU HAD TO REMOVE HIM AND FRAME HIM, AS THE BEAST...
FOR THE DEATH OF HIS SORCERERS.
LEAVING YOU SECRETLY FREE...
TO EXPERIMENT ON THAT SWORD UNTIL YOU CAN TRANSFORM BACK.
IT'S NOT THAT EASY.
DO YOU KNOW WHY I FAILED FIVE YEARS AGO?
DID YOU EVER STOP TO WONDER WHY A METAMORPHOSIS ARTIFACT WAS A SWORD?

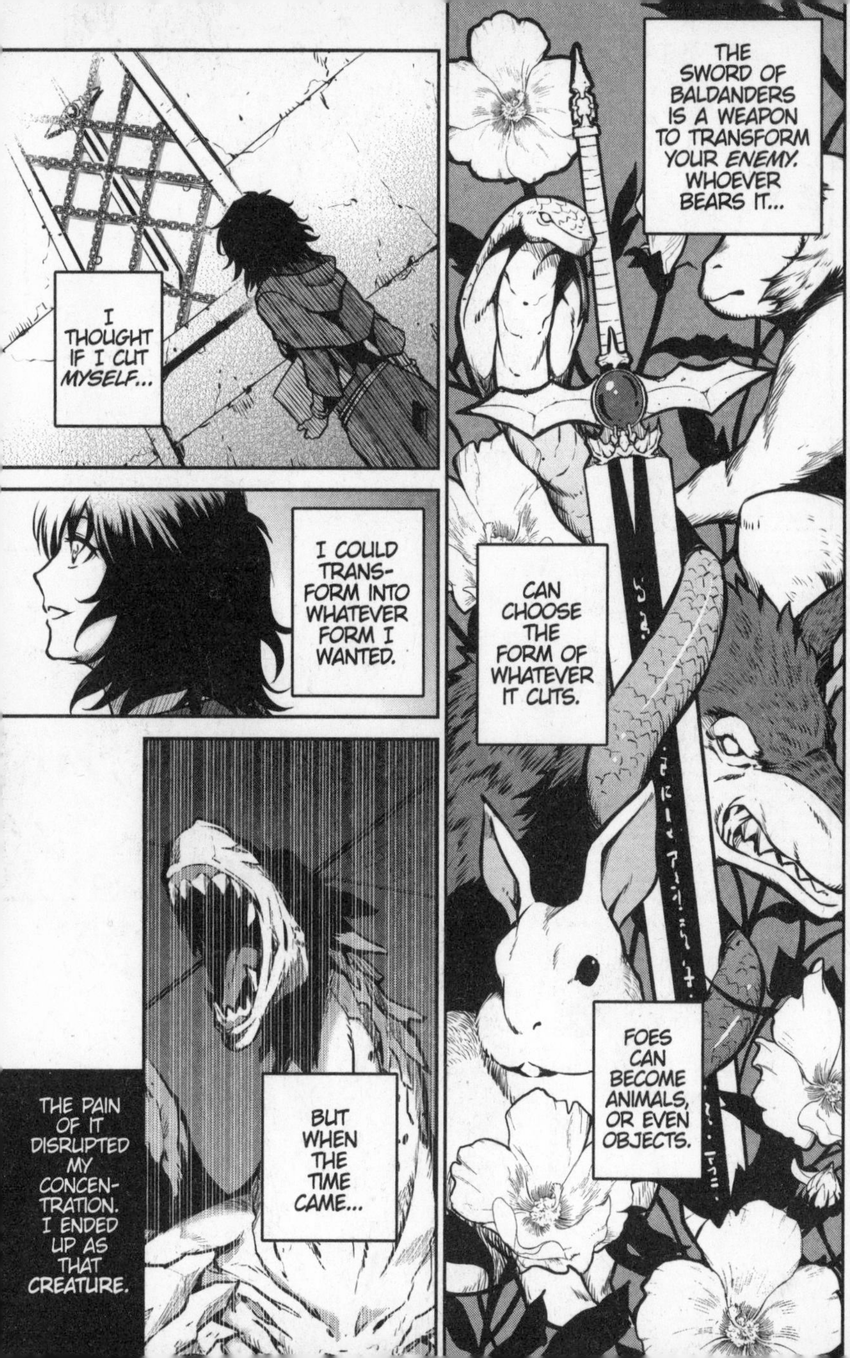
THE SWORD OF BALDANDERS IS A WEAPON TO TRANSFORM YOUR *ENEMY.* WHOEVER BEARS IT...
CAN CHOOSE THE FORM OF WHATEVER IT CUTS.
FOES CAN BECOME ANIMALS, OR EVEN OBJECTS.
I THOUGHT IF I CUT *MYSELF*...
I COULD TRANSFORM INTO WHATEVER FORM I WANTED.
BUT WHEN THE TIME CAME...
THE PAIN OF IT DISRUPTED MY CONCENTRATION. I ENDED UP AS THAT CREATURE.

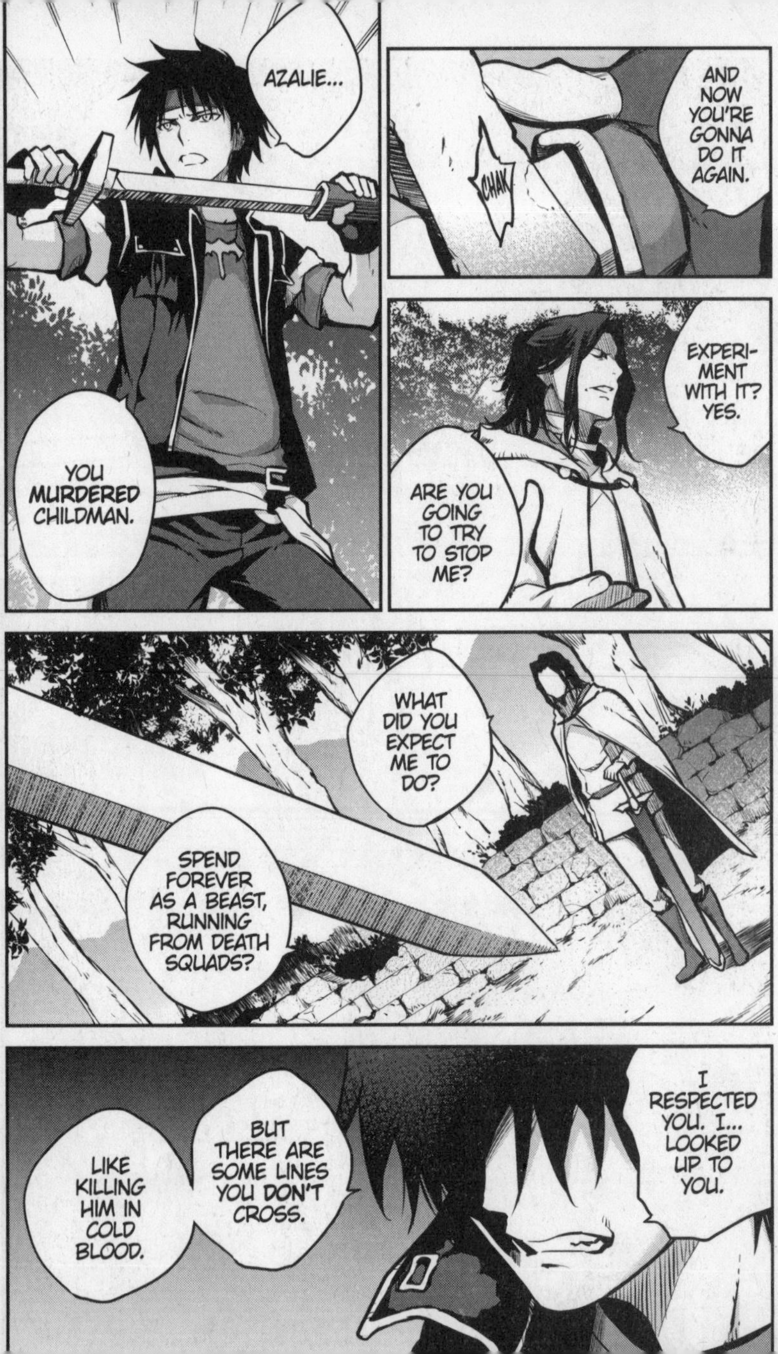
AND NOW YOU'RE GONNA DO IT AGAIN.
CHAK
EXPERIMENT WITH IT? YES.
ARE YOU GOING TO TRY TO STOP ME?
AZALIE...
YOU MURDERED CHILDMAN.
WHAT DID YOU EXPECT ME TO DO?
SPEND FOREVER AS A BEAST, RUNNING FROM DEATH SQUADS?
I RESPECTED YOU. I... LOOKED UP TO YOU.
BUT THERE ARE SOME LINES YOU DON'T CROSS.
LIKE KILLING HIM IN COLD BLOOD.

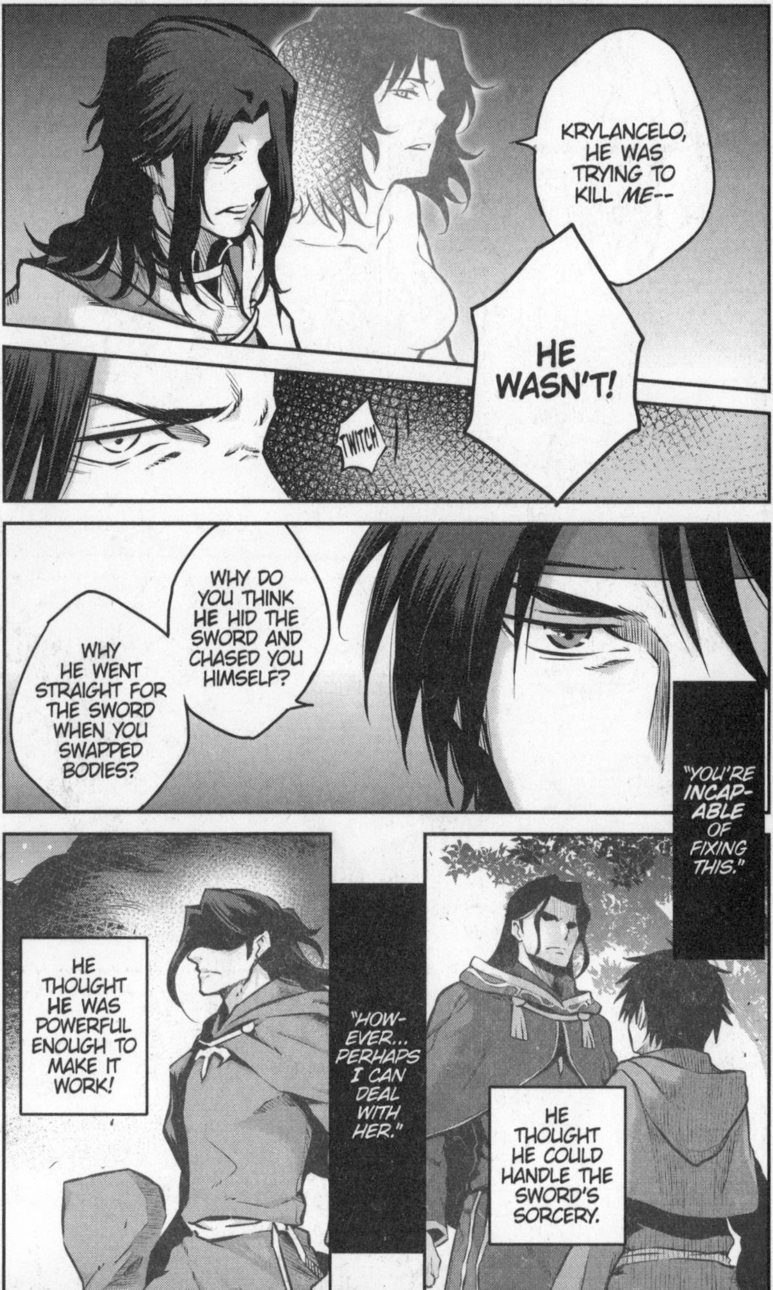
KRYLANCELO, HE WAS TRYING TO KILL *ME*--
HE WASN'T!
TWITCH
WHY DO YOU THINK HE HID THE SWORD AND CHASED YOU HIMSELF?
WHY HE WENT STRAIGHT FOR THE SWORD WHEN YOU SWAPPED BODIES?
"YOU'RE INCAPABLE OF FIXING THIS."
HE THOUGHT HE COULD HANDLE THE SWORD'S SORCERY.
"HOWEVER... PERHAPS I CAN DEAL WITH HER."
HE THOUGHT HE WAS POWERFUL ENOUGH TO MAKE IT WORK!

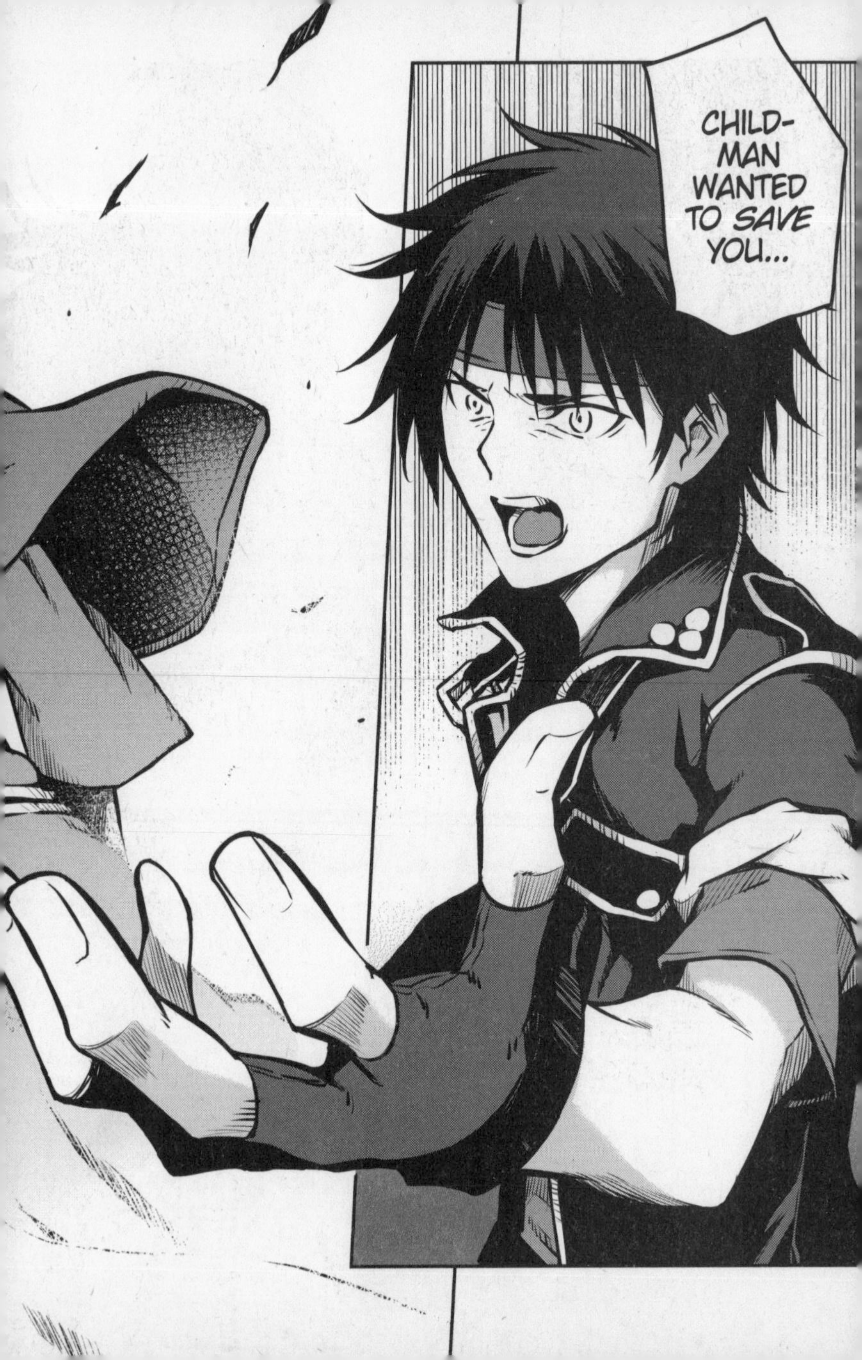
CHILD-MAN WANTED TO SAVE YOU...

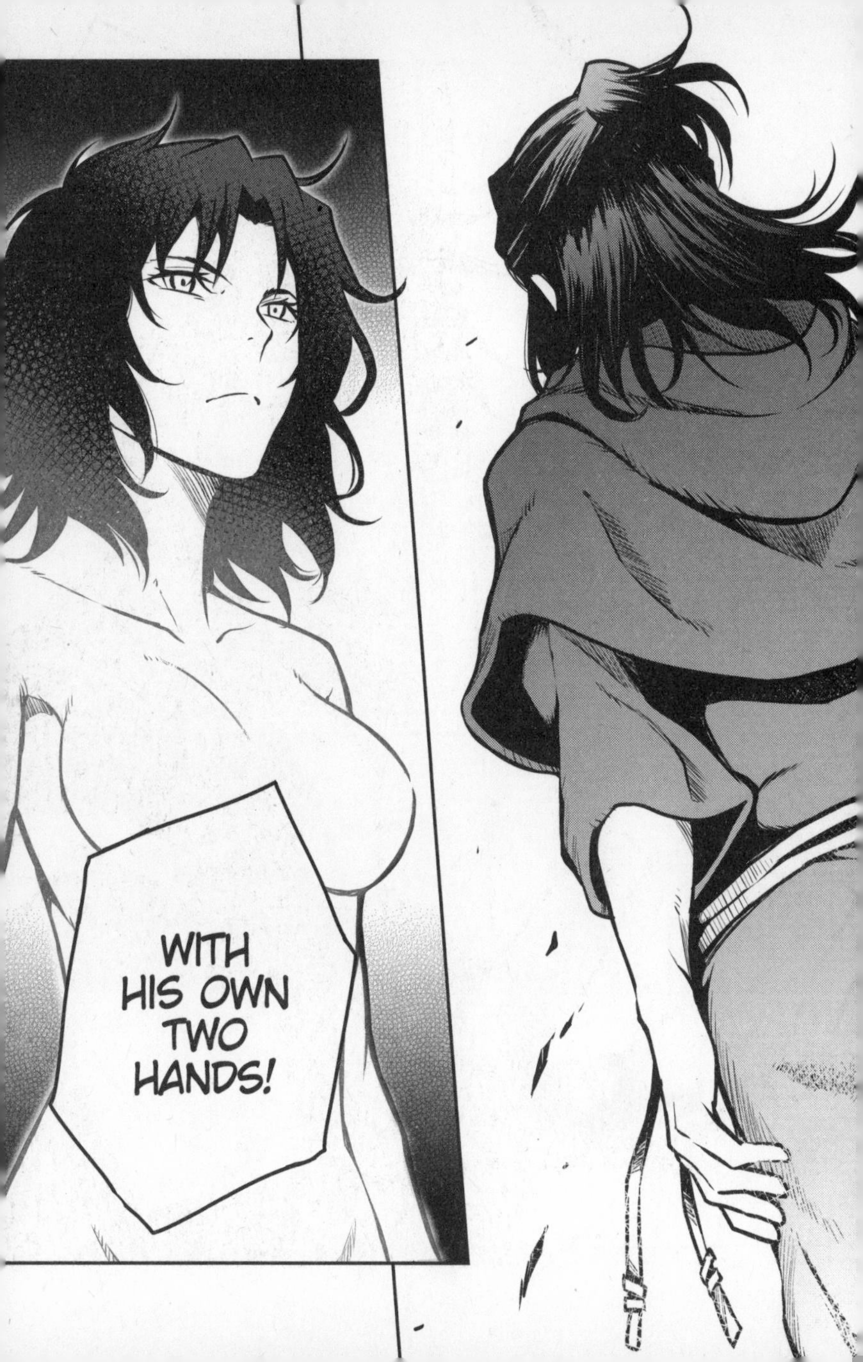
WITH HIS OWN TWO HANDS!

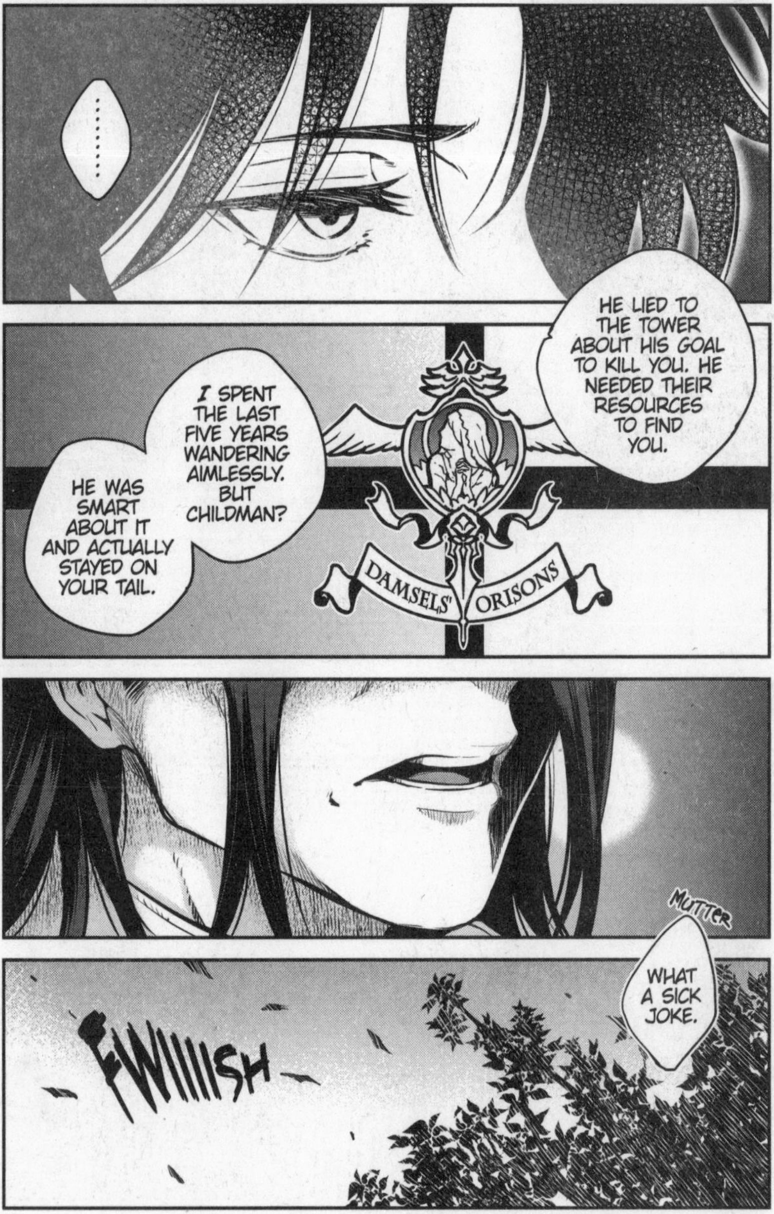
……
HE LIED TO THE TOWER ABOUT HIS GOAL TO KILL YOU. HE NEEDED THEIR RESOURCES TO FIND YOU.
I SPENT THE LAST FIVE YEARS WANDERING AIMLESSLY. BUT CHILDMAN?
HE WAS SMART ABOUT IT AND ACTUALLY STAYED ON YOUR TAIL.
DAMSELS' ORISONS
MUTTER
WHAT A SICK JOKE.
FWIIIIISH

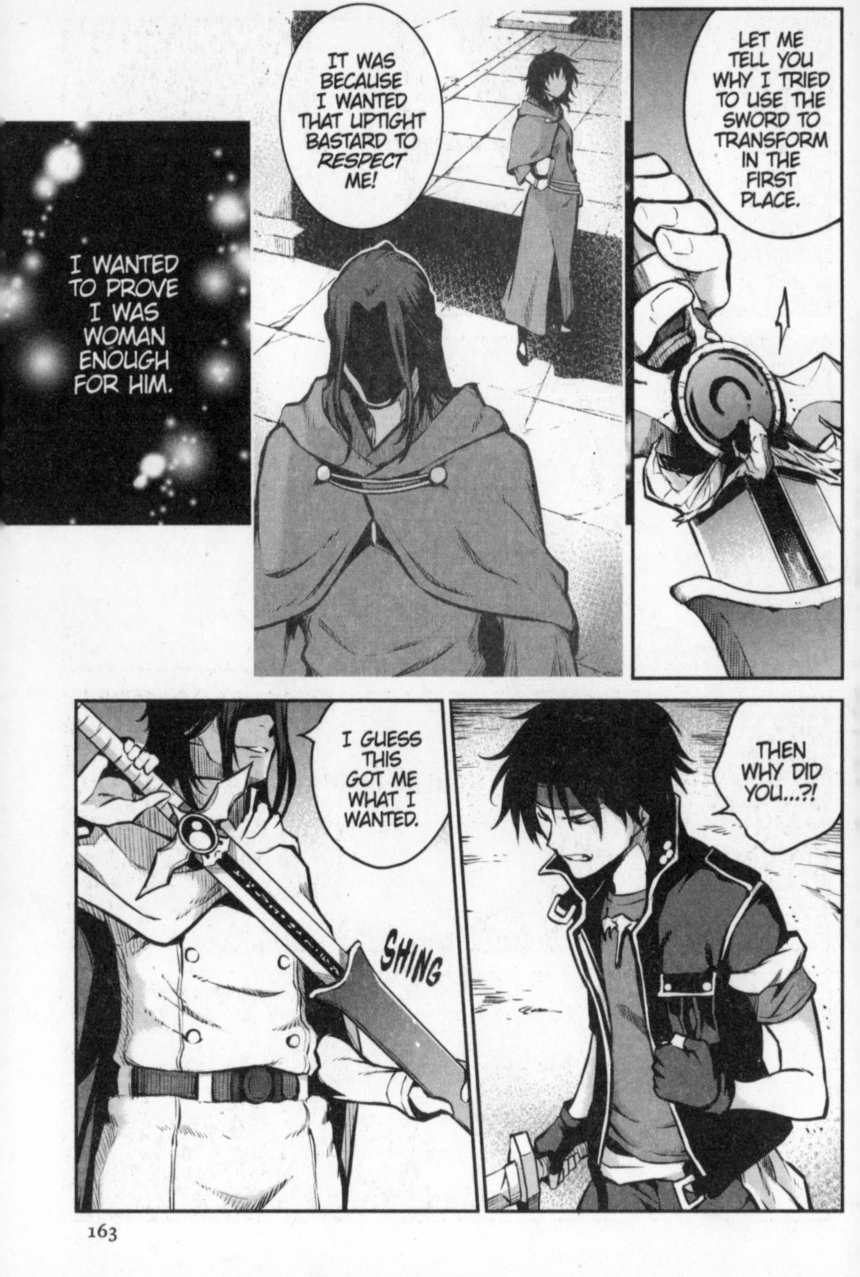
LET ME TELL YOU WHY I TRIED TO USE THE SWORD TO TRANSFORM IN THE FIRST PLACE.
IT WAS BECAUSE I WANTED THAT UPTIGHT BASTARD TO *RESPECT* ME!
I WANTED TO PROVE I WAS WOMAN ENOUGH FOR HIM.
THEN WHY DID YOU...?!
I GUESS THIS GOT ME WHAT I WANTED.
SHING

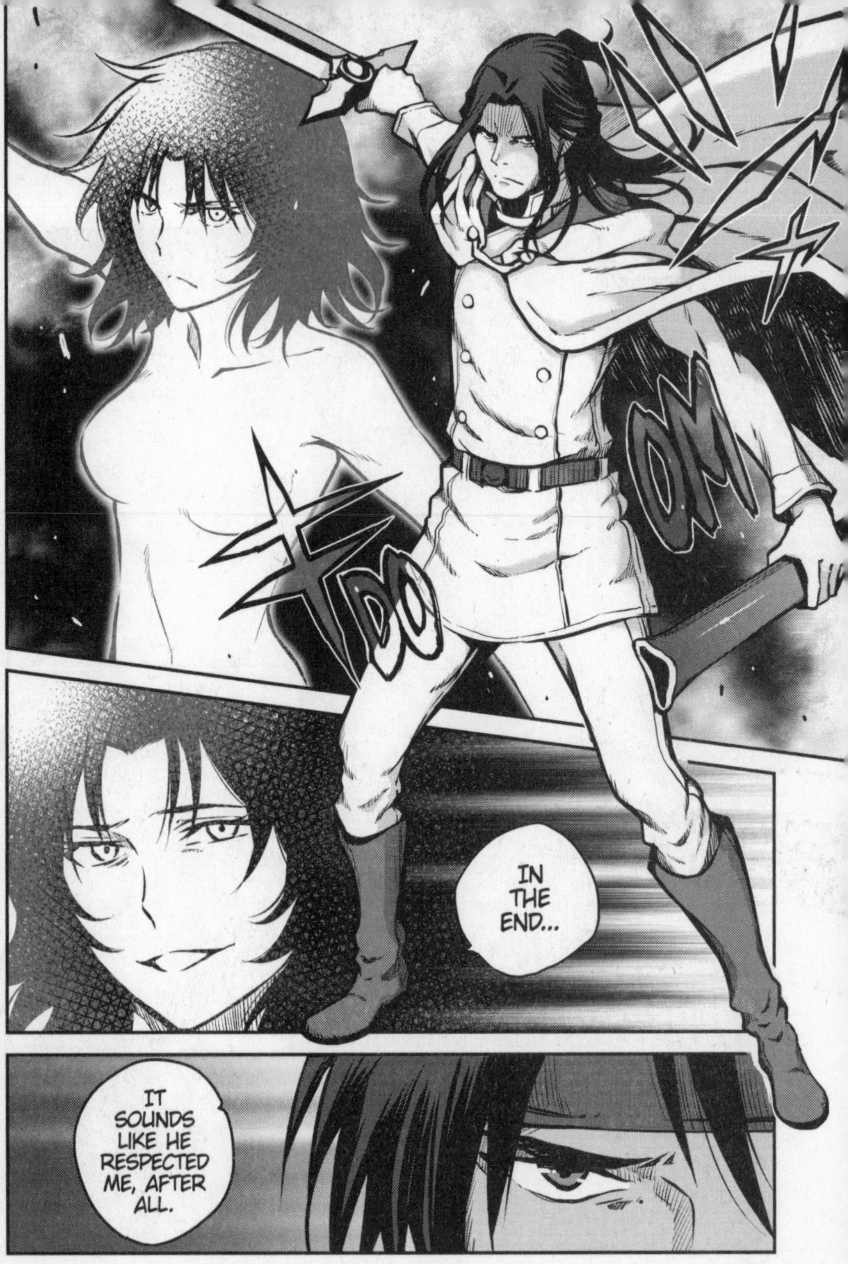
DO
OM
IN THE END...
IT SOUNDS LIKE HE RESPECTED ME, AFTER ALL.

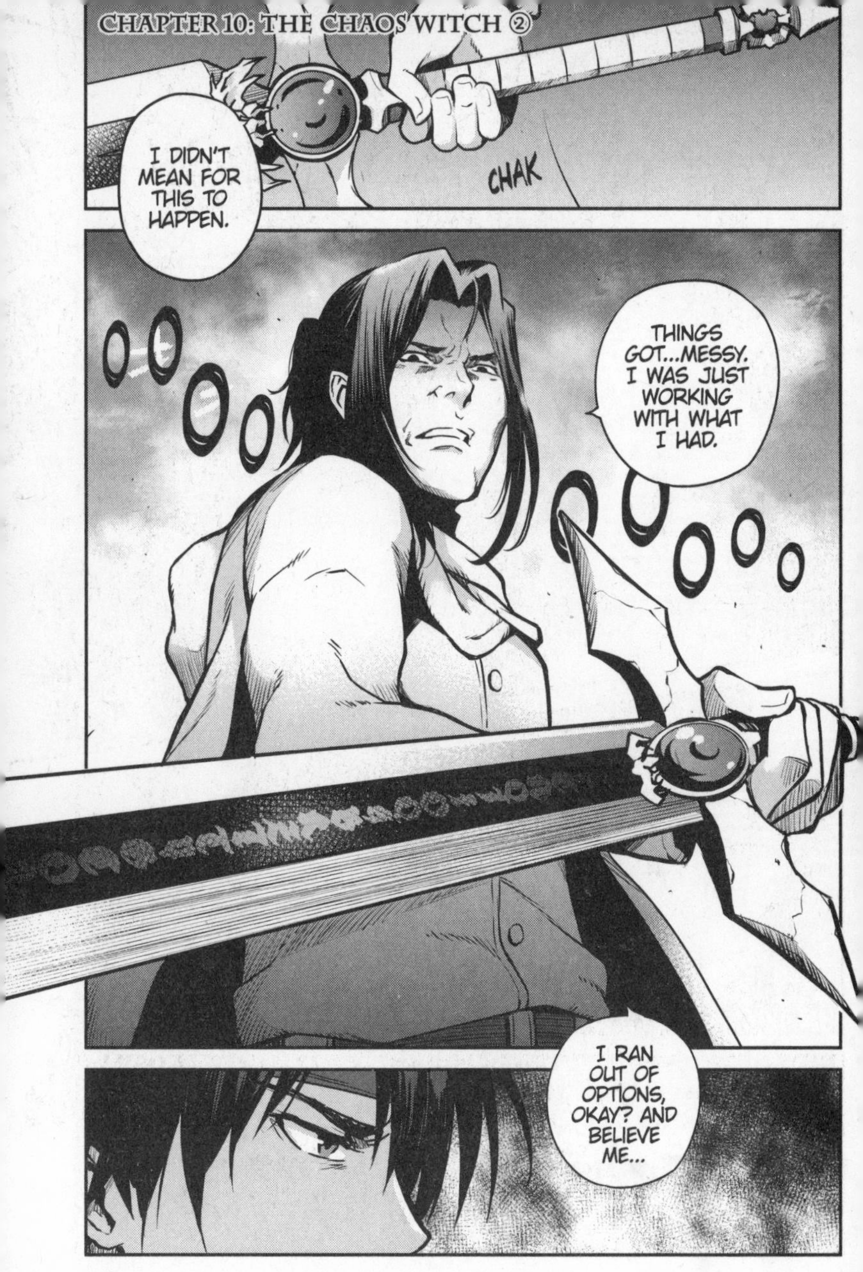
CHAK
I DIDN'T MEAN FOR THIS TO HAPPEN.
THINGS GOT...MESSY. I WAS JUST WORKING WITH WHAT I HAD.
I RAN OUT OF OPTIONS, OKAY? AND BELIEVE ME...

I WISH THERE'D BEEN ANOTHER WAY.

CHAPTER 10: THE CHAOS WITCH ②

Sorcerous Stabber ORPHEN

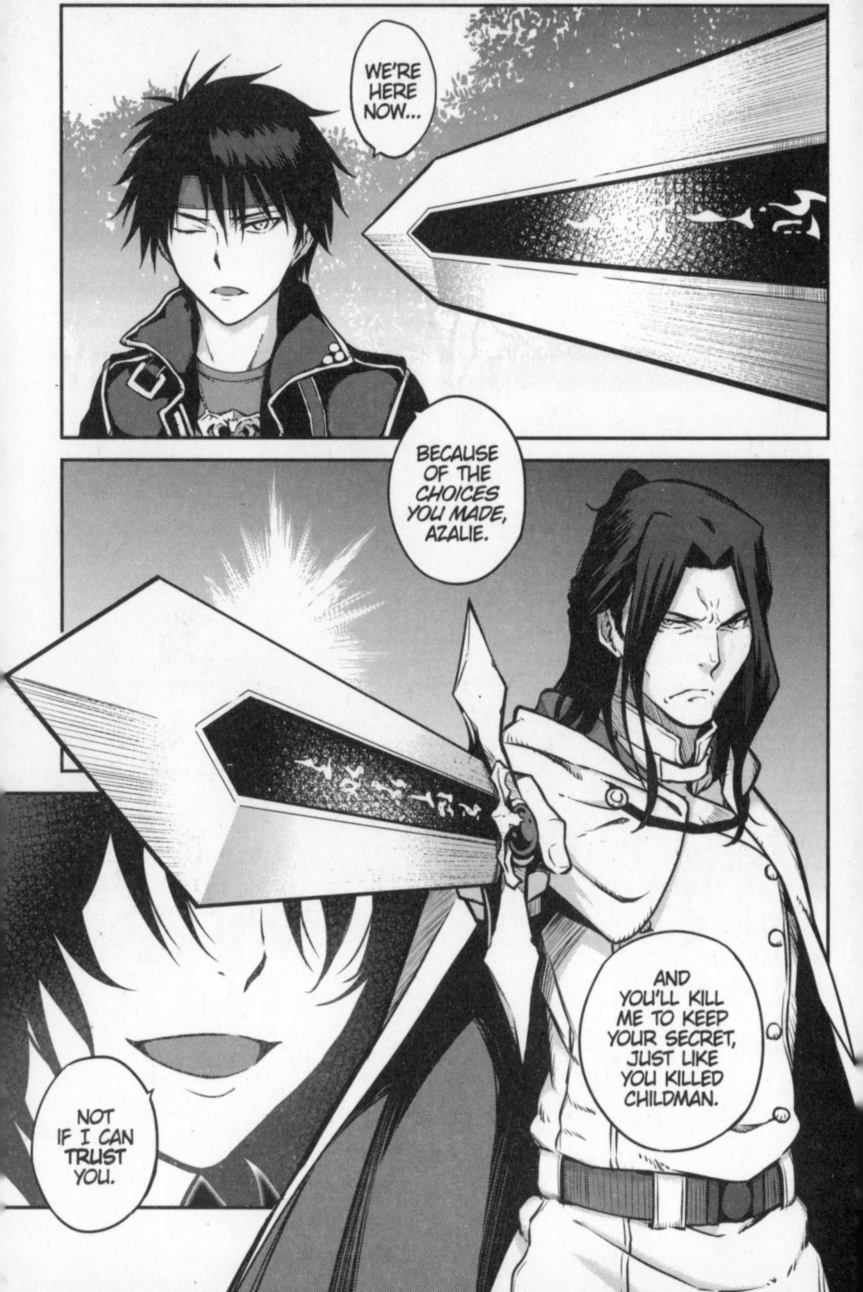
WE'RE HERE NOW...
BECAUSE OF THE CHOICES YOU MADE, AZALIE.
AND YOU'LL KILL ME TO KEEP YOUR SECRET, JUST LIKE YOU KILLED CHILDMAN.
NOT IF I CAN TRUST YOU.

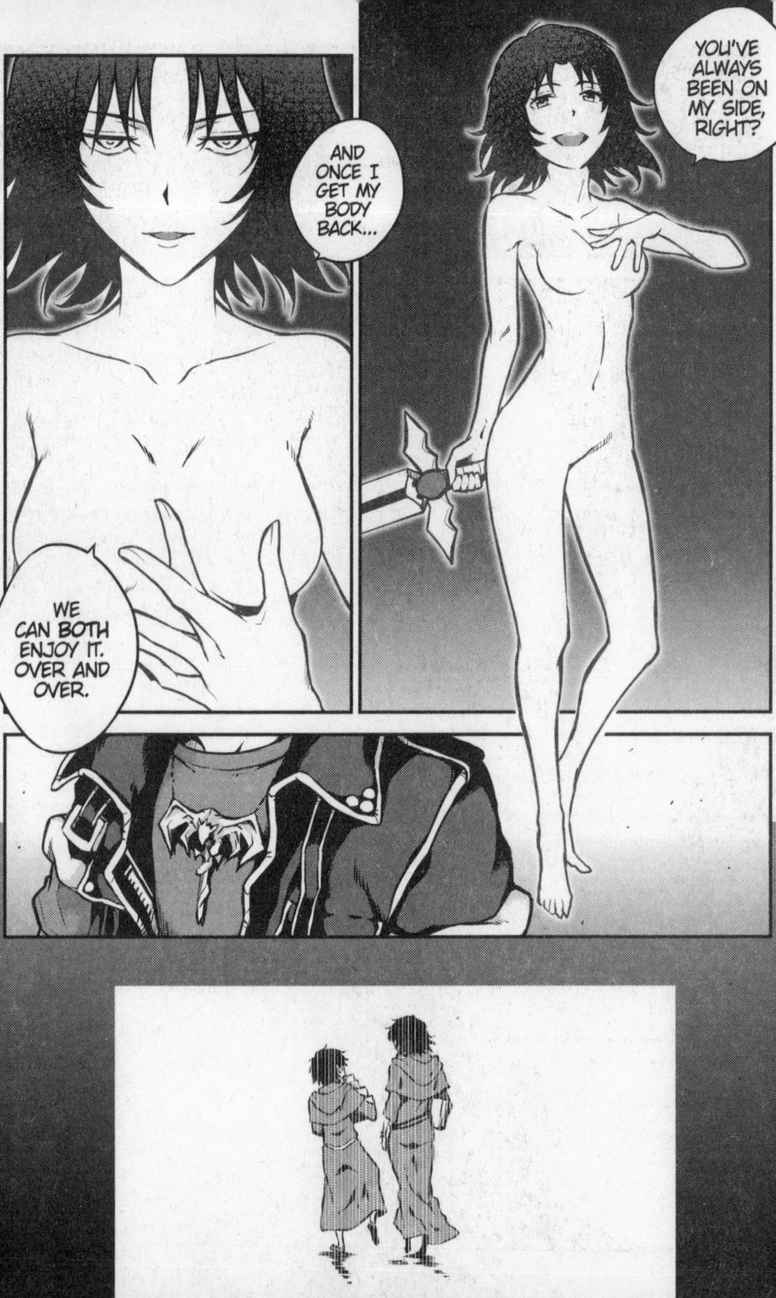
YOU'VE ALWAYS BEEN ON MY SIDE, RIGHT?
AND ONCE I GET MY BODY BACK...
WE CAN BOTH ENJOY IT. OVER AND OVER.

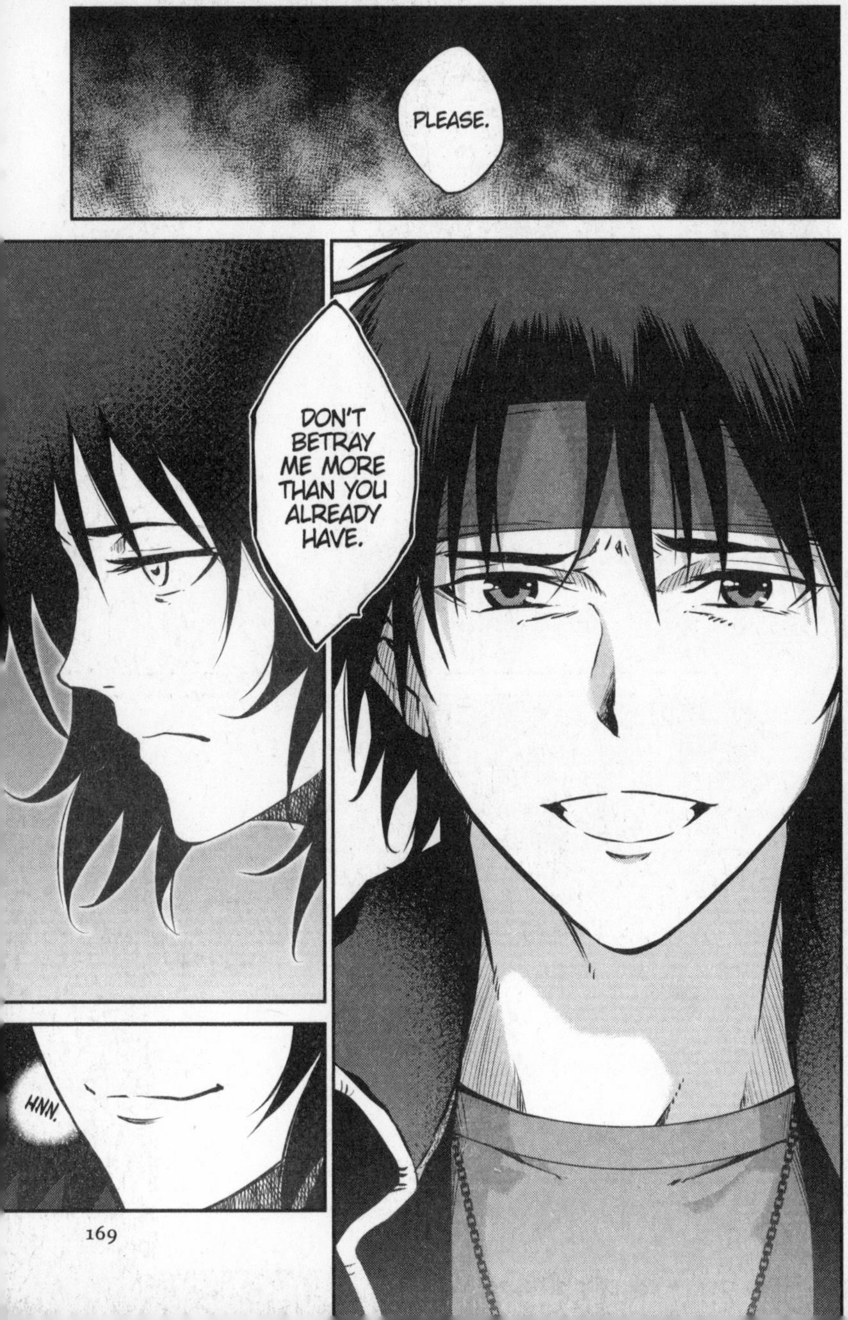
PLEASE.
DON'T BETRAY ME MORE THAN YOU ALREADY HAVE.
HNN.

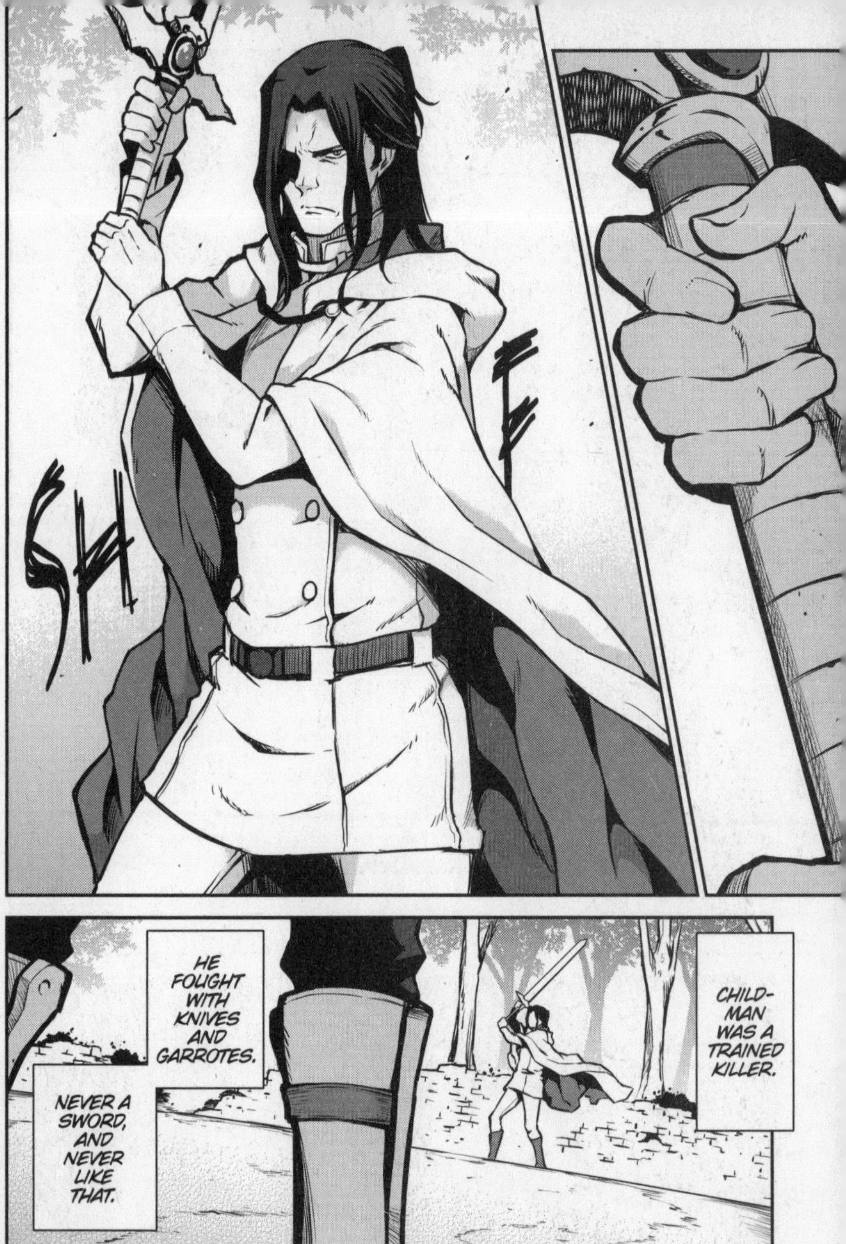
CHILD-MAN WAS A TRAINED KILLER.
HE FOUGHT WITH KNIVES AND GARROTES.
NEVER A SWORD, AND NEVER LIKE THAT.

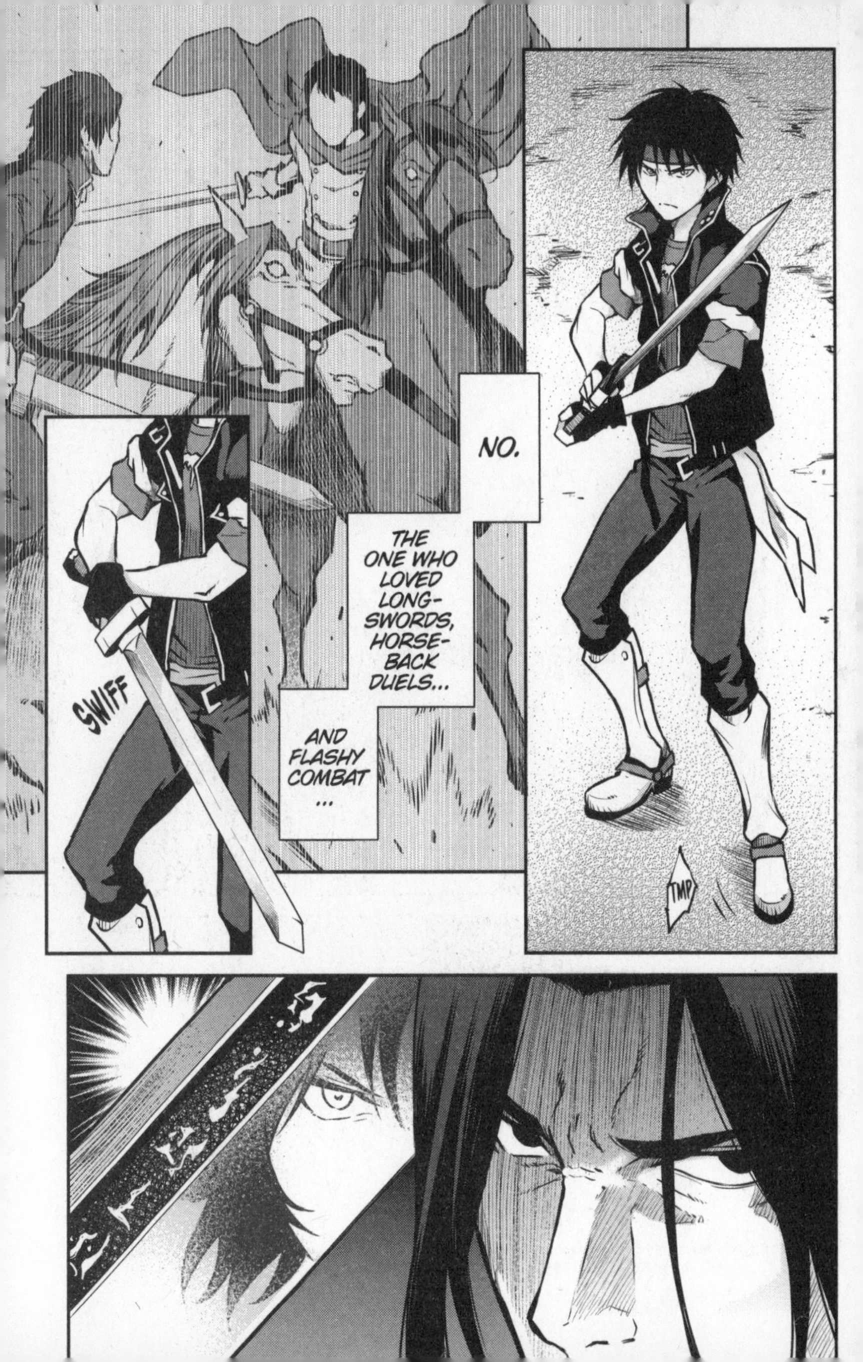
TMP
NO.
THE ONE WHO LOVED LONG-SWORDS, HORSE-BACK DUELS...
AND FLASHY COMBAT ...
SWIFF

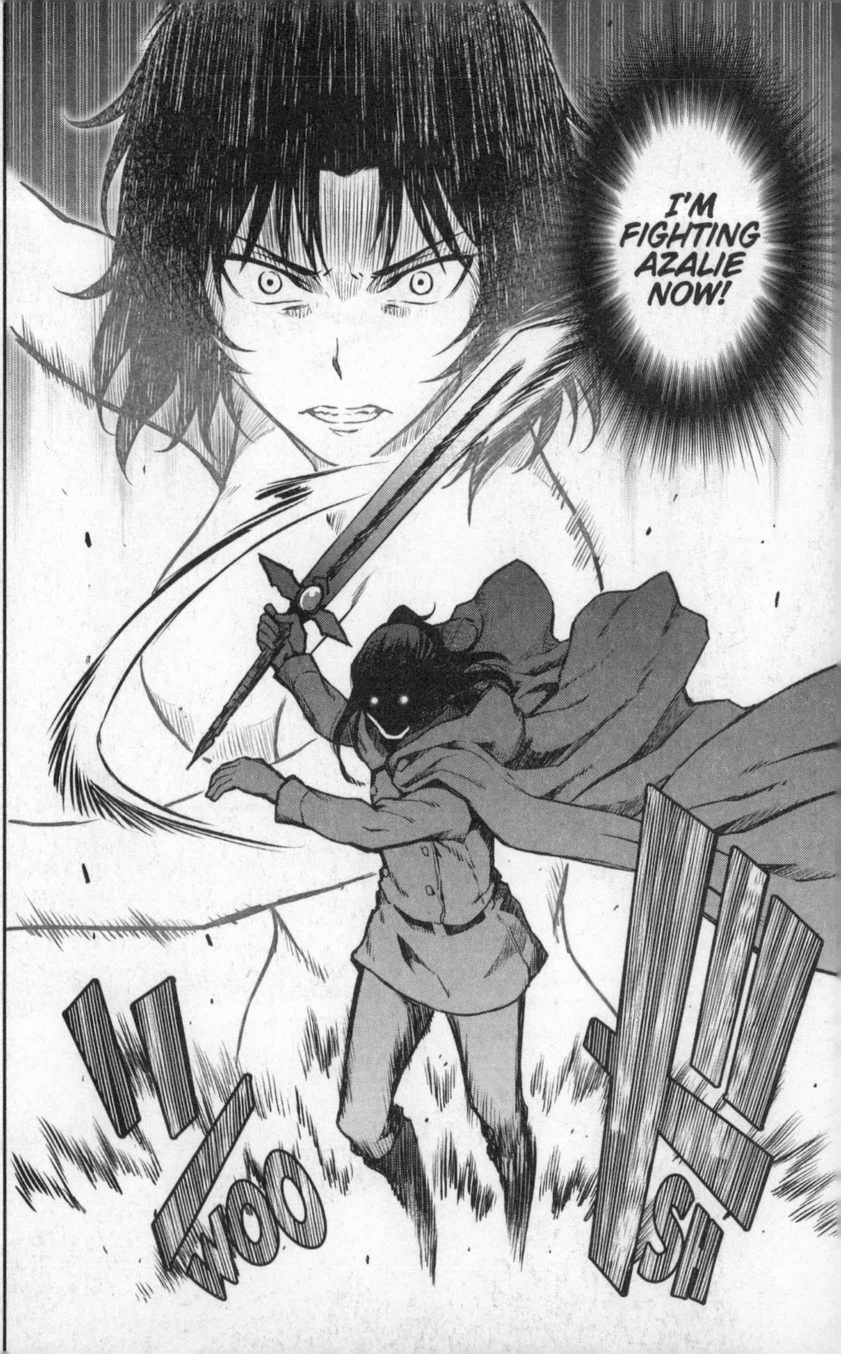
I'M FIGHTING AZALIE NOW!
WHOOSH

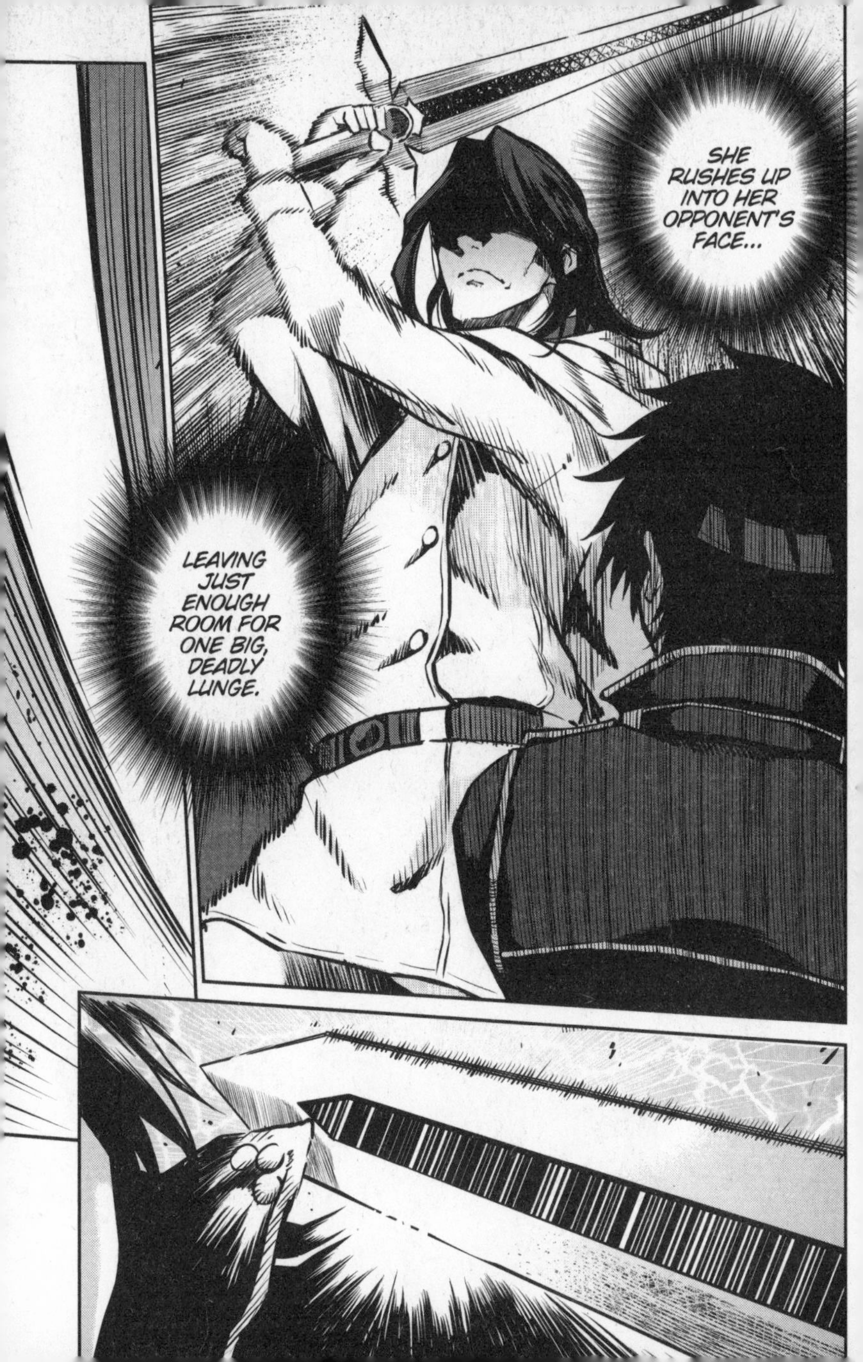
SHE RUSHES UP INTO HER OPPONENT'S FACE...
LEAVING JUST ENOUGH ROOM FOR ONE BIG, DEADLY LUNGE.

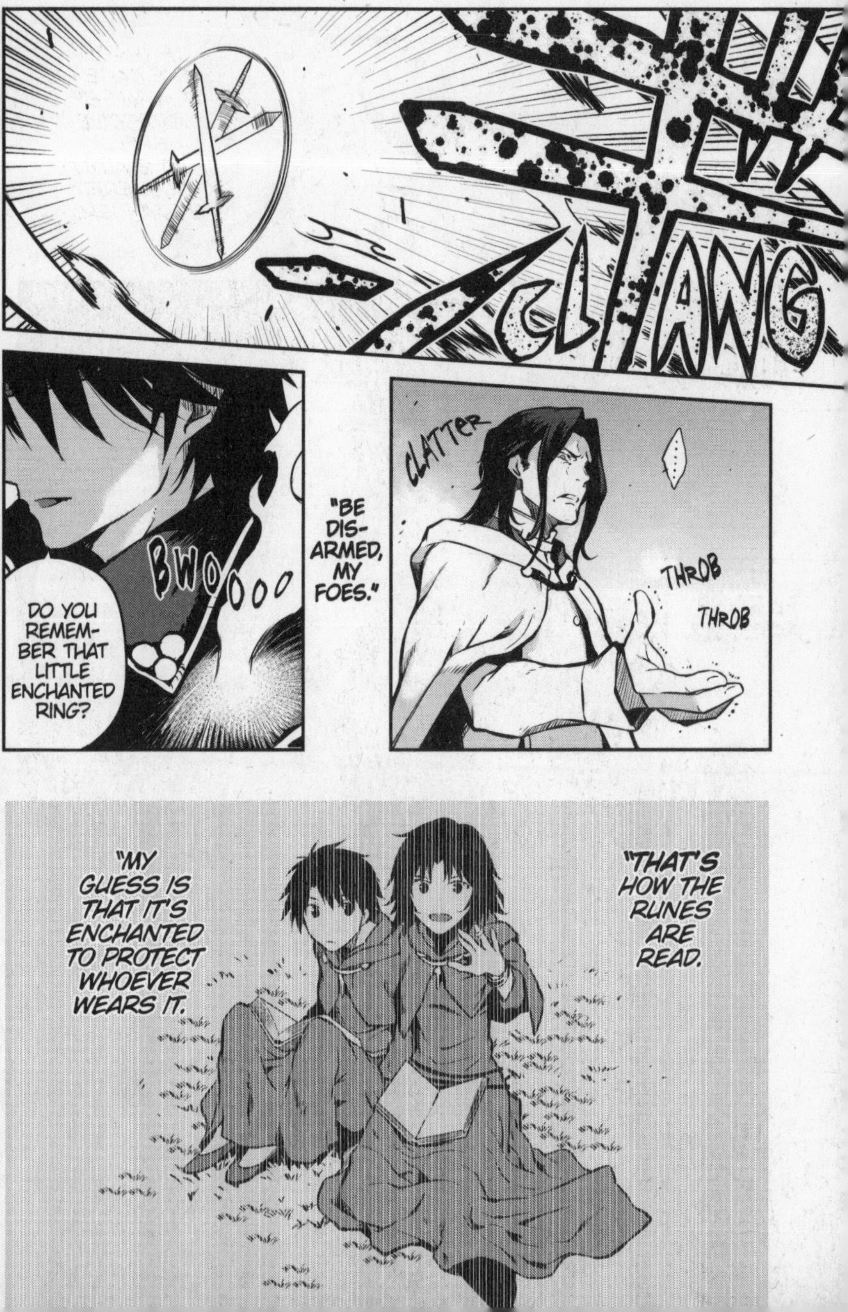
CLANG
CLATTER
THROB
THROB
"BE DISARMED, MY FOES."
BWOOOO
DO YOU REMEMBER THAT LITTLE ENCHANTED RING?
"THAT'S HOW THE RUNES ARE READ.
"MY GUESS IS THAT IT'S ENCHANTED TO PROTECT WHOEVER WEARS IT.

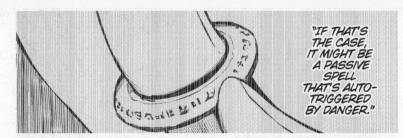

"IF THAT'S THE CASE, IT MIGHT BE A PASSIVE SPELL THAT'S AUTO-TRIGGERED BY DANGER."

TOO SMALL TO WEAR...

BUT EASY TO SWALLOW.

PAT

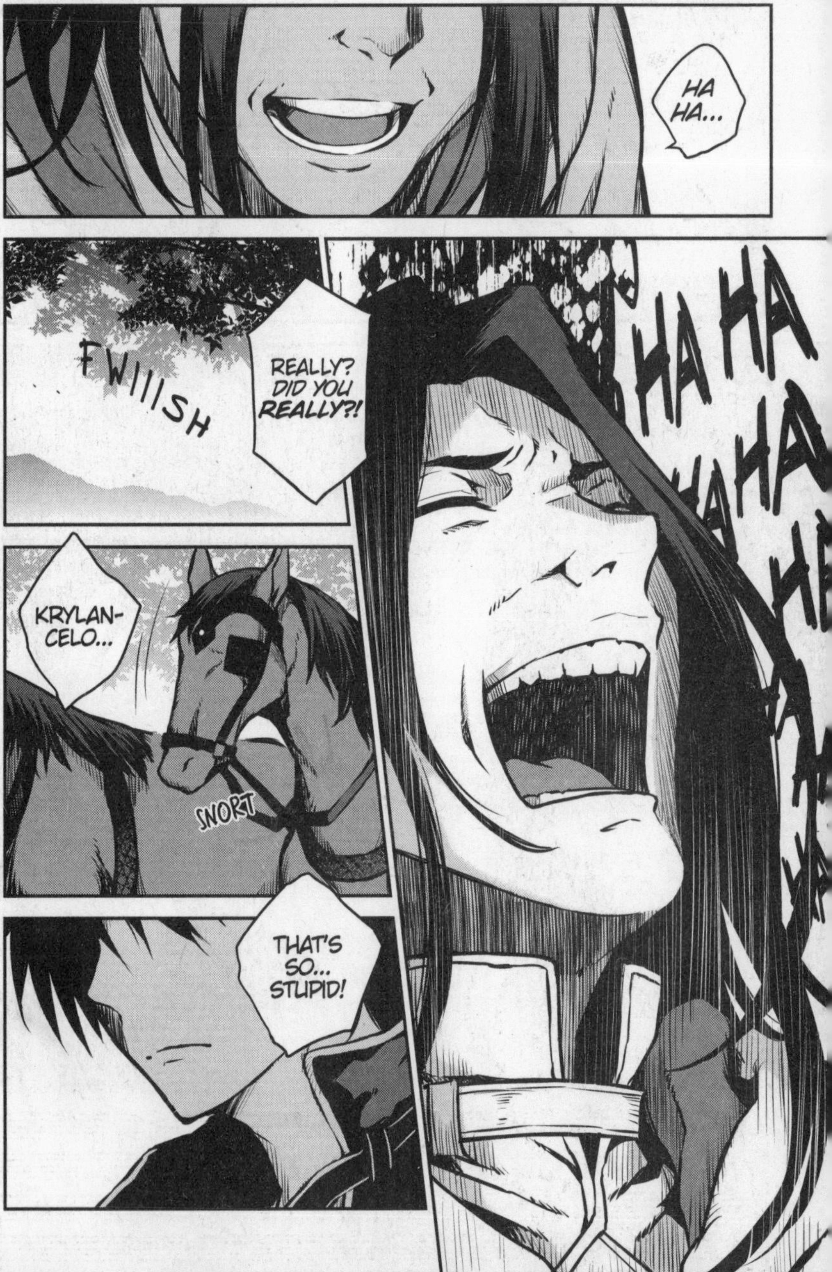
HA HA...
HA HA
HA HA
HA HA
REALLY? DID YOU REALLY?!
FWIIISH
KRYLAN-CELO...
SNORT
THAT'S SO... STUPID!

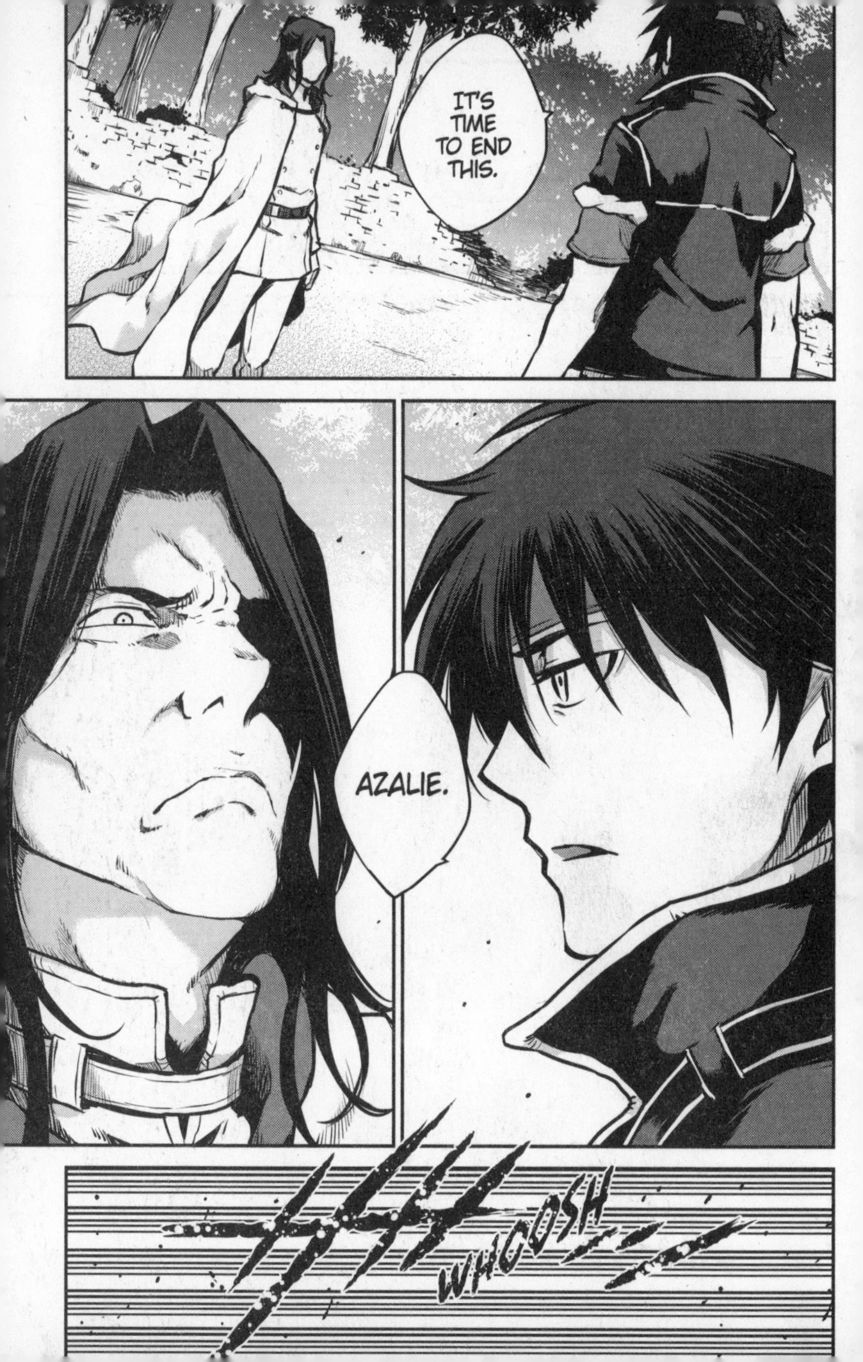
IT'S TIME TO END THIS.
AZALIE.
WHOOSH

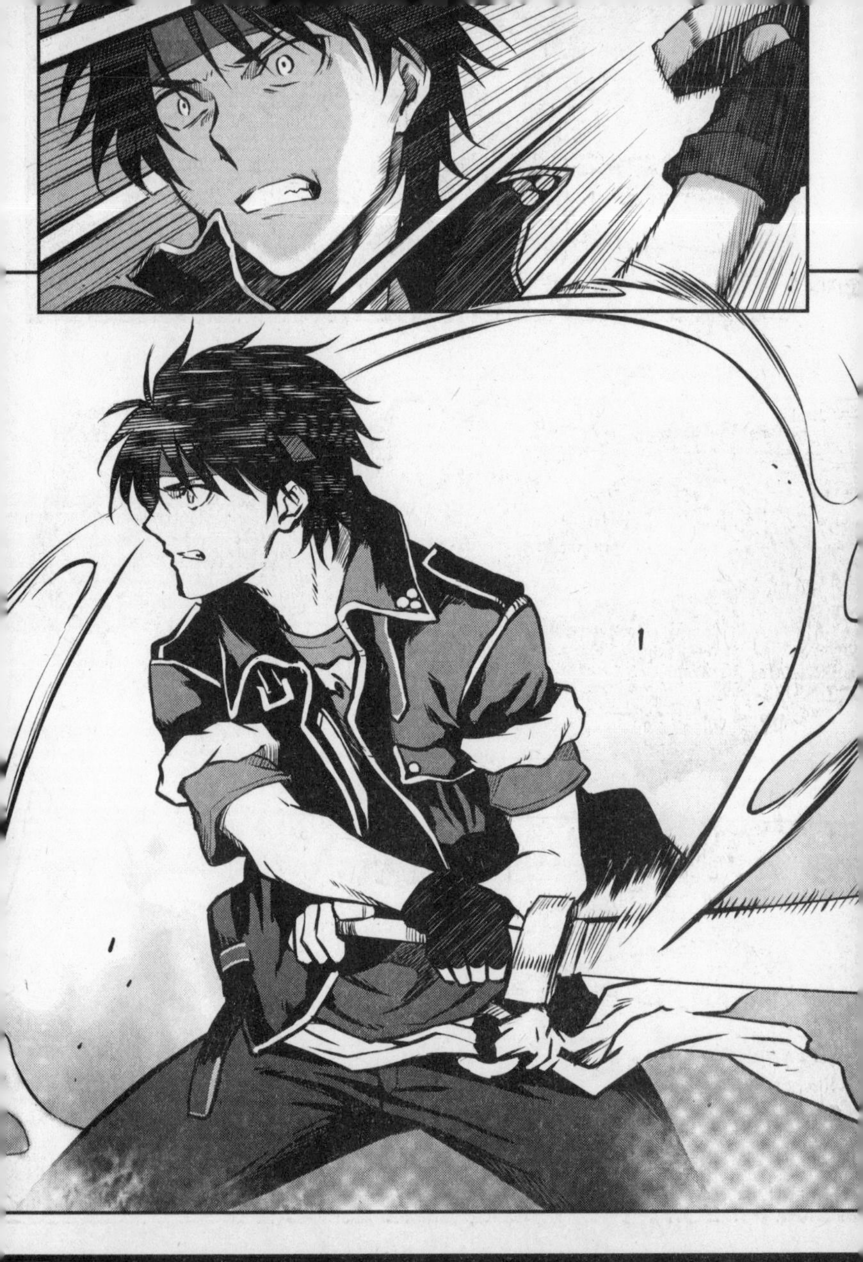

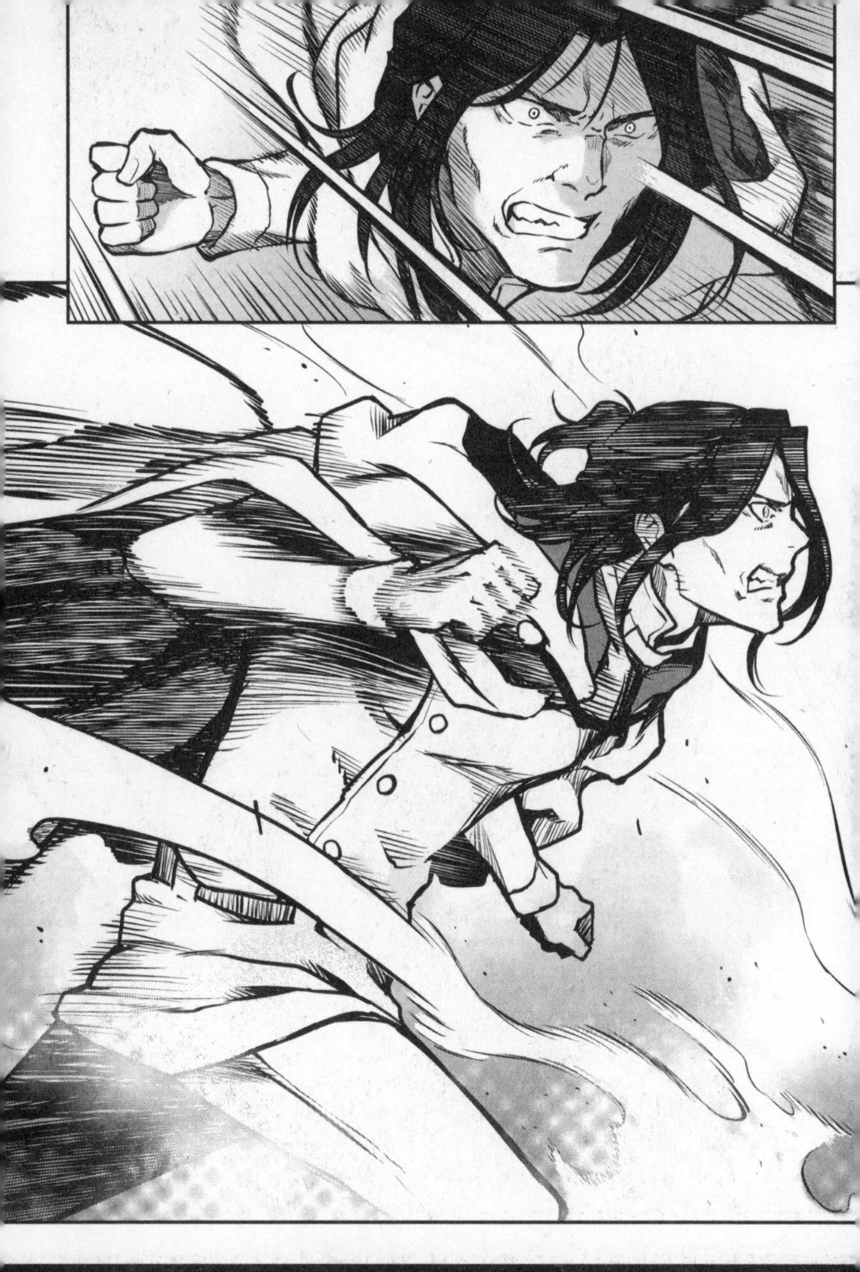

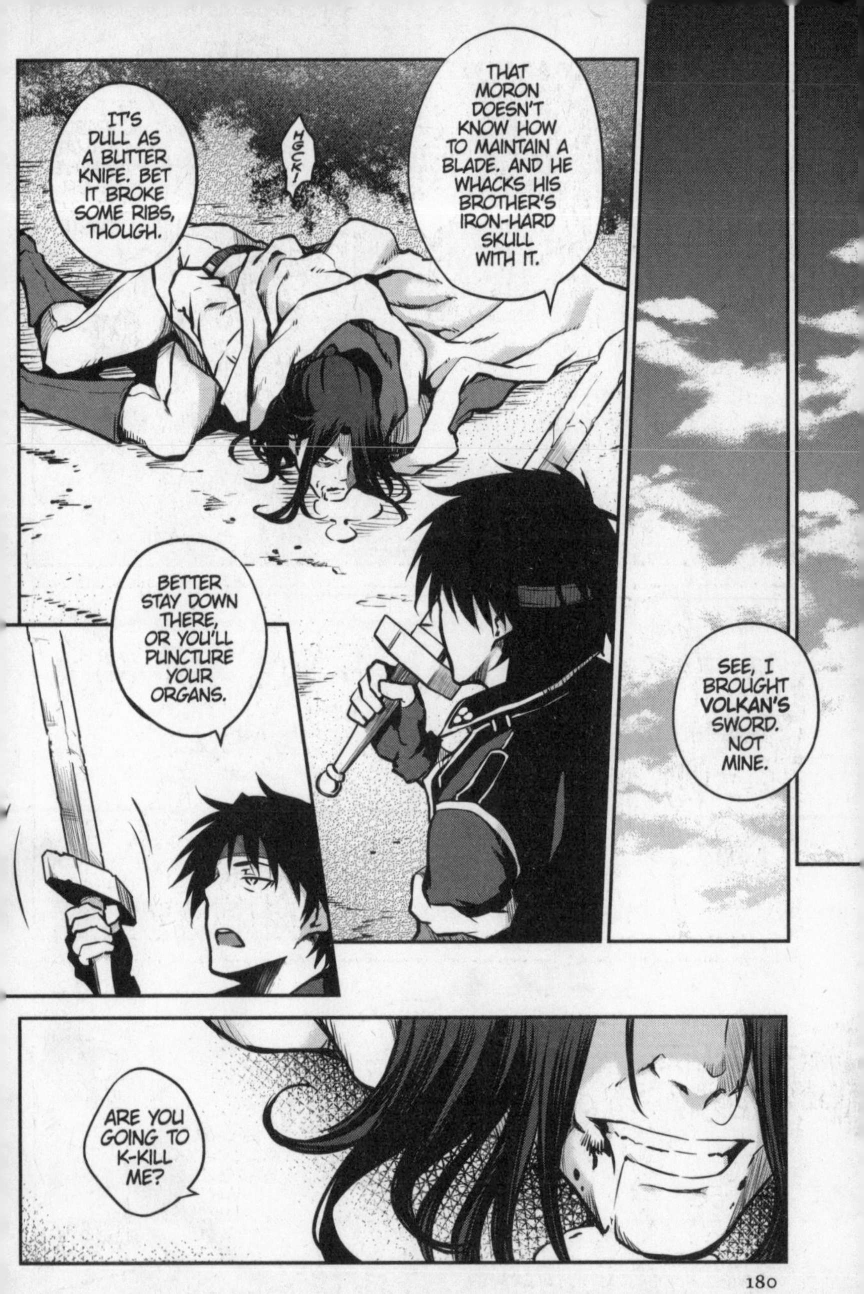

SEE, I BROUGHT VOLKAN'S SWORD. NOT MINE.
THAT MORON DOESN'T KNOW HOW TO MAINTAIN A BLADE. AND HE WHACKS HIS BROTHER'S IRON-HARD SKULL WITH IT.
HGCK!
IT'S DULL AS A BUTTER KNIFE. BET IT BROKE SOME RIBS, THOUGH.
BETTER STAY DOWN THERE, OR YOU'LL PUNCTURE YOUR ORGANS.
ARE YOU GOING TO K-KILL ME?

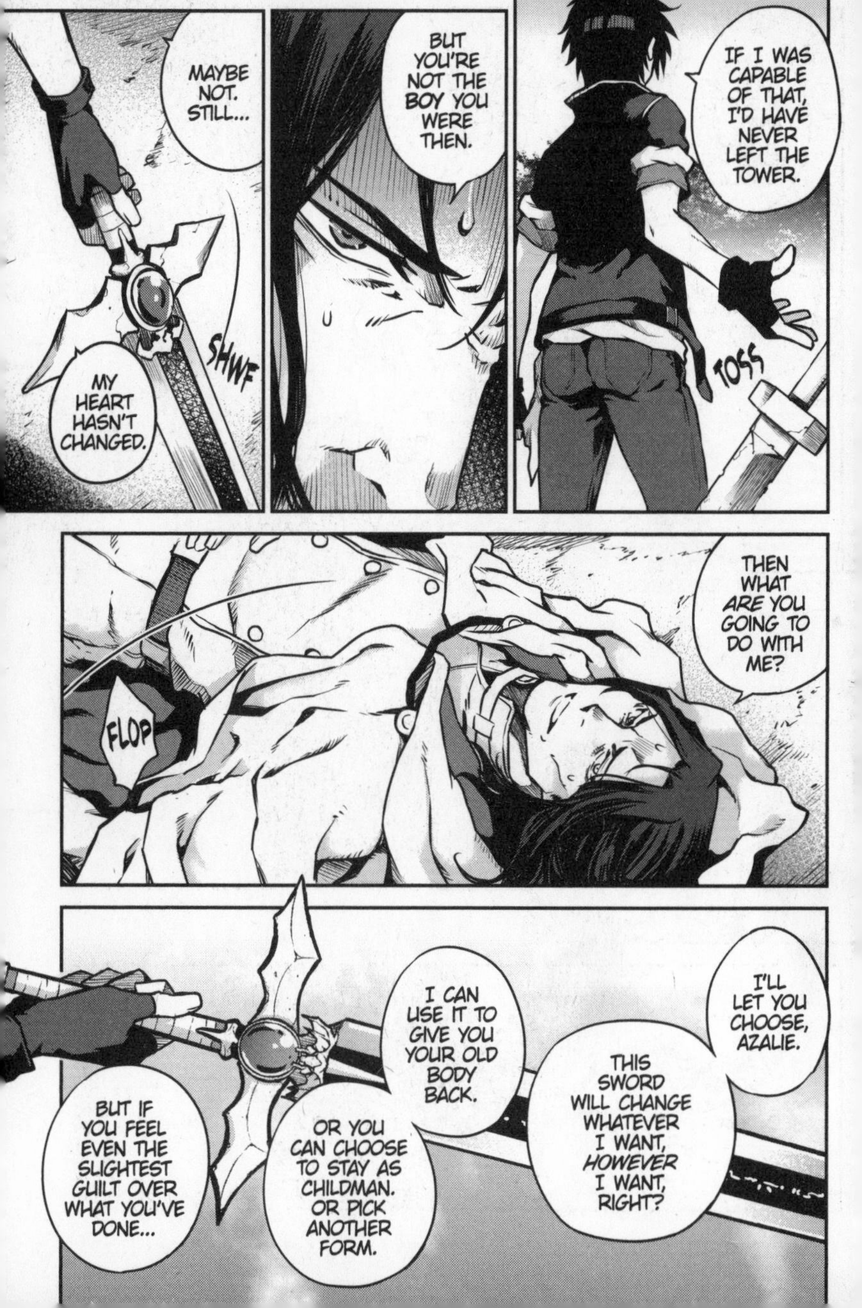
IF I WAS CAPABLE OF THAT, I'D HAVE NEVER LEFT THE TOWER.
TOSS
BUT YOU'RE NOT THE BOY YOU WERE THEN.
MAYBE NOT. STILL...
SHWF
MY HEART HASN'T CHANGED.
THEN WHAT ARE YOU GOING TO DO WITH ME?
FLOP
I'LL LET YOU CHOOSE, AZALIE.
THIS SWORD WILL CHANGE WHATEVER I WANT, *HOWEVER* I WANT, RIGHT?
I CAN USE IT TO GIVE YOU YOUR OLD BODY BACK.
OR YOU CAN CHOOSE TO STAY AS CHILDMAN. OR PICK ANOTHER FORM.
BUT IF YOU FEEL EVEN THE SLIGHTEST GUILT OVER WHAT YOU'VE DONE...

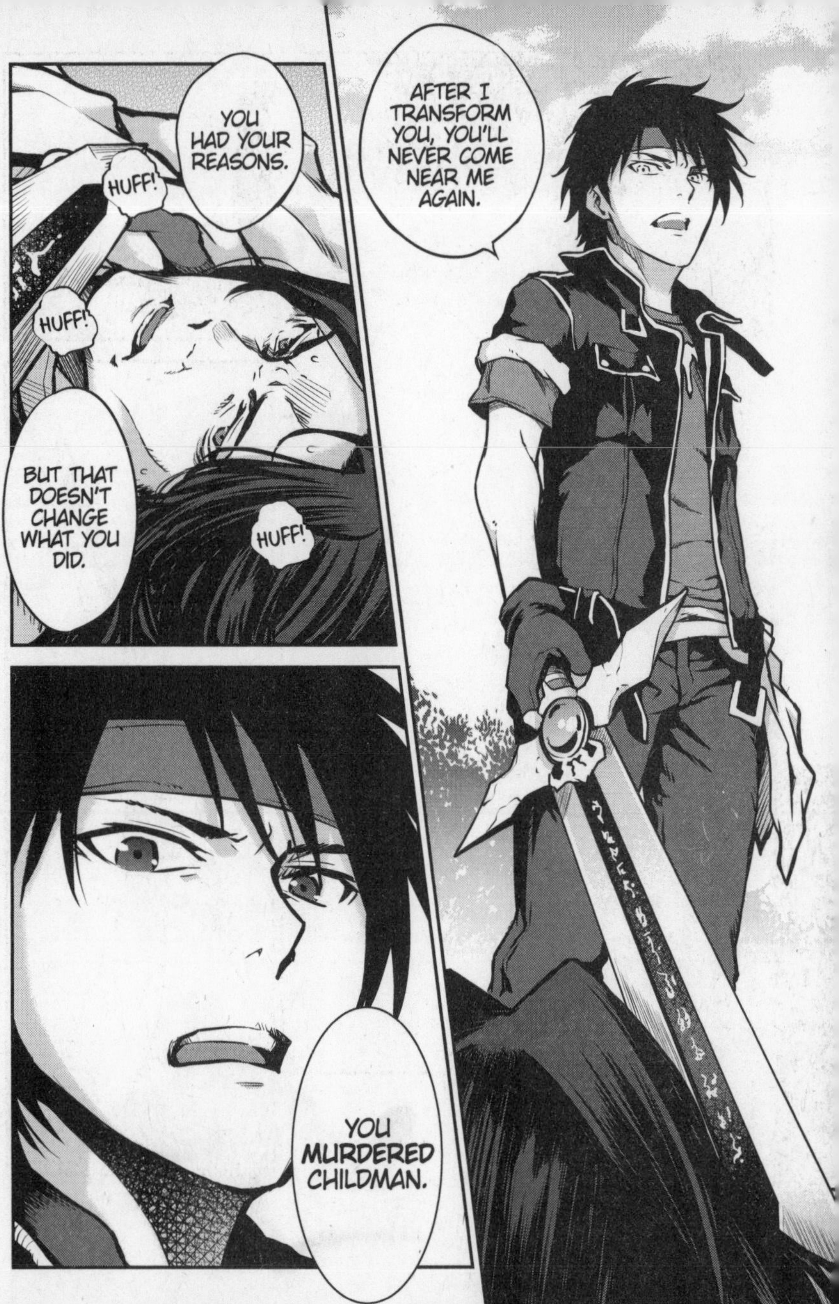
AFTER I TRANSFORM YOU, YOU'LL NEVER COME NEAR ME AGAIN.
YOU HAD YOUR REASONS.
HUFF!
HUFF!
BUT THAT DOESN'T CHANGE WHAT YOU DID.
HUFF!
YOU MURDERED CHILDMAN.

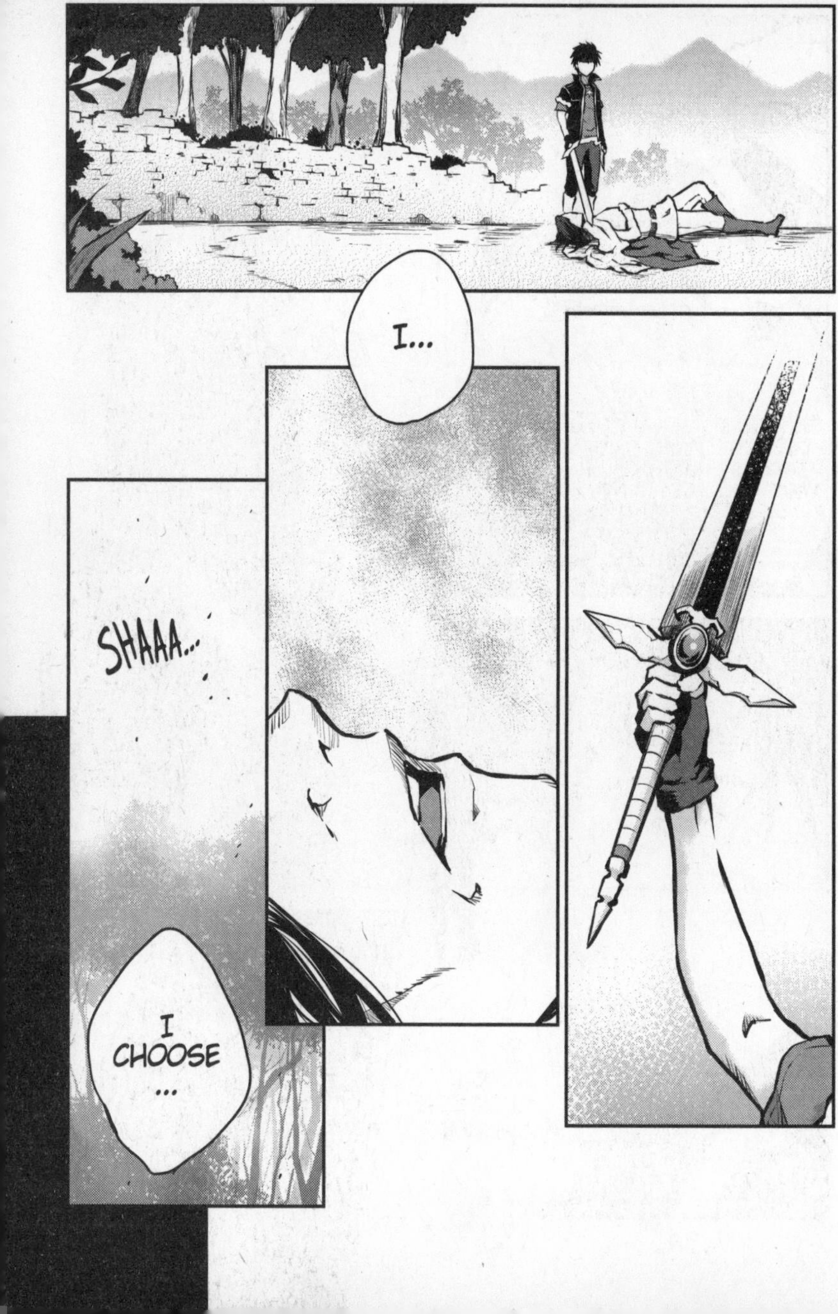
I...
SHAAA...
I CHOOSE ...

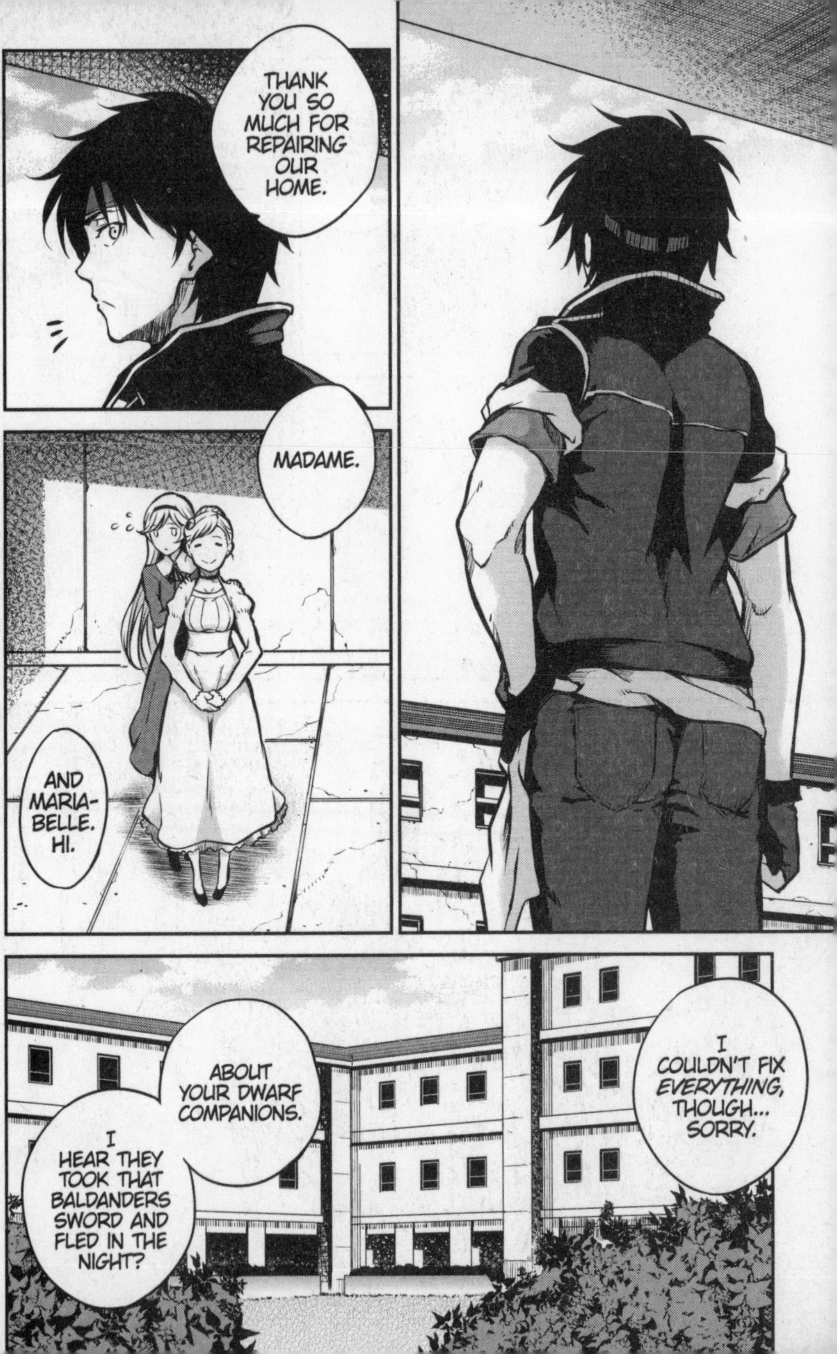

THANK YOU SO MUCH FOR REPAIRING OUR HOME.
MADAME.
AND MARIA-BELLE. HI.
I COULDN'T FIX *EVERYTHING*, THOUGH... SORRY.
ABOUT YOUR DWARF COMPANIONS.
I HEAR THEY TOOK THAT BALDANDERS SWORD AND FLED IN THE NIGHT?

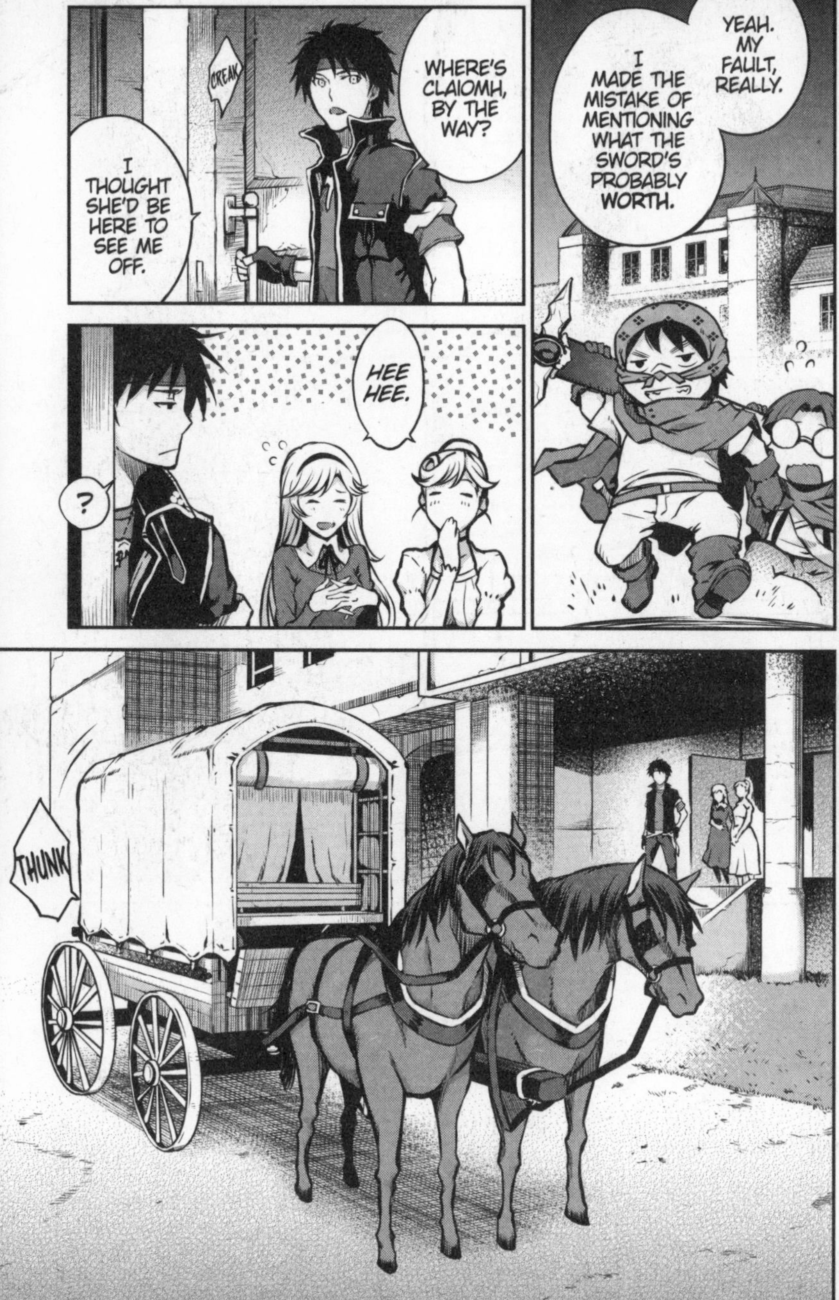

CREAK
WHERE'S CLAIOMH, BY THE WAY?
I THOUGHT SHE'D BE HERE TO SEE ME OFF.
HEE HEE.
?
YEAH. MY FAULT, REALLY.
I MADE THE MISTAKE OF MENTIONING WHAT THE SWORD'S PROBABLY WORTH.
THUNK

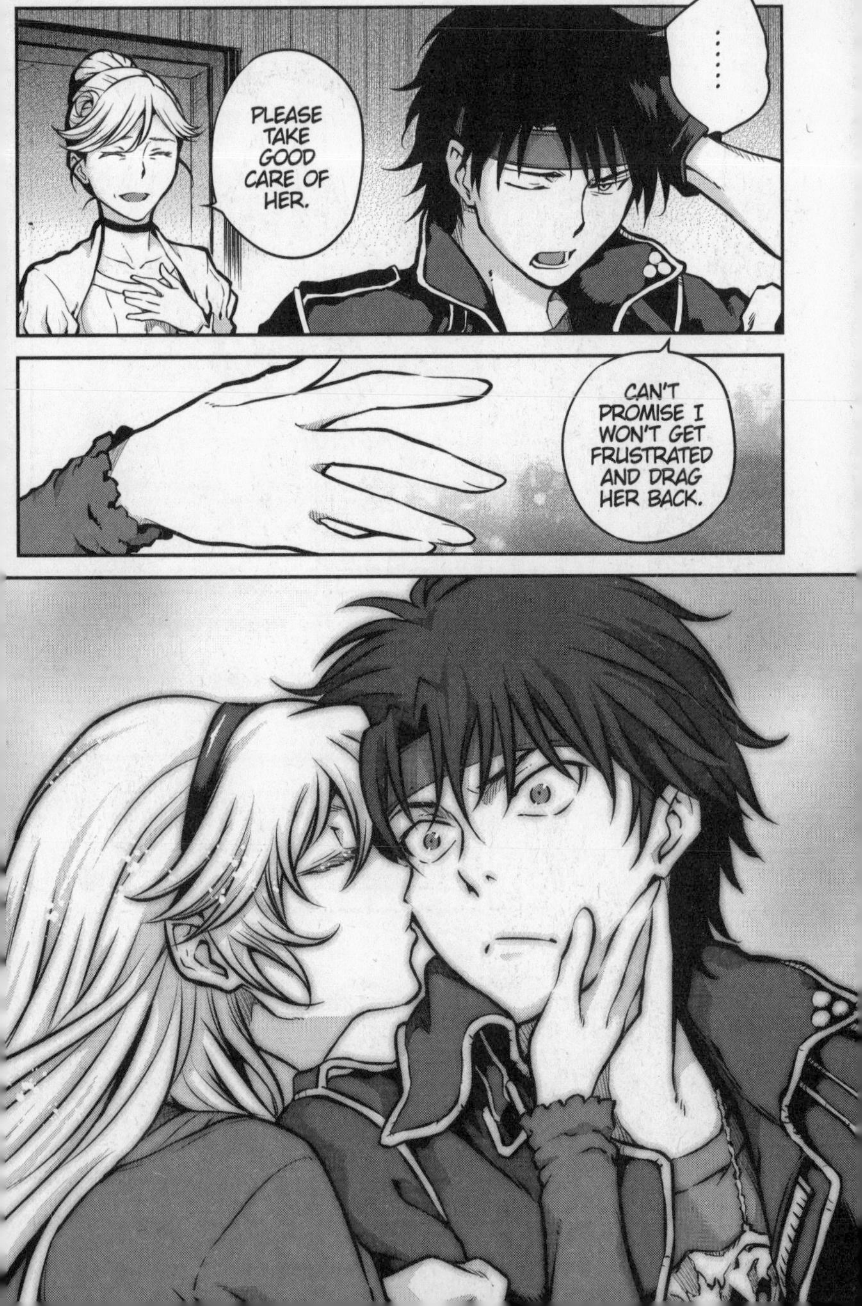
......
PLEASE TAKE GOOD CARE OF HER.
CAN'T PROMISE I WON'T GET FRUSTRATED AND DRAG HER BACK.

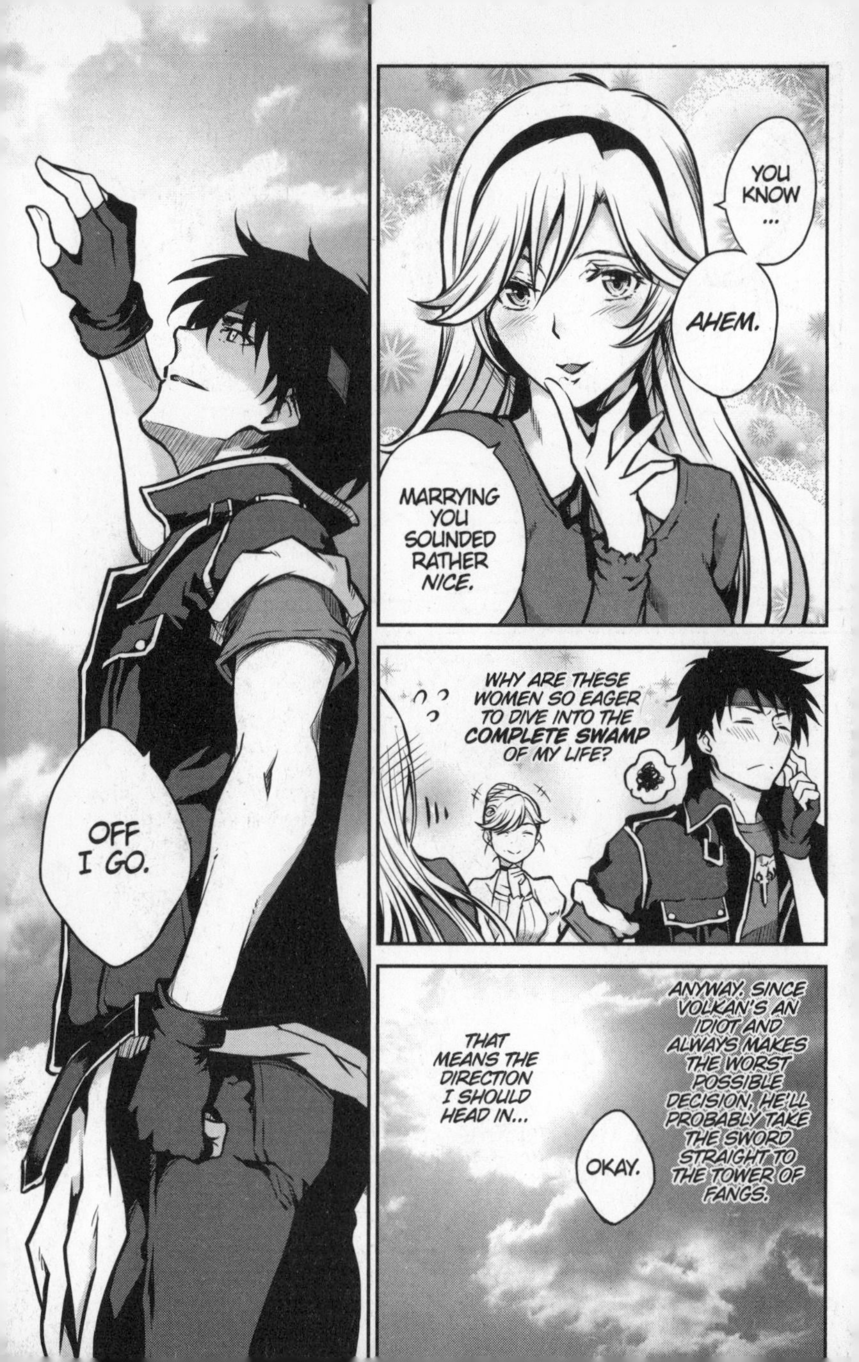
YOU KNOW ...
AHEM.
MARRYING YOU SOUNDED RATHER NICE.
WHY ARE THESE WOMEN SO EAGER TO DIVE INTO THE COMPLETE SWAMP OF MY LIFE?
ANYWAY. SINCE VOLKAN'S AN IDIOT AND ALWAYS MAKES THE WORST POSSIBLE DECISION, HE'LL PROBABLY TAKE THE SWORD STRAIGHT TO THE TOWER OF FANGS.
THAT MEANS THE DIRECTION I SHOULD HEAD IN...
OKAY.
OFF I GO.

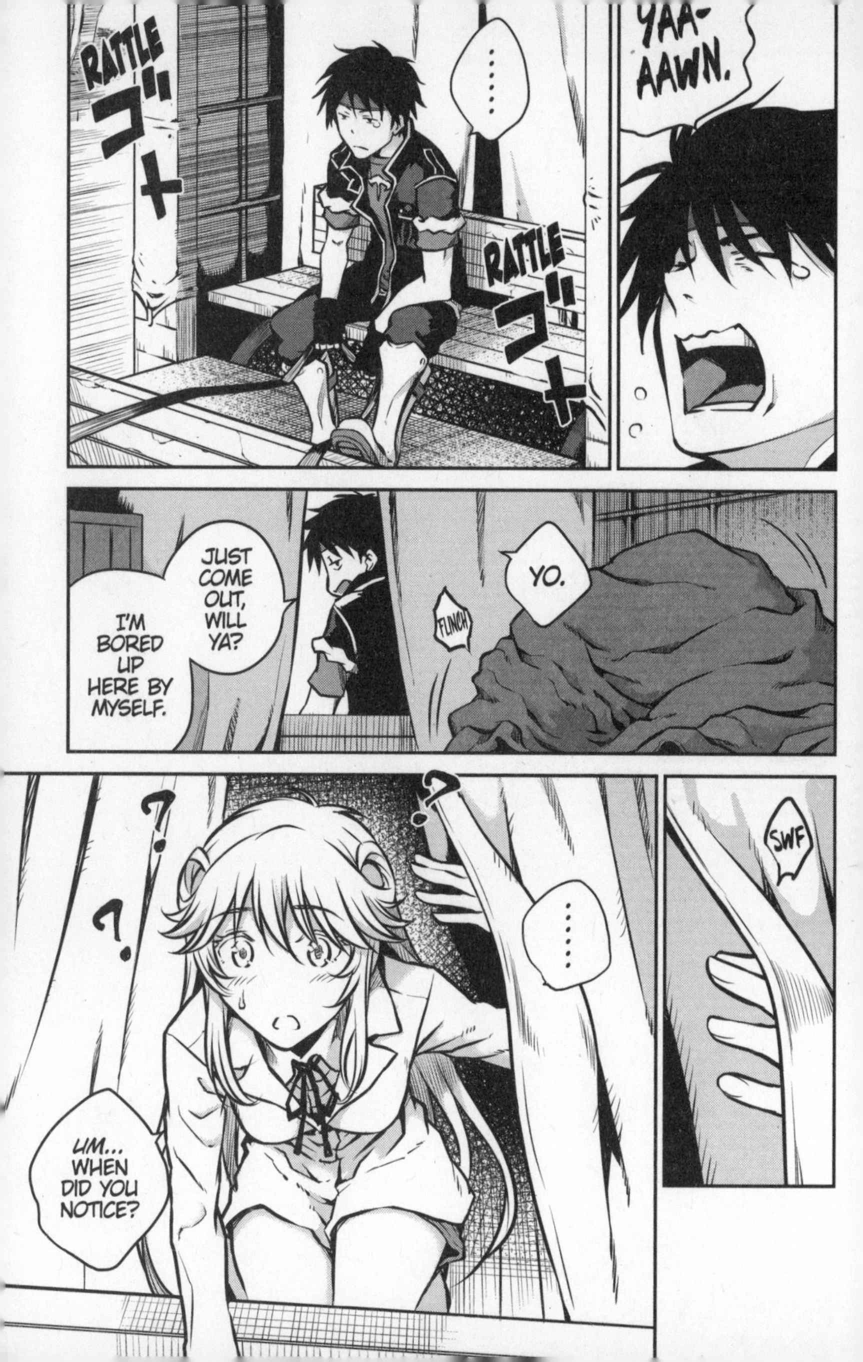
YAA-AAWN.
......
RATTLE
RATTLE
YO.
FLINCH
JUST COME OUT, WILL YA?
I'M BORED UP HERE BY MYSELF.
SWF
?
?
?
......
UM... WHEN DID YOU NOTICE?

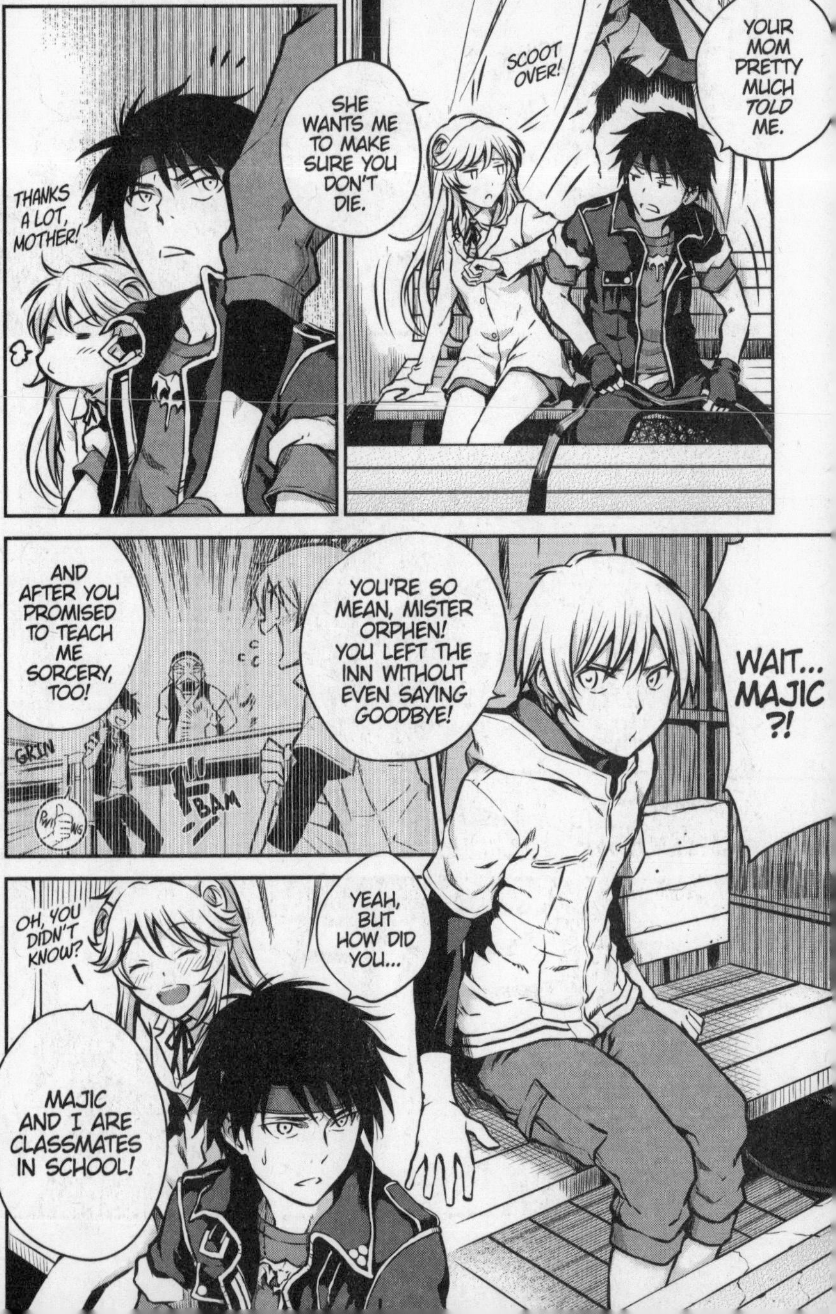
YOUR MOM PRETTY MUCH TOLD ME.
SCOOT OVER!
SHE WANTS ME TO MAKE SURE YOU DON'T DIE.
THANKS A LOT, MOTHER!
YOU'RE SO MEAN, MISTER ORPHEN! YOU LEFT THE INN WITHOUT EVEN SAYING GOODBYE!
AND AFTER YOU PROMISED TO TEACH ME SORCERY, TOO!
GRIN
BAM
WAIT... MAJIC ?!
YEAH, BUT HOW DID YOU...
OH, YOU DIDN'T KNOW?
MAJIC AND I ARE CLASSMATES IN SCHOOL!

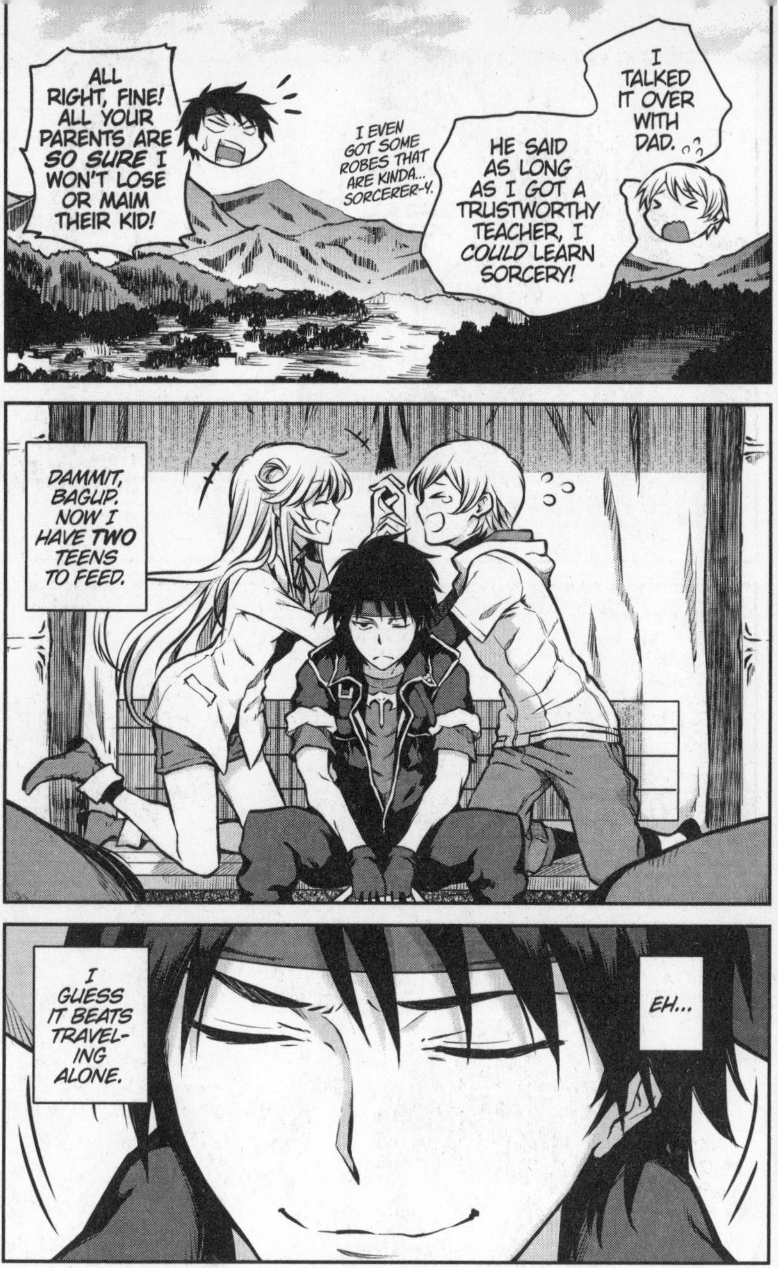
I TALKED IT OVER WITH DAD.
HE SAID AS LONG AS I GOT A TRUSTWORTHY TEACHER, I COULD LEARN SORCERY!
I EVEN GOT SOME ROBES THAT ARE KINDA... SORCERER-Y.
ALL RIGHT, FINE! ALL YOUR PARENTS ARE SO SURE I WON'T LOSE OR MAIM THEIR KID!
DAMMIT, BAGUP. NOW I HAVE TWO TEENS TO FEED.
EH...
I GUESS IT BEATS TRAVEL-ING ALONE.

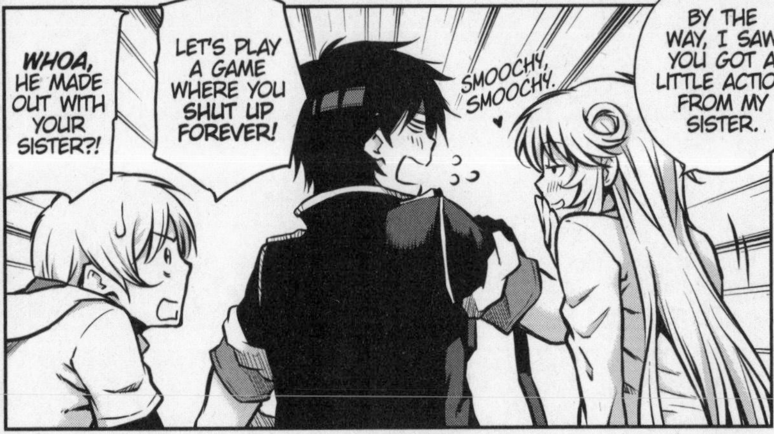
BY THE WAY, I SAW YOU GOT A LITTLE ACTION FROM MY SISTER.
SMOOCHY, SMOOCHY.
LET'S PLAY A GAME WHERE YOU SHUT UP FOREVER!
WHOA, HE MADE OUT WITH YOUR SISTER?!

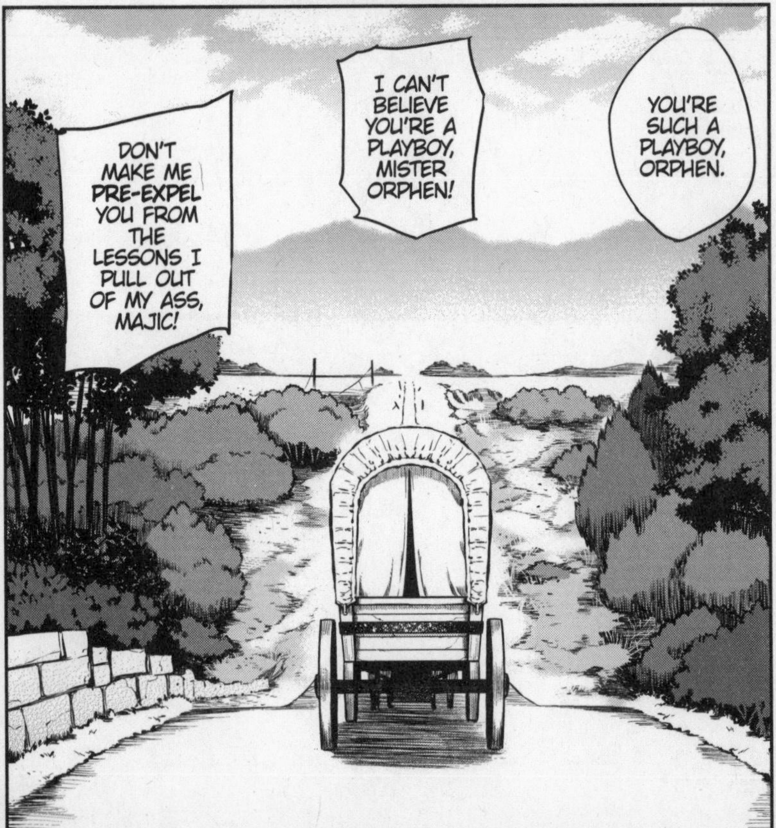
YOU'RE SUCH A PLAYBOY, ORPHEN.
I CAN'T BELIEVE YOU'RE A PLAYBOY, MISTER ORPHEN!
DON'T MAKE ME PRE-EXPEL YOU FROM THE LESSONS I PULL OUT OF MY ASS, MAJIC!

THE END

SEVEN SEAS ENTERTAINMENT PRESENTS

SORCEROUS STABBER ORPHEN

Heed My Call, Beast! Part II

story by **YOSHINOBU AKITA** / art by **MURAJI**

TRANSLATION
Adrienne Beck

ADAPTATION
Lianne Sentar

LETTERING AND RETOUCH
Ray Steeves

COVER DESIGN
KC Fabellon

PROOFREADER
Janet Houck
Danielle King

EDITOR
J.P. Sullivan

PRODUCTION MANAGER
Lissa Pattillo

MANAGING EDITOR
Julie Davis

EDITOR-IN-CHIEF
Adam Arnold

PUBLISHER
Jason DeAngelis

First published in Japan in 2017 by KADOKAWA CORPORATION, Tokyo.
English translation rights arranged with KADOKAWA CORPORATION, Tokyo.

Seven Seas press and purchase enquiries can be sent to Marketing Manager Lianne Sentar at press@gomanga.com. Information regarding the distribution and purchase of digital editions is available from Digital Manager CK Russell at digital@gomanga.com.

ISBN: 978-1-64275-075-1

Printed in Canada

First Printing: July 2019

10 9 8 7 6 5 4 3 2 1

FOLLOW US ONLINE: ***www.sevenseasentertainment.com***

READING DIRECTIONS

This book reads from ***right to left***, Japanese style. If this is your first time reading manga, you start reading from the top right panel on each page and take it from there. If you get lost, just follow the numbered diagram here. It may seem backwards at first, but you'll get the hang of it! Have fun!!

1
2
3
4
5
6
7
8
9

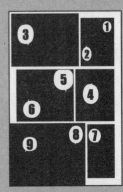